IMMORTAL HOUNDS

1

Ryo Yasohachi

VERTICAL COMICS

Table of Contents

Characters

Tousai Precinct

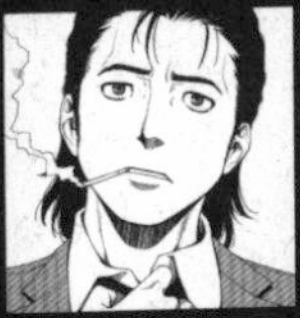

Kenzaki
Investigating the source of RDS (a fatal communicable disease).

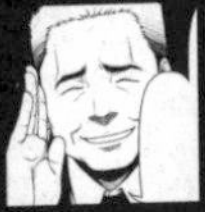

Shigematsu
Kenzaki's senior age-wise though his rank at work is lower. Nicknamed "Shige."

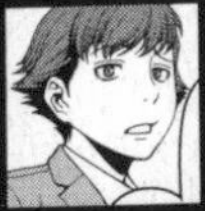

Wakabayashi
Kenzaki's underling.

Escape Artists

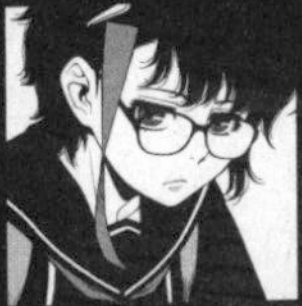

Rin
Works to spread RDS.

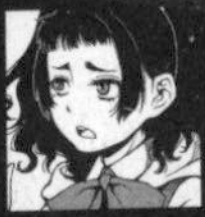

Kiriko
Rin's sister. Training to become an escape artist.

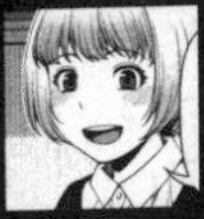

Ikumi Kenzaki
Kenzaki's younger sister.

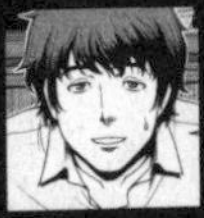

Teruyoshi Kouda
Ikumi's lover.

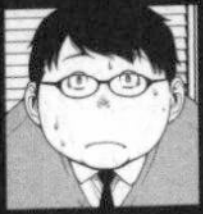

Takamiya
Suspected of having deep ties to RDS.

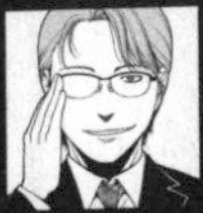

Kanai
Works for the UN Disease Control Office. Has a complex relationship with Kenzaki.

1

Death by Pistol is Best

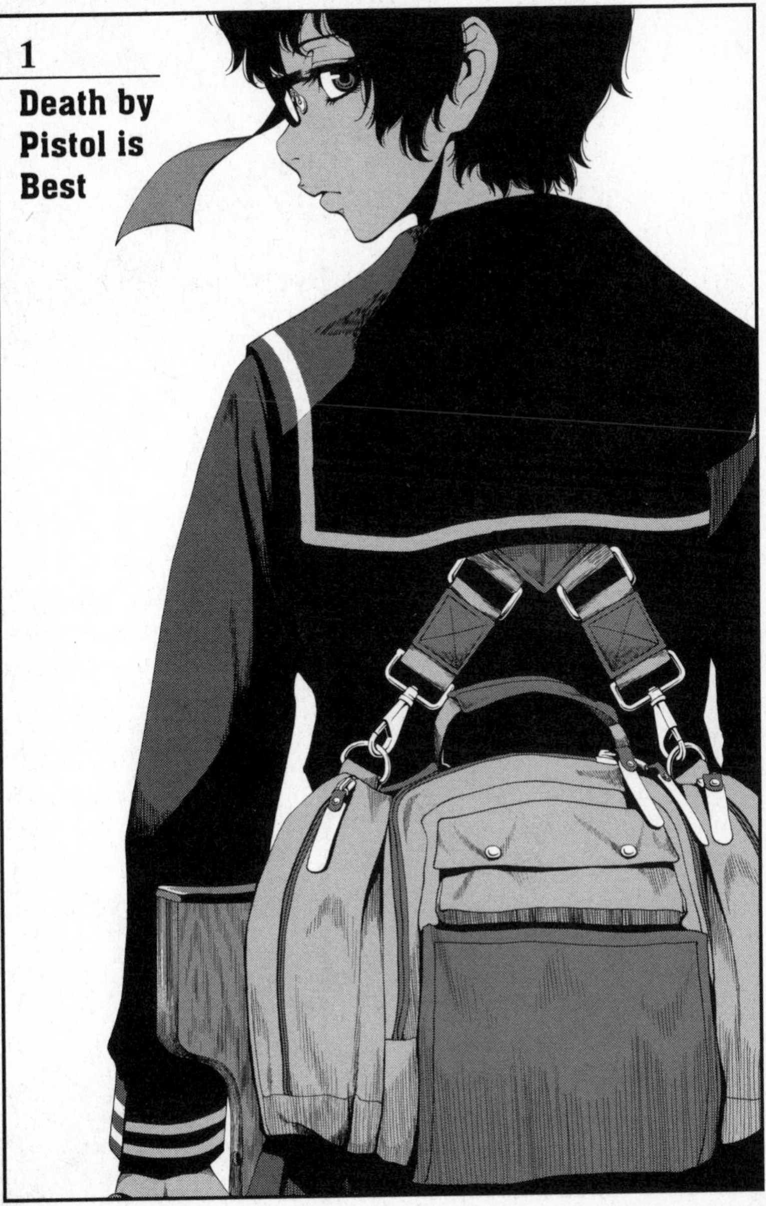

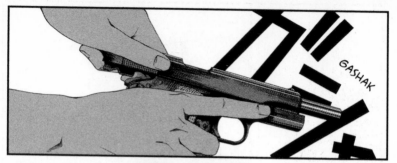

GASHAK

haa

haa

haa

haa

Yes... please...

Hey, Ikumi,

do I really have to?

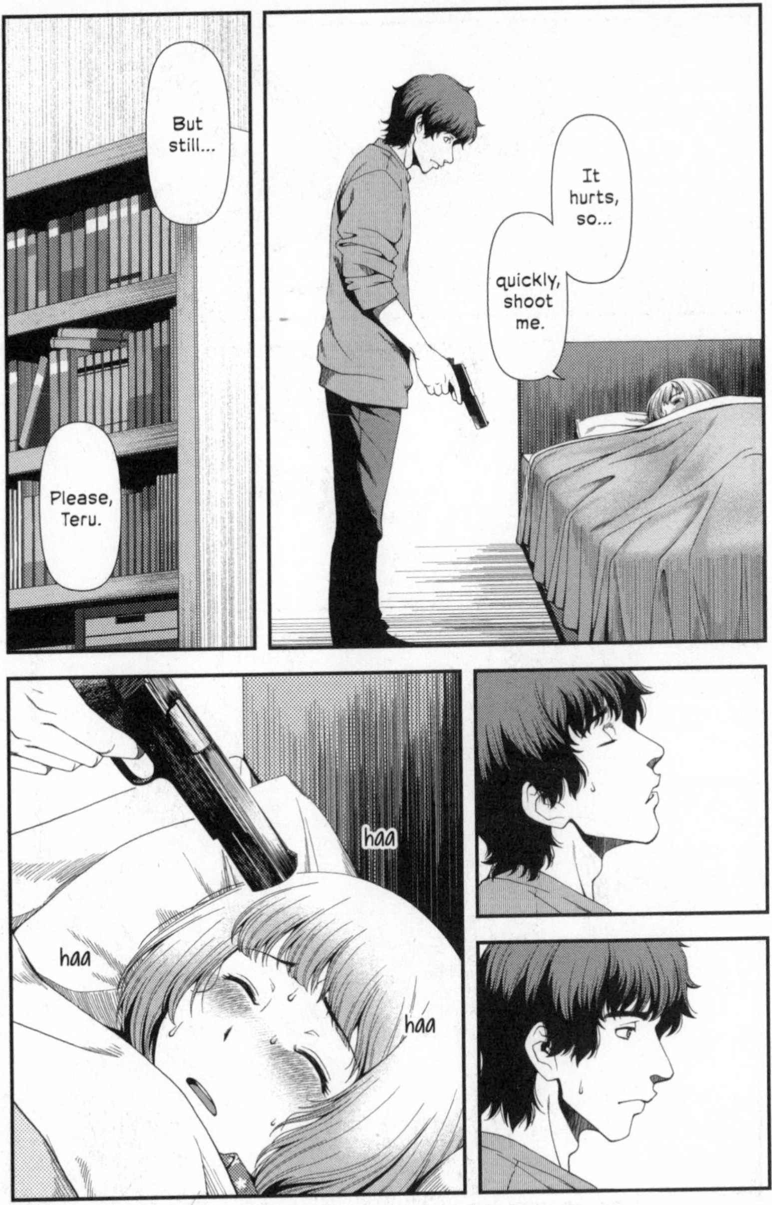
It hurts, so...
quickly, shoot me.
But still...
Please, Teru.
haa
haa
haa

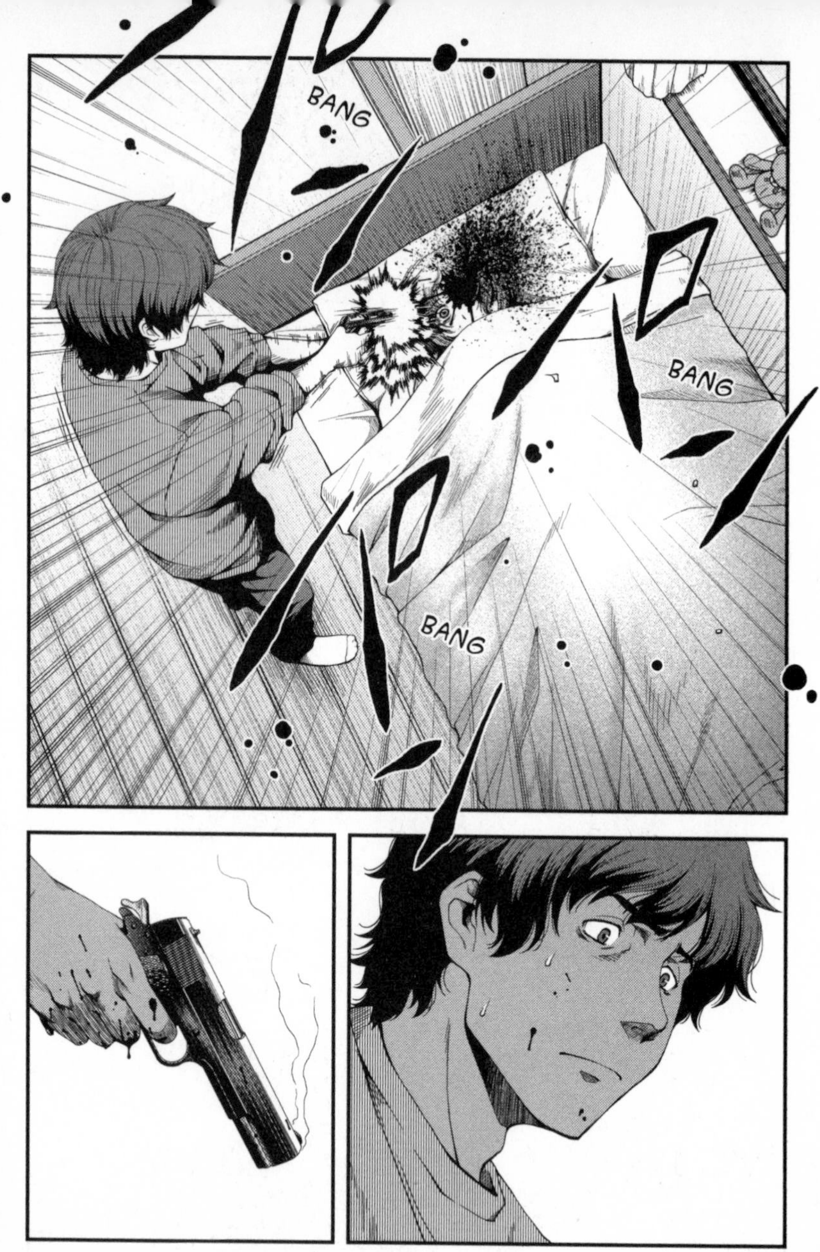
BANG
BANG
BANG

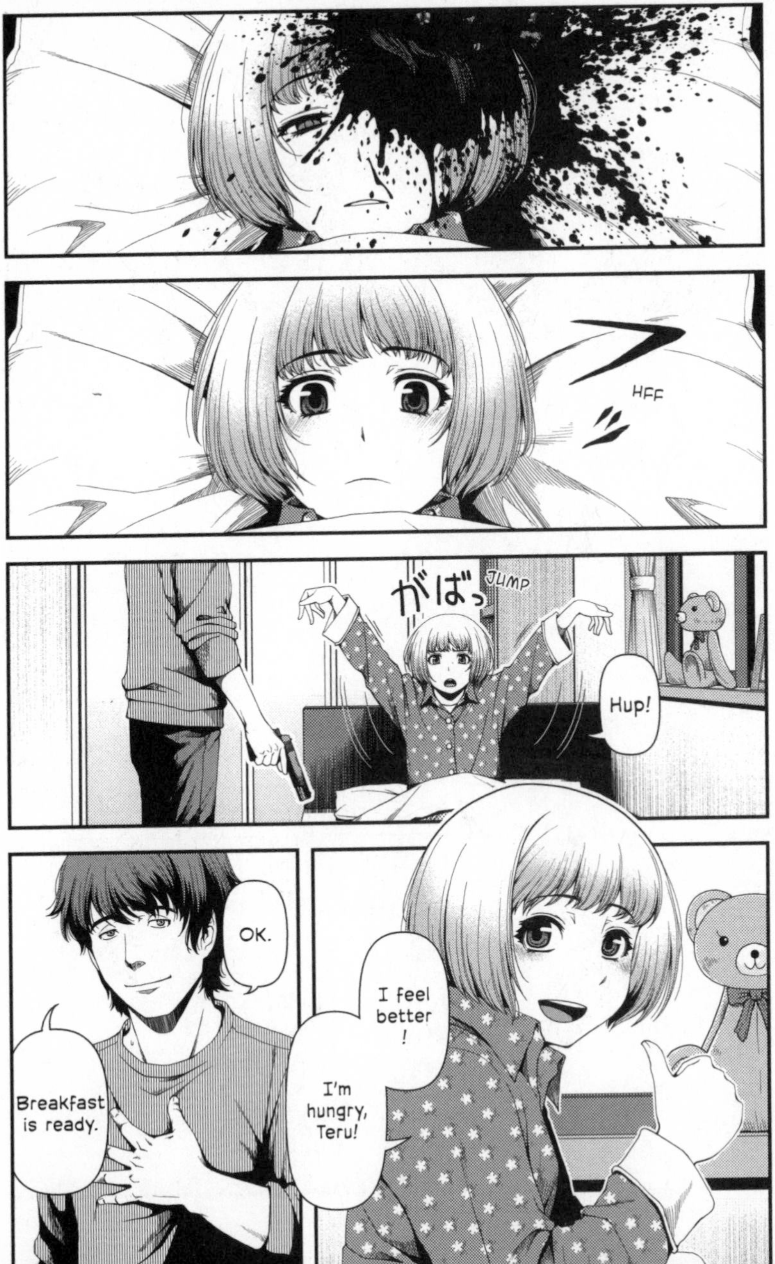
HFF
がばっ JUMP
Hup!
I feel better!
I'm hungry, Teru!
OK.
Breakfast is ready.

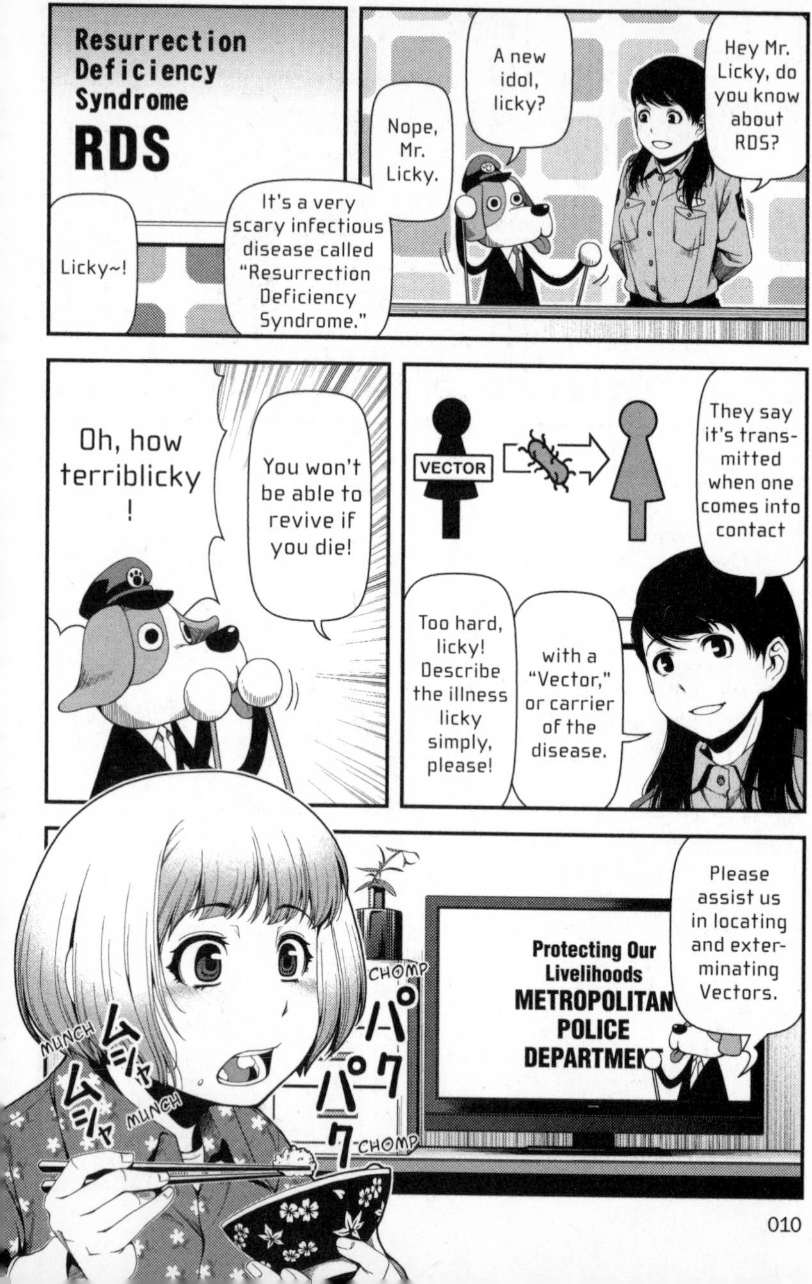
Hey Mr. Licky, do you know about RDS?
A new idol, licky?
Nope, Mr. Licky.
Resurrection Deficiency Syndrome
RDS
It's a very scary infectious disease called "Resurrection Deficiency Syndrome."
Licky~!
They say it's trans- mitted when one comes into contact
VECTOR
with a "Vector," or carrier of the disease.
Too hard, licky! Describe the illness licky simply, please!
You won't be able to revive if you die!
Oh, how terriblicky !
Please assist us in locating and exter- minating Vectors.
Protecting Our Livelihoods
METROPOLITAN POLICE DEPARTMEN
パクパク
CHOMP
CHOMP
ムシャムシャ
MUNCH
MUNCH

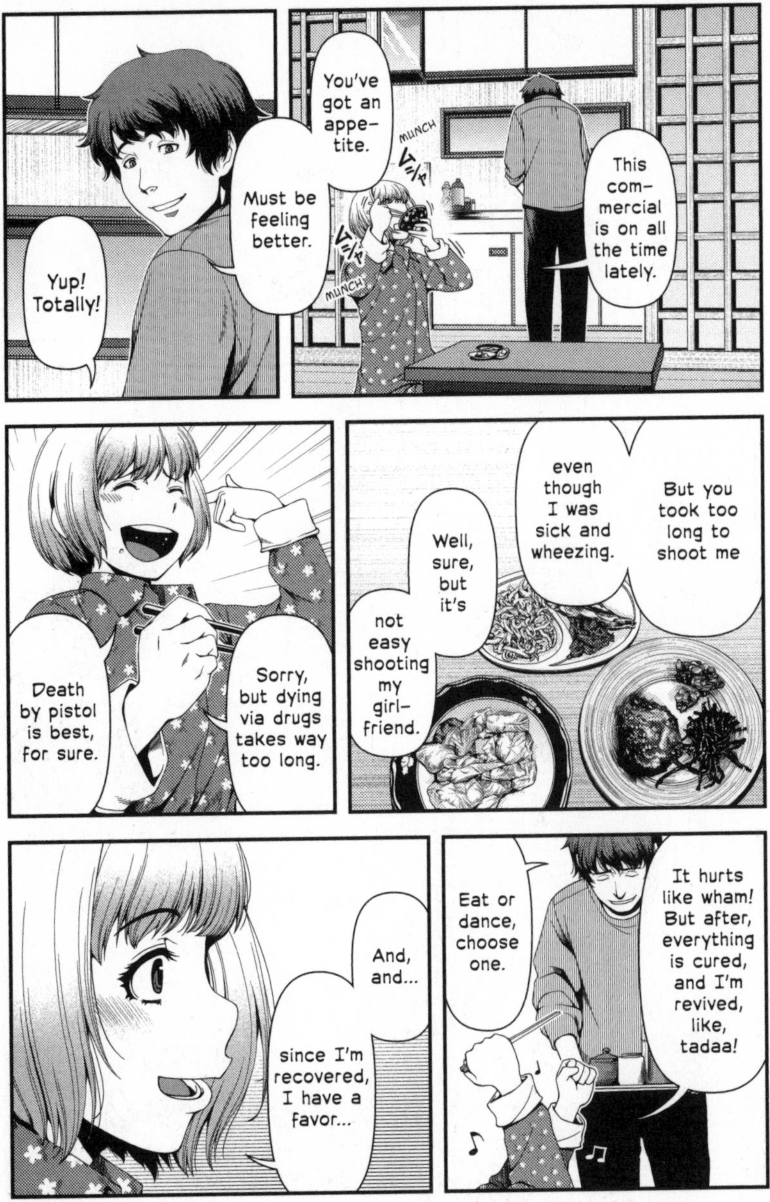
This commercial is on all the time lately.
MUNCH
ムシャ
You've got an appetite.
MUNCH
ムシャ
Must be feeling better.
Yup! Totally!
But you took too long to shoot me
even though I was sick and wheezing.
Well, sure, but it's
not easy shooting my girlfriend.
Sorry, but dying via drugs takes way too long.
Death by pistol is best, for sure.
It hurts like wham! But after, everything is cured, and I'm revived, like, tadaa!
Eat or dance, choose one.
And, and...
since I'm recovered, I have a favor...

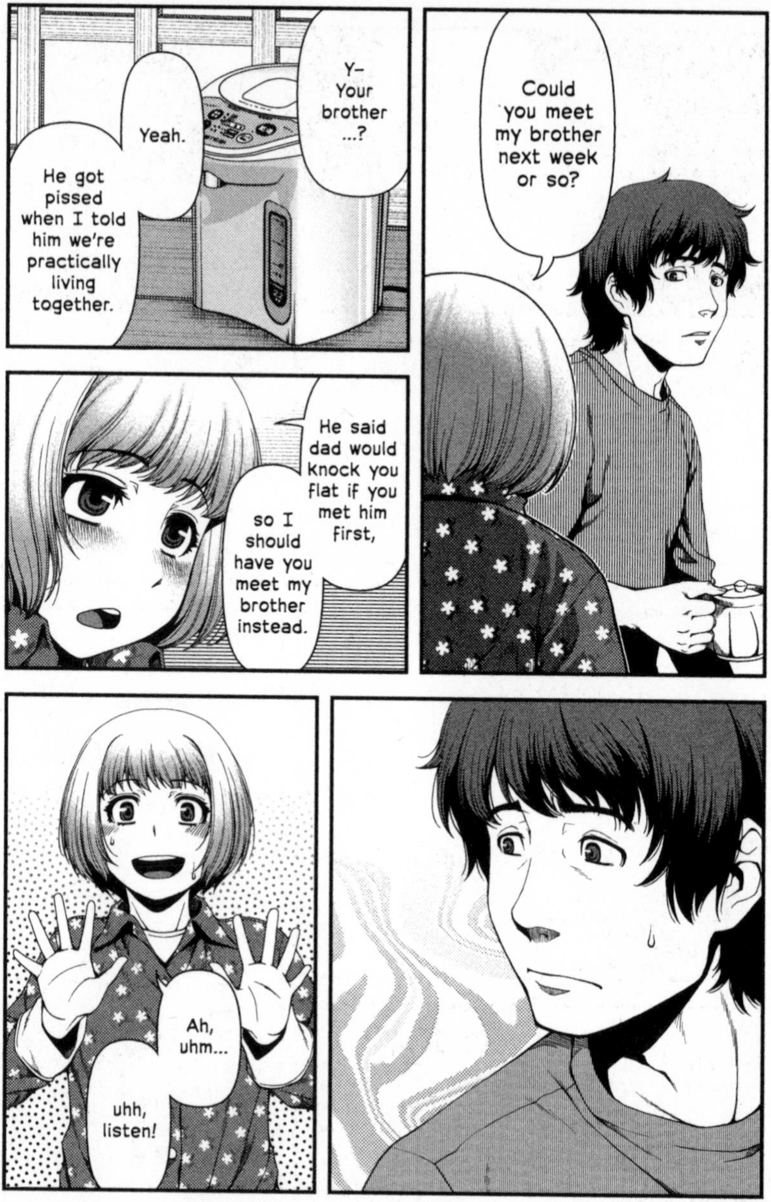
Could you meet my brother next week or so?
Y– Your brother ...?
Yeah.
He got pissed when I told him we're practically living together.
He said dad would knock you flat if you met him first,
so I should have you meet my brother instead.
Ah, uhm...
uhh, listen!

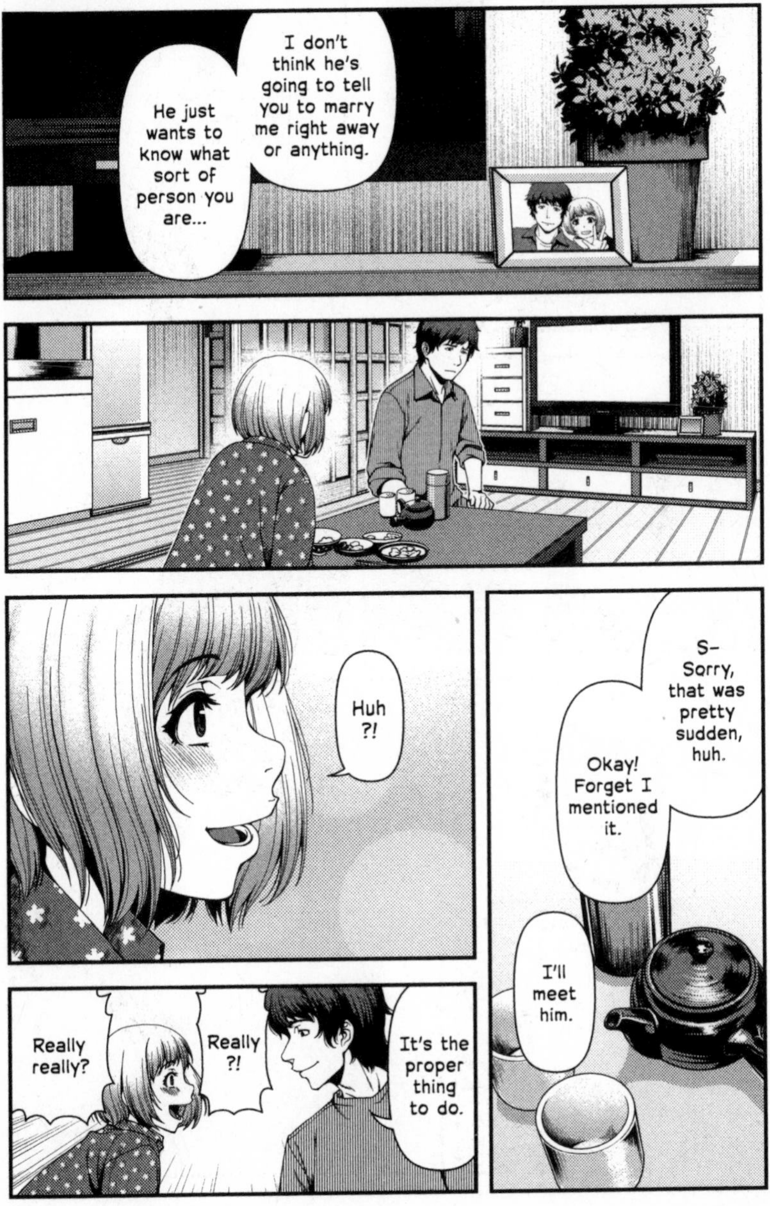
I don't think he's going to tell you to marry me right away or anything.
He just wants to know what sort of person you are...
S-Sorry, that was pretty sudden, huh.
Okay! Forget I mentioned it.
I'll meet him.
Huh?!
It's the proper thing to do.
Really?!
Really really?

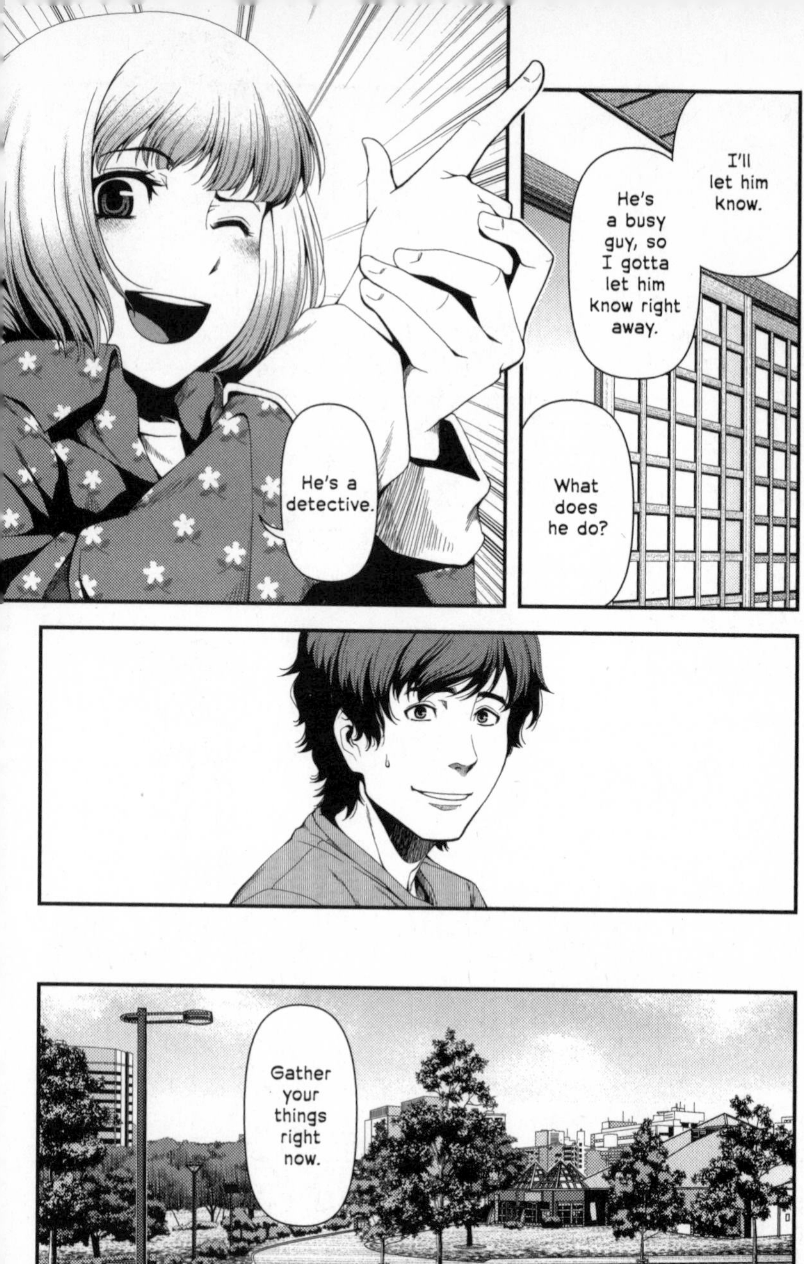
I'll let him know.
He's a busy guy, so I gotta let him know right away.
What does he do?
He's a detective.
Gather your things right now.

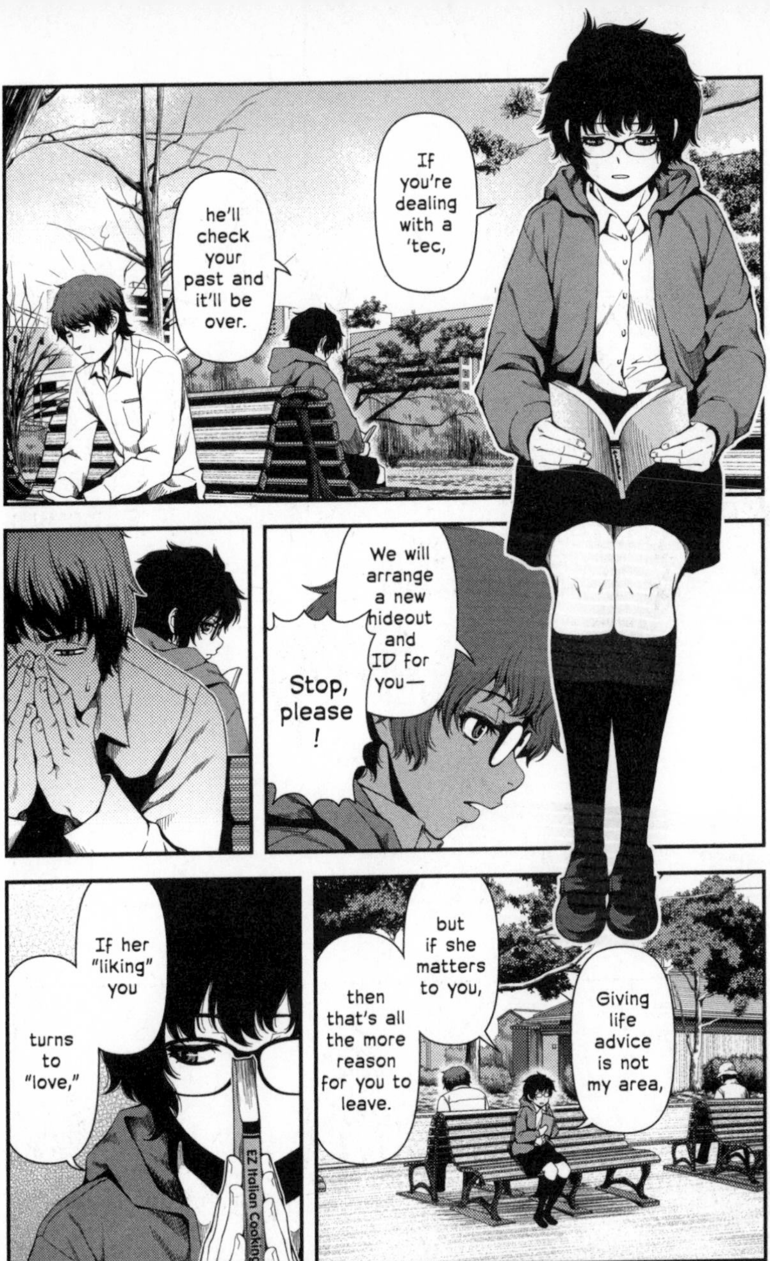

If you're dealing with a 'tec,
he'll check your past and it'll be over.
We will arrange a new hideout and ID for you—
Stop, please!
Giving life advice is not my area,
but if she matters to you,
then that's all the more reason for you to leave.
If her "liking" you
turns to "love,"
EZ Italian Cooking

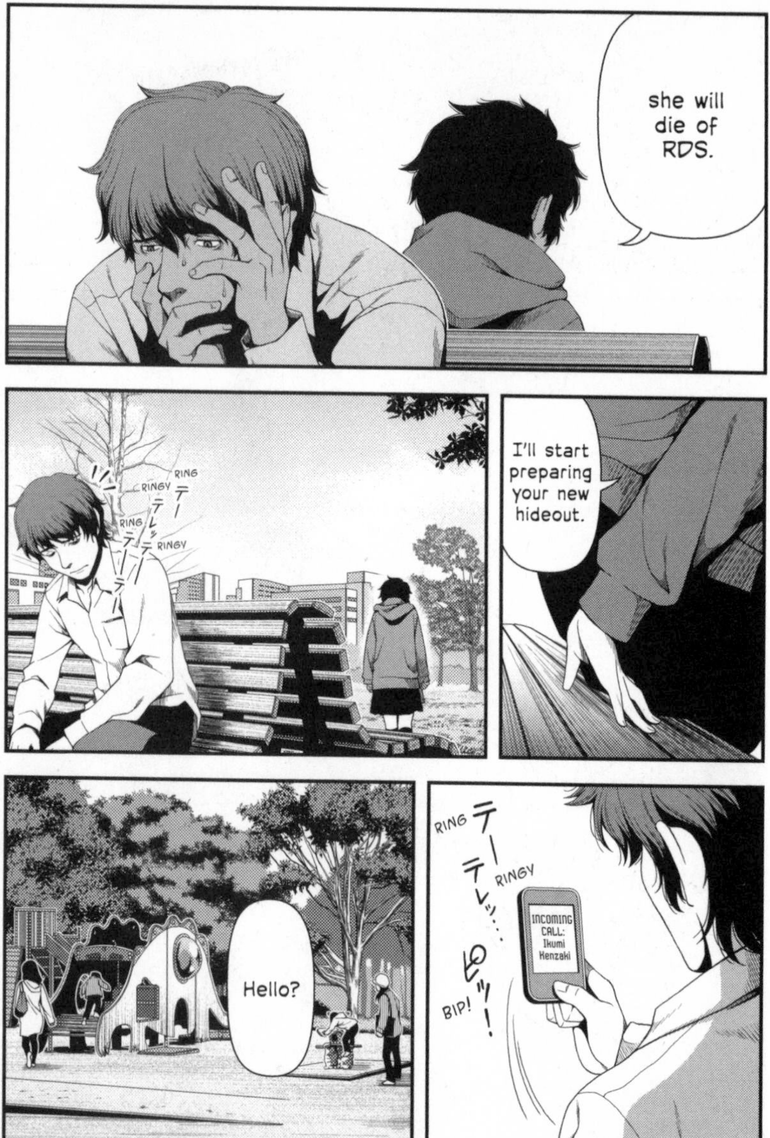
she will die of RDS.
I'll start preparing your new hideout.
RING
RINGY
RING
RINGY
RING
テー
RINGY
テレッ…
INCOMING CALL: Ikumi Kenzaki
BIP!
ピッ!
Hello?

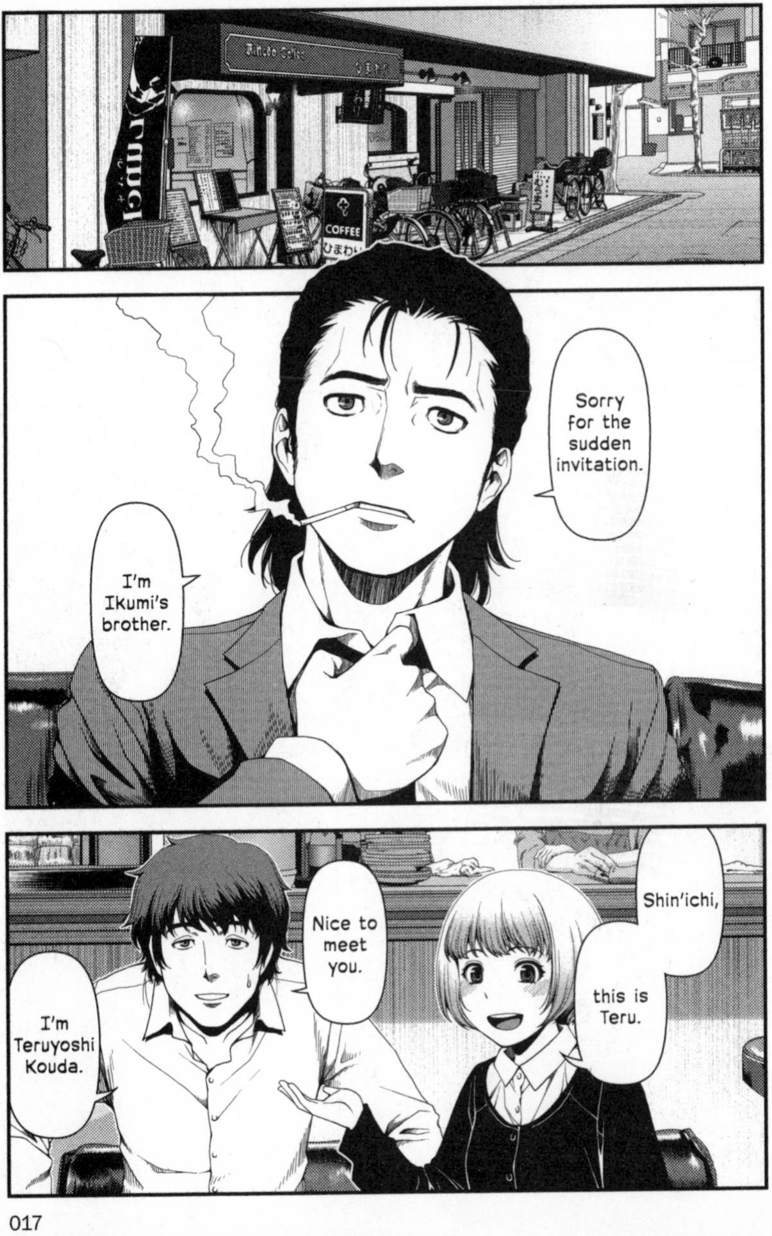
COFFEE
Sorry for the sudden invitation.
I'm Ikumi's brother.
Shin'ichi, this is Teru.
Nice to meet you.
I'm Teruyoshi Kouda.

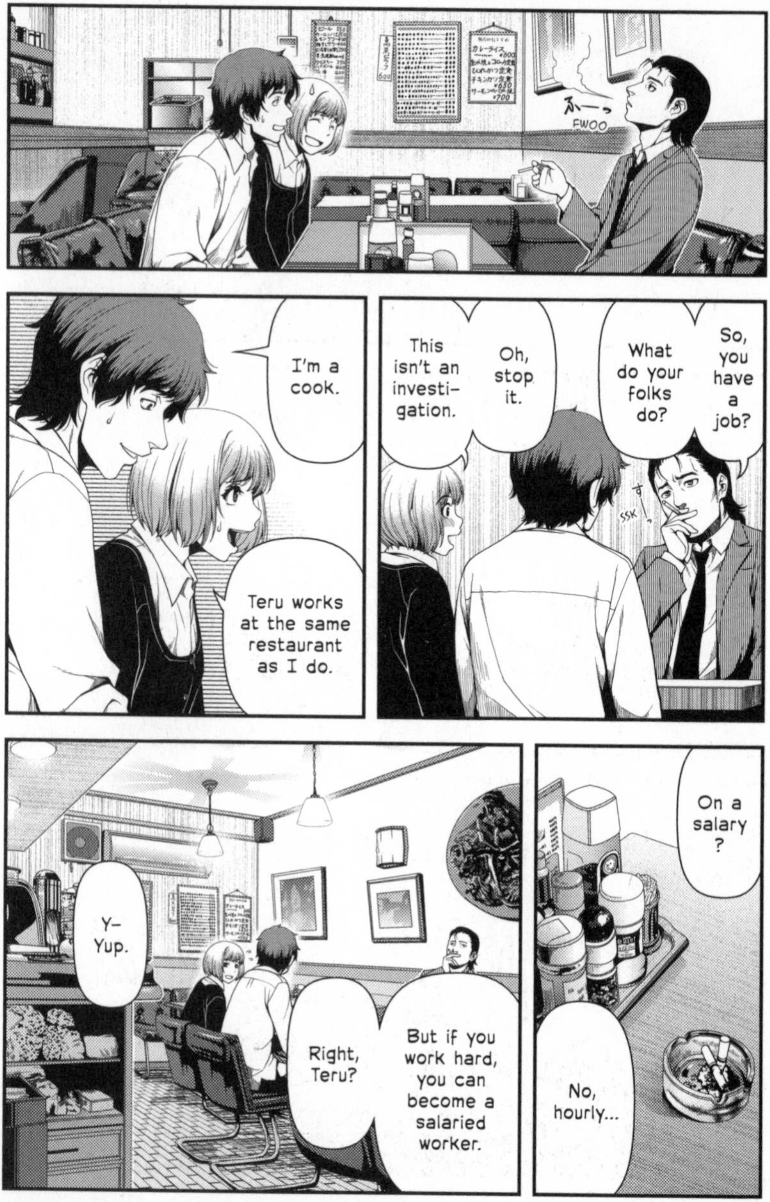
ふーっ
FWOO
So, you have a job?
What do your folks do?
Oh, stop it.
This isn't an investigation.
す
SSK
I'm a cook.
Teru works at the same restaurant as I do.
On a salary?
No, hourly...
But if you work hard, you can become a salaried worker.
Right, Teru?
Y-Yup.

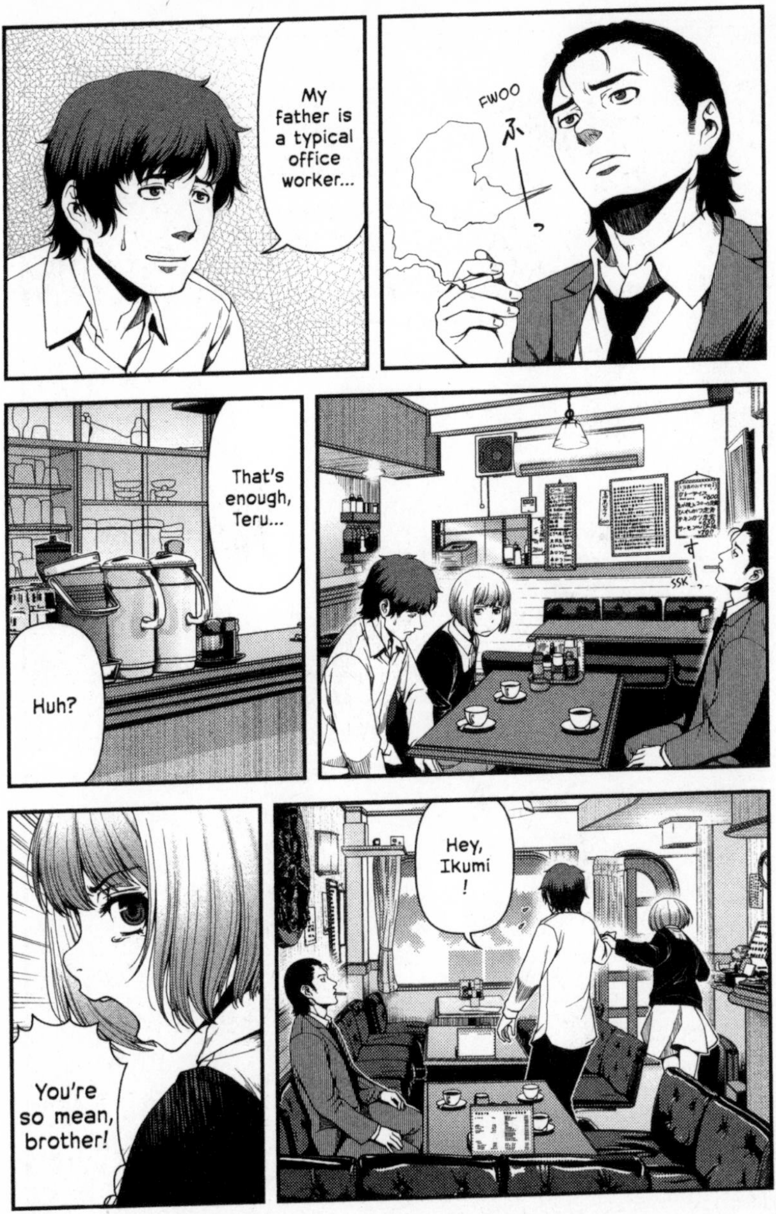
FWOO
ふーっ
My father is a typical office worker...
SSK
すーっ
That's enough, Teru...
Huh?
Hey, Ikumi!
You're so mean, brother!

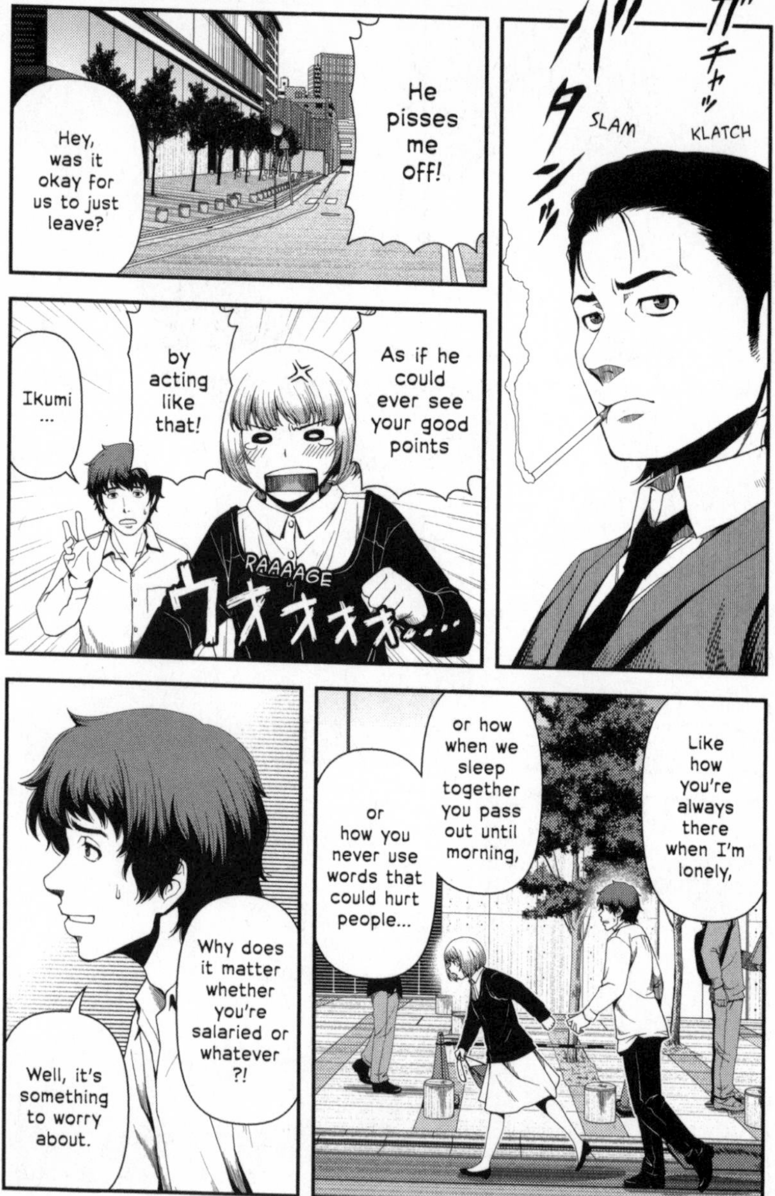
ガチャッ
KLATCH
バタンッ
SLAM
He pisses me off!
Hey, was it okay for us to just leave?
As if he could ever see your good points
by acting like that!
Ikumi ...
ウオオオオ…
RAAAAGE
Like how you're always there when I'm lonely,
or how when we sleep together you pass out until morning,
or how you never use words that could hurt people...
Why does it matter whether you're salaried or whatever ?!
Well, it's something to worry about.

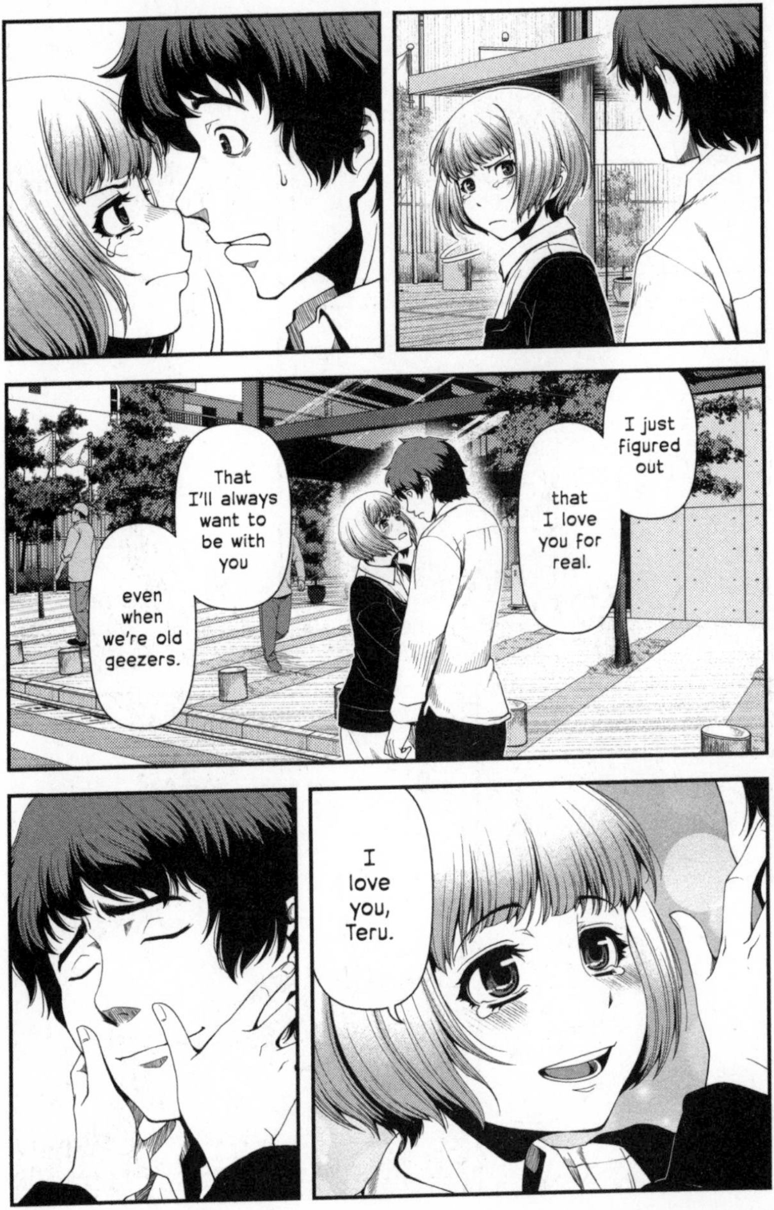
I just figured out
that I love you for real.
That I'll always want to be with you
even when we're old geezers.
I love you, Teru.

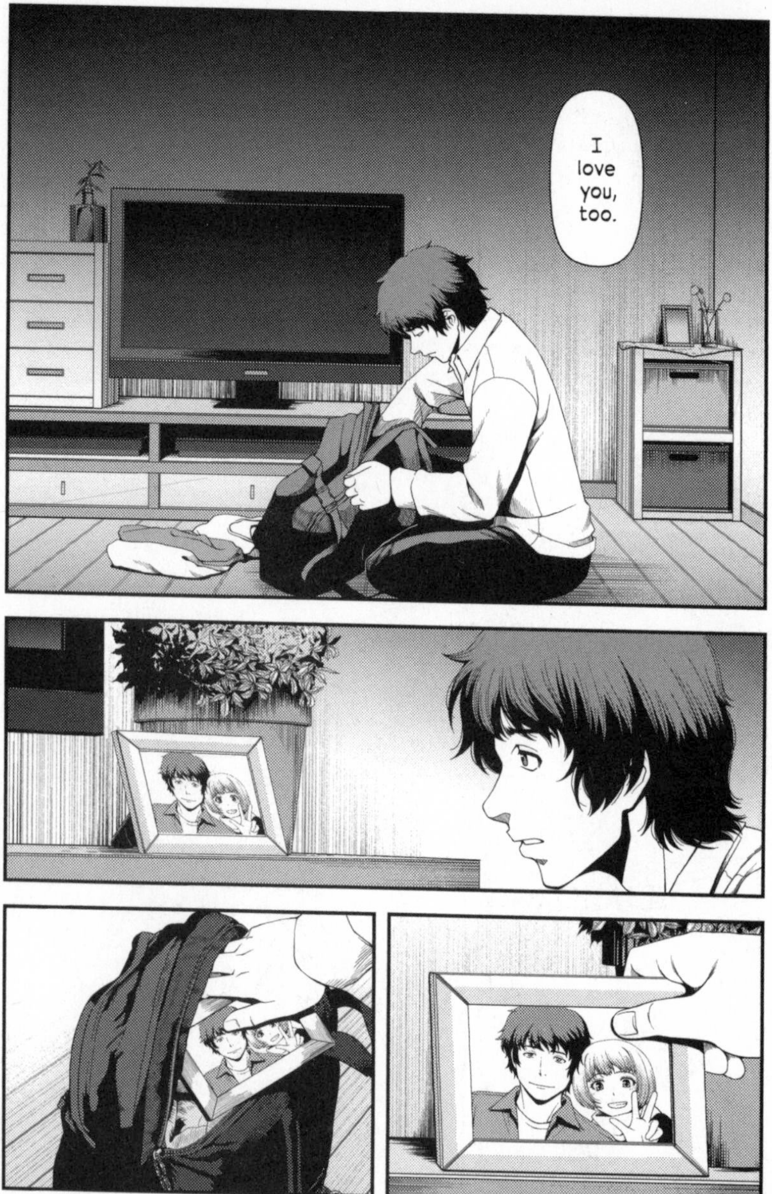
I love you, too.

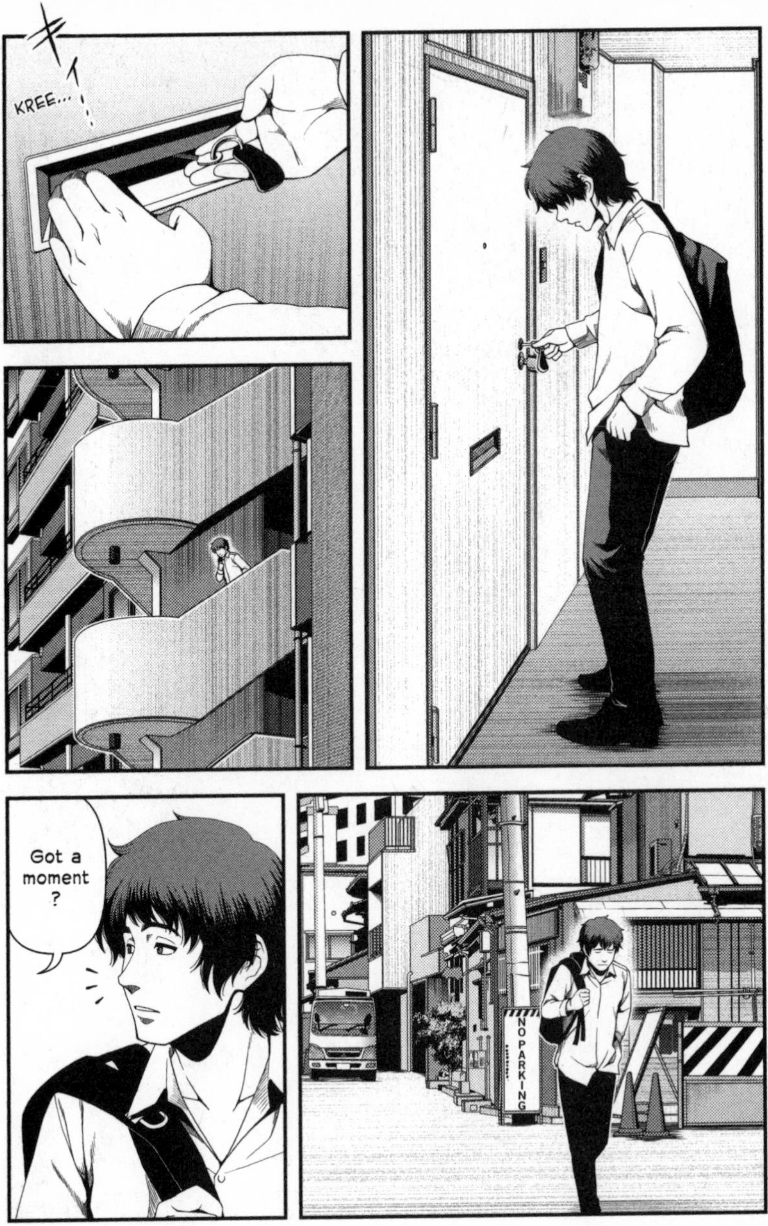

キィ
KREE...
NO PARKING
Got a moment?

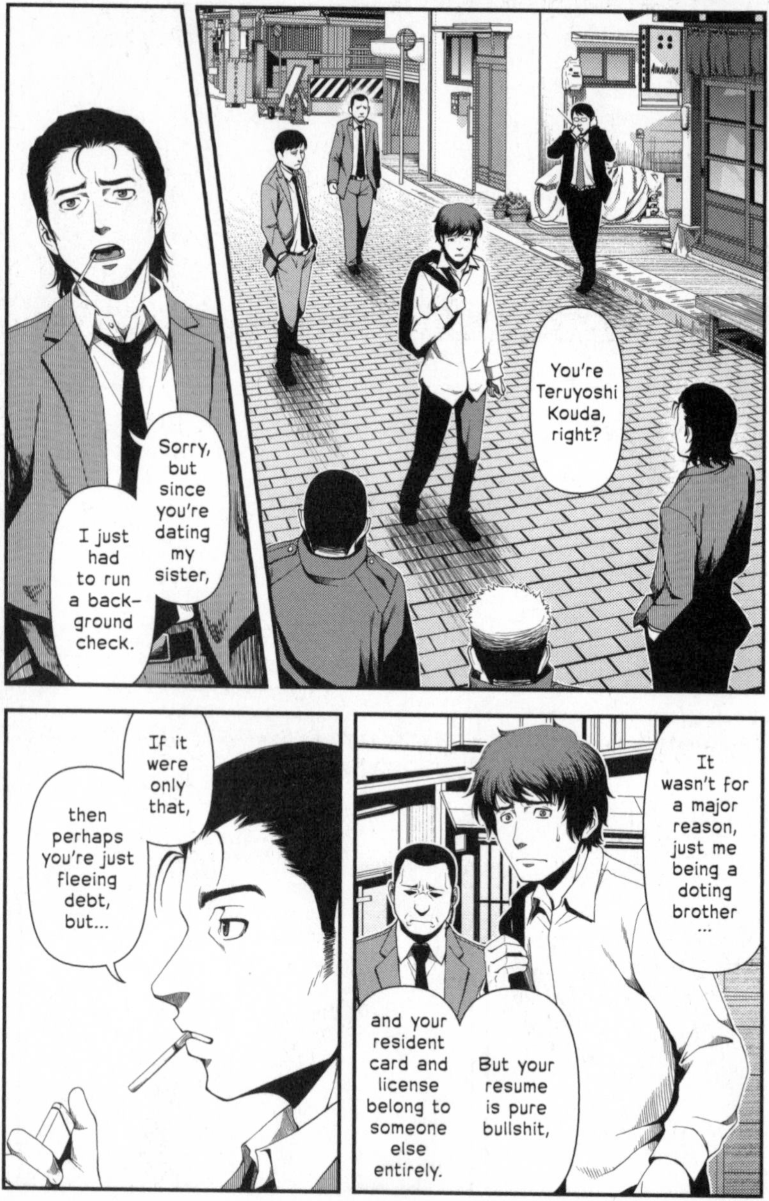
You're Teruyoshi Kouda, right?
Sorry, but since you're dating my sister,
I just had to run a back-ground check.
It wasn't for a major reason, just me being a doting brother ...
But your resume is pure bullshit,
and your resident card and license belong to someone else entirely.
If it were only that,
then perhaps you're just fleeing debt, but...

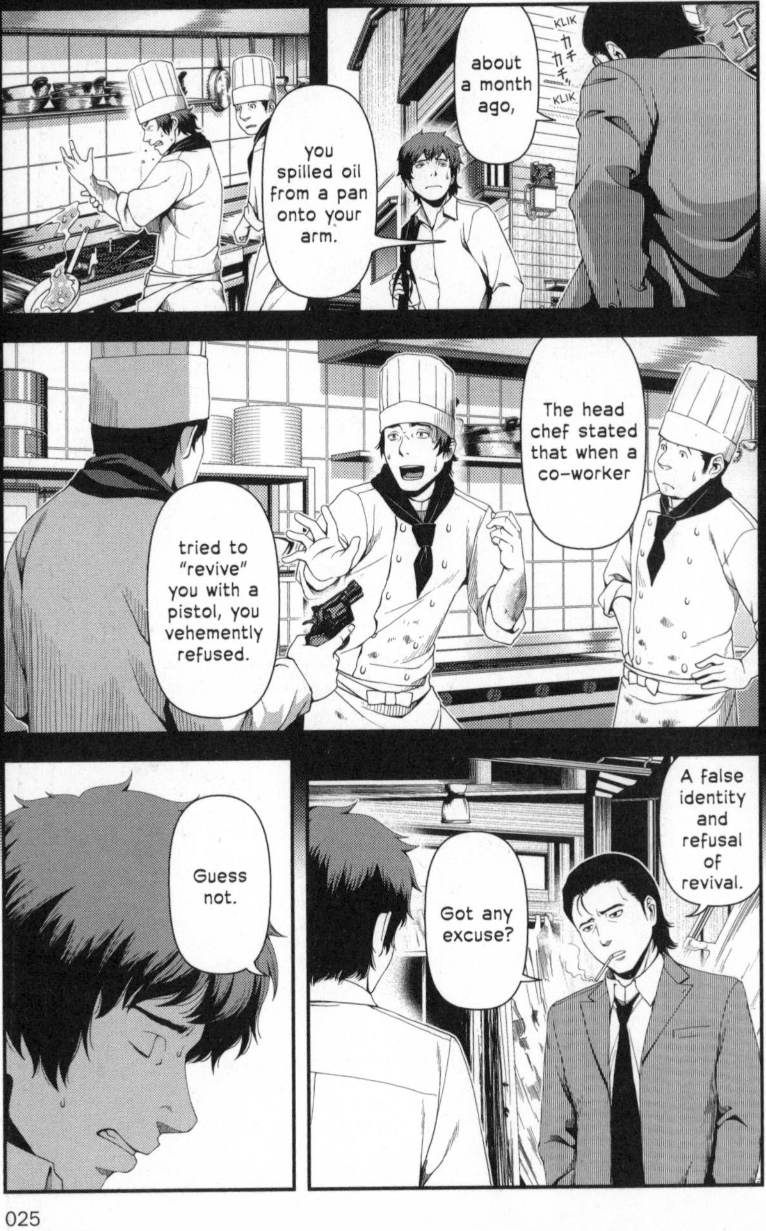
about a month ago,
KLIK
カチ
カチ
KLIK
you spilled oil from a pan onto your arm.
The head chef stated that when a co-worker
tried to "revive" you with a pistol, you vehemently refused.
A false identity and refusal of revival.
Got any excuse?
Guess not.

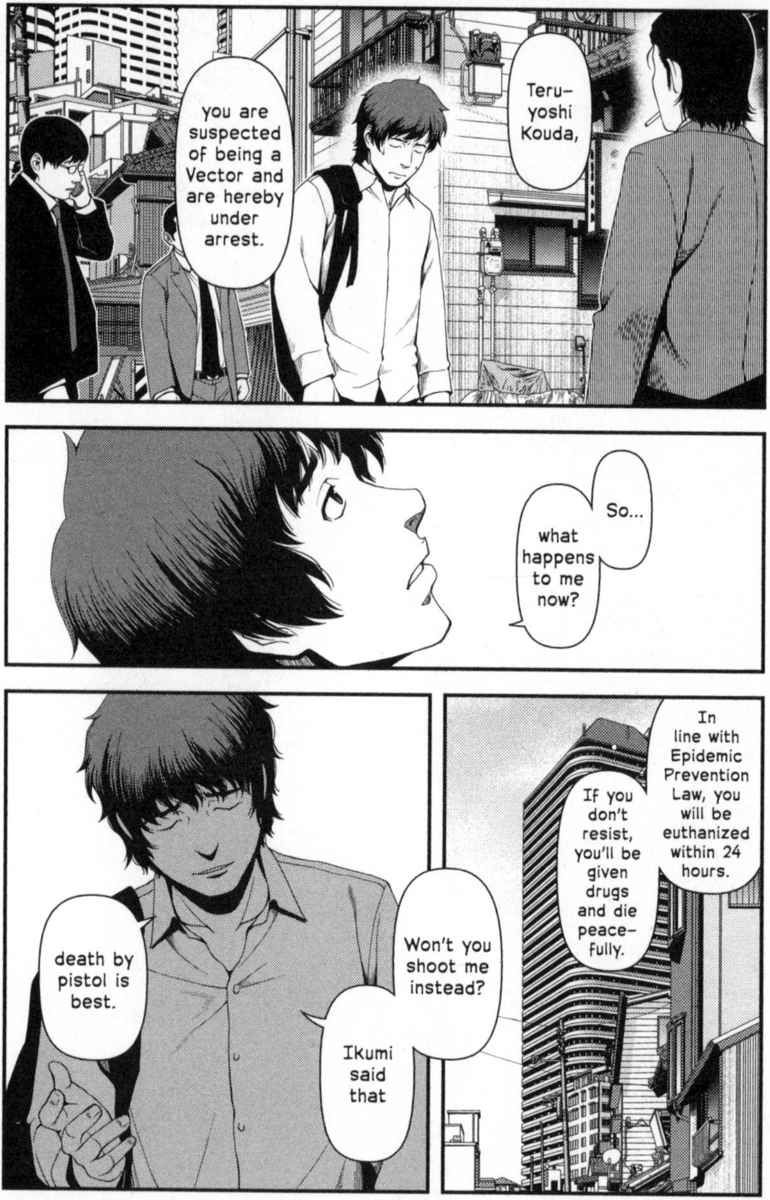
Teru-yoshi Kouda,
you are suspected of being a Vector and are hereby under arrest.
So...
what happens to me now?
In line with Epidemic Prevention Law, you will be euthanized within 24 hours.
If you don't resist, you'll be given drugs and die peace-fully.
Won't you shoot me instead?
Ikumi said that
death by pistol is best.

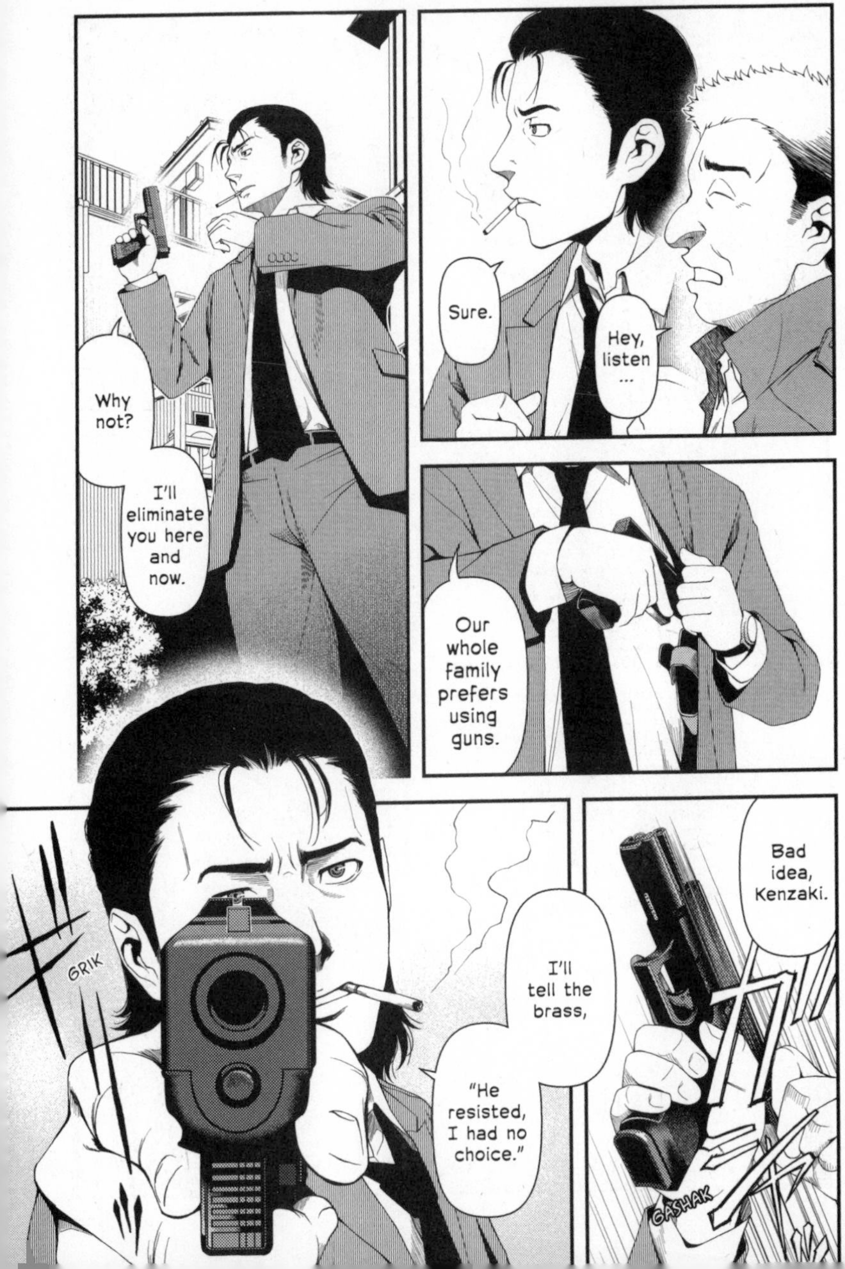
Hey, listen ...
Sure.
Our whole family prefers using guns.
Why not?
I'll eliminate you here and now.
Bad idea, Kenzaki.
GASHAK
I'll tell the brass,
"He resisted, I had no choice."
GRIK

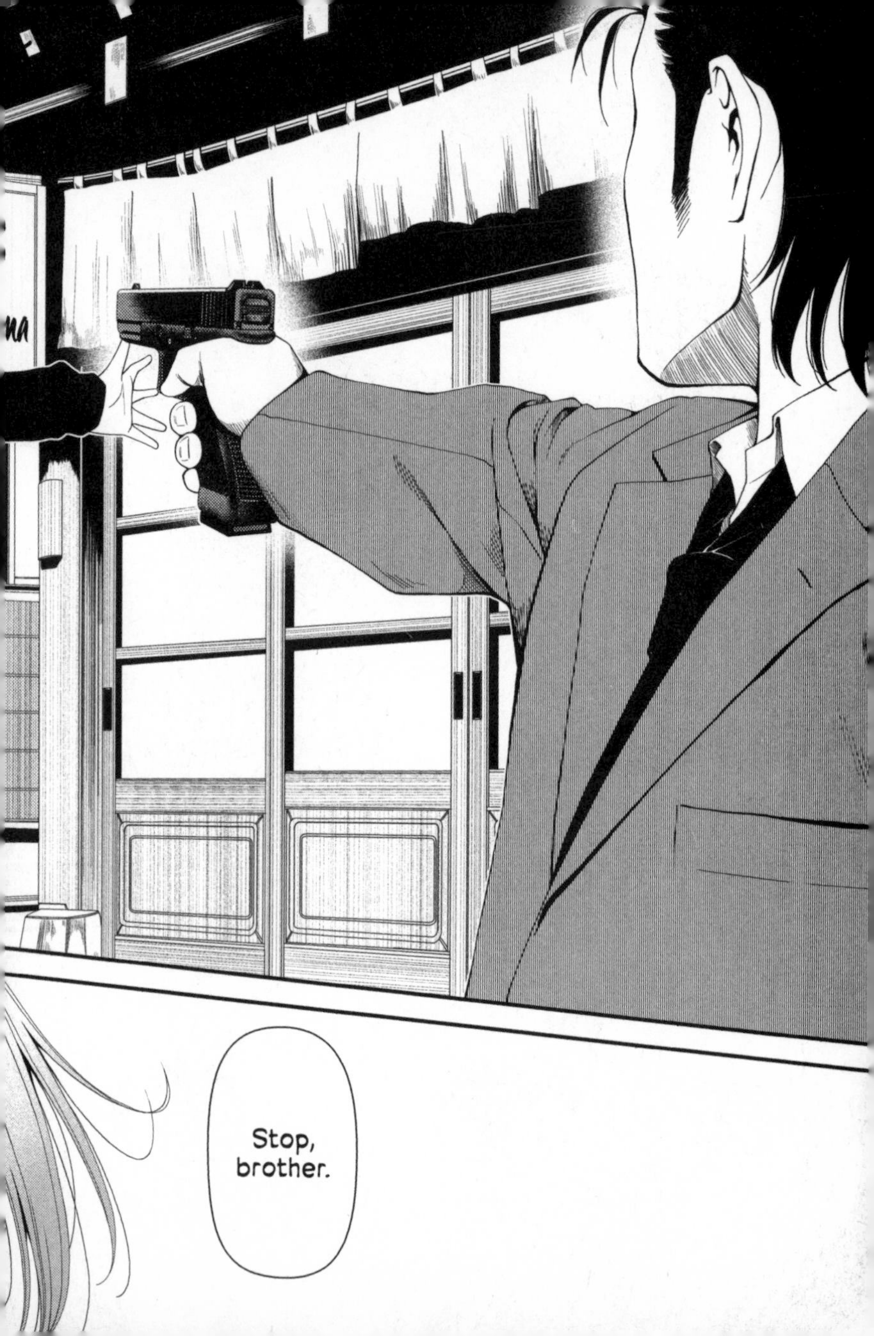
Stop, brother.

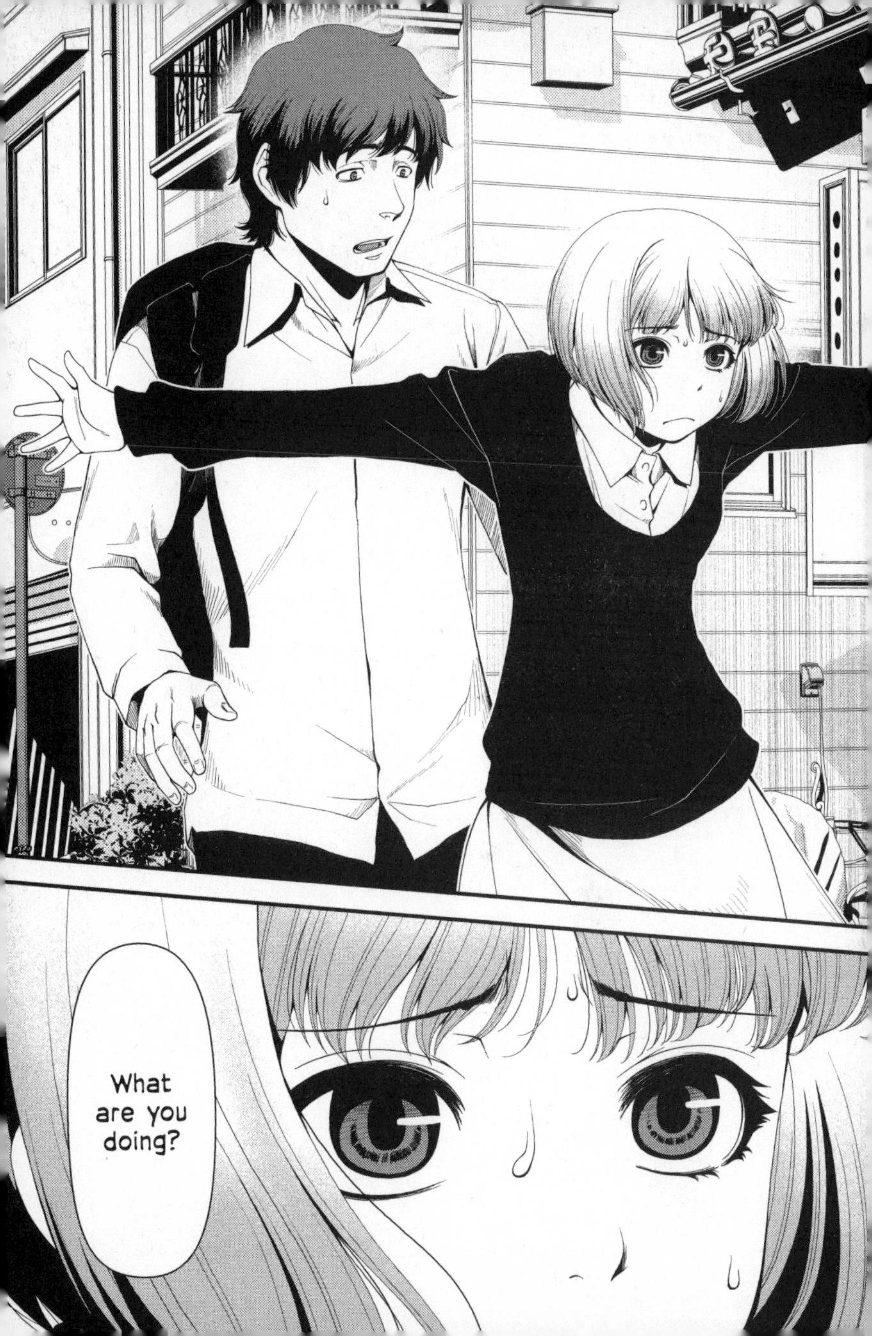
What are you doing?

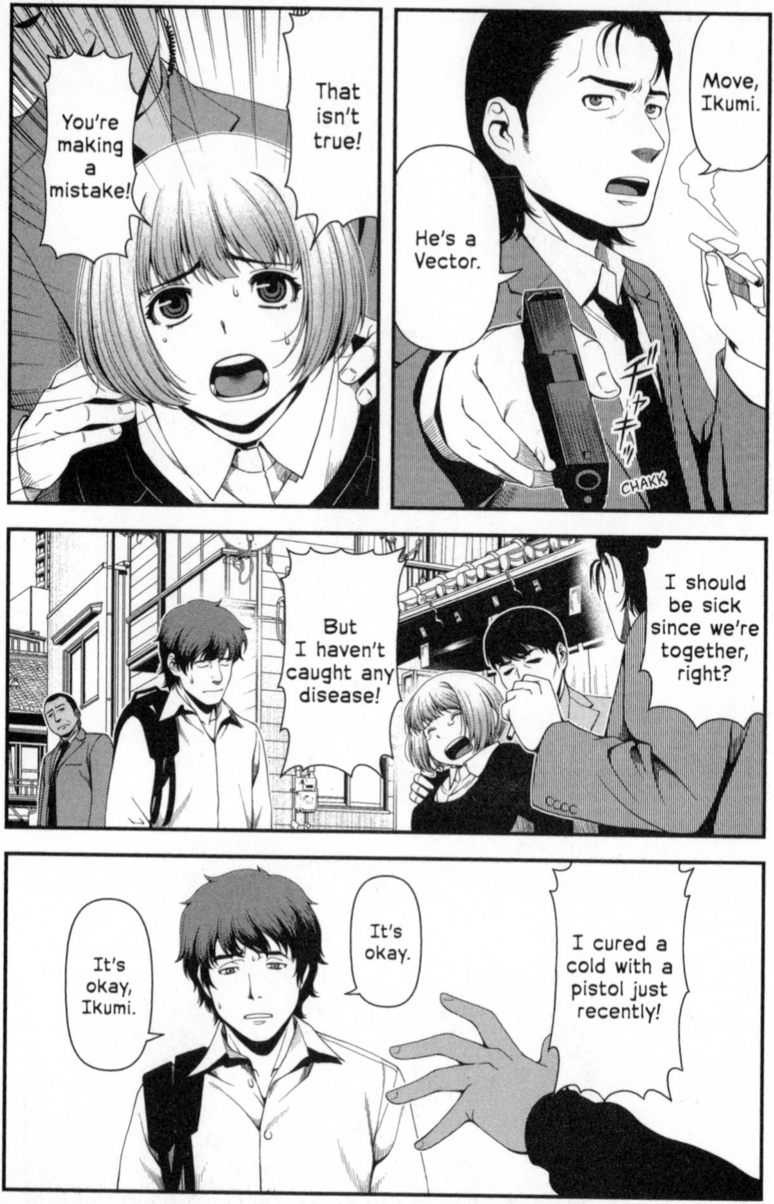
Move, Ikumi.
He's a Vector.
CHAKK
That isn't true!
You're making a mistake!
I should be sick since we're together, right?
But I haven't caught any disease!
I cured a cold with a pistol just recently!
It's okay.
It's okay, Ikumi.

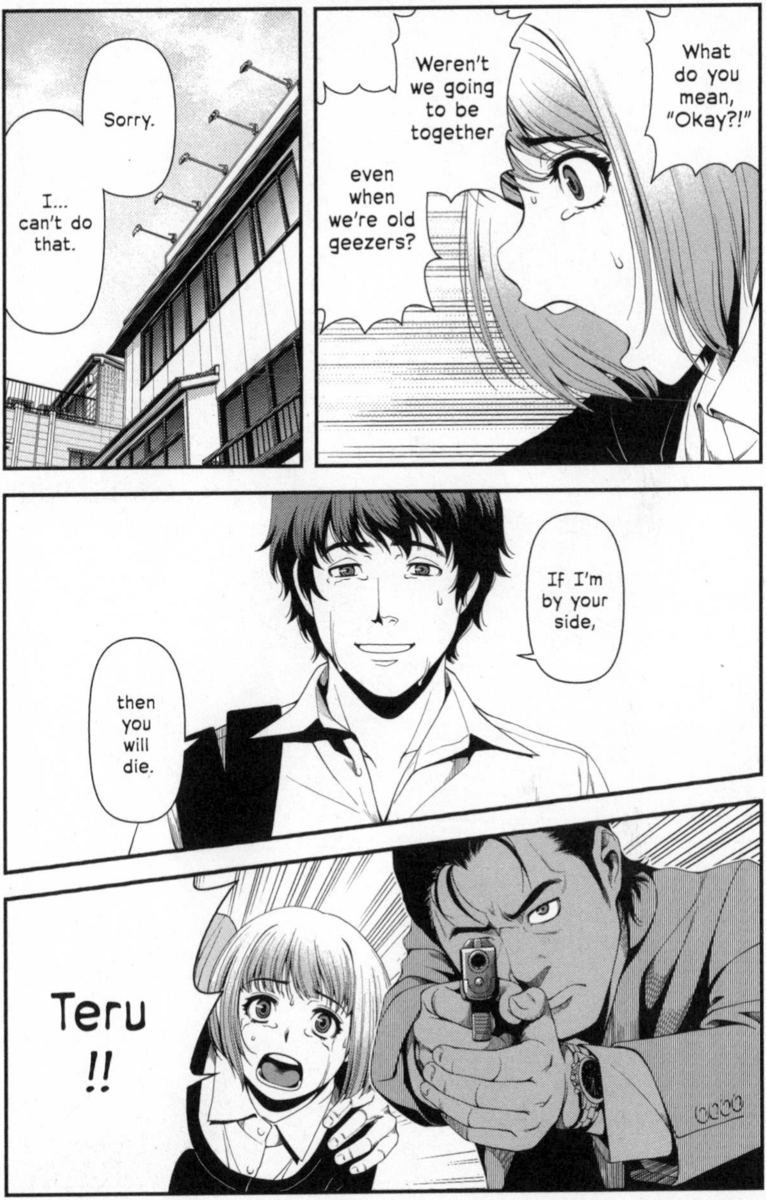
What do you mean, "Okay?!"
Weren't we going to be together
even when we're old geezers?
Sorry.
I... can't do that.
If I'm by your side,
then you will die.
Teru!!

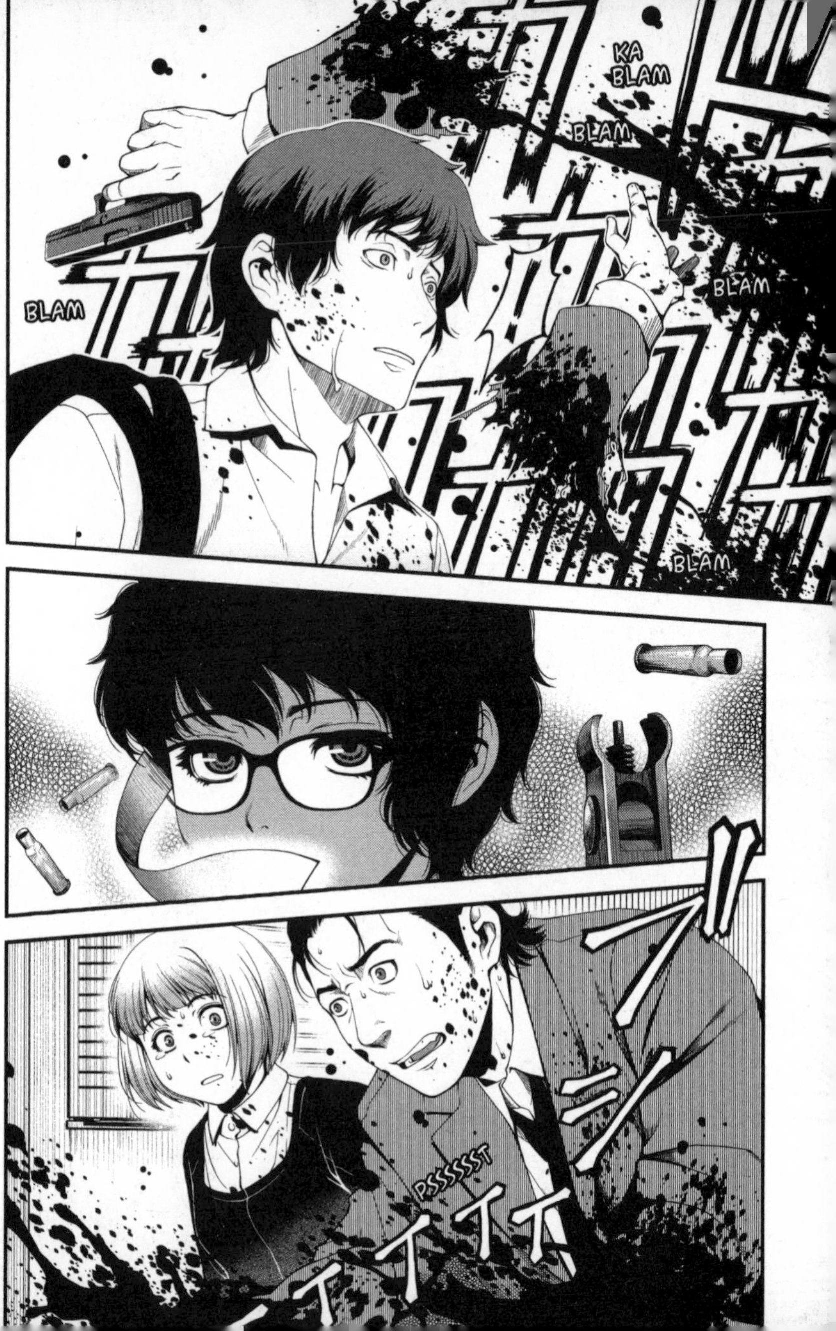
KA
BLAM
BLAM
BLAM
BLAM
BLAM
PSSSSSST

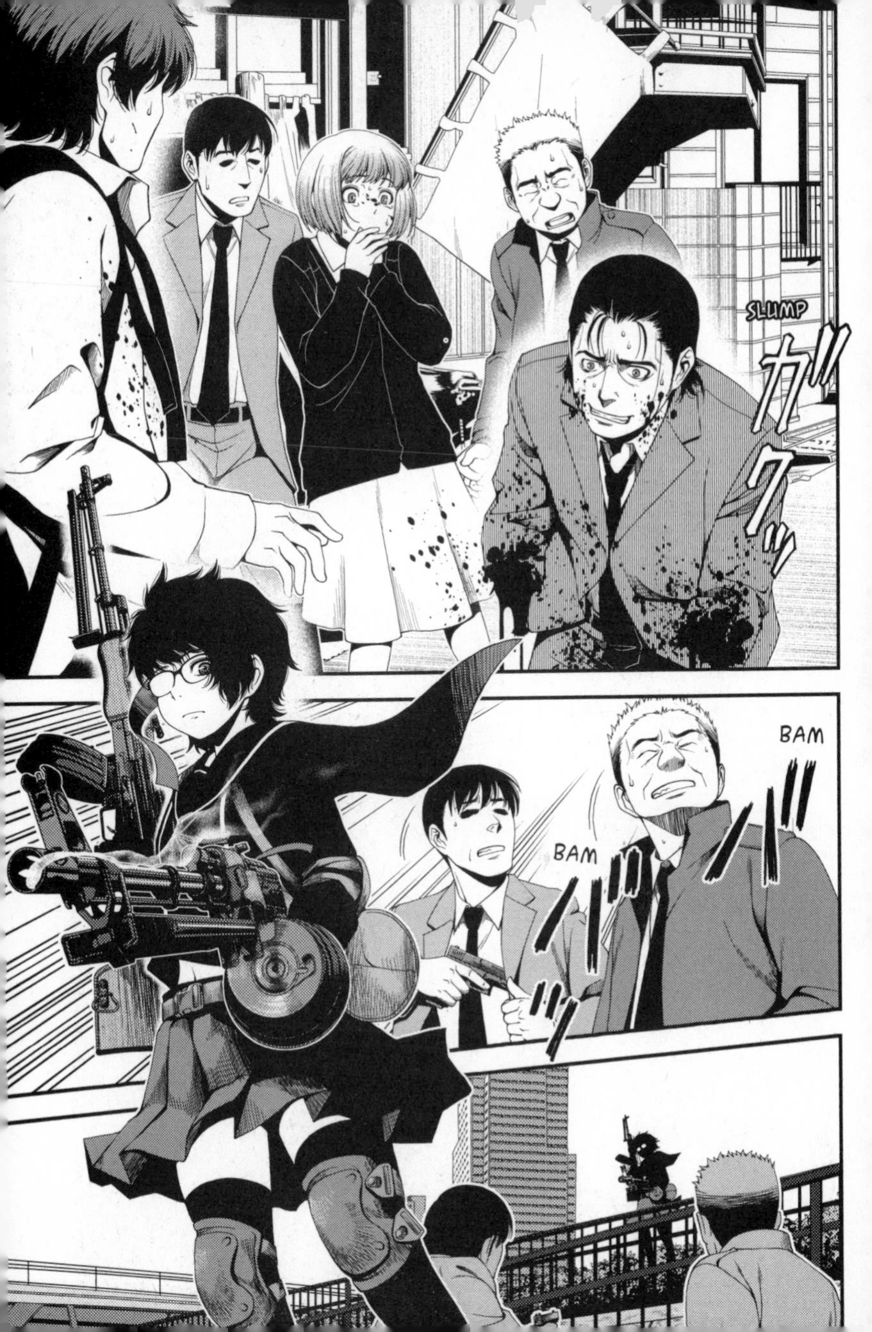
SLUMP
ガクッ
BAM
BAM

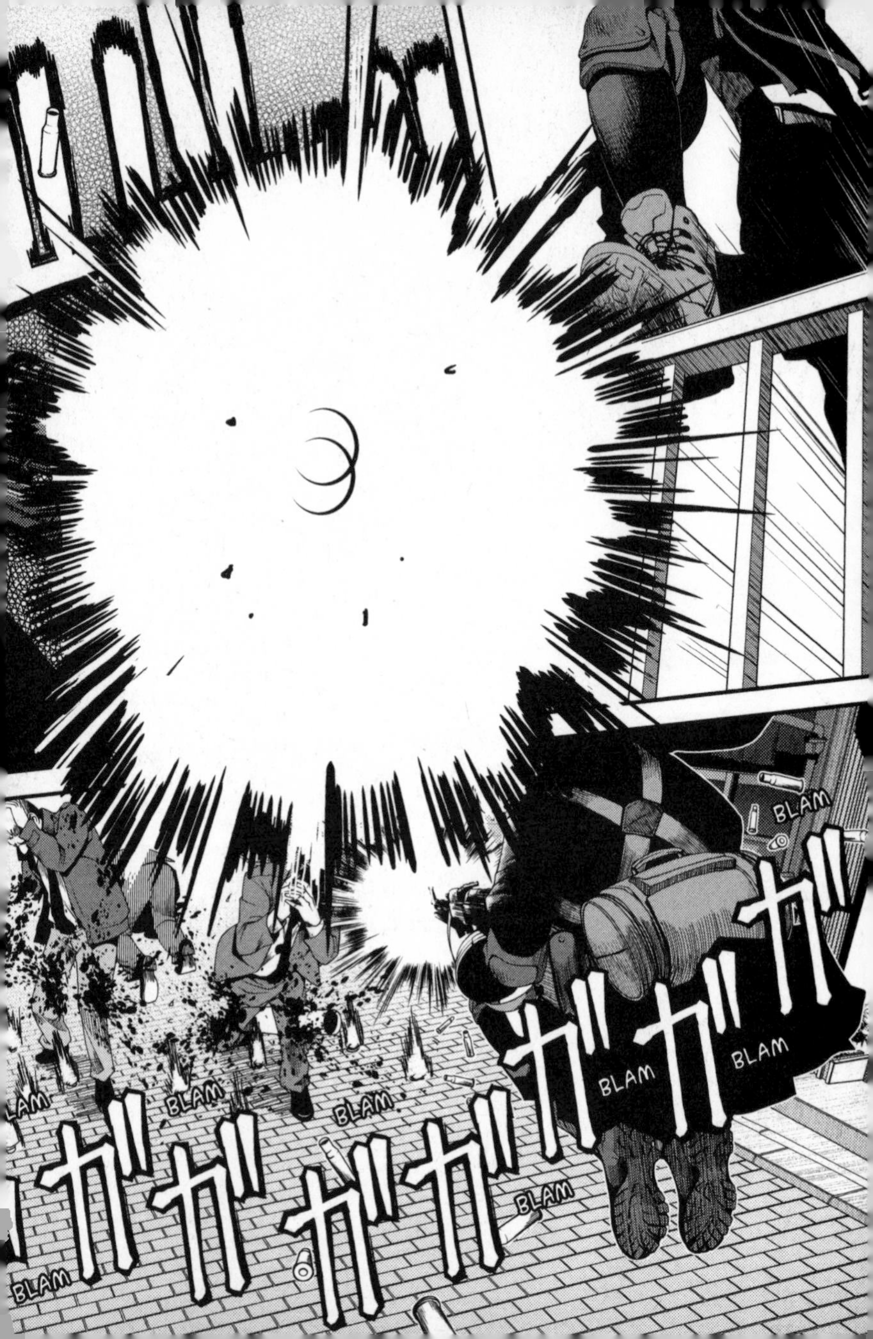
BLAM
ガガガ
BLAM
BLAM
BLAM
BLAM
BLAM
BLAM
BLAM
ガガガガガ

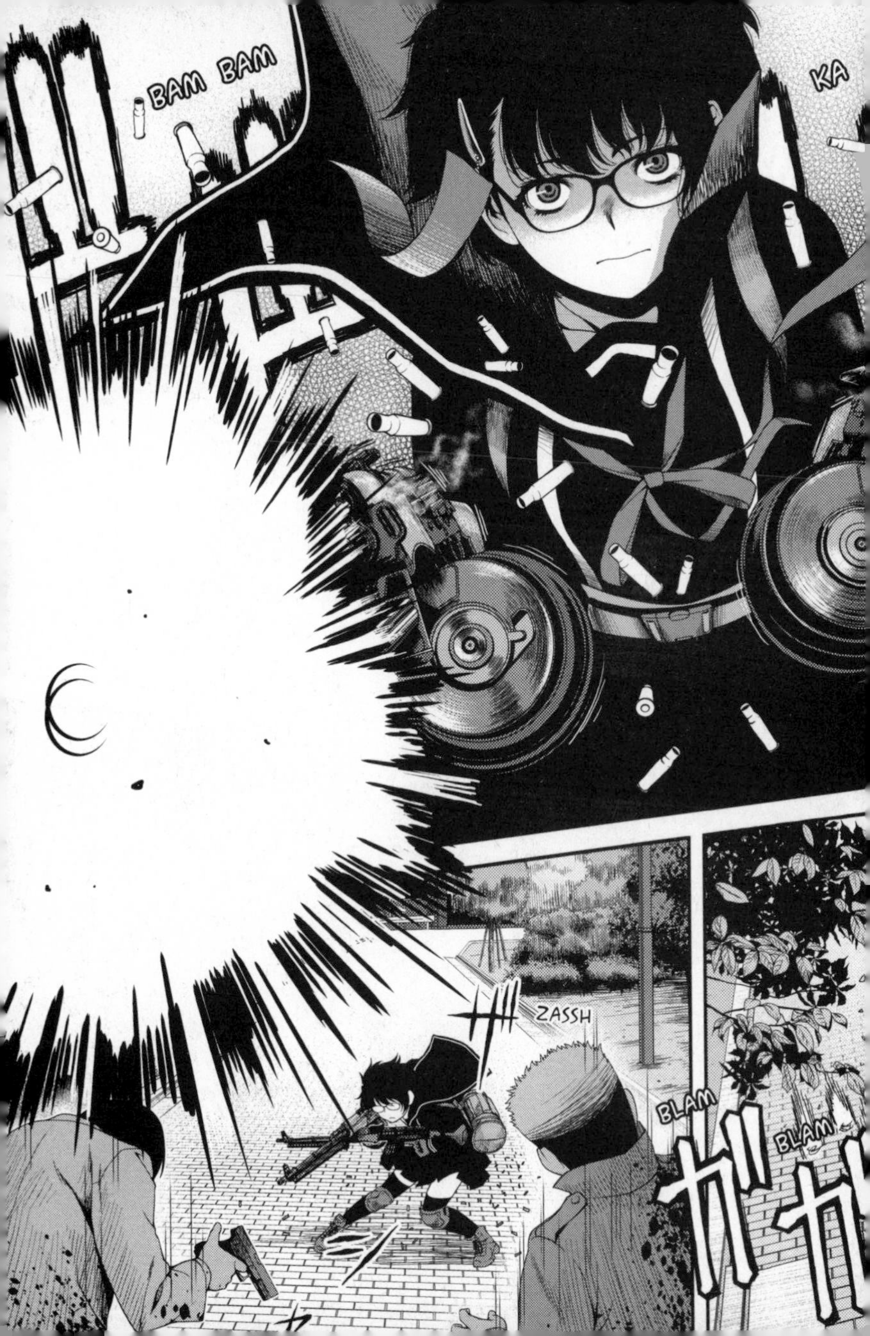
KA
BAM BAM
BLAM
BLAM
ZASSH

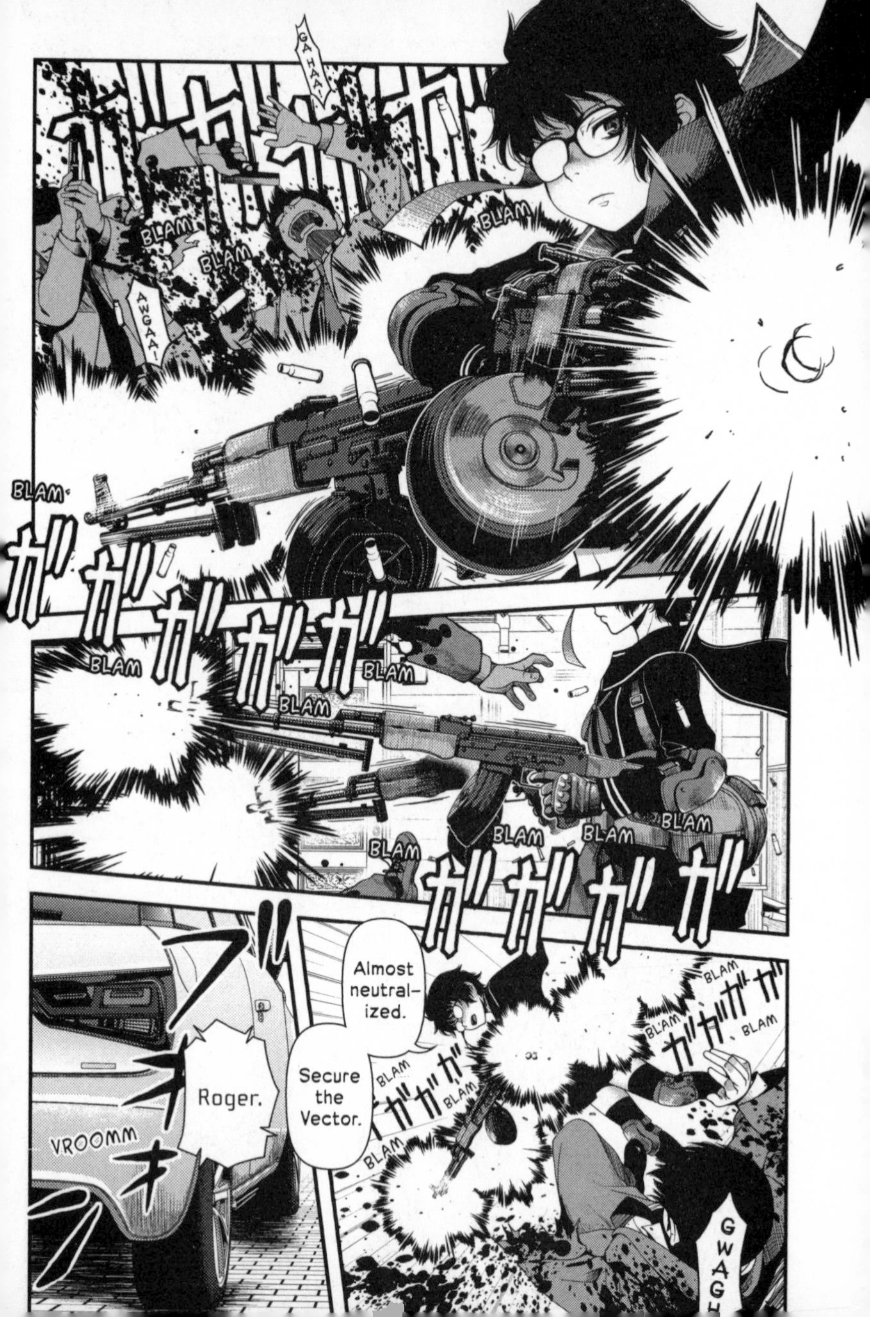

BLAM
GA HAA!
BLAM
BLAM
AWGAA!
BLAM
ガガガガガ
BLAM
BLAM
BLAM
BLAM
BLAM
BLAM
BLAM
ガガガガガ
Almost neutral-ized.
Secure the Vector.
BLAM
ガガガガ
BLAM
BLAM
BLAM
ガガガ
BLAM
BLAM
GWAGH
Roger.
VROOMM

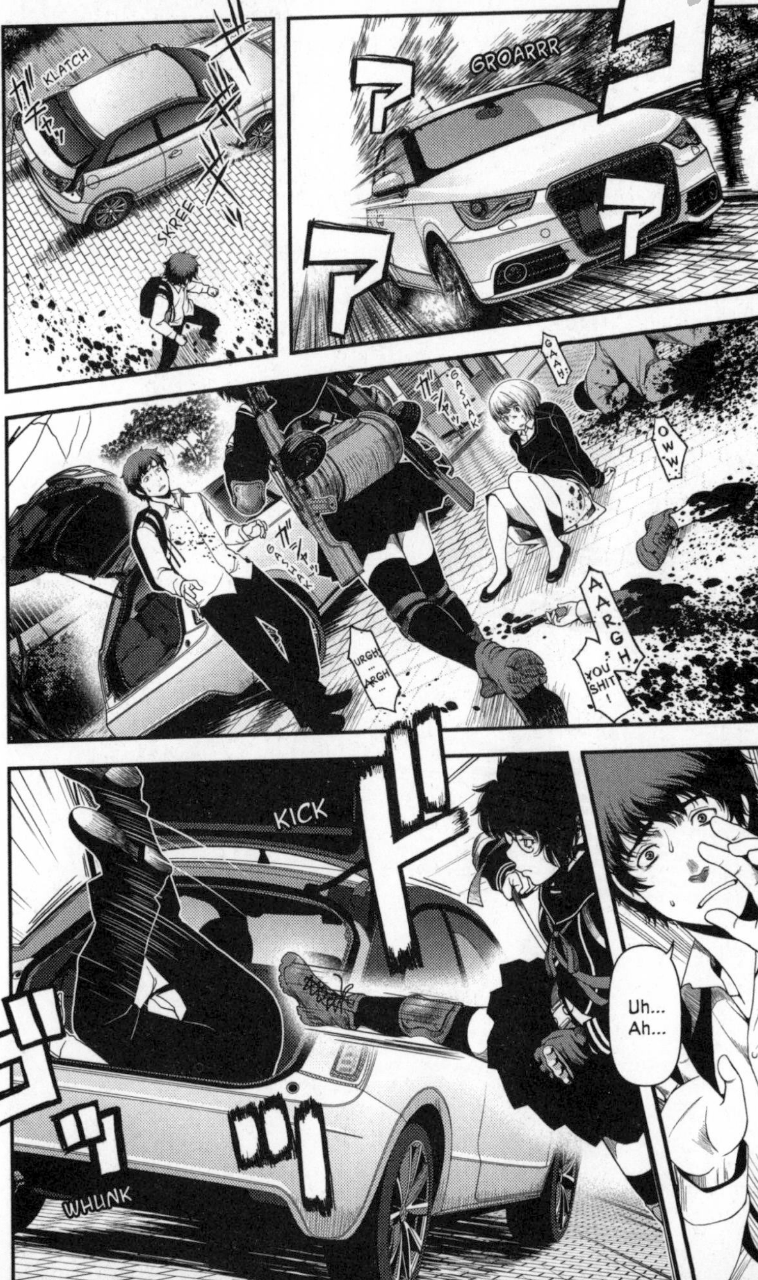
GROARRR
KLATCH
SKREE
GAAH!
GASHAK
OWW...
AARGH.
YOU SHIT!
URGH... ARGH...
Uh... Ah...
KICK
WHUNK

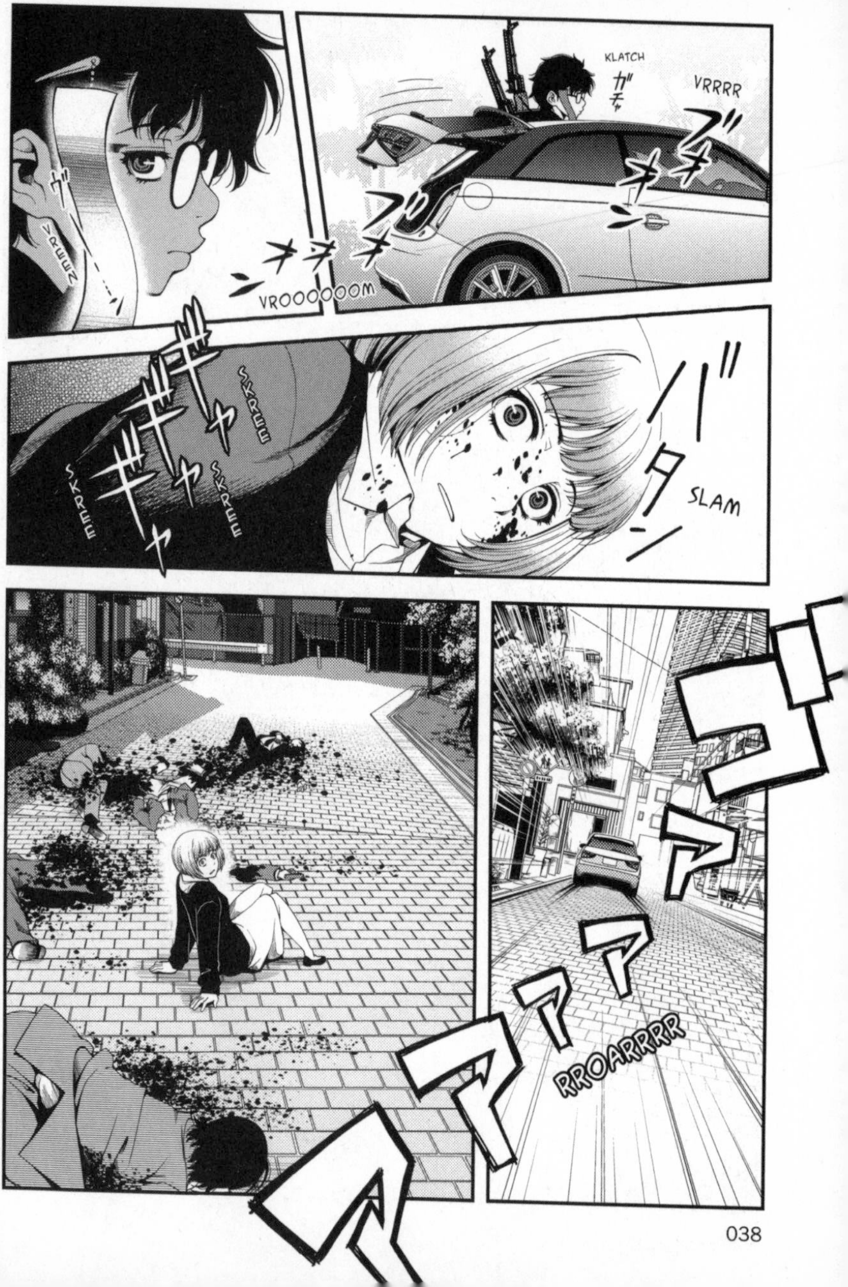

KLATCH
ガチャ
VRRRR
ブオオン
ブオオオン
VROOOOOOM
VREEEN
バタン
SLAM
ギャギャギャ
SKREE
SKREE
SKREE
ゴアアアアア
RROARRRR

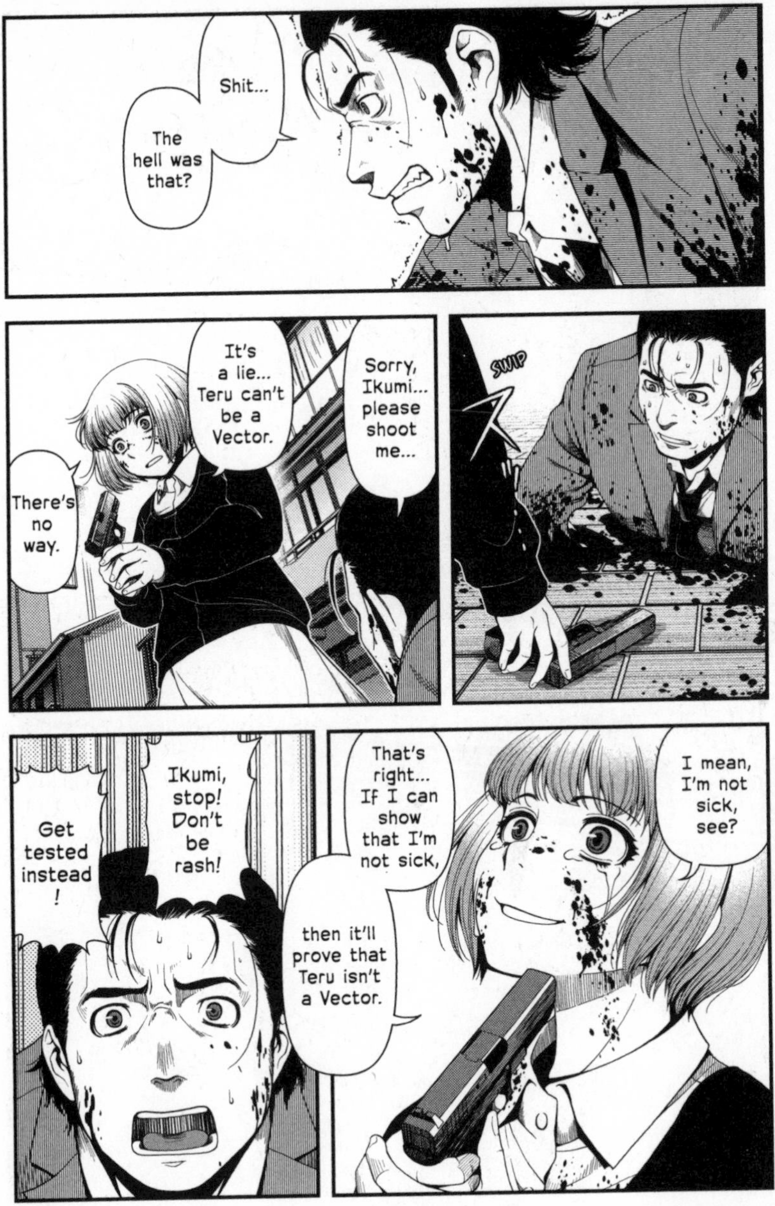
Shit...
The hell was that?
SWIP
Sorry, Ikumi... please shoot me...
It's a lie... Teru can't be a Vector.
There's no way.
I mean, I'm not sick, see?
That's right... If I can show that I'm not sick,
then it'll prove that Teru isn't a Vector.
Ikumi, stop! Don't be rash!
Get tested instead!

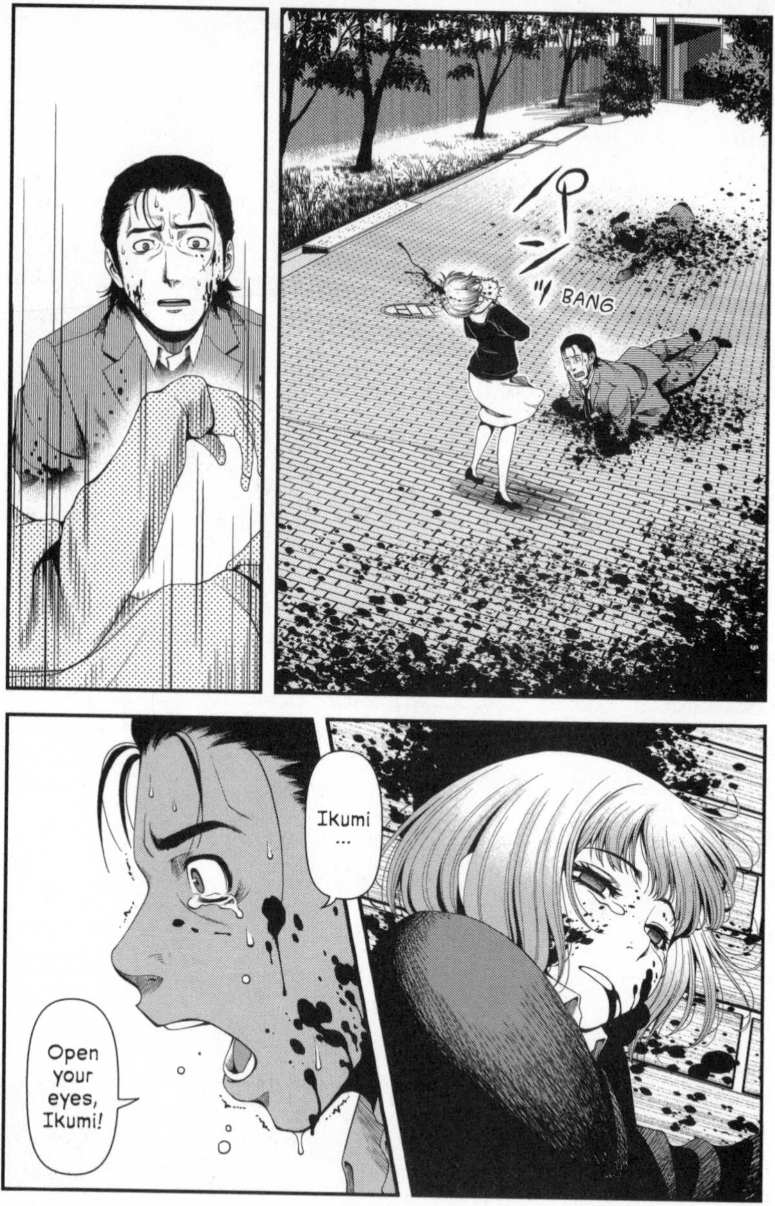
BANG
Ikumi ...
Open your eyes, Ikumi!

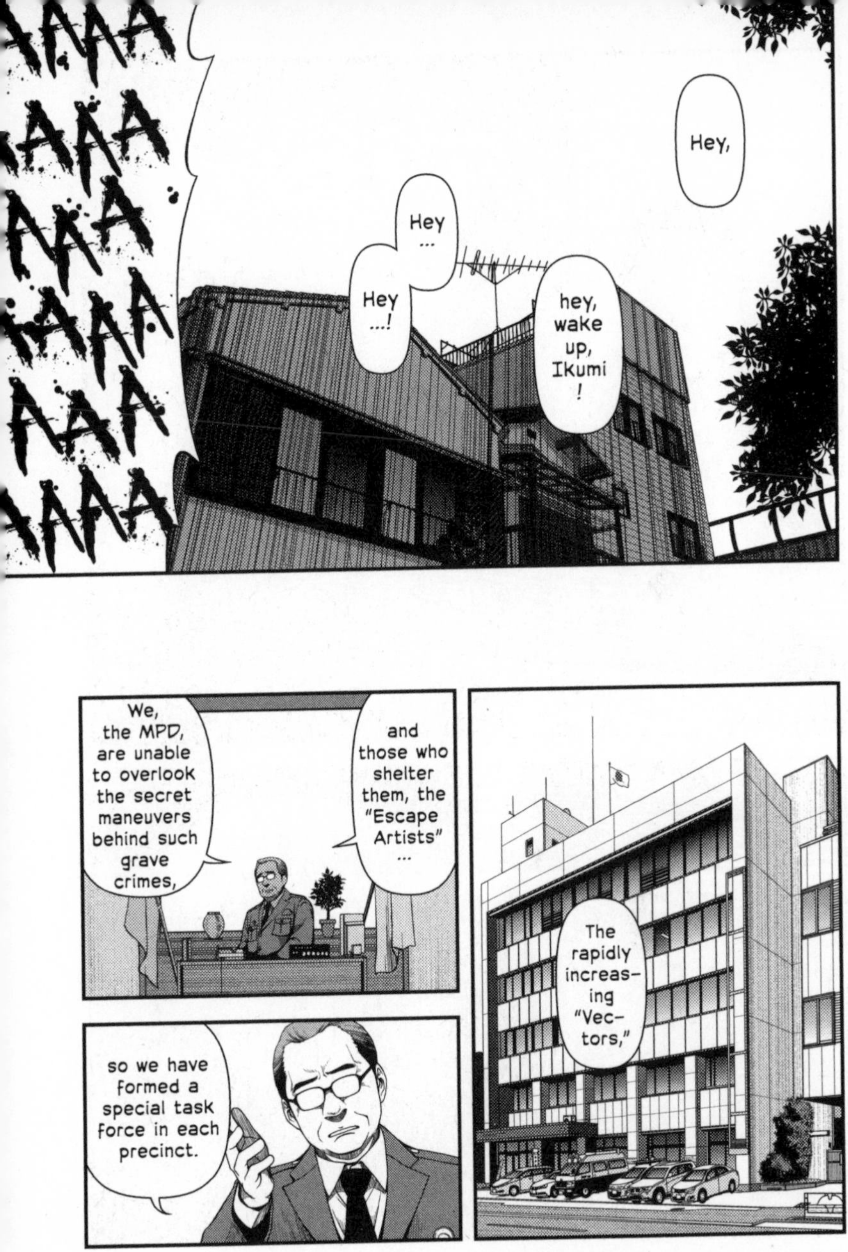

Hey,
Hey ...
Hey ...!
hey, wake up, Ikumi!
AAAAAAAAAAAAAAAAAAAAA
The rapidly increasing "Vectors,"
and those who shelter them, the "Escape Artists" ...
We, the MPD, are unable to overlook the secret maneuvers behind such grave crimes,
so we have formed a special task force in each precinct.

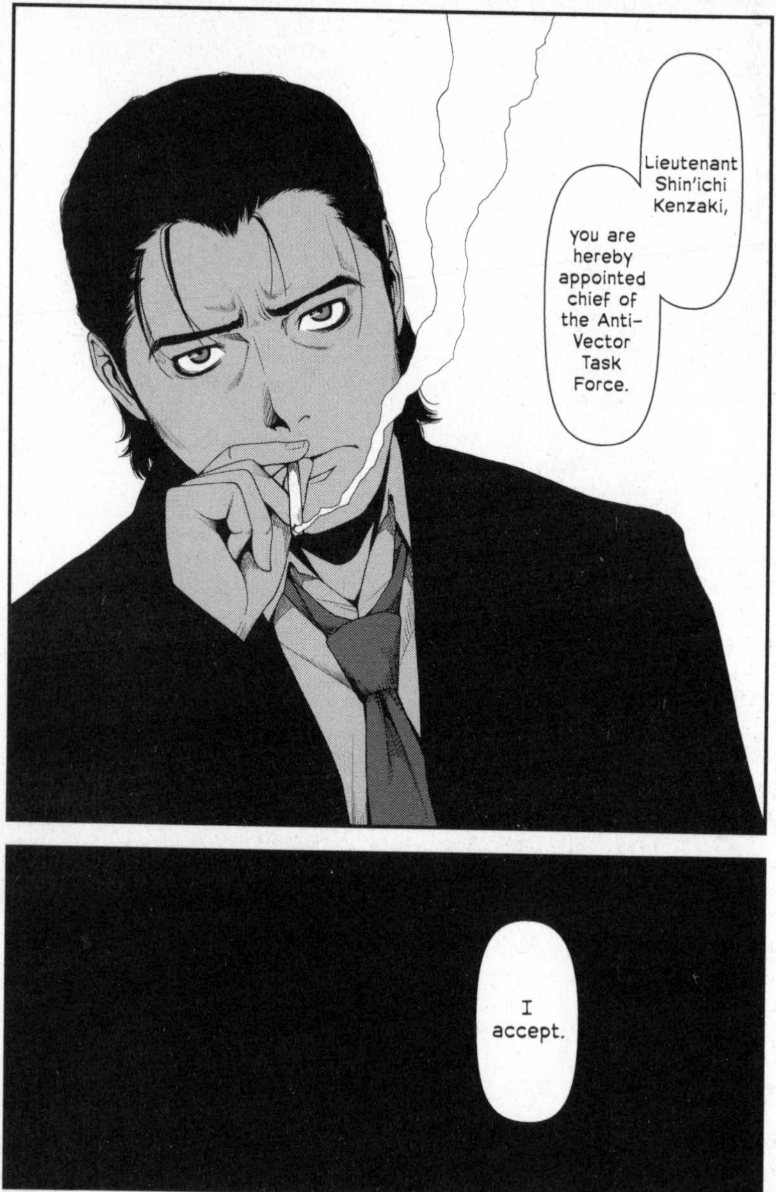
Lieutenant Shin'ichi Kenzaki,
you are hereby appointed chief of the Anti-Vector Task Force.
I accept.

End of Chapter 1

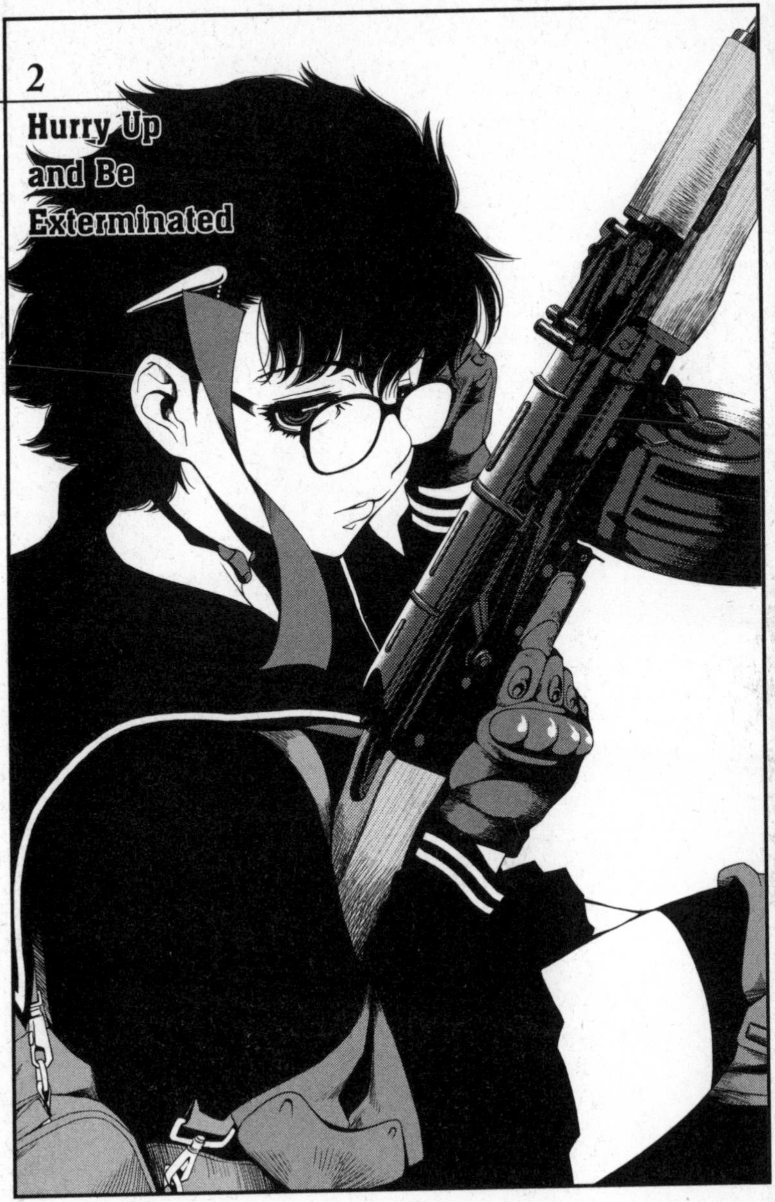
2
Hurry Up
and Be
Exterminated

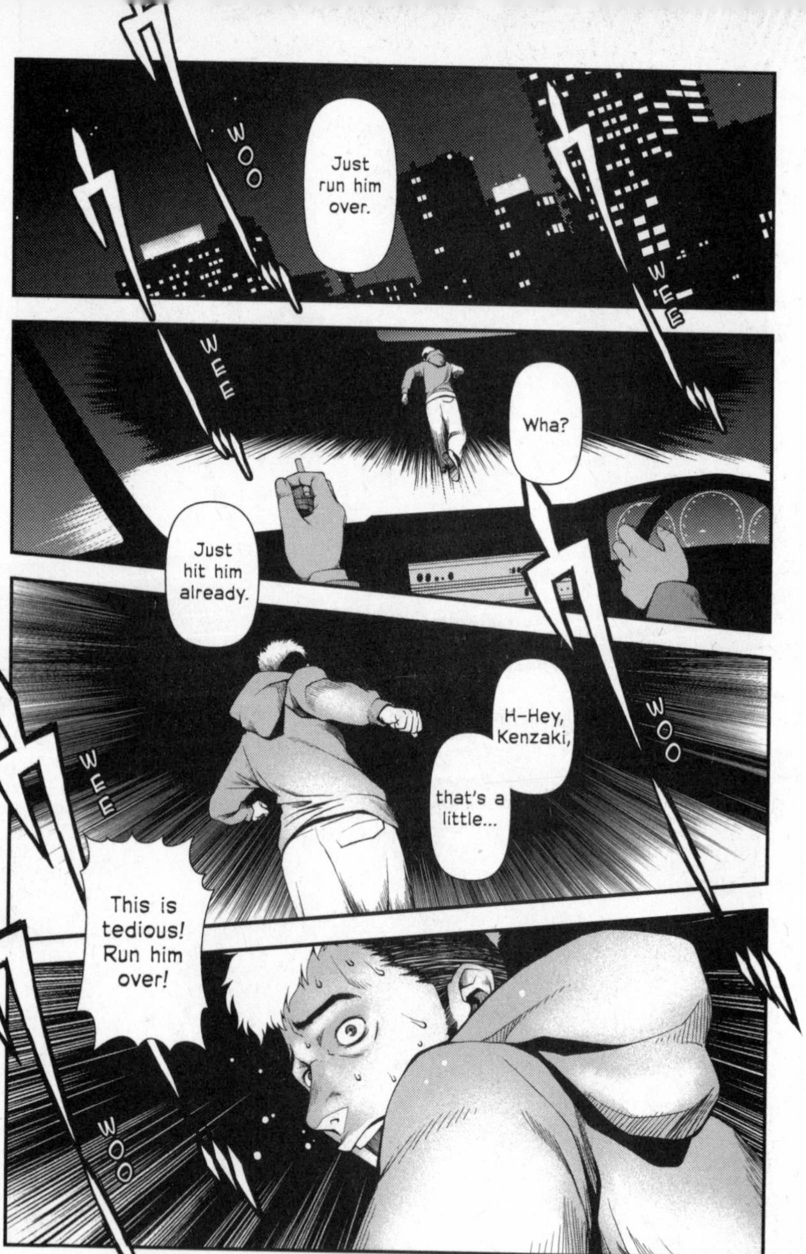
WEE
Just run him over.
WOO
Wha?
WEE
Just hit him already.
WOO
H-Hey, Kenzaki,
that's a little...
WEE
This is tedious! Run him over!
WOO

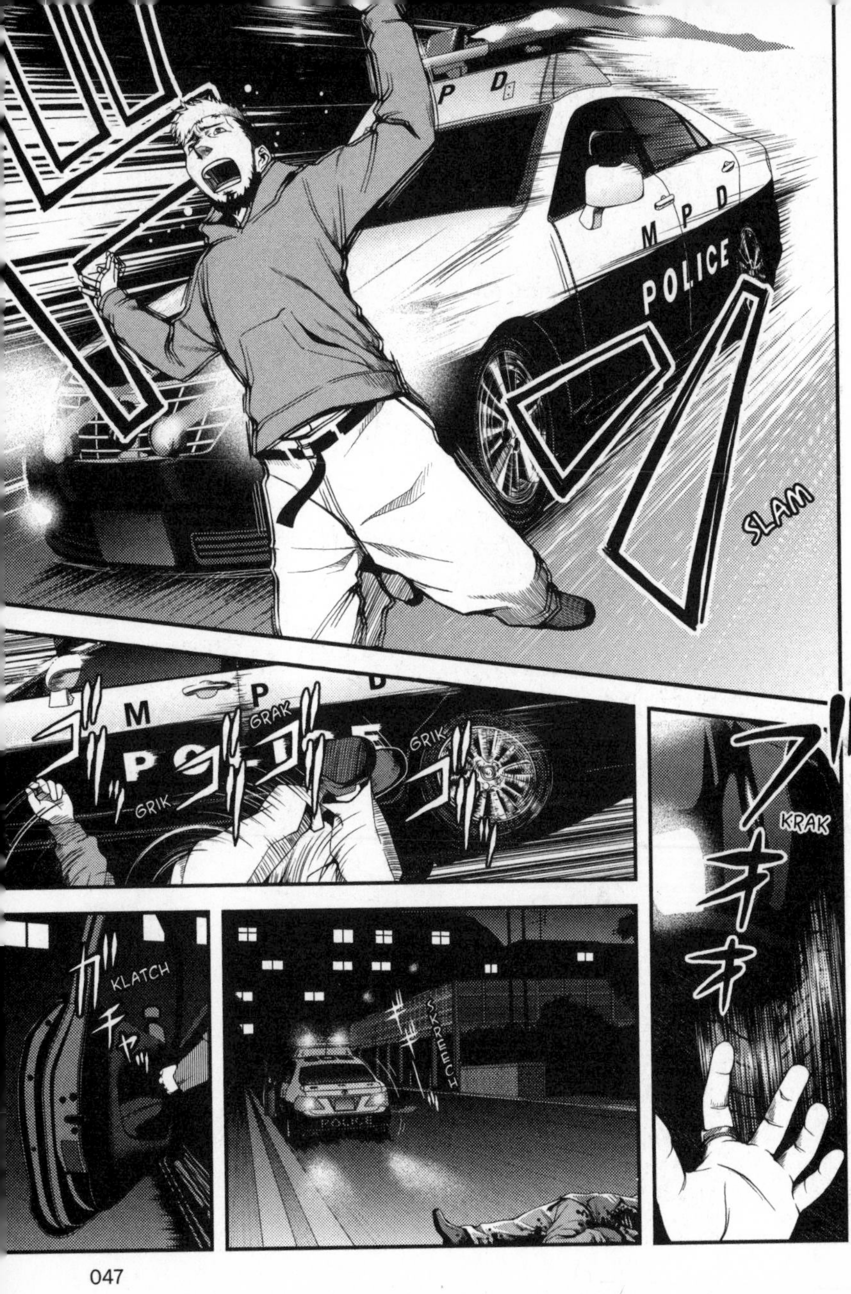
MPD
MPD
POLICE
SLAM
KRAK
MPD
GRAK
GRIK
GRIK
SKREECH
KLATCH

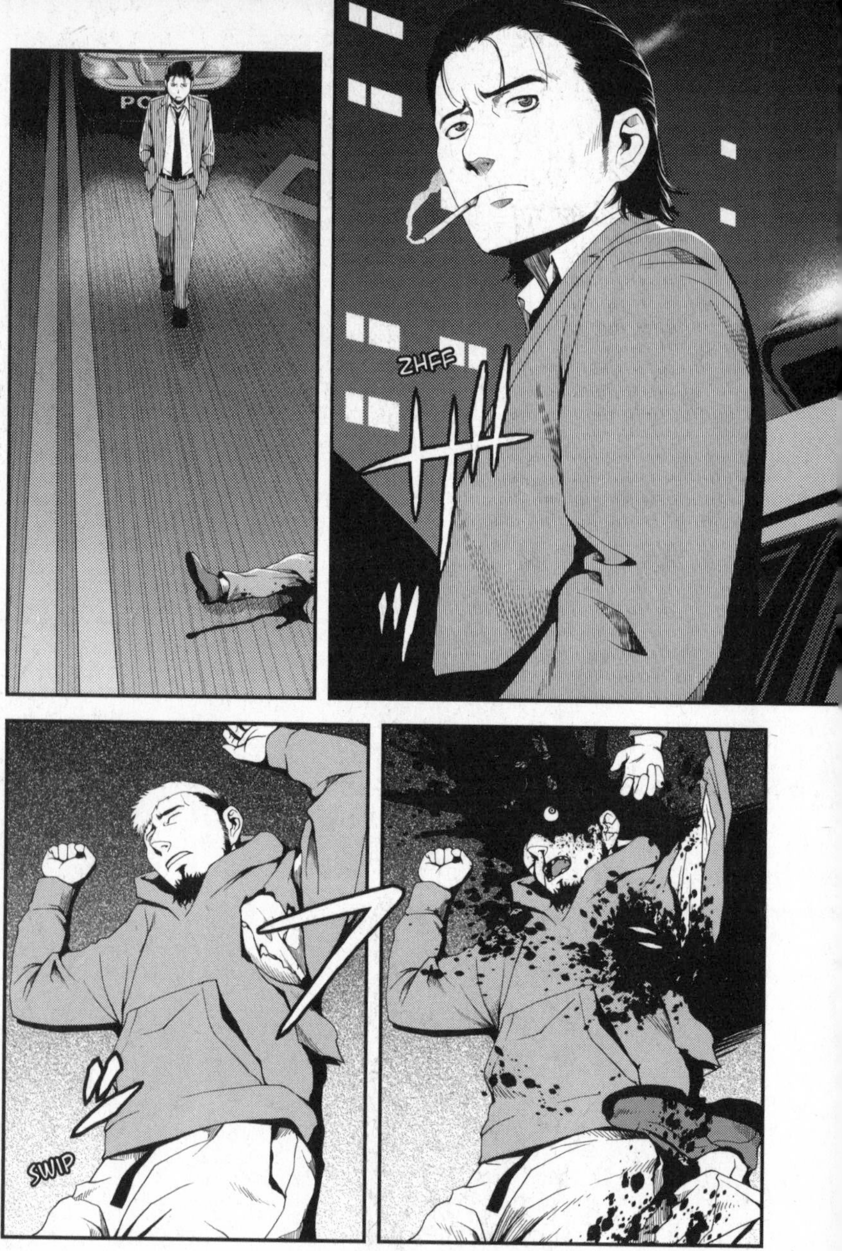
ZHFF
SWIP

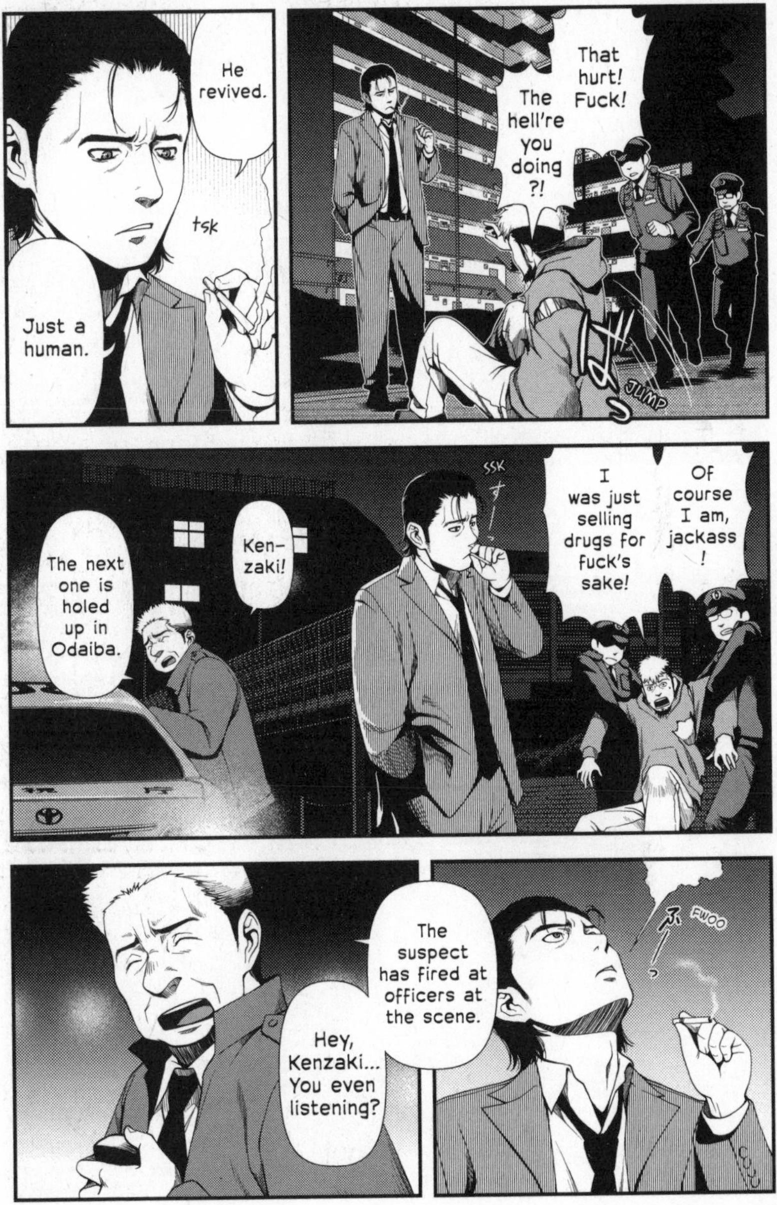

That hurt! Fuck!
The hell're you doing ?!
JUMP
He revived.
tsk
Just a human.
Of course I am, jackass!
I was just selling drugs for fuck's sake!
SSK
Ken-zaki!
The next one is holed up in Odaiba.
FWOO
The suspect has fired at officers at the scene.
Hey, Kenzaki... You even listening?

The suspect has forged ID.

Waka-bayashi is already on the way.

Okay.

Let's hurry!

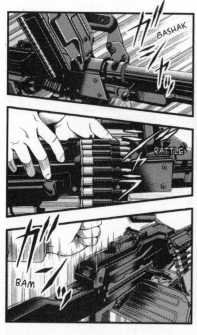

GASHAK

RATTLE

BAM

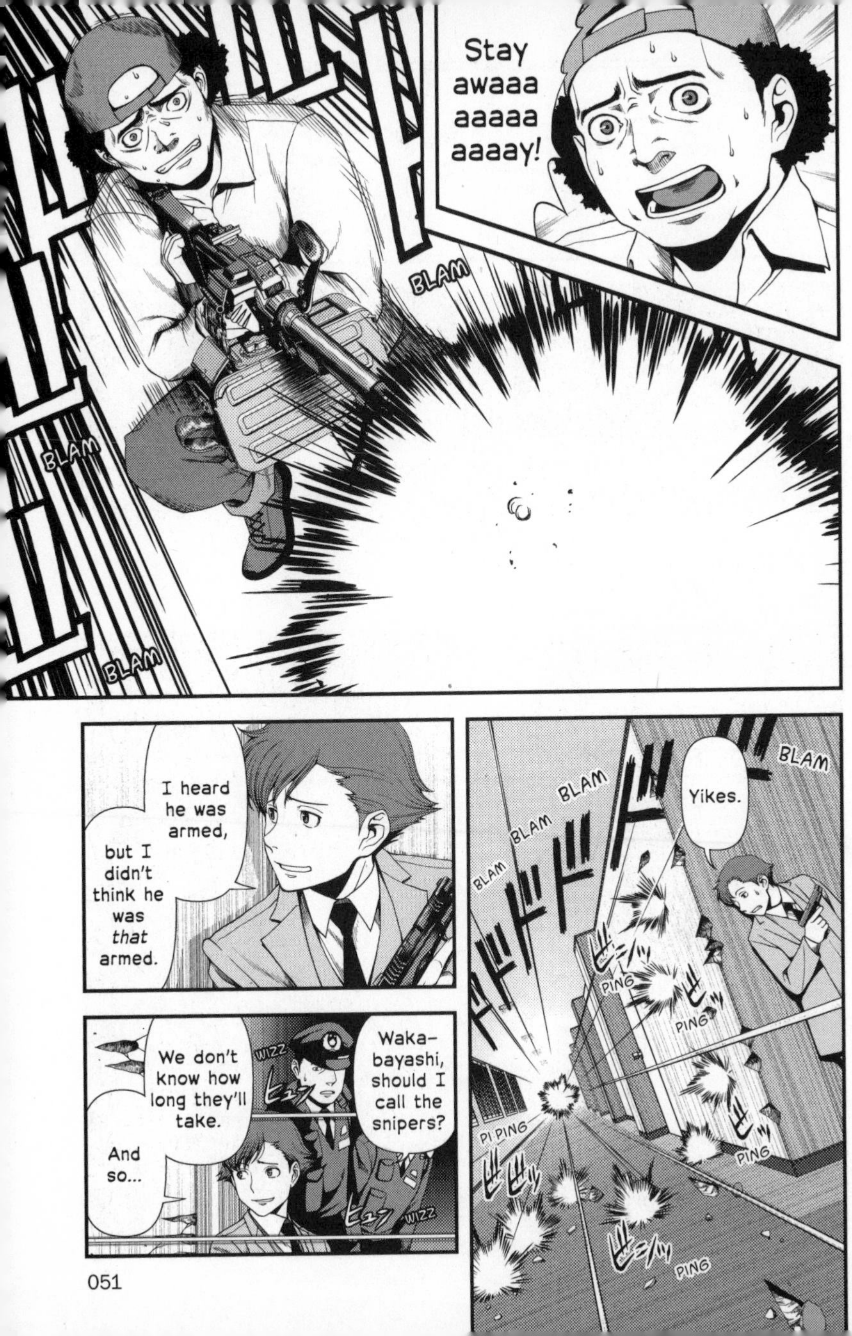
Stay awaaa aaaaa aaaay!
BLAM
BLAM
BLAM
BLAM
BLAM
BLAM
BLAM
Yikes.
PING
PING
PI PING
PING
PING
I heard he was armed,
but I didn't think he was *that* armed.
WIZZ
Waka-bayashi, should I call the snipers?
We don't know how long they'll take.
And so...
WIZZ

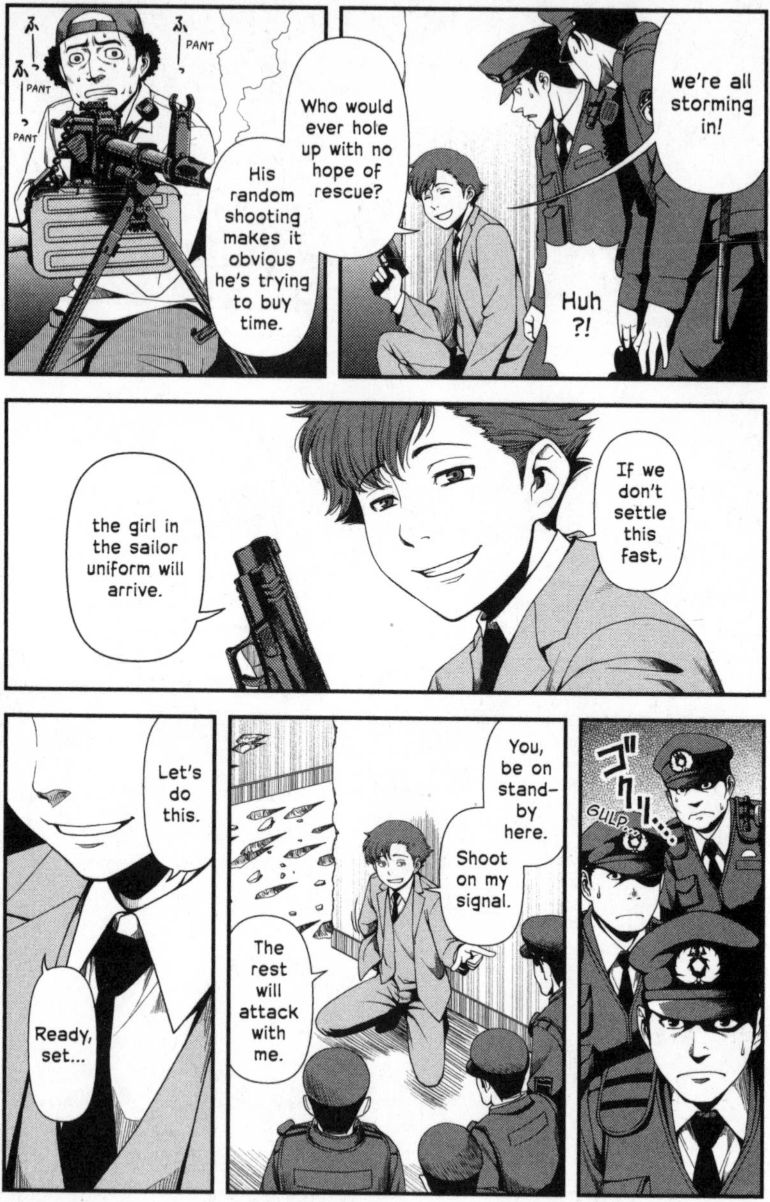

we're all storming in!
Huh ?!
Who would ever hole up with no hope of rescue?
ふーっ
PANT
ふーっ
PANT
ふーっ
PANT
His random shooting makes it obvious he's trying to buy time.
If we don't settle this fast,
the girl in the sailor uniform will arrive.
ゴクリ…
GULP…
You, be on stand-by here.
Shoot on my signal.
The rest will attack with me.
Let's do this.
Ready, set...

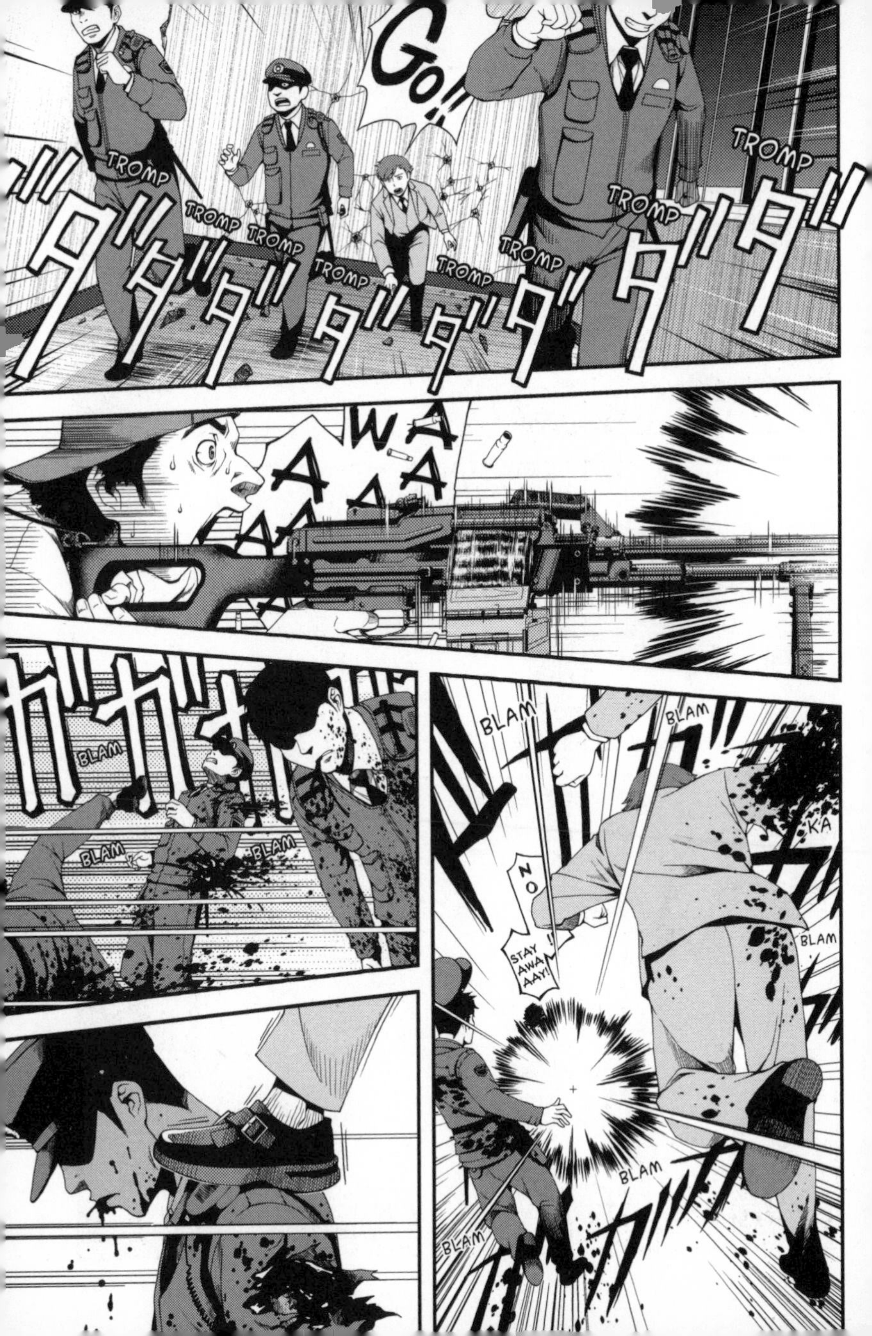
GO!!
TROMP
TROMP
TROMP
TROMP
TROMP
TROMP
TROMP
TROMP
WAAAAAA
BLAM
BLAM
KA
NO!
STAY AWAAAY!
BLAM
BLAM
BLAM
BLAM
BLAM
BLAM

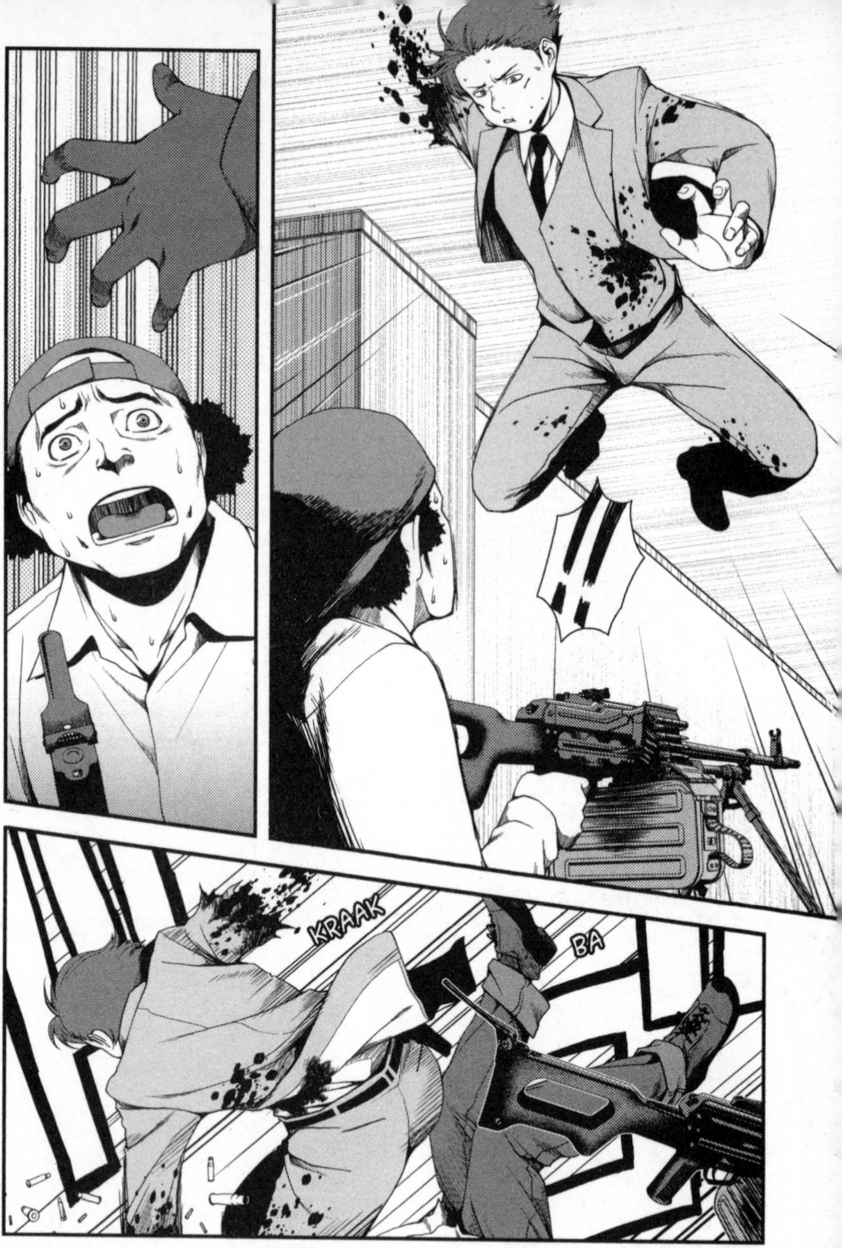
KRAAK
BA

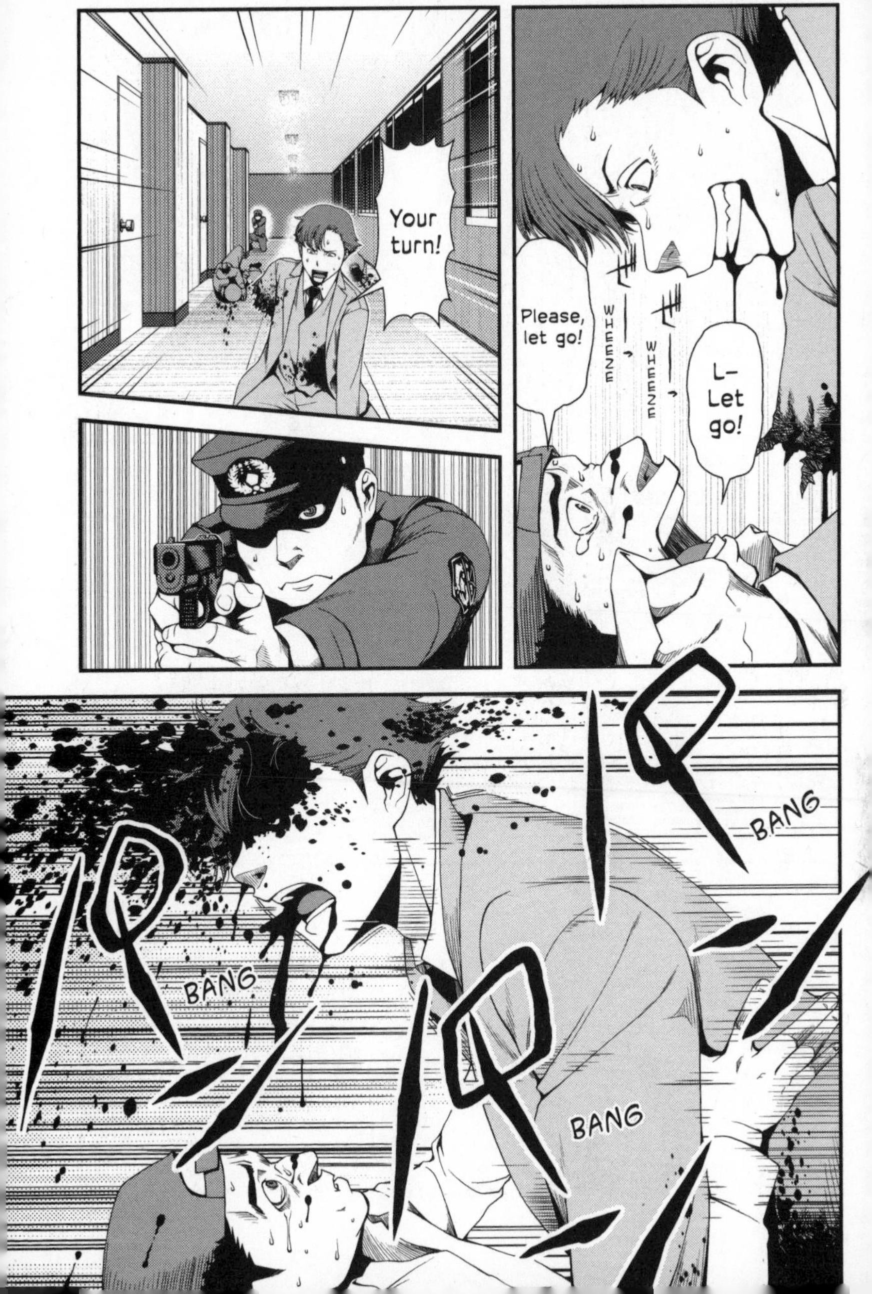
L-
Let go!
WHEEZE
WHEEZE
Please, let go!
Your turn!
BANG
BANG
BANG

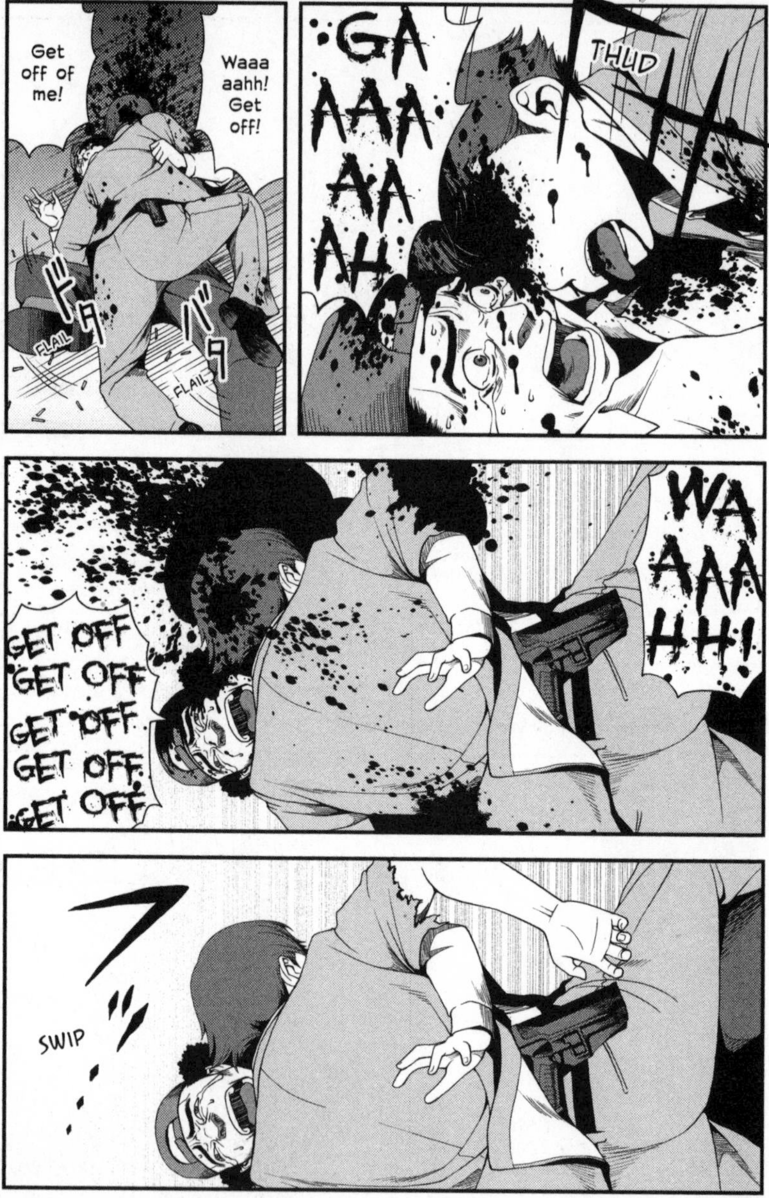
GAAAAAAAH
THUD
Waaa aahh! Get off!
Get off of me!
ドタ
FLAIL
バタ
FLAIL
WAAAAHH!
GET OFF GET OFF GET OFF GET OFF GET OFF
SWIP

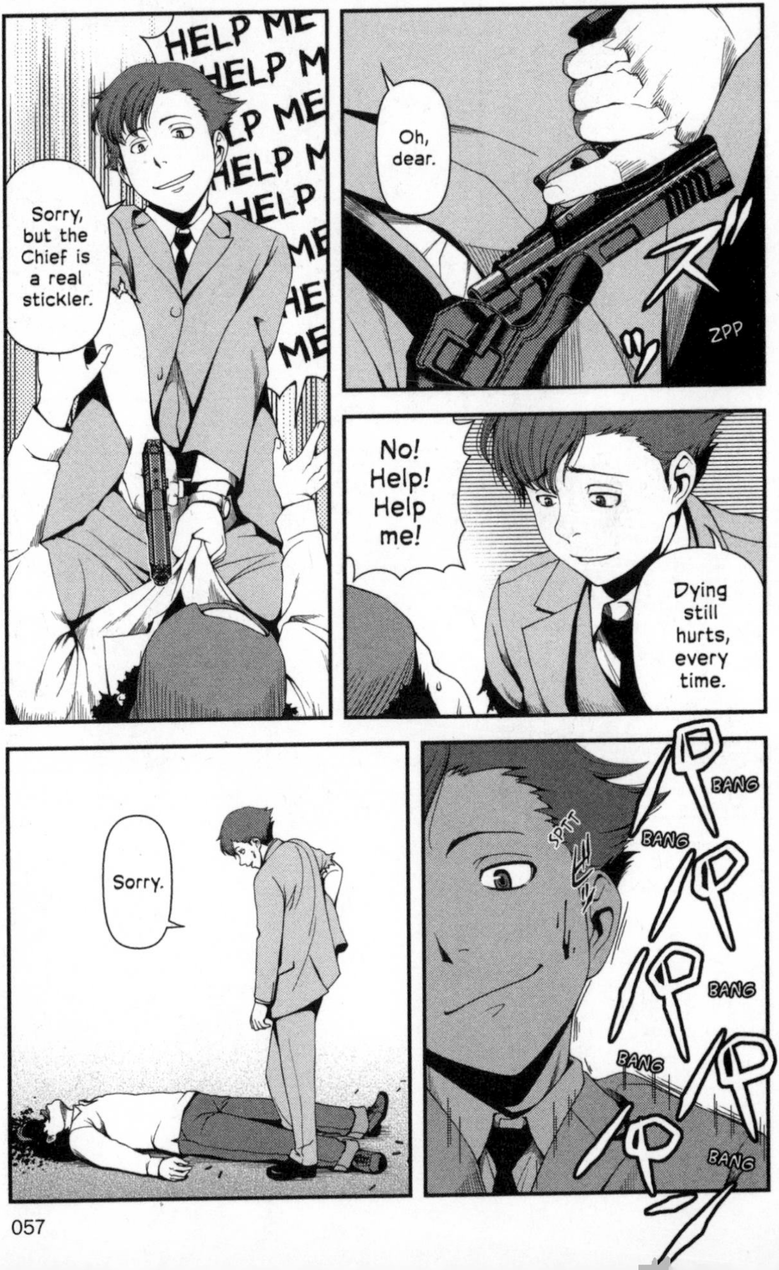
Oh, dear.
ZPP
No! Help! Help me!
Dying still hurts, every time.
HELP ME HELP ME HELP ME HELP ME HELP ME HELP ME
Sorry, but the Chief is a real stickler.
BANG
BANG
BANG
BANG
BANG
SPTT
Sorry.

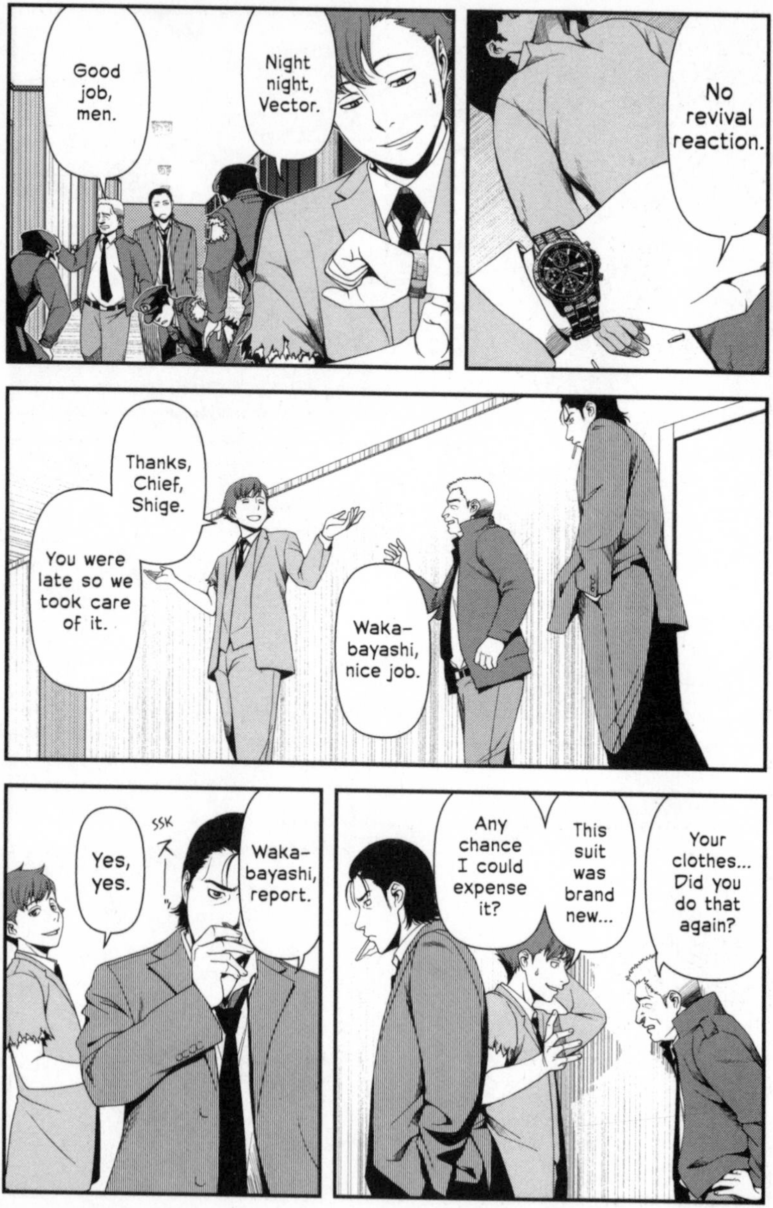
No revival reaction.
Night night, Vector.
Good job, men.
Waka-bayashi, nice job.
Thanks, Chief, Shige.
You were late so we took care of it.
Your clothes... Did you do that again?
This suit was brand new...
Any chance I could expense it?
Waka-bayashi, report.
SSK
スーッ
Yes, yes.

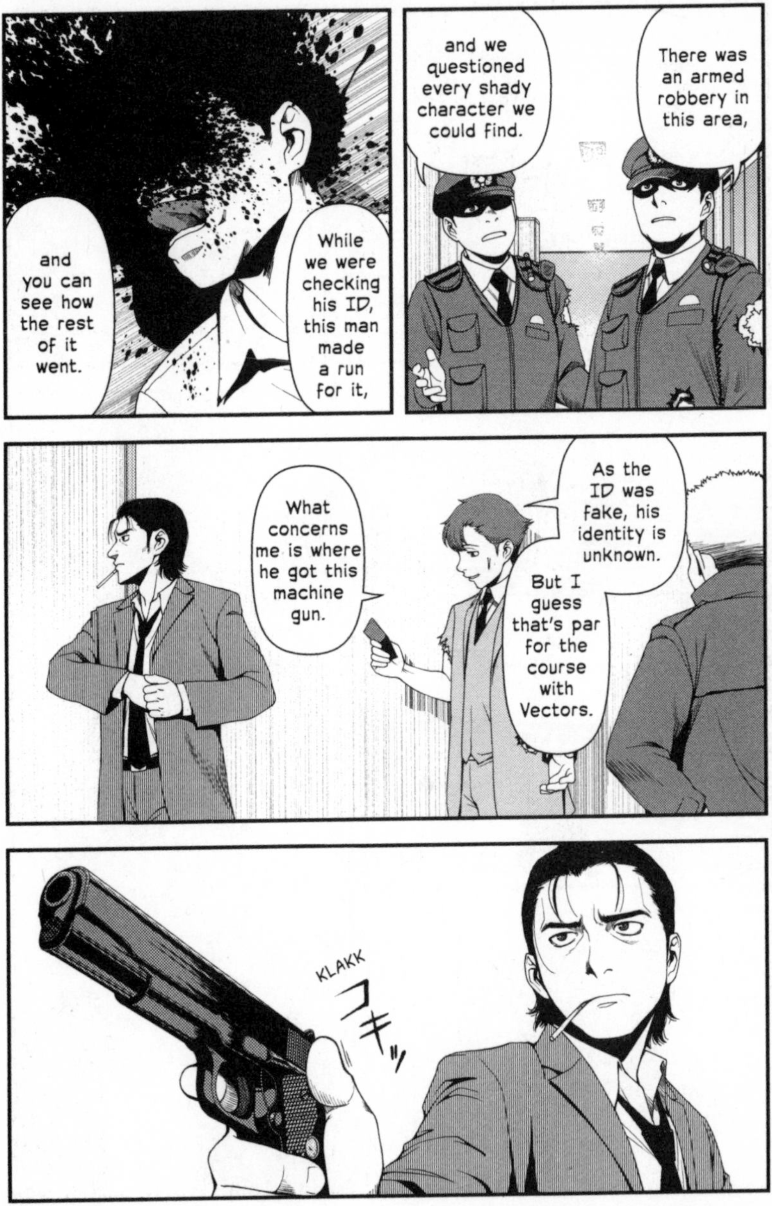
There was an armed robbery in this area,
and we questioned every shady character we could find.
While we were checking his ID, this man made a run for it,
and you can see how the rest of it went.
As the ID was fake, his identity is unknown.
But I guess that's par for the course with Vectors.
What concerns me is where he got this machine gun.
KLAKK

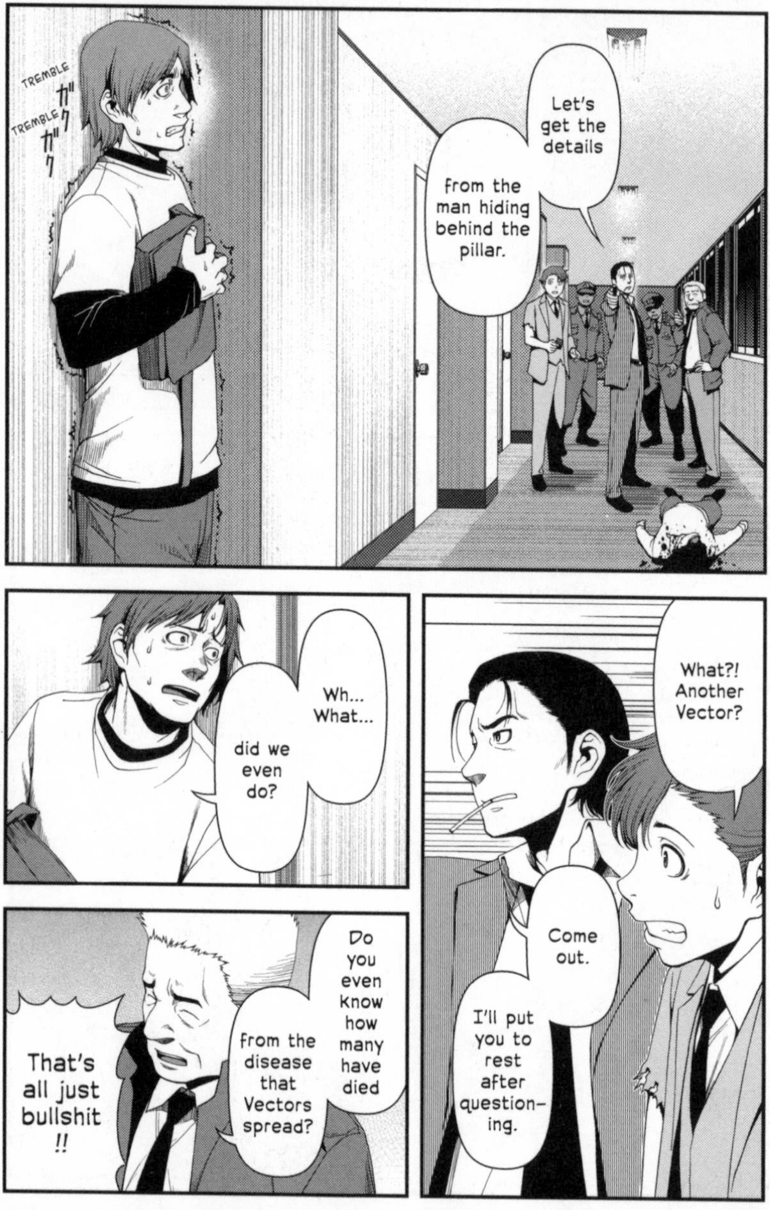
Let's get the details
from the man hiding behind the pillar.
TREMBLE ガク
TREMBLE ガク
What?! Another Vector?
Come out.
I'll put you to rest after question-ing.
Wh... What...
did we even do?
Do you even know how many have died
from the disease that Vectors spread?
That's all just bullshit !!

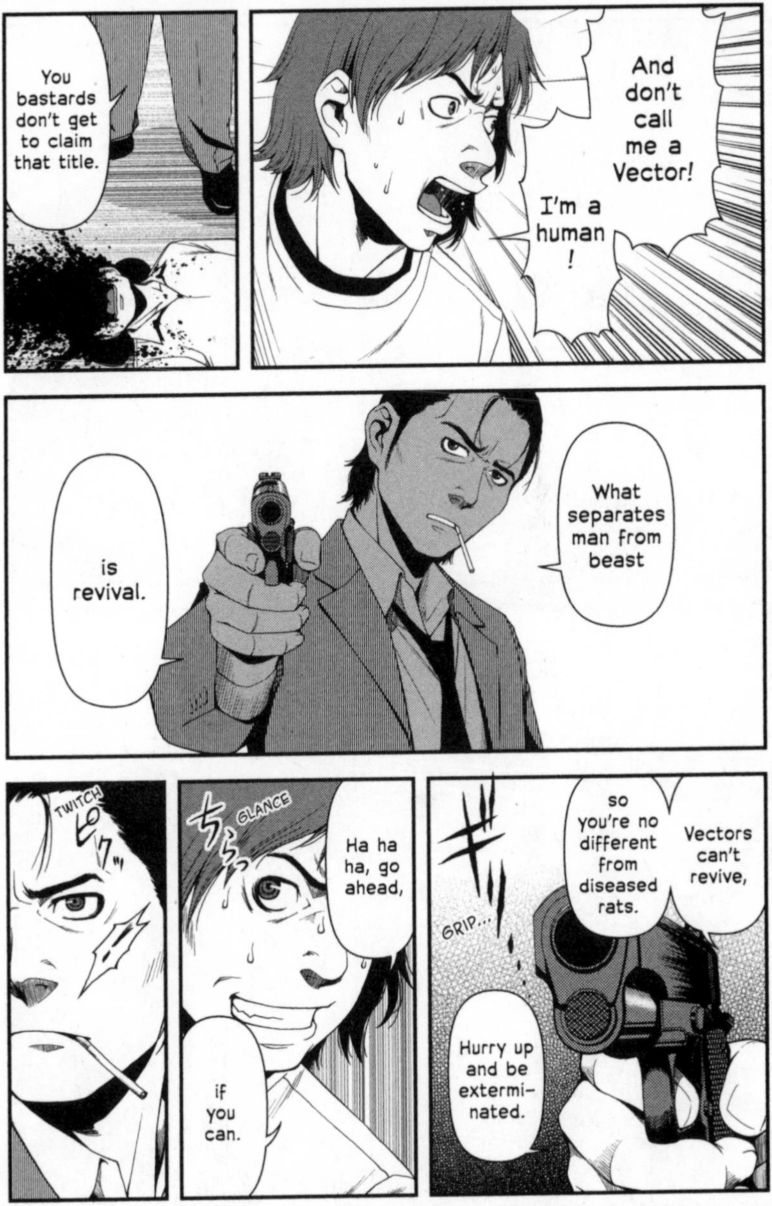
And don't call me a Vector!
I'm a human!
You bastards don't get to claim that title.
What separates man from beast
is revival.
Vectors can't revive,
so you're no different from diseased rats.
GRIP...
Hurry up and be extermi-nated.
GLANCE
Ha ha ha, go ahead,
if you can.
TWITCH

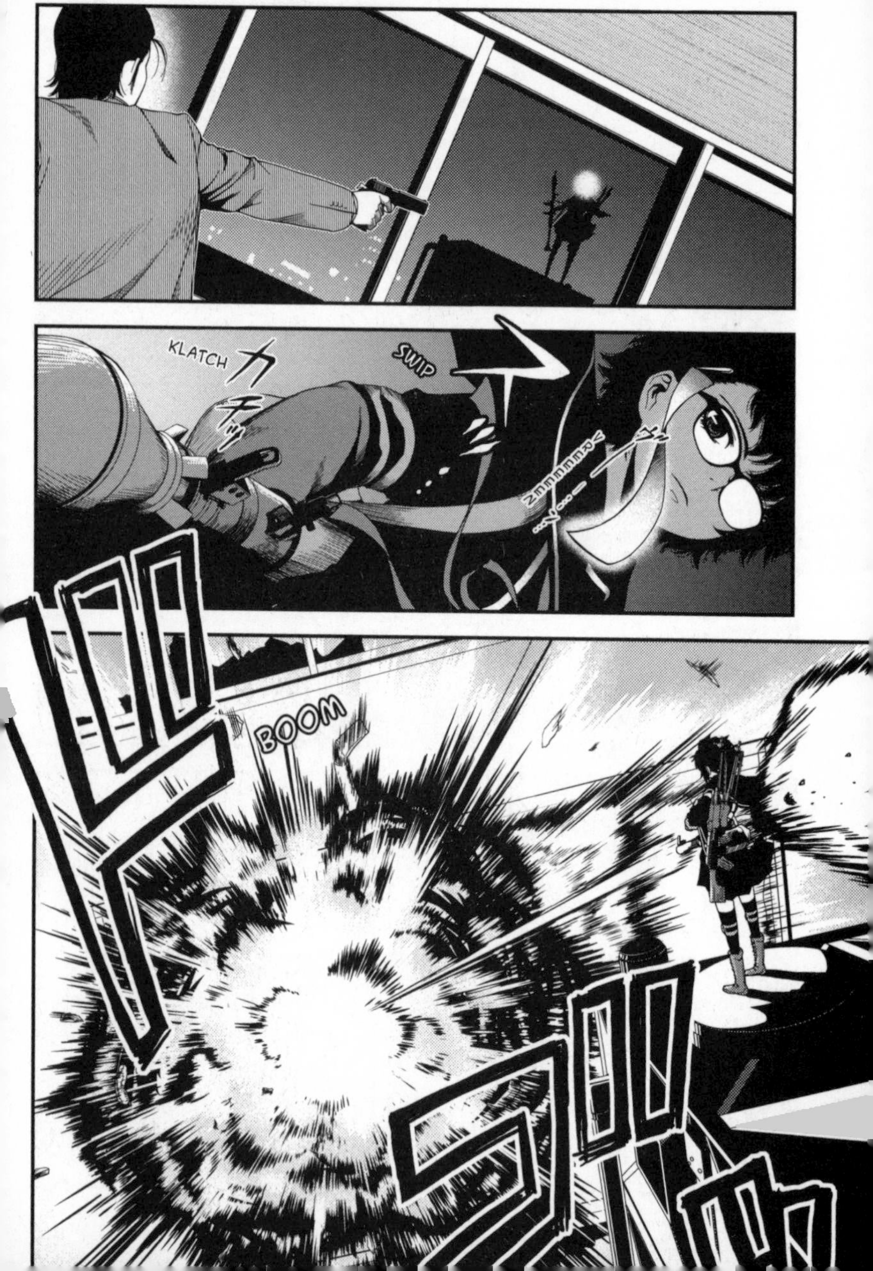
SWIP
KLATCH
カチッ
BOOM

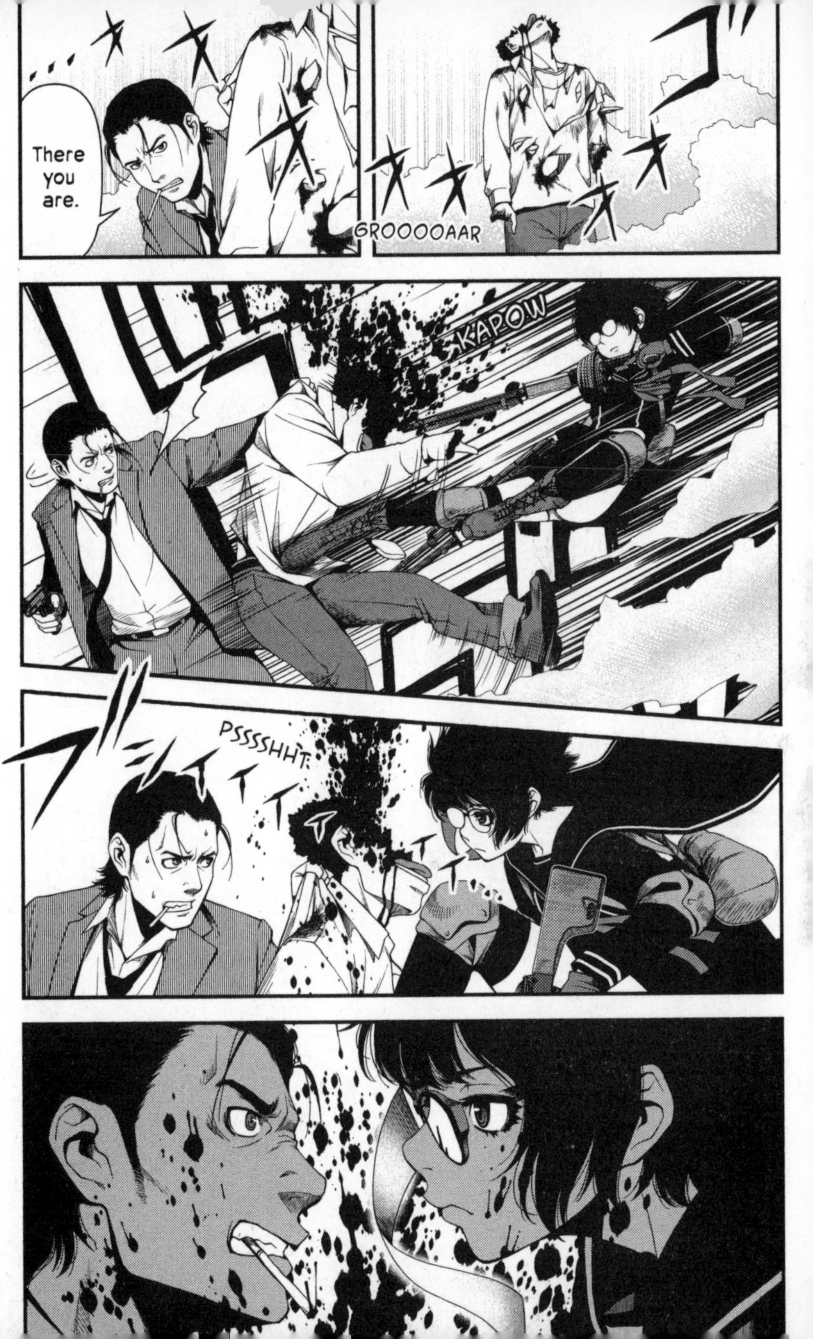
GROOOOAAR
...
There you are.
KAPOW
PSSSSHHT

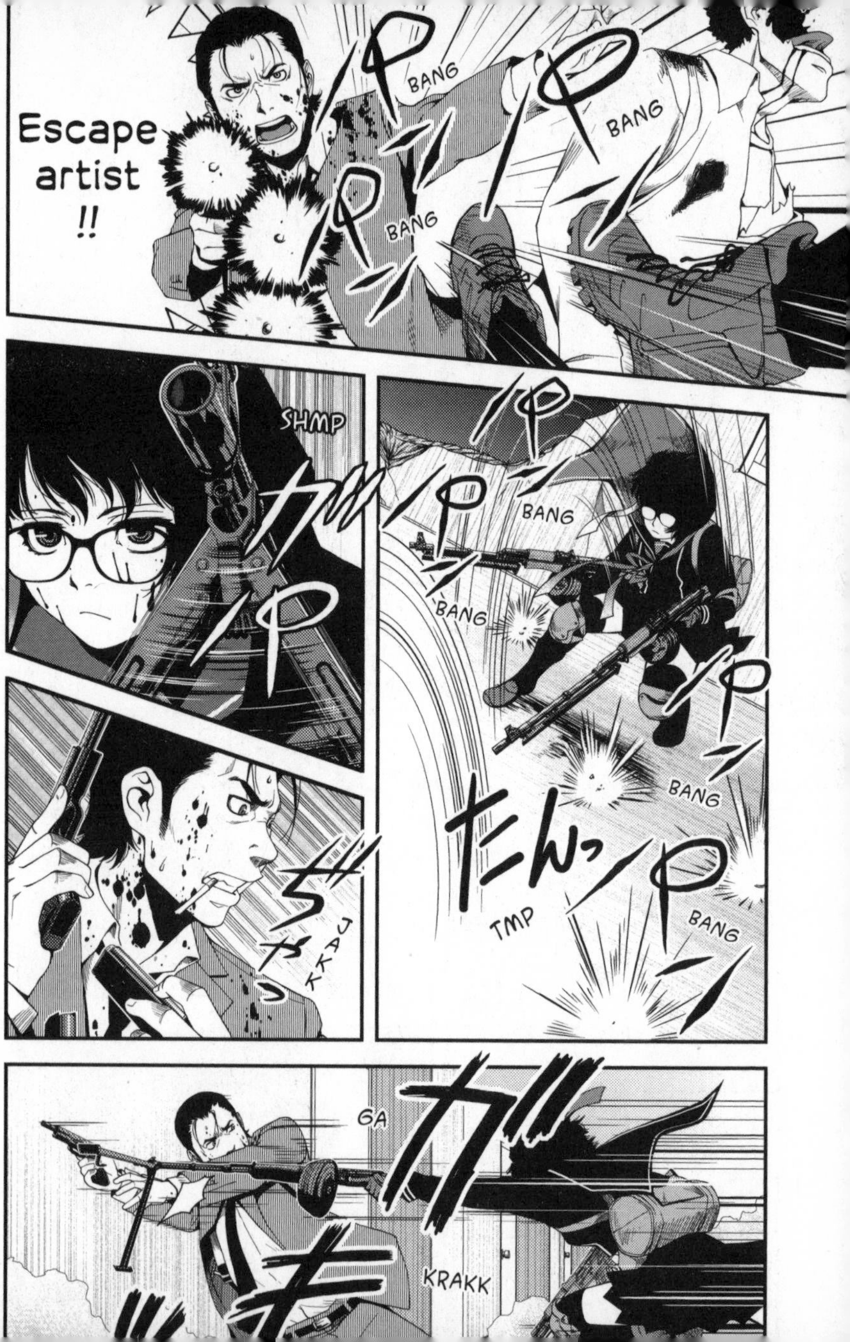
BANG
BANG
Escape artist !!
BANG
BANG
BANG
BANG
TMP
BANG
SHMP
JAKK
GA
KRAKK

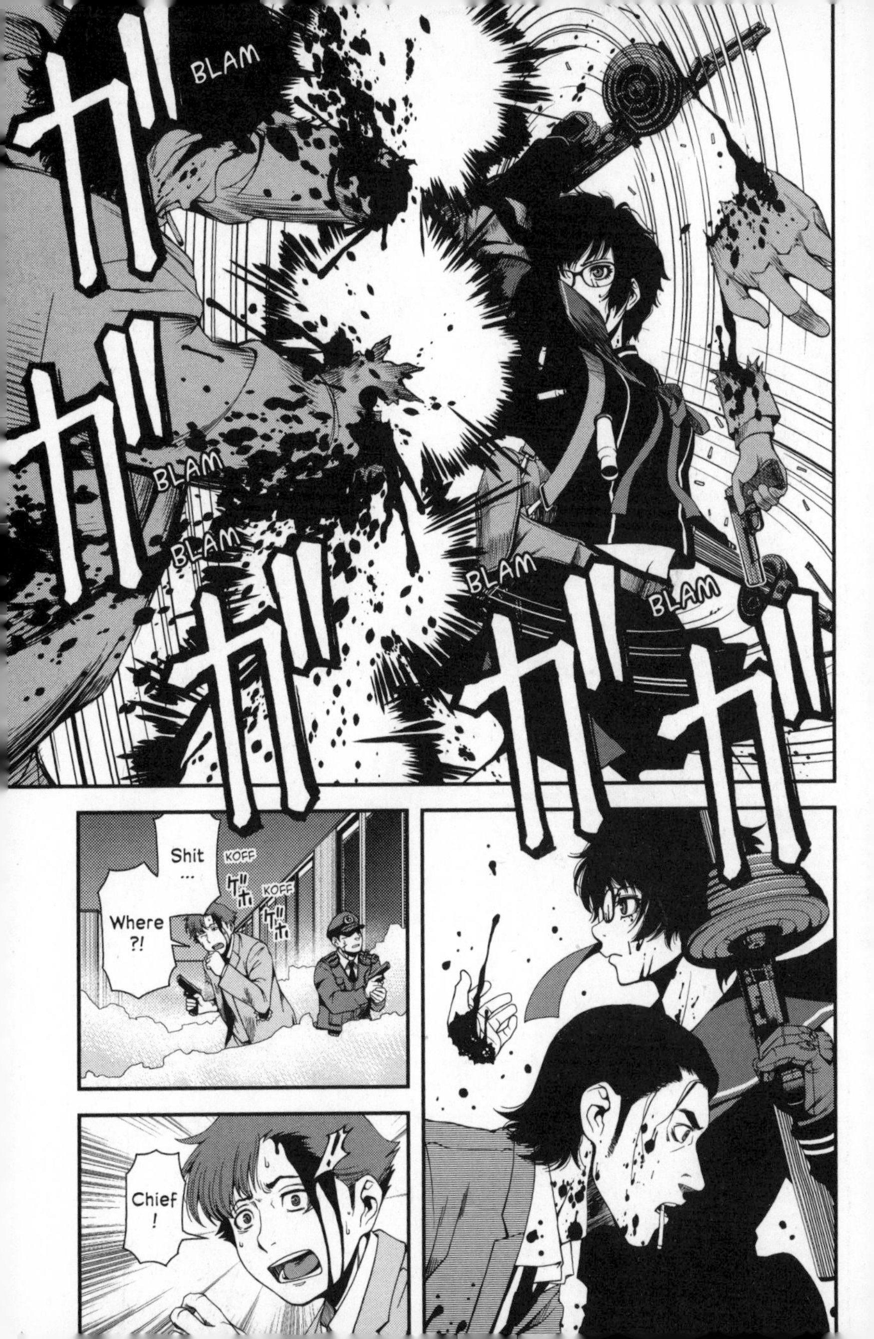

BLAM
BLAM
BLAM
BLAM
BLAM
Shit ...
KOFF
KOFF
Where ?!
Chief !

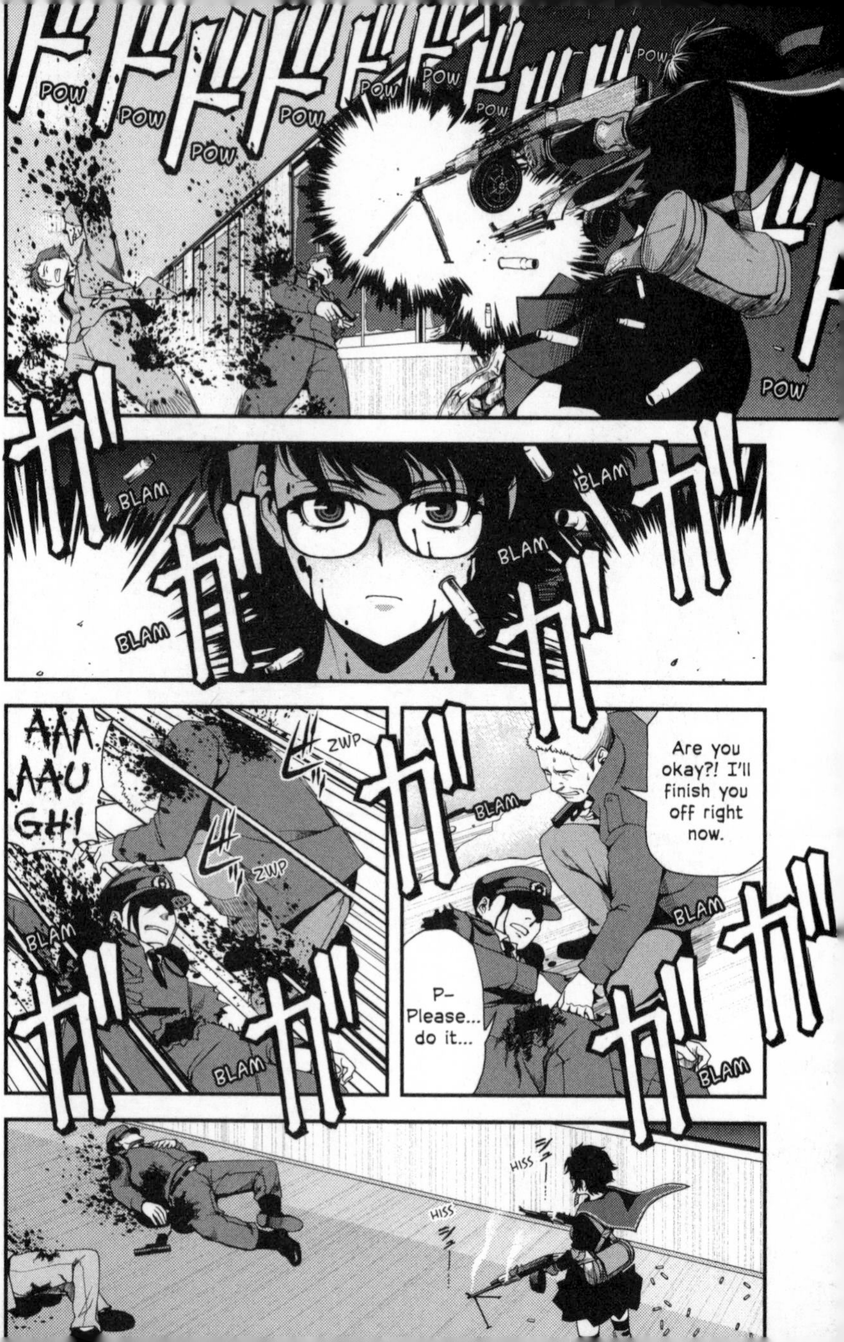
POW
POW
POW
POW
POW
POW
POW
POW
POW
POW
BLAM
BLAM
BLAM
BLAM
Are you okay?! I'll finish you off right now.
BLAM
P– Please... do it...
BLAM
BLAM
AAAAAUGH!
ZWP
ZWP
BLAM
BLAM
HISS
HISS

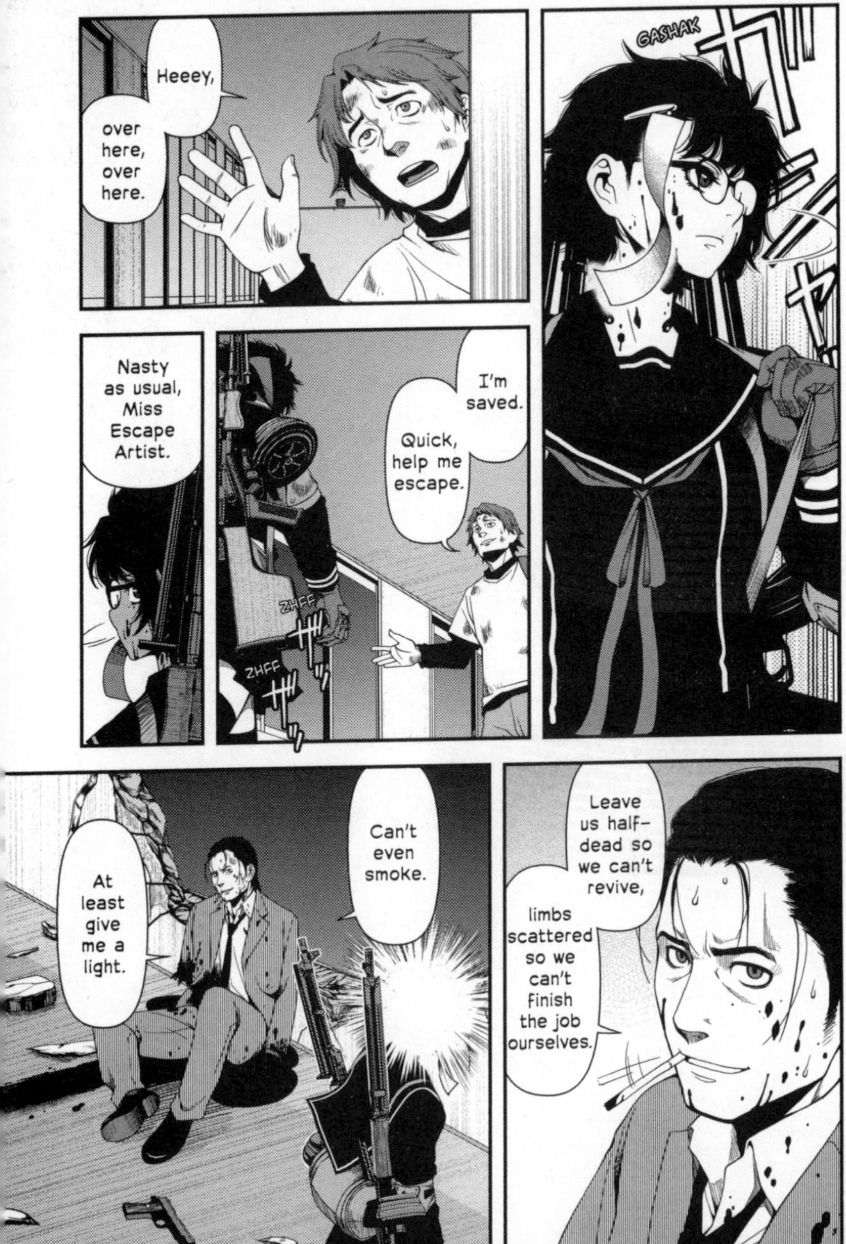
GASHAK
Heeey,
over here, over here.
I'm saved.
Quick, help me escape.
ZHFF
ZHFF
Nasty as usual, Miss Escape Artist.
Leave us half-dead so we can't revive,
limbs scattered so we can't finish the job ourselves.
Can't even smoke.
At least give me a light.

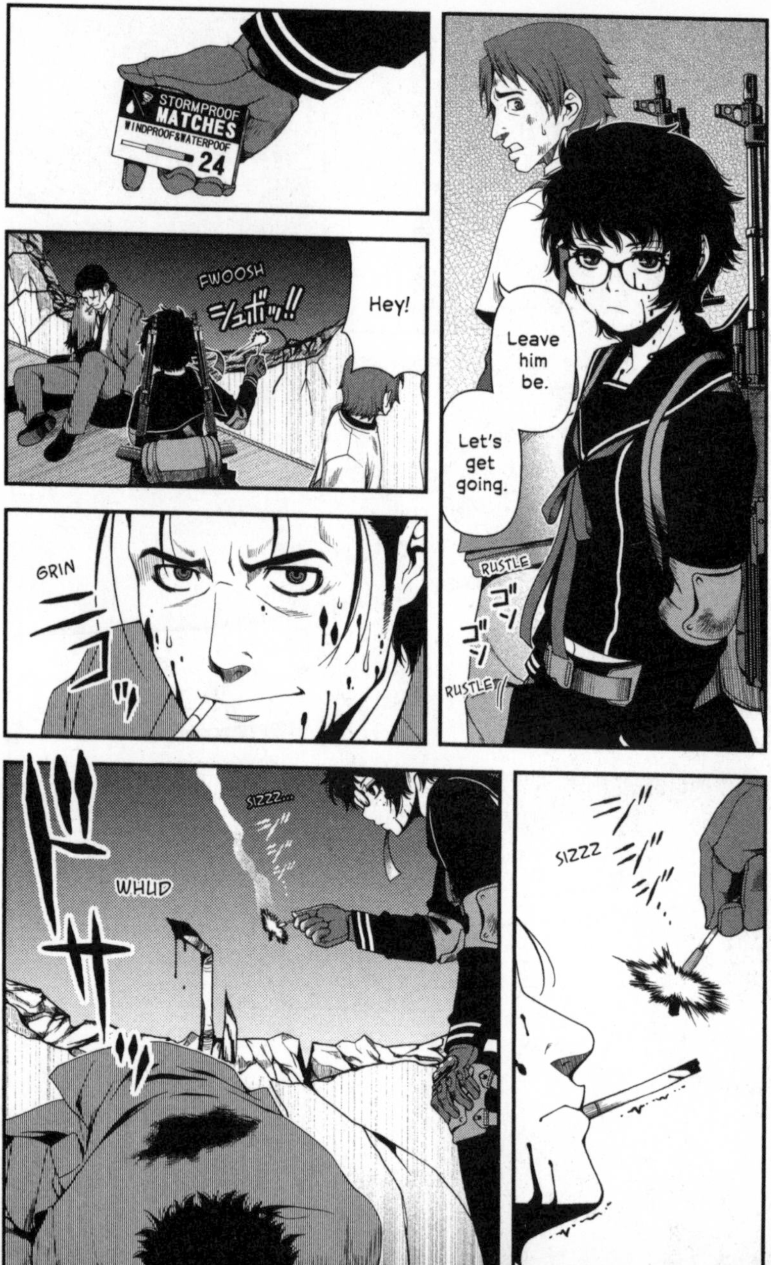
Leave him be.
Let's get going.
RUSTLE
RUSTLE
STORMPROOF
MATCHES
WINDPROOF&WATERPOOF
24
FWOOSH
シュボッ!!
Hey!
GRIN
SIZZZ
SIZZZ...
WHUD

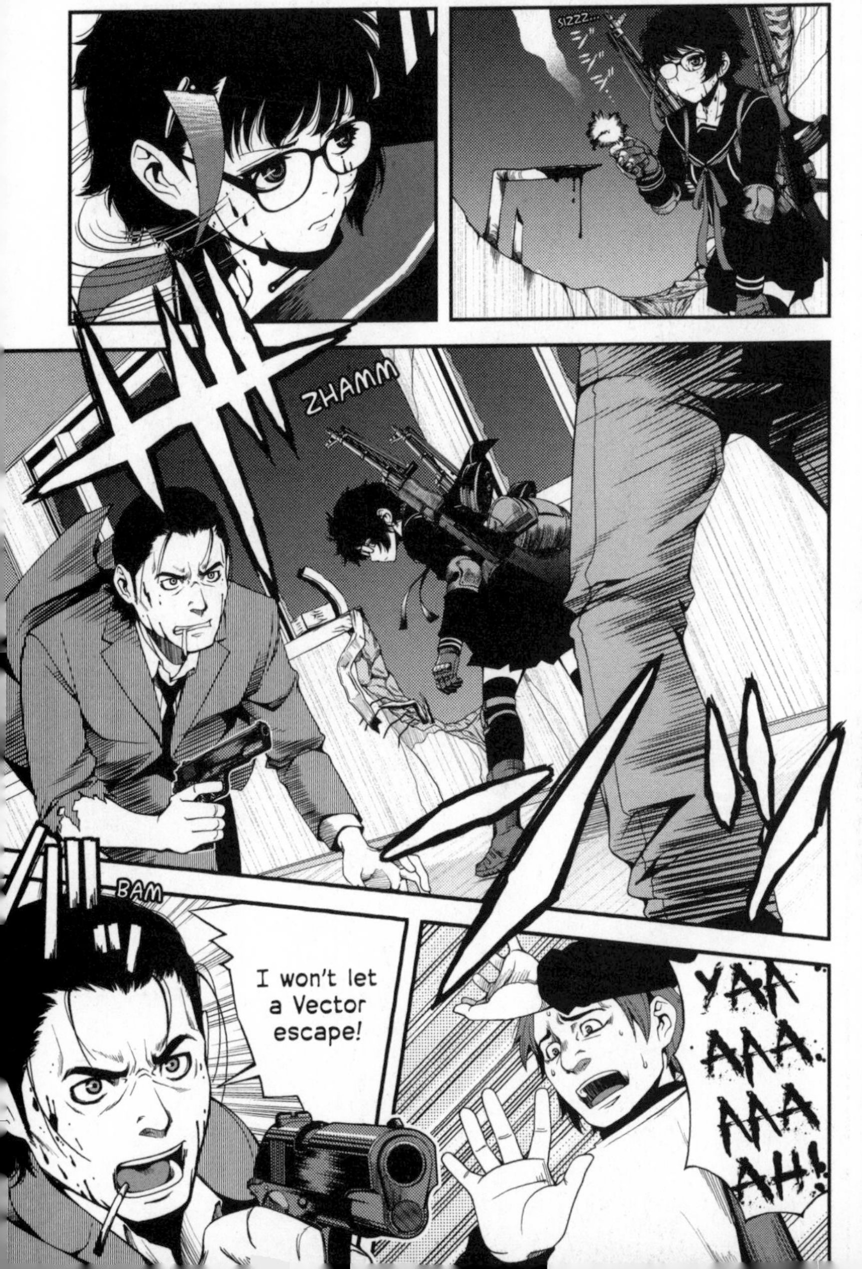

SIZZZ...
ZHAMM
YAA AAA. AAA AH!!
BAM
I won't let a Vector escape!

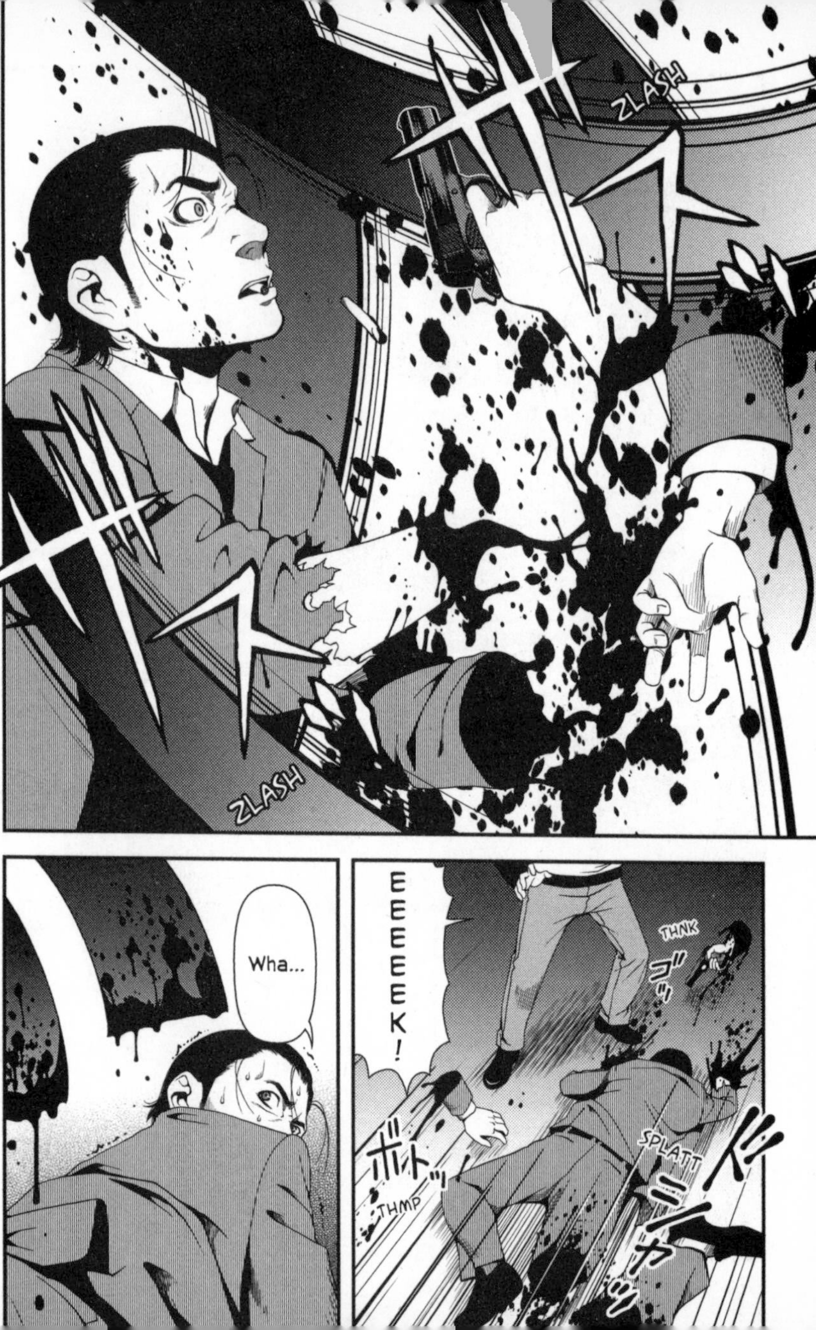
ZLASH
ZLASH
EEEEEEK!
THNK
ゴッ
SPLATT
ボトッ
THMP
Wha...

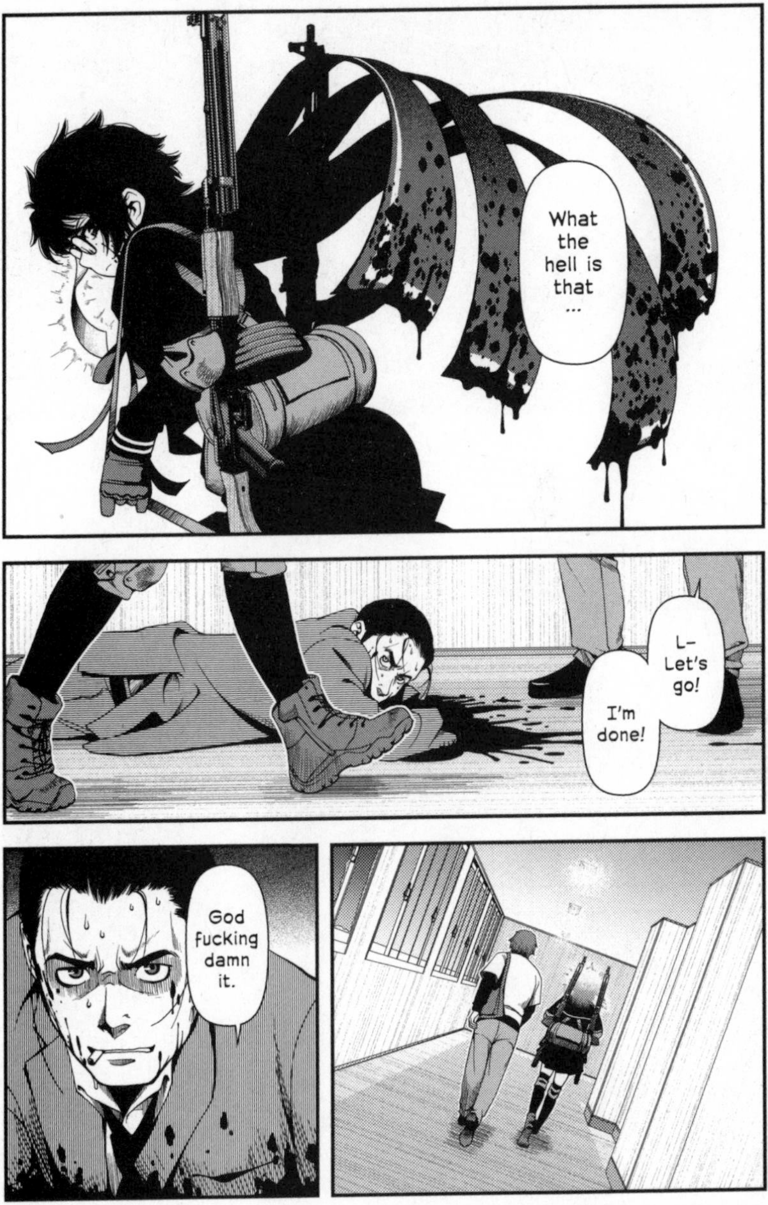
What the hell is that ...
L- Let's go!
I'm done!
God fucking damn it.

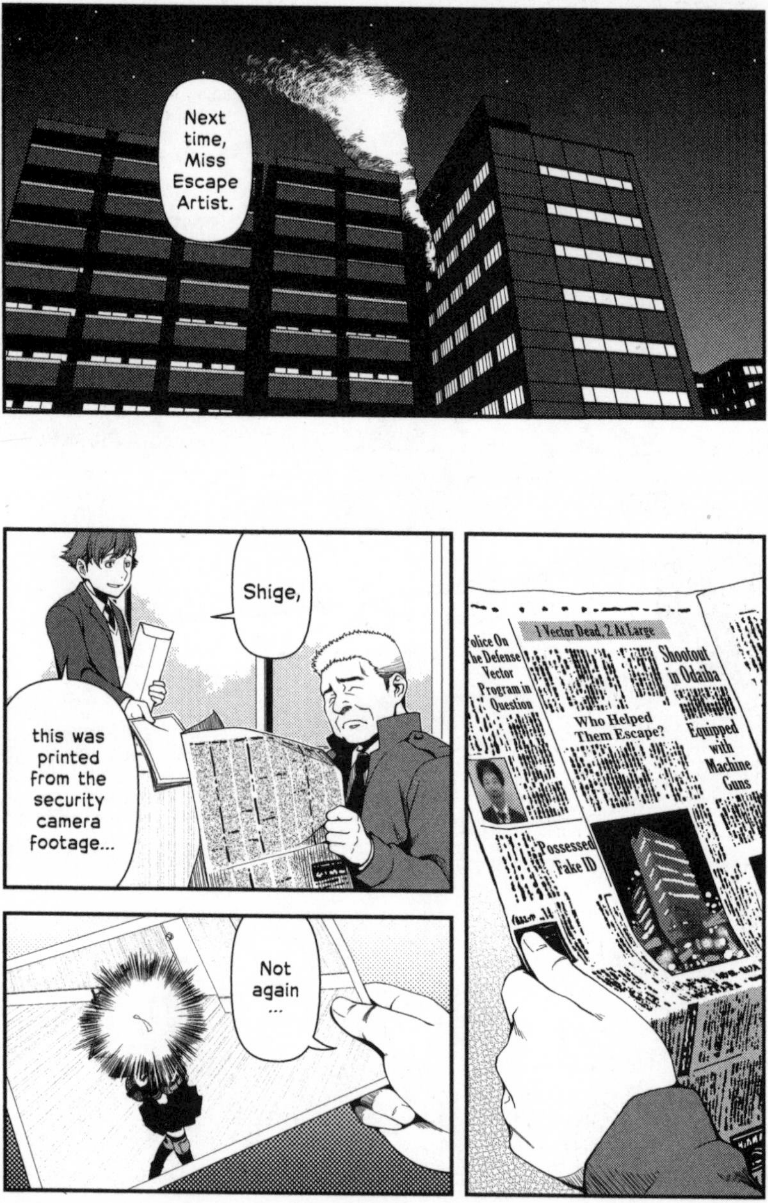

Next time, Miss Escape Artist.
1 Vector Dead, 2 At Large
olice On he Defense Vector Program in Question
Shootout in Odaiba
Who Helped Them Escape?
Equipped with Machine Guns
Possessed Fake ID
Shige,
this was printed from the security camera footage...
Not again ...

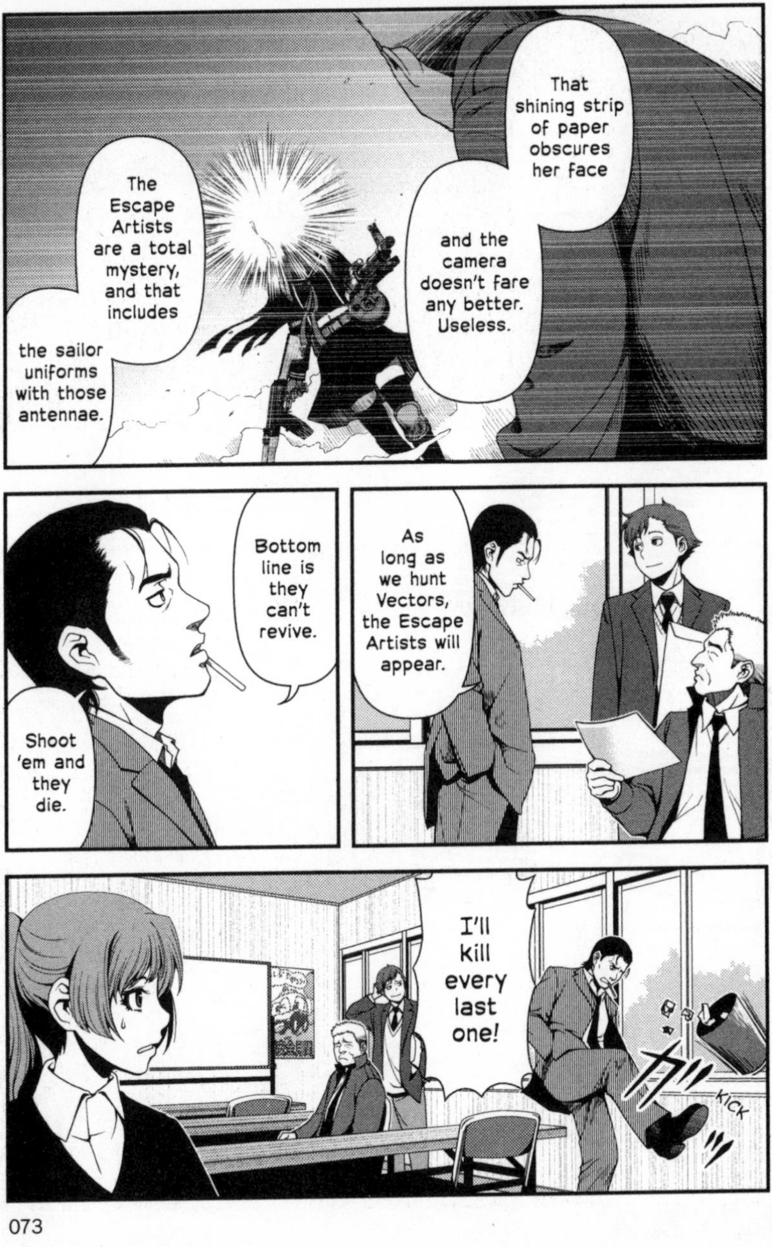
That shining strip of paper obscures her face
and the camera doesn't fare any better. Useless.
The Escape Artists are a total mystery, and that includes
the sailor uniforms with those antennae.
As long as we hunt Vectors, the Escape Artists will appear.
Bottom line is they can't revive.
Shoot 'em and they die.
I'll kill every last one!
KICK

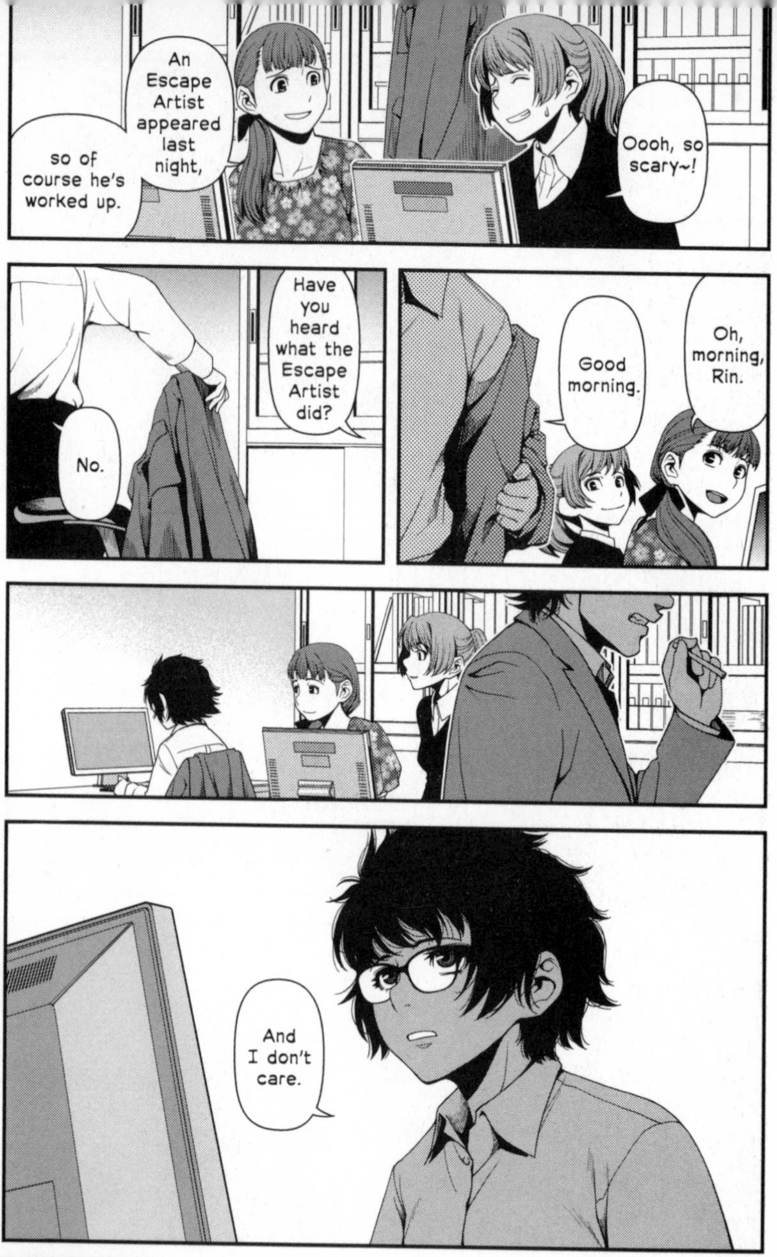
Oooh, so scary~!
An Escape Artist appeared last night,
so of course he's worked up.
Oh, morning, Rin.
Good morning.
Have you heard what the Escape Artist did?
No.
And I don't care.

End of Chapter 2

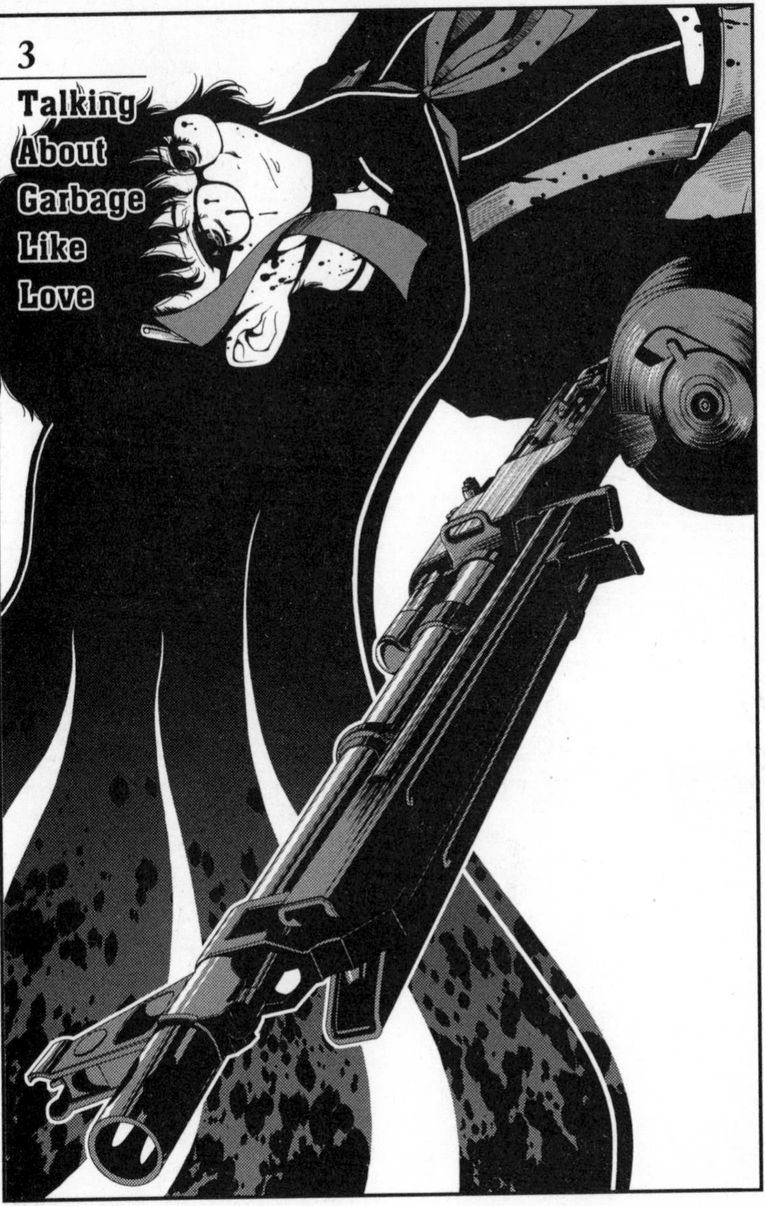
3
Talking About Garbage Like Love

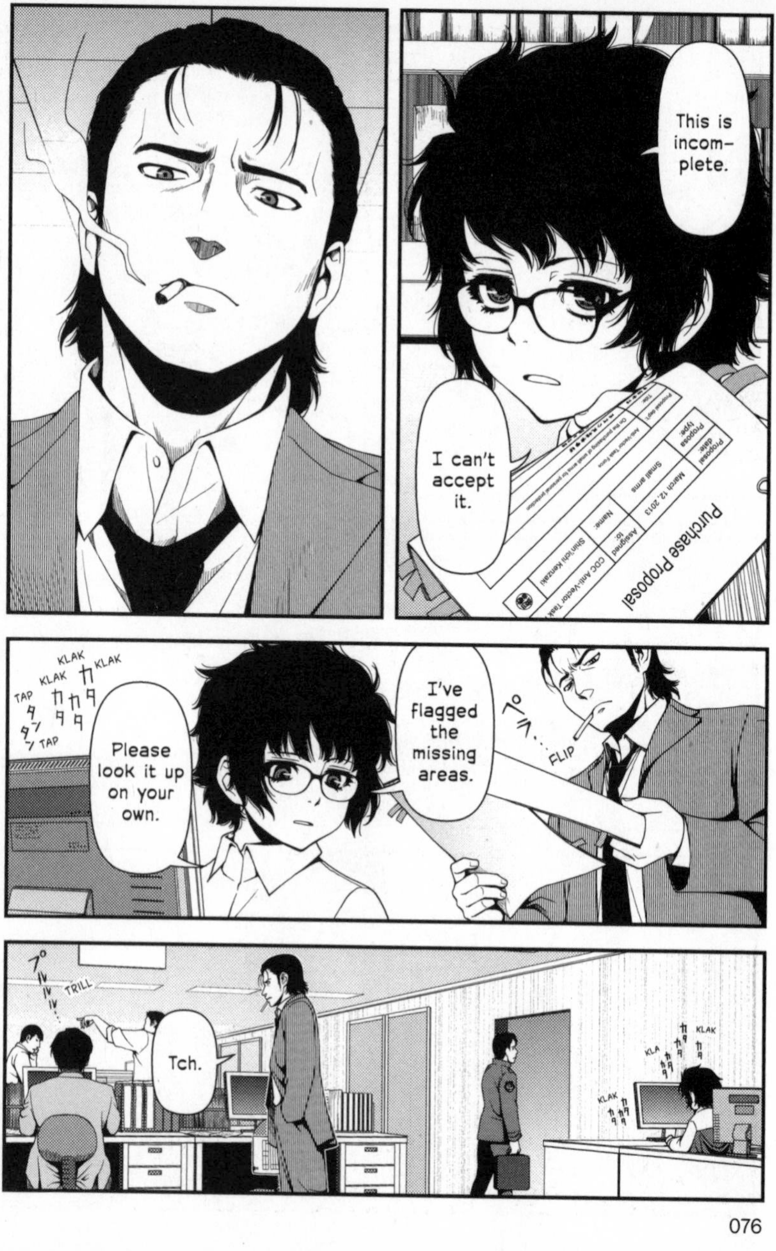
This is incomplete.
I can't accept it.
Purchase Proposal
Proposal date:
March 12, 2013
Assigned to:
CDC Anti-Vector Task
Proposal type:
Small arms
Name:
Shinichi Kenzaki
FLIP
I've flagged the missing areas.
Please look it up on your own.
KLAK KLAK KLAK
TAP TAP
KLAK
KLA
KLAK
Tch.
TRILL

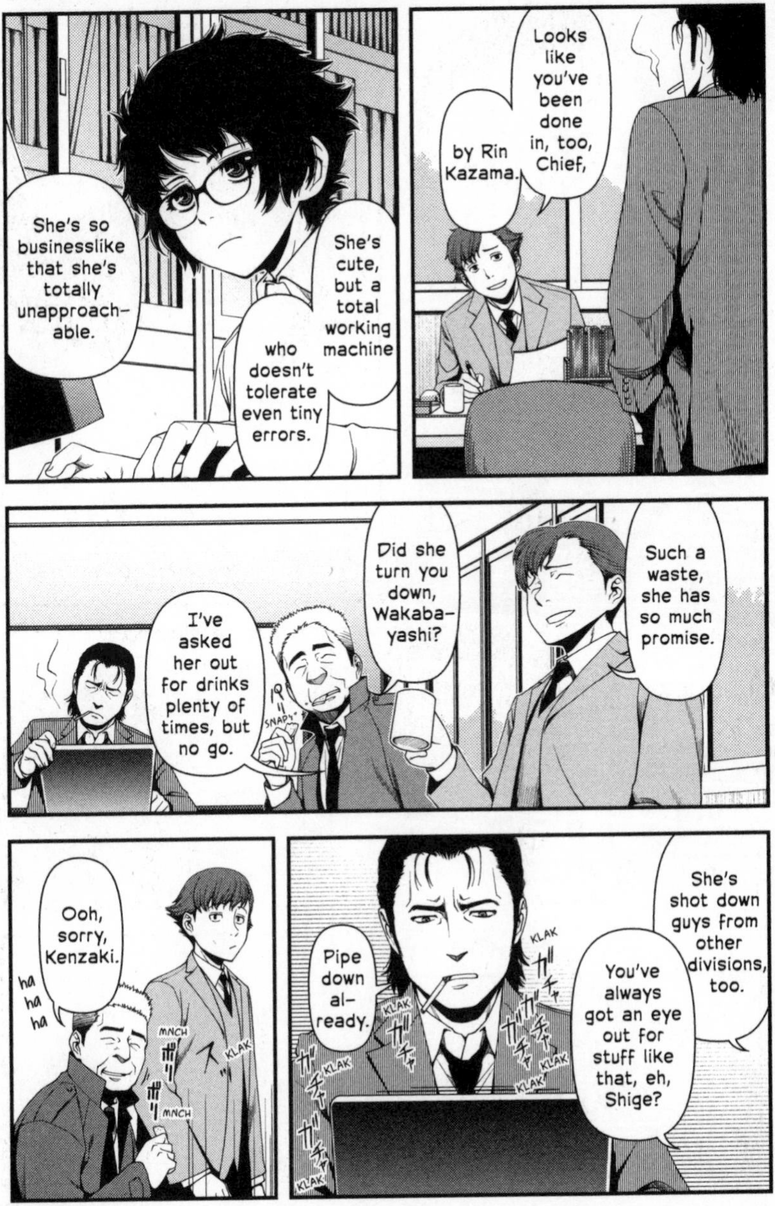
Looks like you've been done in, too, Chief,
by Rin Kazama.
She's cute, but a total working machine
who doesn't tolerate even tiny errors.
She's so businesslike that she's totally unapproachable.
Such a waste, she has so much promise.
Did she turn you down, Wakabayashi?
I've asked her out for drinks plenty of times, but no go.
SNAP
She's shot down guys from other divisions, too.
You've always got an eye out for stuff like that, eh, Shige?
KLAK ガチャ
Pipe down already.
KLAK ガチャ
Ooh, sorry, Kenzaki.
ha ha ha
MNCH ボリ
KLAK
MNCH ボリ

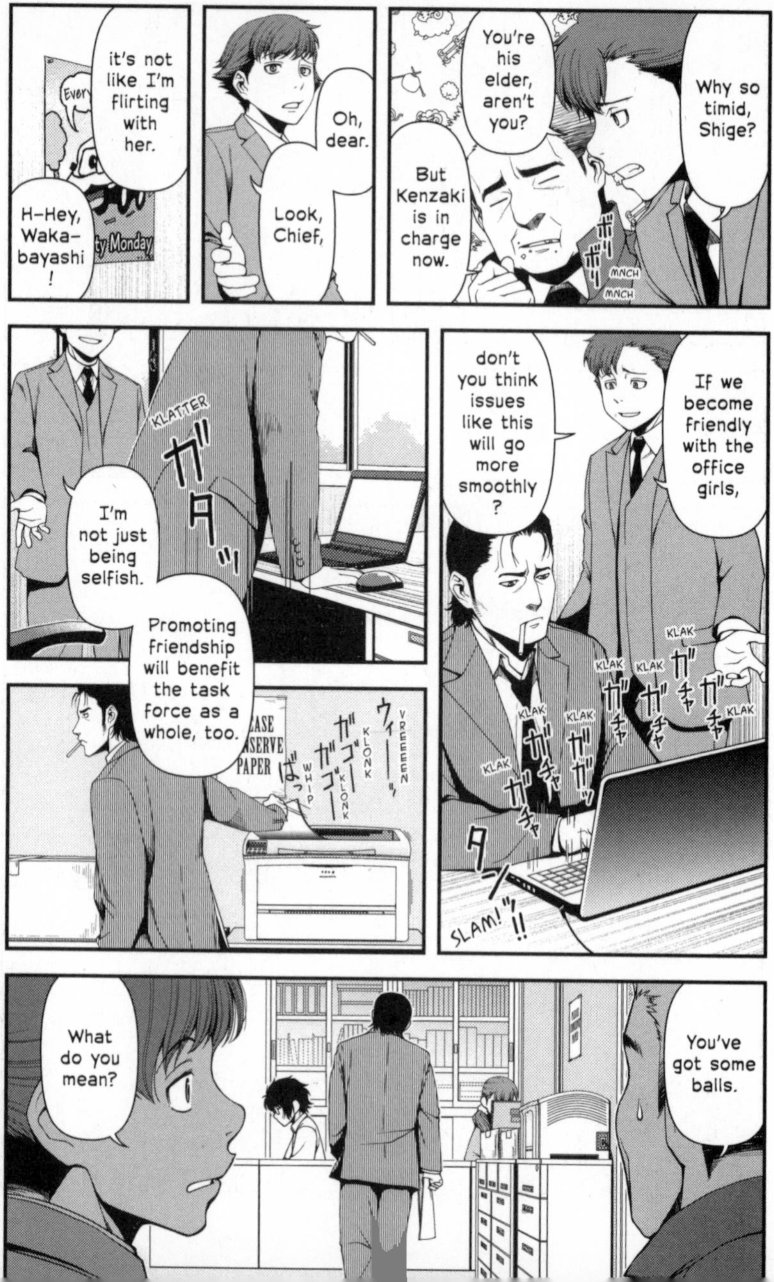
Why so timid, Shige?
You're his elder, aren't you?
But Kenzaki is in charge now.
ボリボリ
MNCH
MNCH
Oh, dear.
Look, Chief,
it's not like I'm flirting with her.
H-Hey, Waka-bayashi!
If we become friendly with the office girls,
don't you think issues like this will go more smoothly?
KLAK
ガチャ
KLAK
ガチャ
KLAK
ガチャ
KLAK
ガガッ
KLAK
ガチャ
KLAK
ガチャ
KLAK
タン!!
SLAM!!
KLATTER
ガタッ
I'm not just being selfish.
Promoting friendship will benefit the task force as a whole, too.
ウィーーッ
VREEEEN
ガゴーガゴー
KLONK
KLONK
ばっ
WHIP
PAPER
You've got some balls.
What do you mean?

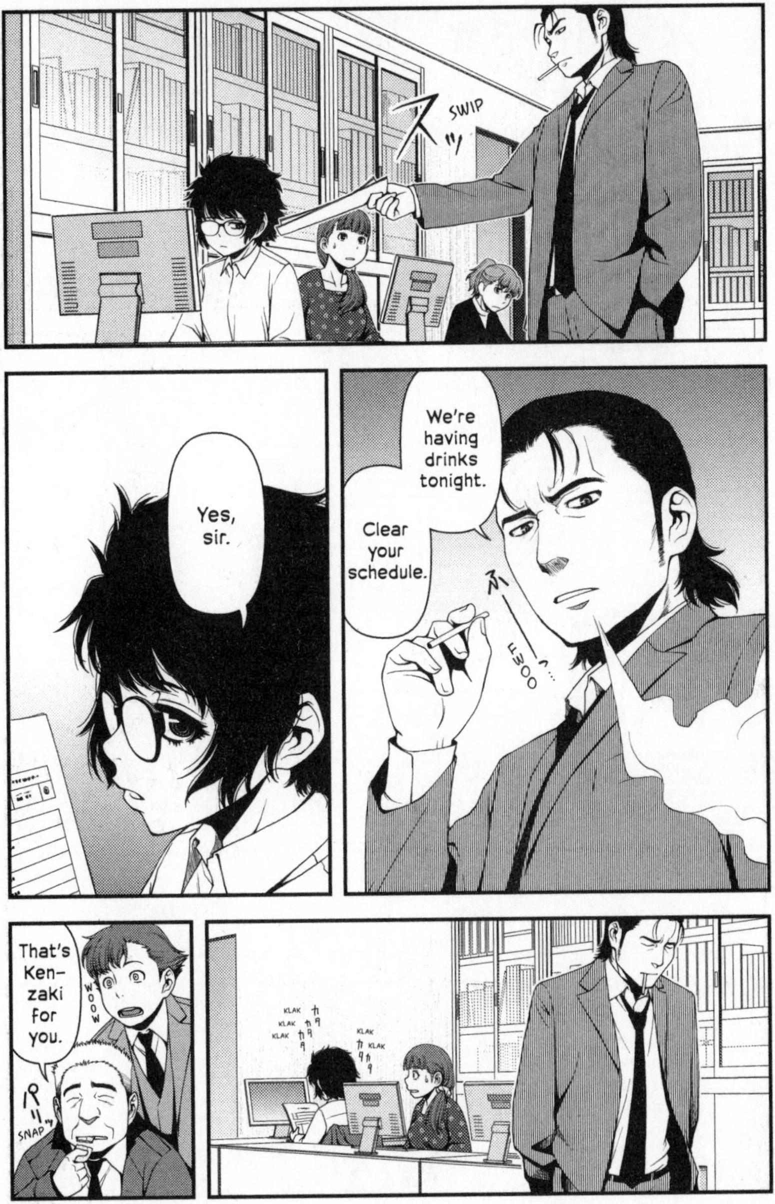
スッ
SWIP
We're having drinks tonight.
Clear your schedule.
ふー
FWOO...
Yes, sir.
KLAK KLAK KLAK
カタ カタ カタ
KLAK KLAK
カタ カタ
That's Ken-zaki for you.
WOOW
パリッ
SNAP

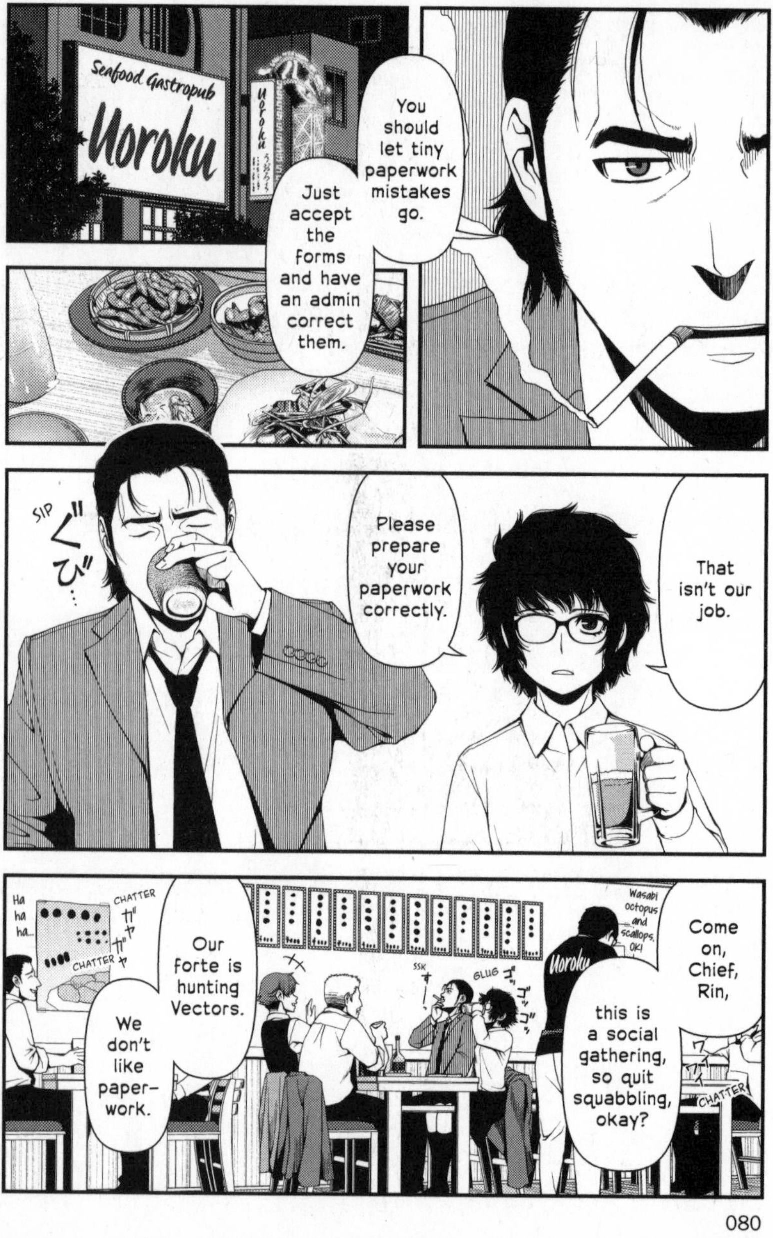

You should let tiny paperwork mistakes go.
Seafood Gastropub Uoroku
Uoroku
Just accept the forms and have an admin correct them.
That isn't our job.
Please prepare your paperwork correctly.
SIP
Come on, Chief, Rin,
this is a social gathering, so quit squabbling, okay?
CHATTER
Wasabi octopus and scallops, OK!
Uoroku
GLUG
SSK
Our forte is hunting Vectors.
We don't like paper-work.
CHATTER
CHATTER
Ha ha ha...

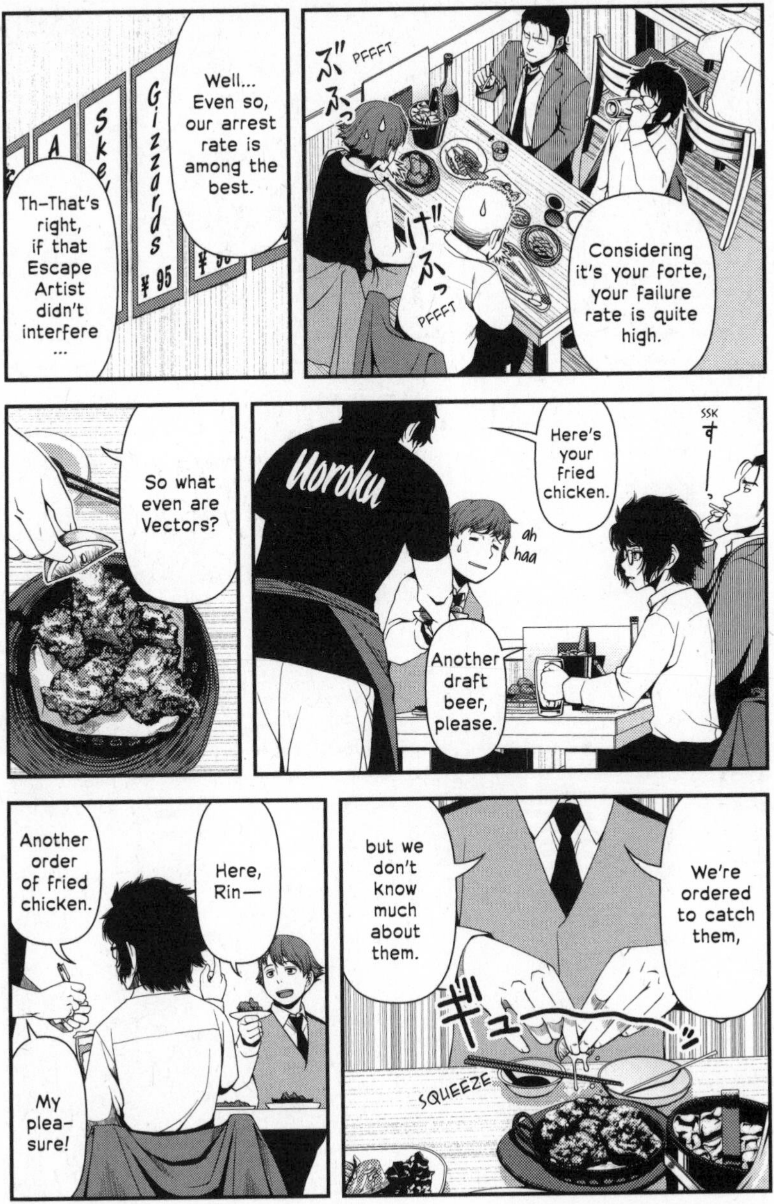
ぶふっ
PFFFT
Considering it's your forte, your failure rate is quite high.
げふっ
PFFFT
Well... Even so, our arrest rate is among the best.
Gizzards
¥ 95
Th-That's right, if that Escape Artist didn't interfere ...
SSK
す—
Here's your fried chicken.
Uoroku
ah haa
Another draft beer, please.
So what even are Vectors?
We're ordered to catch them,
but we don't know much about them.
ギュ——ッ
SQUEEZE
Here, Rin—
Another order of fried chicken.
My plea-sure!

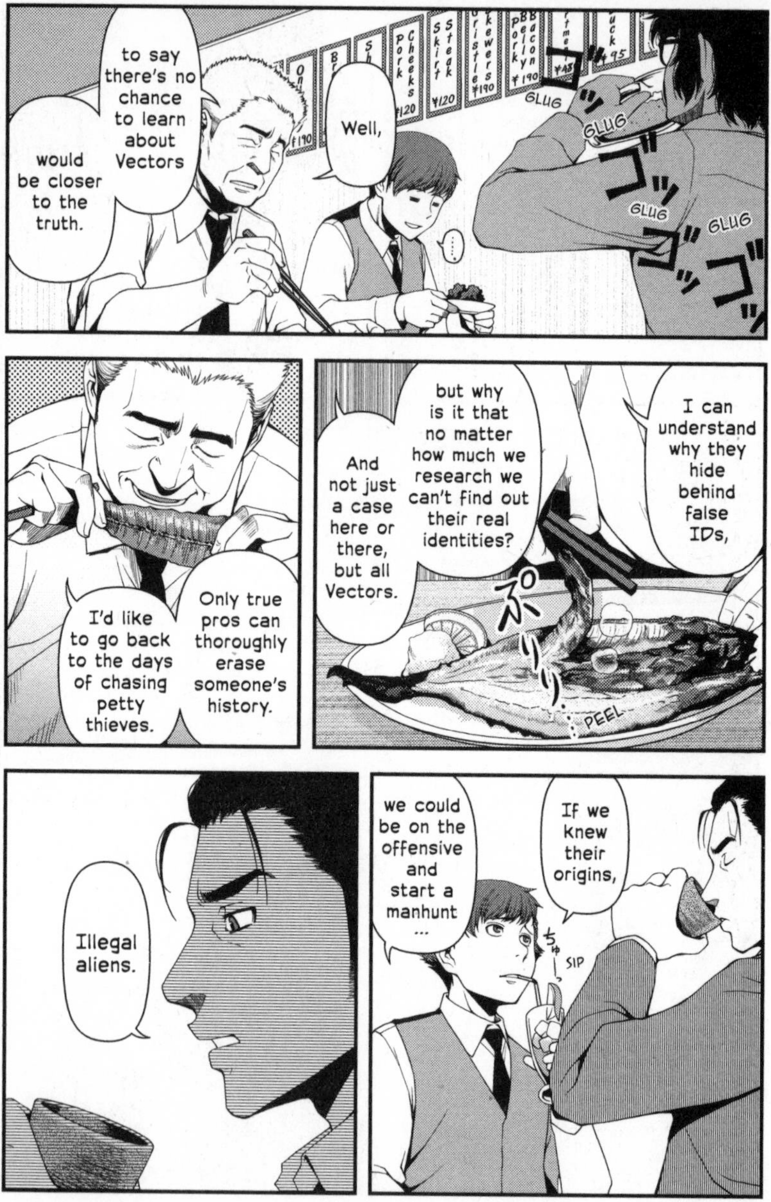
Duck ¥95
Bacon Belly ¥190
Pork ¥190
Gristle Skewers ¥190
Skirt Steak ¥120
Pork Cheeks ¥120
¥190
GLUG
GLUG
GLUG
GLUG
Well,
to say there's no chance to learn about Vectors
would be closer to the truth.
......
I can understand why they hide behind false IDs,
but why is it that no matter how much we research we can't find out their real identities?
And not just a case here or there, but all Vectors.
PEEL
Only true pros can thoroughly erase someone's history.
I'd like to go back to the days of chasing petty thieves.
If we knew their origins,
we could be on the offensive and start a manhunt ...
SIP
Illegal aliens.

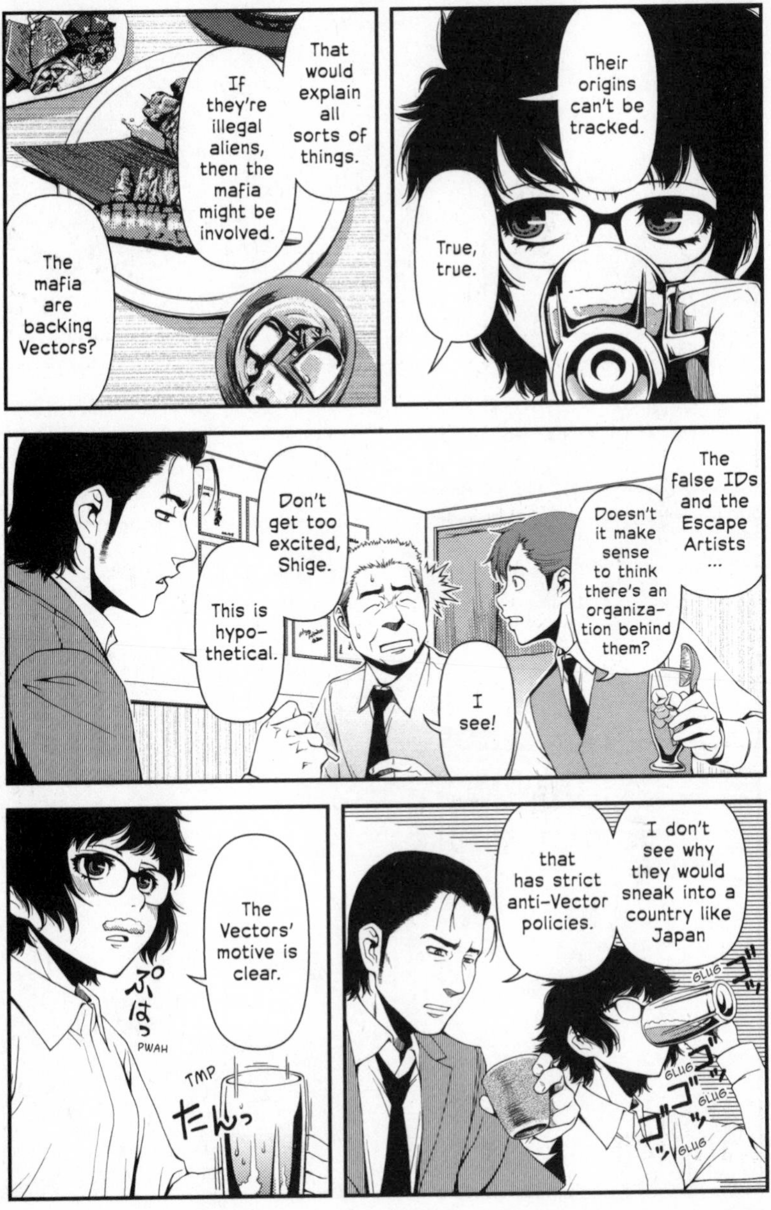
Their origins can't be tracked.
True, true.
That would explain all sorts of things.
If they're illegal aliens, then the mafia might be involved.
The mafia are backing Vectors?
The false IDs and the Escape Artists ...
Doesn't it make sense to think there's an organization behind them?
I see!
Don't get too excited, Shige.
This is hypothetical.
I don't see why they would sneak into a country like Japan
that has strict anti-Vector policies.
GLUG
GLUG
GLUG
GLUG
The Vectors' motive is clear.
ぷはっ
PWAH
TMP
たんっ

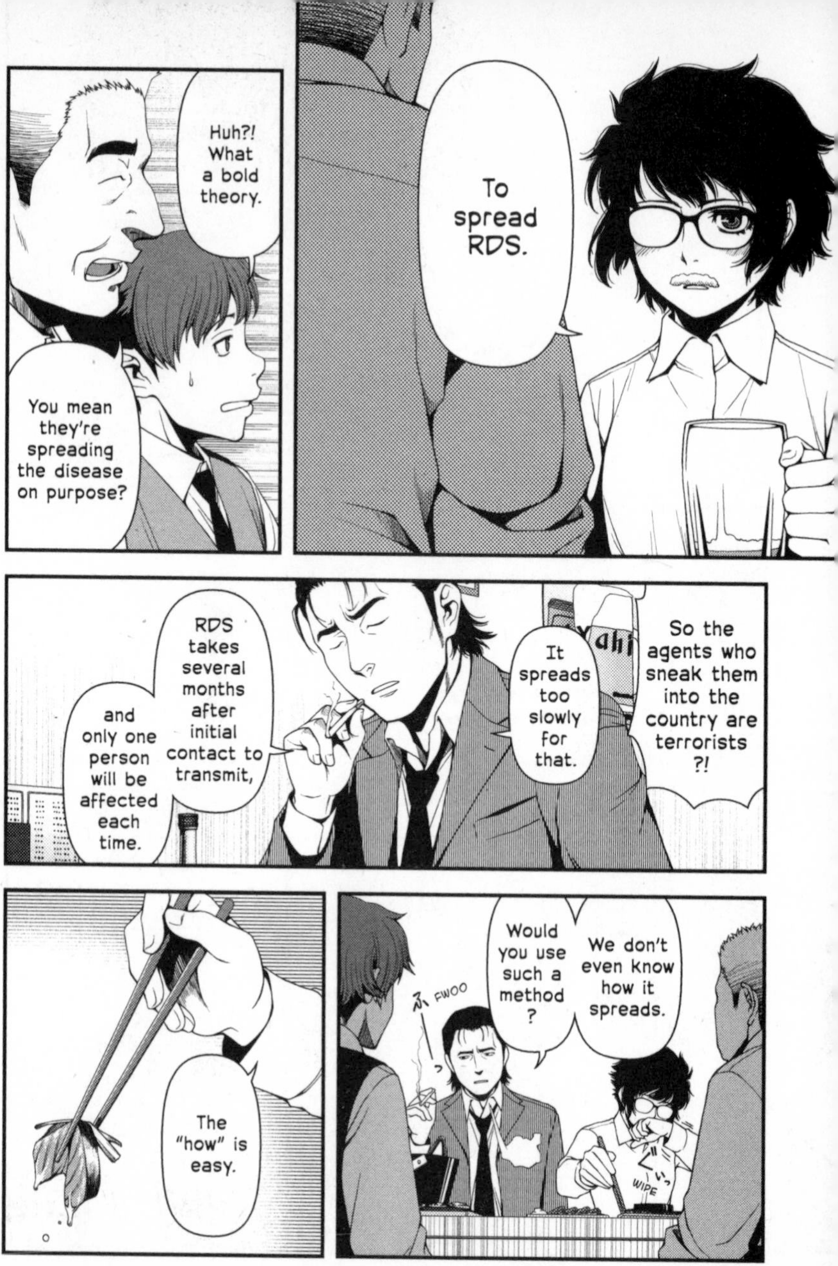

To spread RDS.
Huh?! What a bold theory.
You mean they're spreading the disease on purpose?
So the agents who sneak them into the country are terrorists?!
It spreads too slowly for that.
RDS takes several months after initial contact to transmit,
and only one person will be affected each time.
We don't even know how it spreads.
Would you use such a method?
FWOO
WIPE
The "how" is easy.

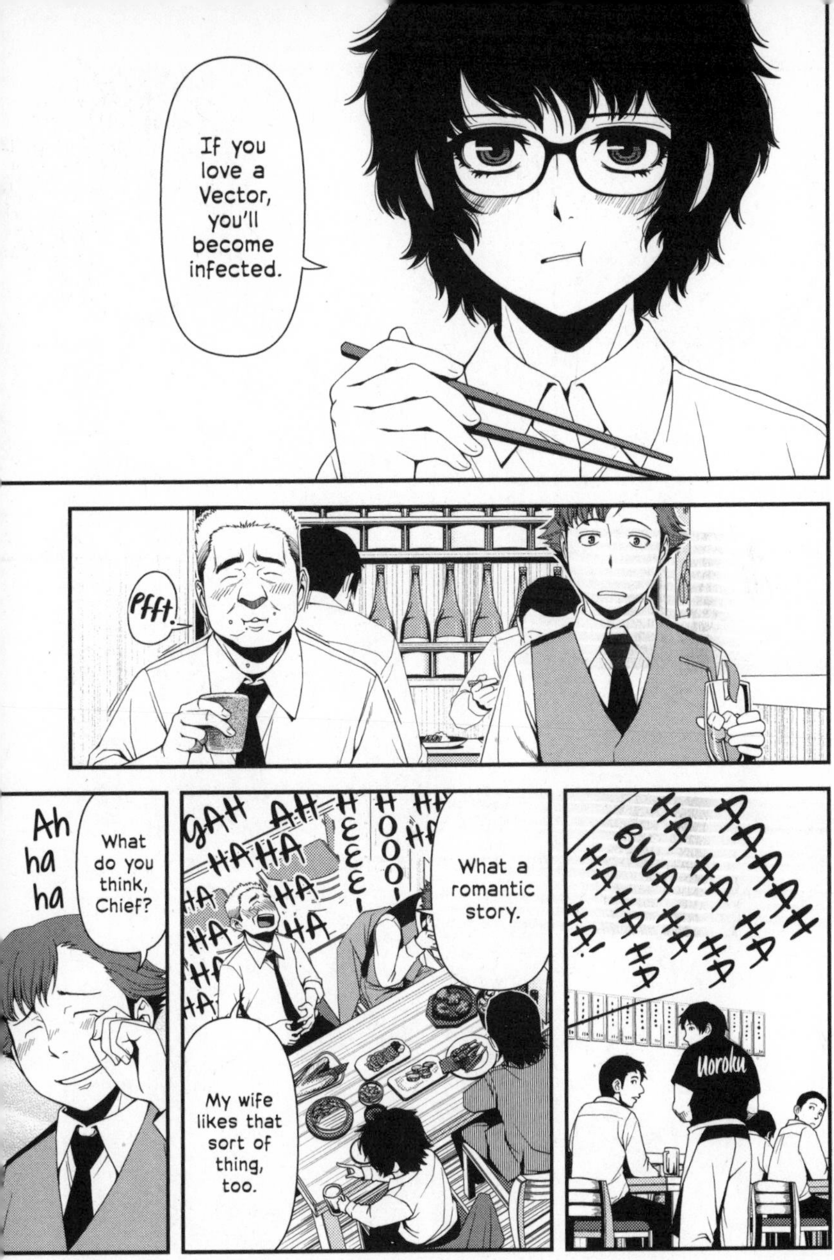
If you love a Vector, you'll become infected.
Pfft.
AAAAAH HA HA HA HA HA HA BWA HA HA HA HA!
What a romantic story.
My wife likes that sort of thing, too.
GAH AH HA HA HA HA HA HA HA
HEEE!
HOOO!
Uoroku
What do you think, Chief?
Ah ha ha

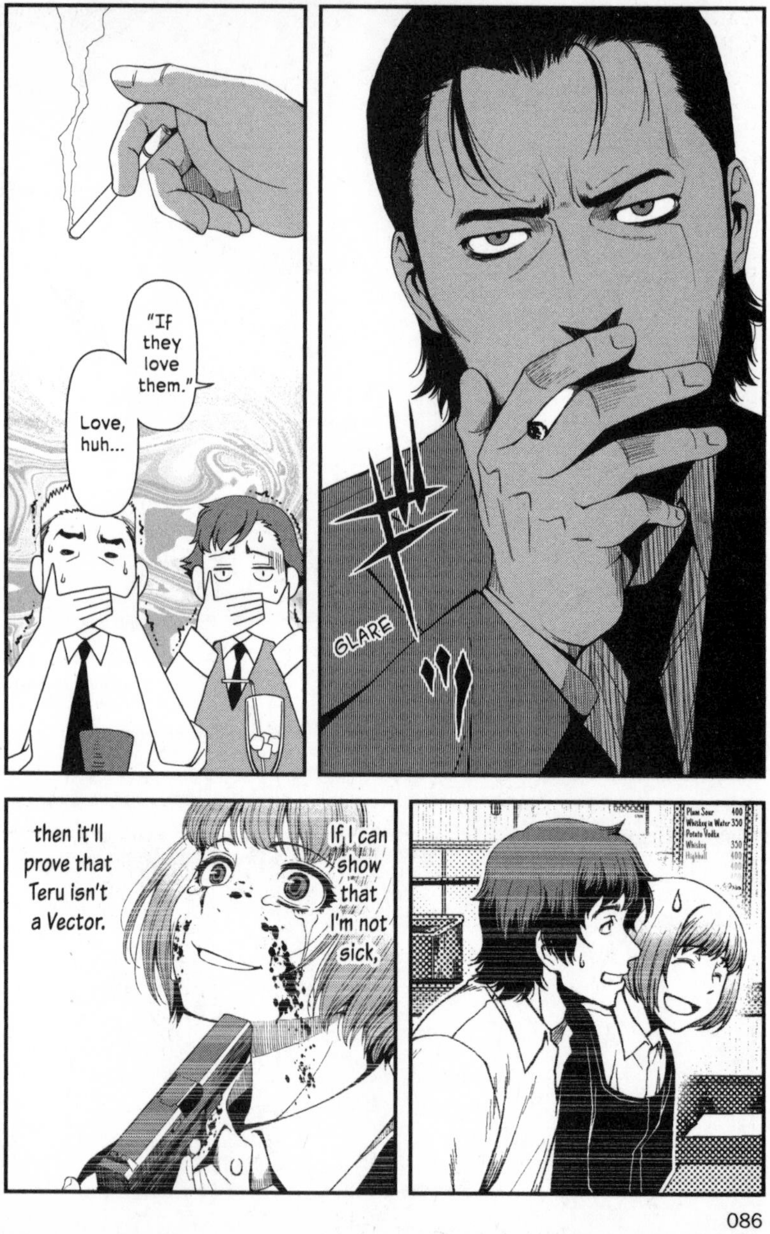
GLARE
"If they love them."
Love, huh...
Plum Sour 400
Whiskey in Water 350
Potato Vodka
Whiskey 350
Highball
If I can show that I'm not sick,
then it'll prove that Teru isn't a Vector.

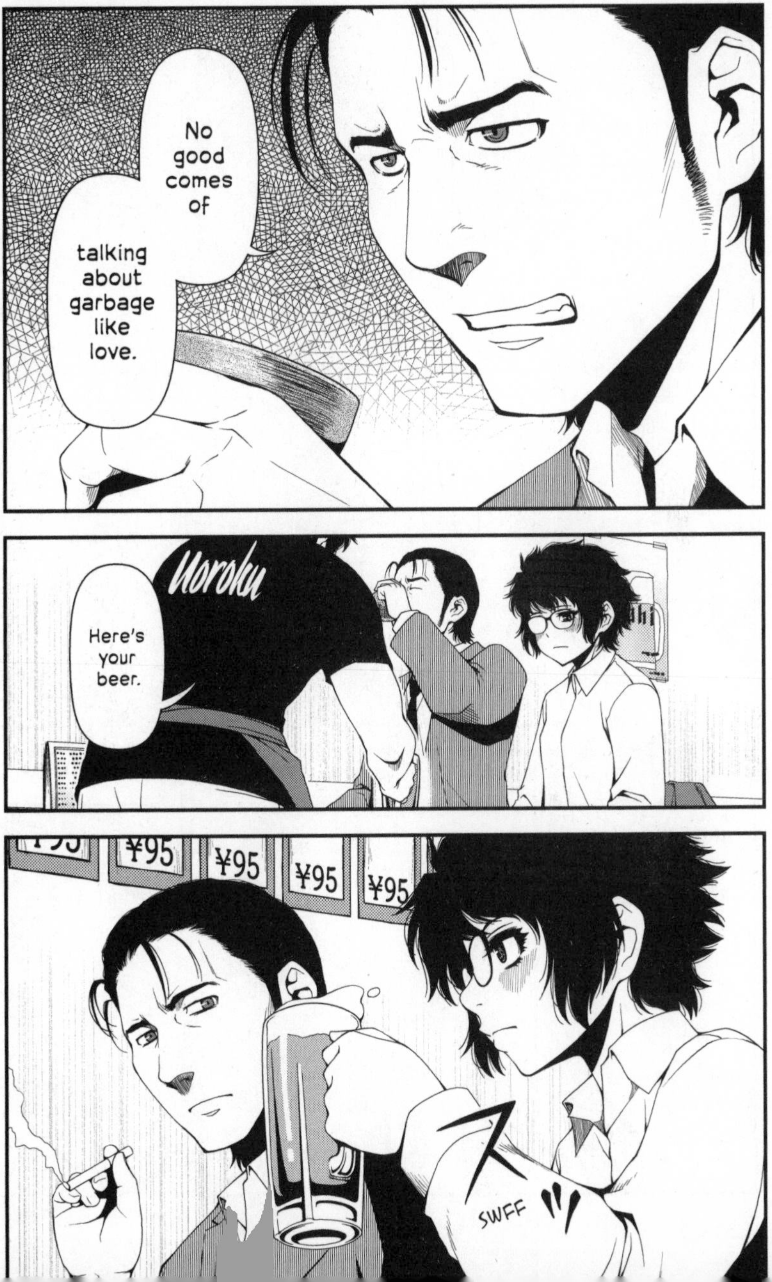
No good comes of
talking about garbage like love.
Uoroku
Here's your beer.
¥95
¥95
¥95
¥95
SWFF

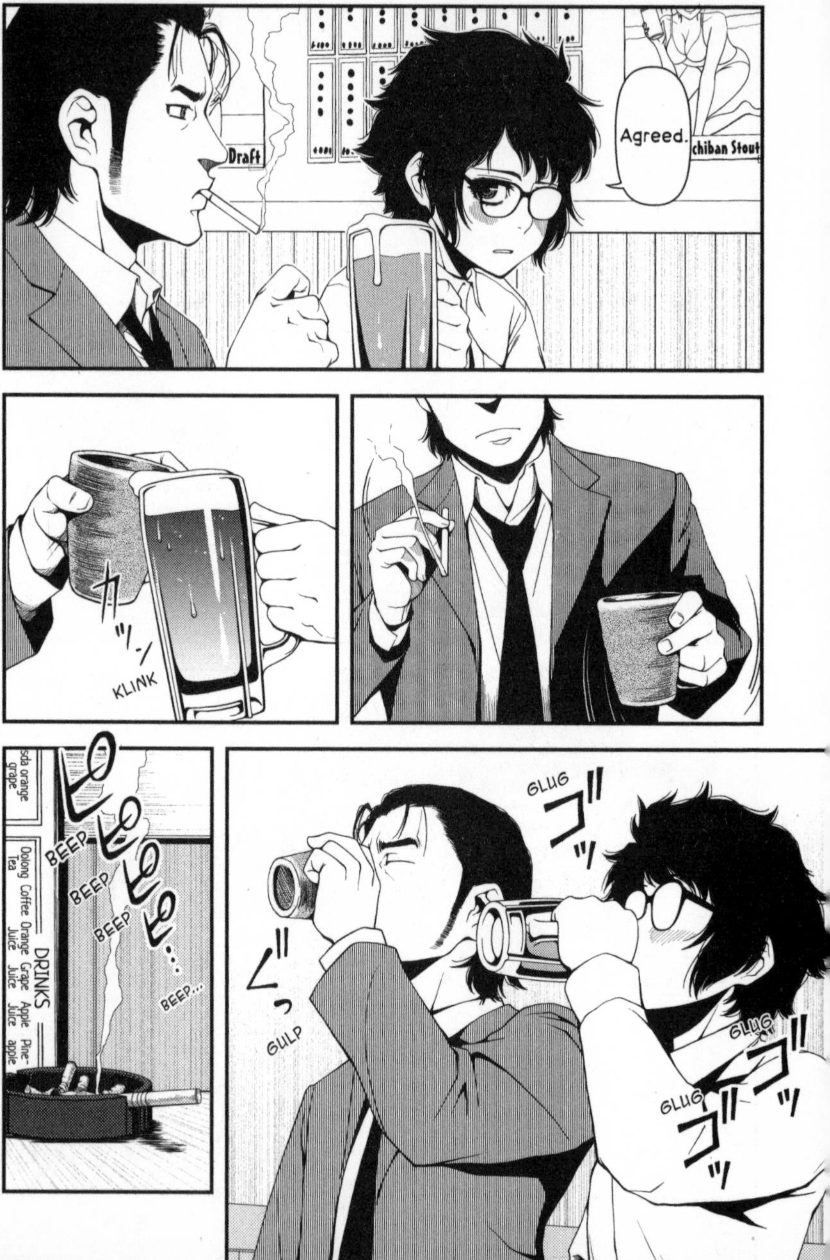
Draft
chiban Stout
Agreed.
ガツン
KLINK
GLUG
ゴッ
GLUG
ゴッ
GLUG
ゴッ
ぐっ
GULP
ピ BEEP
ピ BEEP
ピ BEEP
ピ…
BEEP...
sda orange grape
DRINKS
Oolong Tea
Coffee
Orange Juice
Grape Juice
Apple Juice
Pine-apple

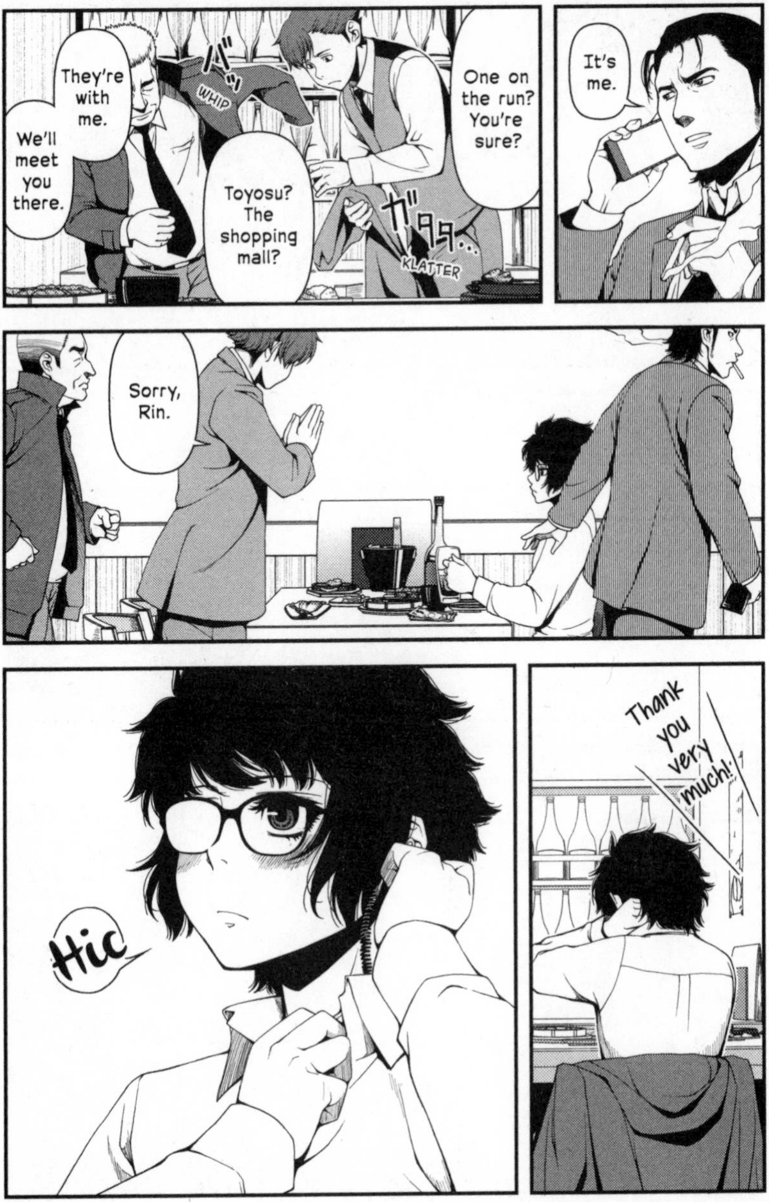
It's me.
One on the run? You're sure?
バッ
WHIP
They're with me.
Toyosu? The shopping mall?
ガタタ…
KLATTER
We'll meet you there.
Sorry, Rin.
Thank you very much!
Hic

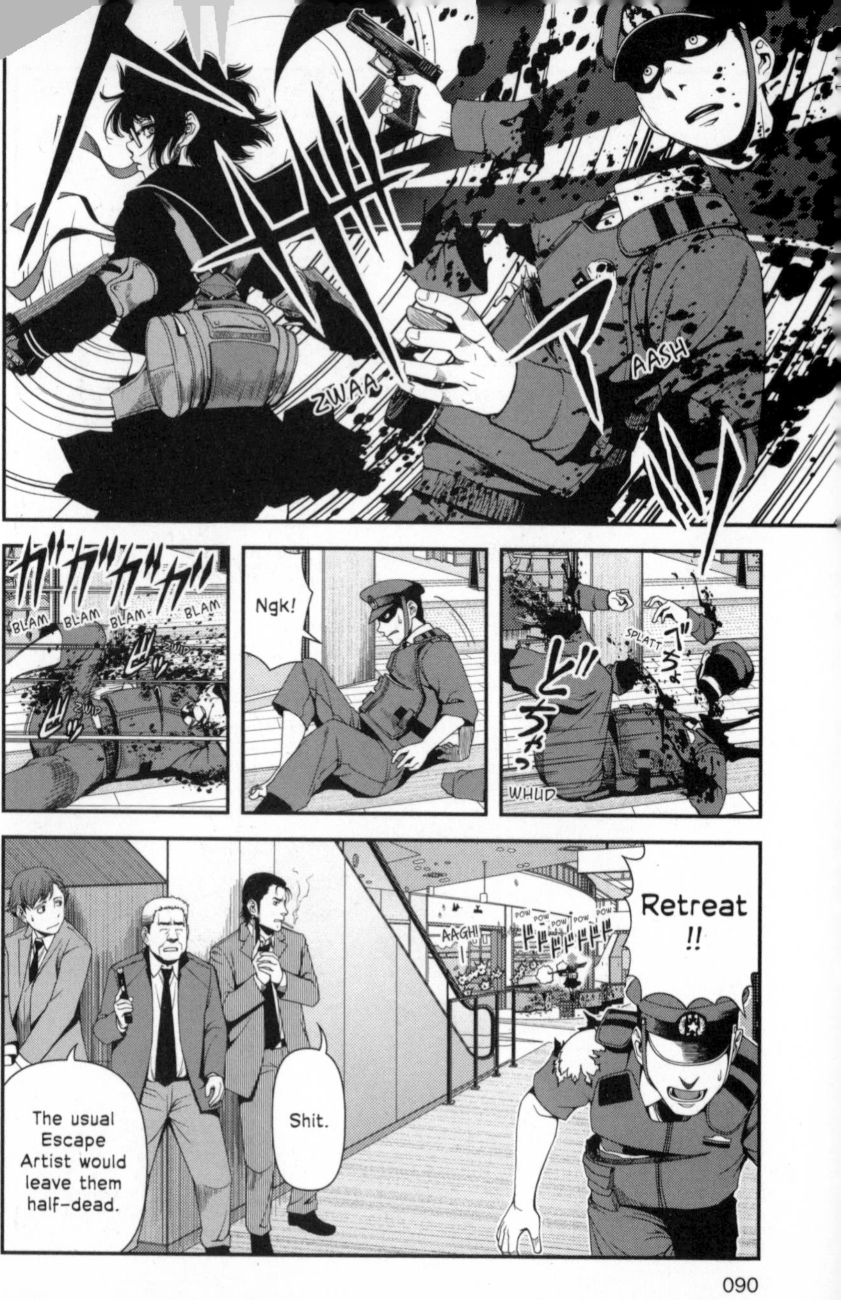
AASH
ZWAA
SPLATT
べちょ
どちゃっ
WHUD
Ngk!
ガガガガガ
BLAM BLAM BLAM BLAM
ビッ
ZWIP
ビッ
ZWIP
Retreat !!
AAGH!!
POW POW POW POW POW
Shit.
The usual Escape Artist would leave them half-dead.

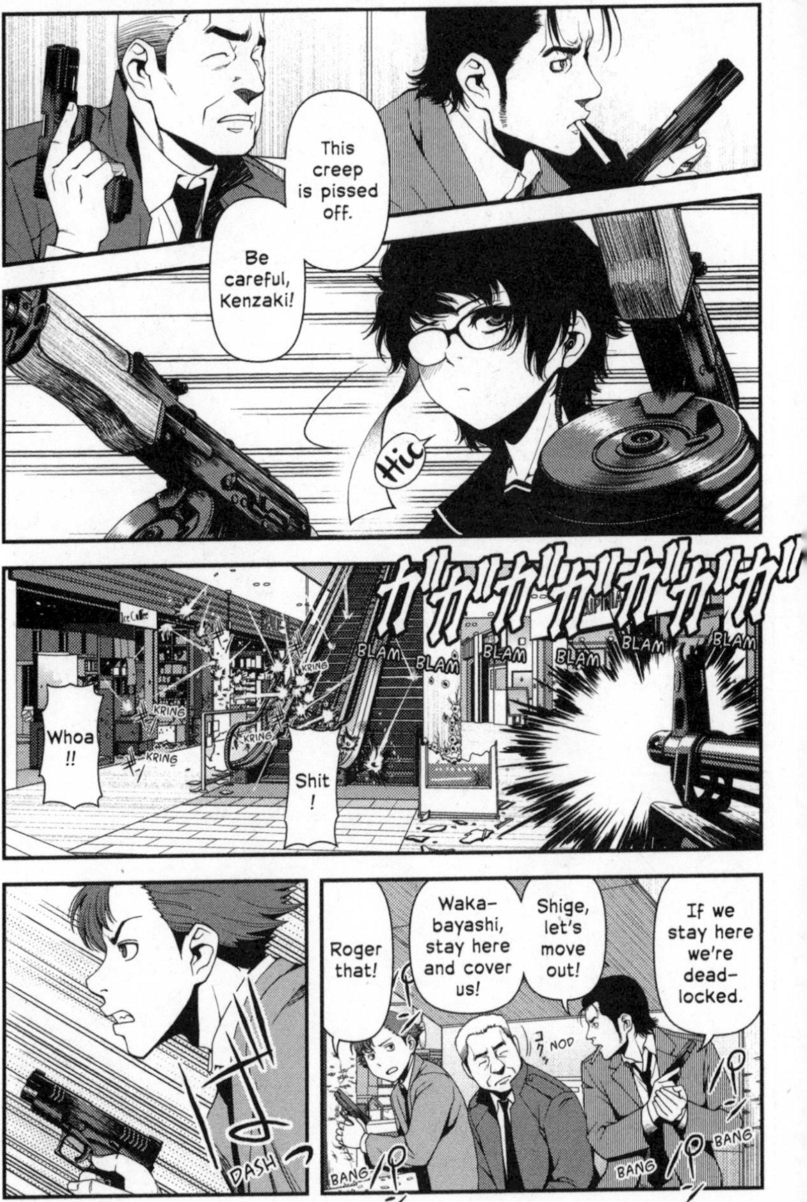

This creep is pissed off.
Be careful, Kenzaki!
Hic
ガガガガガガガ
BLAM BLAM BLAM BLAM BLAM BLAM
KRING KRING KRING KRING
Whoa !!
Shit !
If we stay here we're dead-locked.
Shige, let's move out!
NOD
Waka-bayashi, stay here and cover us!
Roger that!
BANG BANG BANG
DASH

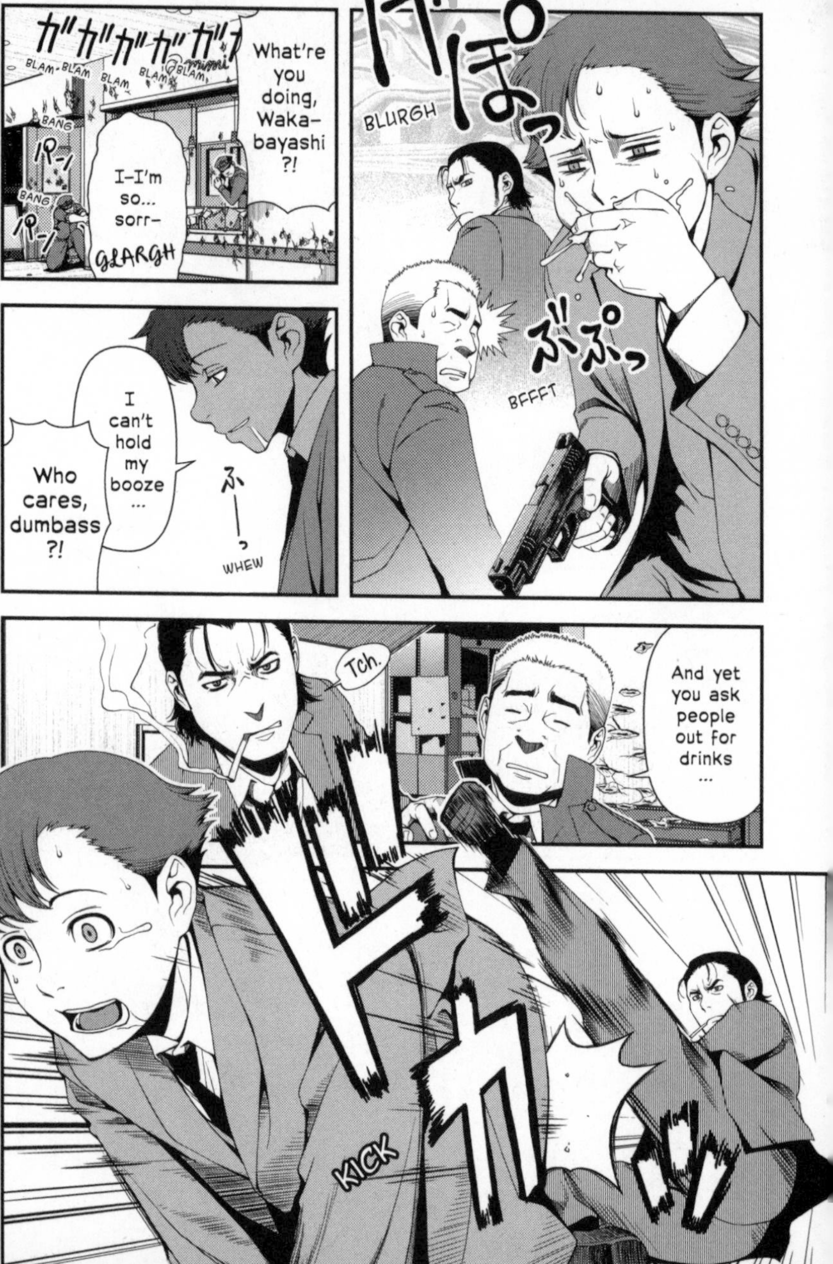
げぽっ
BLURGH
ぶぷっ
BFFFT
ガガガガガ
BLAM-BLAM BLAM BLAM BLAM
BANG
パーン
BANG
パーン
What're you doing, Waka-bayashi?!
I-I'm so... sorr-
GLARGH
I can't hold my booze...
Who cares, dumbass?!
ふーっ
WHEW
And yet you ask people out for drinks...
Tch.
ドカッ
KICK

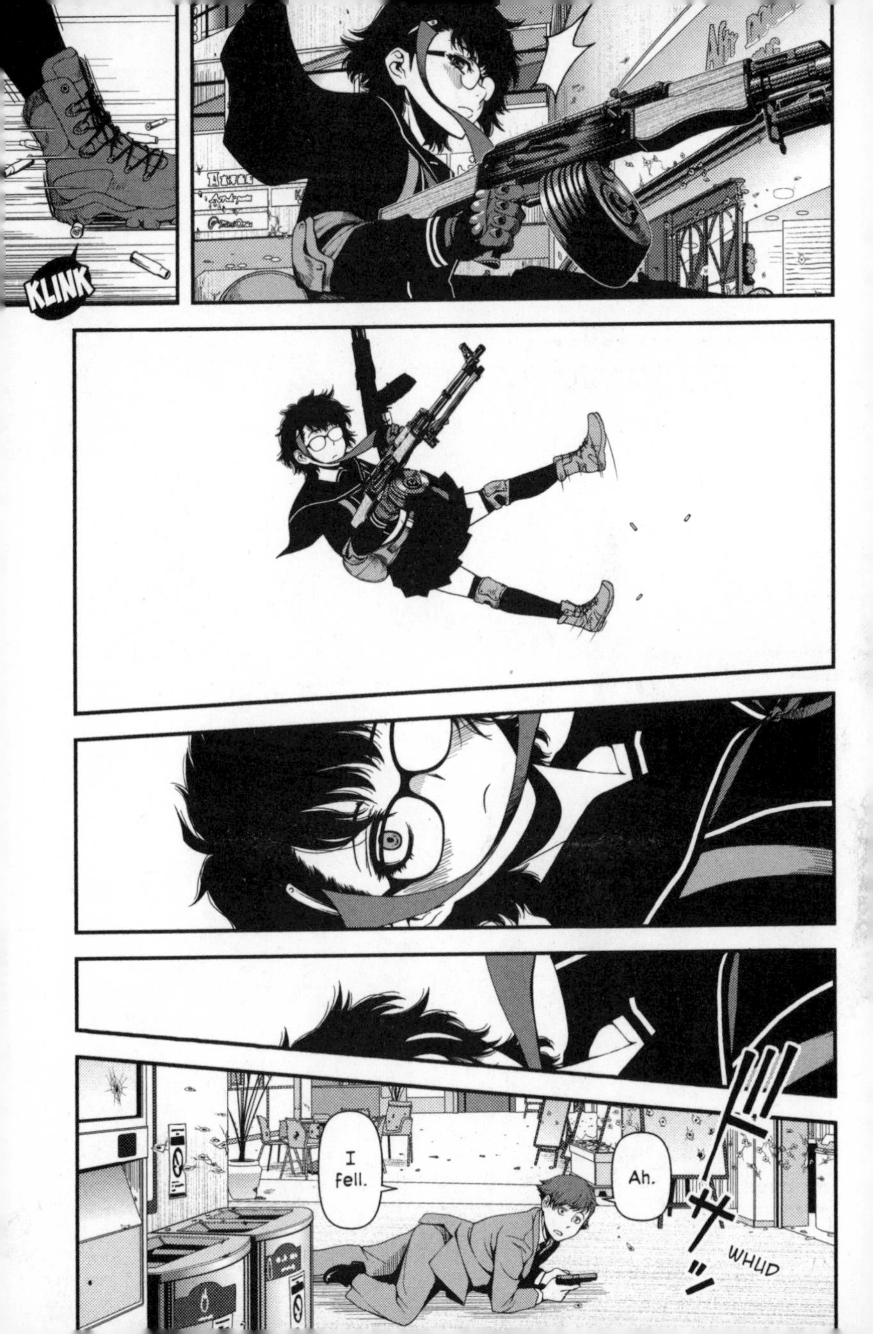

KLINK
Ah.
I fell.
WHUD

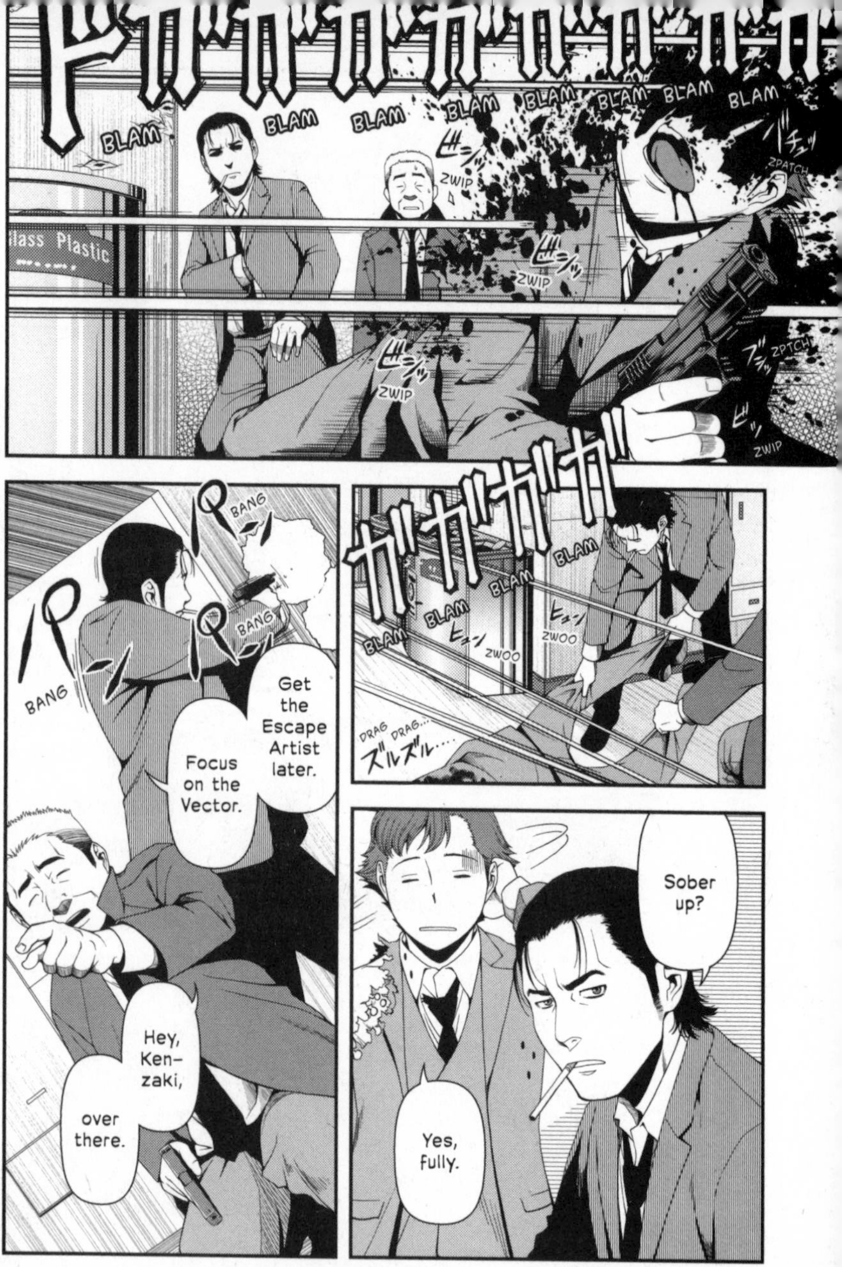
BLAM BLAM BLAM BLAM BLAM BLAM BLAM BLAM
ZPATCH
ZWIP
ZWIP
ZWIP
ZPTCH
ZWIP
ZWIP
ガガガガ
BLAM BLAM BLAM BLAM BLAM
ZWOO
ZWOO
DRAG DRAG...
ズルズル….
Sober up?
Yes, fully.
BANG
BANG
BANG
Get the Escape Artist later.
Focus on the Vector.
Hey, Ken-zaki,
over there.

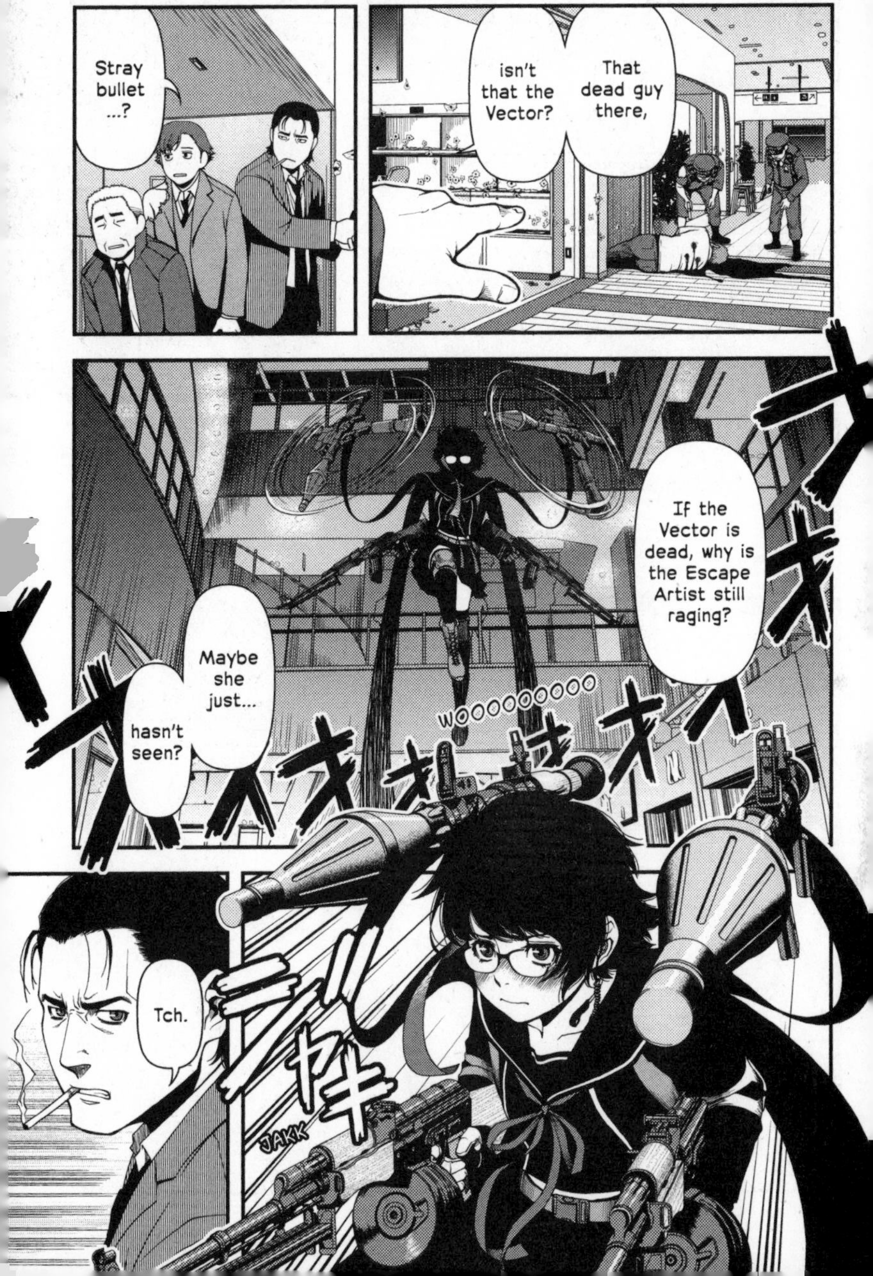
That dead guy there,
isn't that the Vector?
Stray bullet ...?
If the Vector is dead, why is the Escape Artist still raging?
WOOOOOOOOOO
Maybe she just...
hasn't seen?
JAKK
Tch.

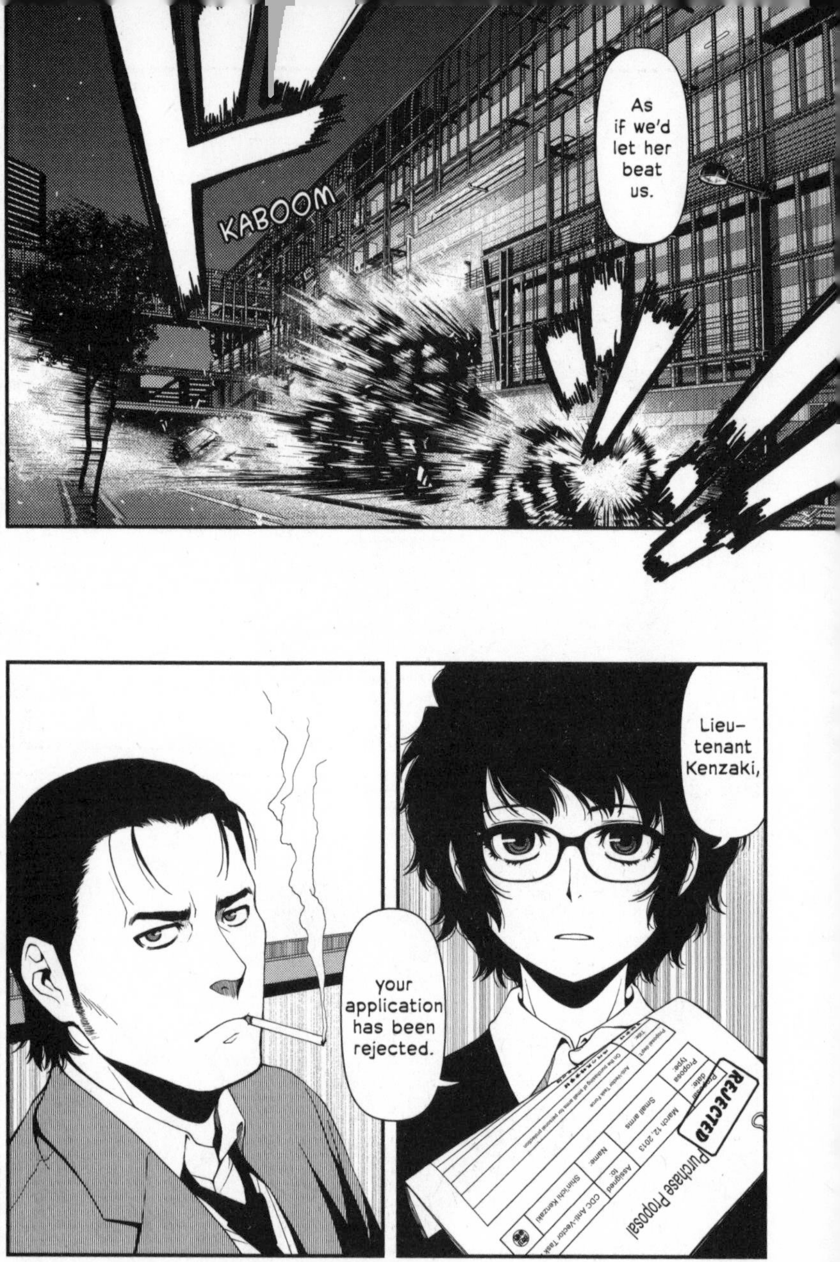
KABOOM
As if we'd let her beat us.
Lieu-tenant Kenzaki,
REJECTED
Purchase Proposal
your application has been rejected.

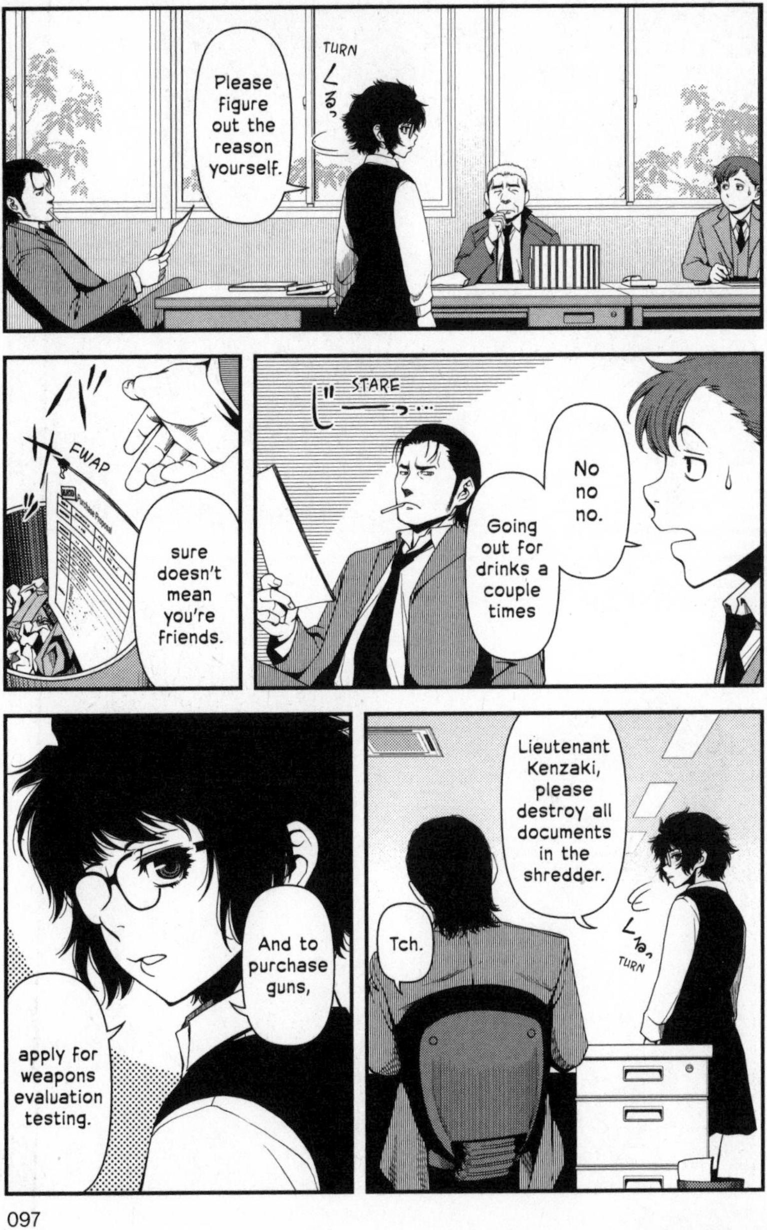
TURN
Please figure out the reason yourself.
STARE
No no no.
Going out for drinks a couple times
FWAP
Purchase Proposal
sure doesn't mean you're friends.
Lieutenant Kenzaki, please destroy all documents in the shredder.
TURN
Tch.
And to purchase guns,
apply for weapons evaluation testing.

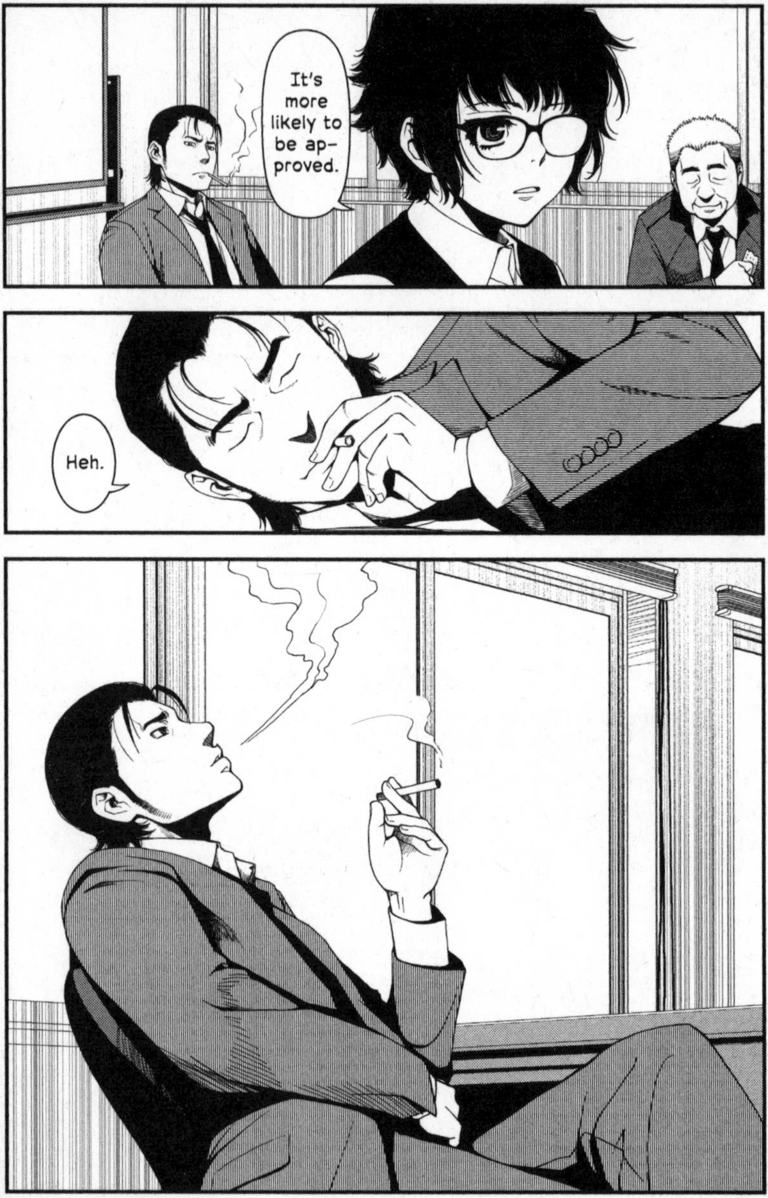
It's more likely to be approved.
Heh.

A Q&A with Mr. Licky and Ms. Policewoman
~WHAT ARE VECTORS?~

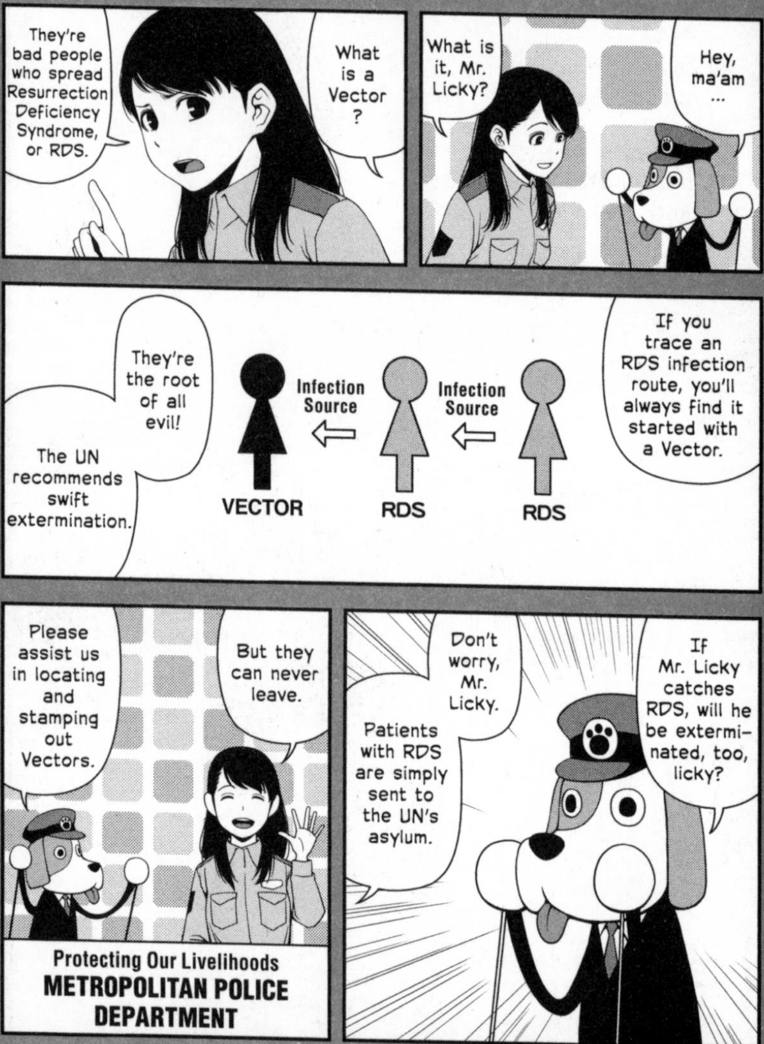
Hey, ma'am ...
What is it, Mr. Licky?
What is a Vector?
They're bad people who spread Resurrection Deficiency Syndrome, or RDS.
If you trace an RDS infection route, you'll always find it started with a Vector.
Infection Source
Infection Source
VECTOR
RDS
RDS
They're the root of all evil!
The UN recommends swift extermination.
If Mr. Licky catches RDS, will he be extermi-nated, too, licky?
Don't worry, Mr. Licky.
Patients with RDS are simply sent to the UN's asylum.
But they can never leave.
Please assist us in locating and stamping out Vectors.
Protecting Our Livelihoods
METROPOLITAN POLICE DEPARTMENT

A Q&A with Mr. Licky and Ms. Policewoman
~HOW TO TELL WHO IS A VECTOR~

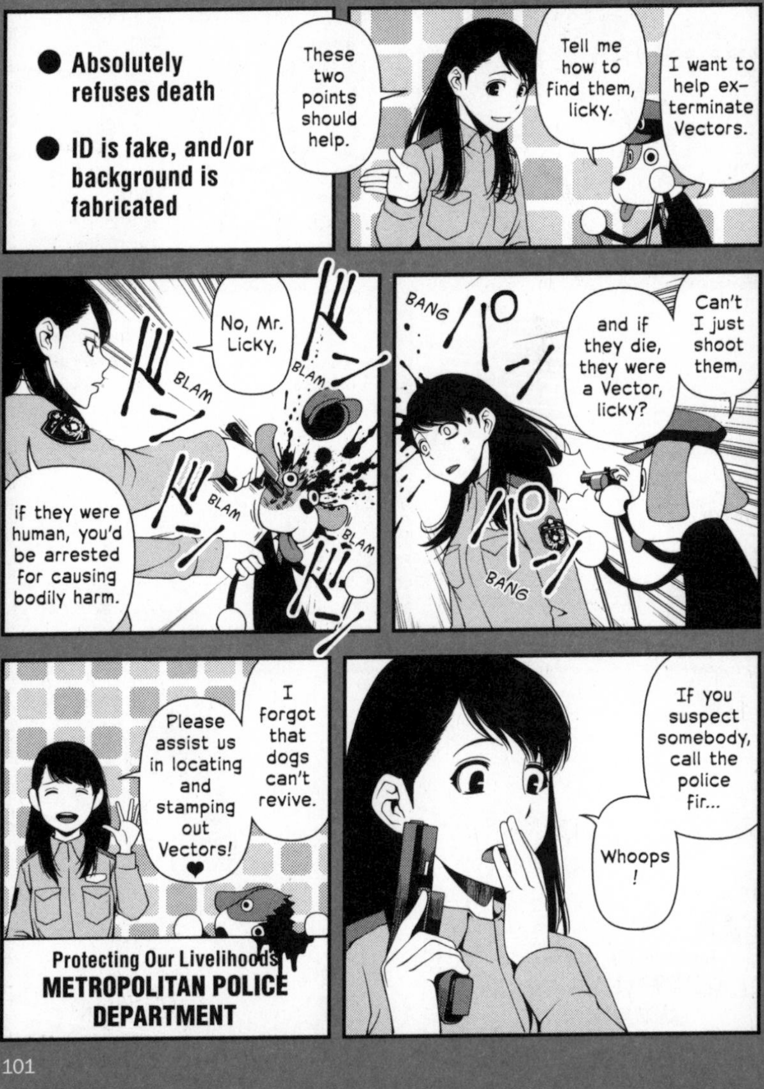

I want to help exterminate Vectors.
Tell me how to find them, licky.
These two points should help.
● Absolutely refuses death
● ID is fake, and/or background is fabricated
Can't I just shoot them,
and if they die, they were a Vector, licky?
BANG
BANG
No, Mr. Licky,
BLAM
BLAM
BLAM
BLAM
if they were human, you'd be arrested for causing bodily harm.
If you suspect somebody, call the police fir...
Whoops!
I forgot that dogs can't revive.
Please assist us in locating and stamping out Vectors! ❤
Protecting Our Livelihoods
METROPOLITAN POLICE DEPARTMENT

A Q&A with Mr. Cluck and Ms. Policewoman
~A VECTOR'S FATE~

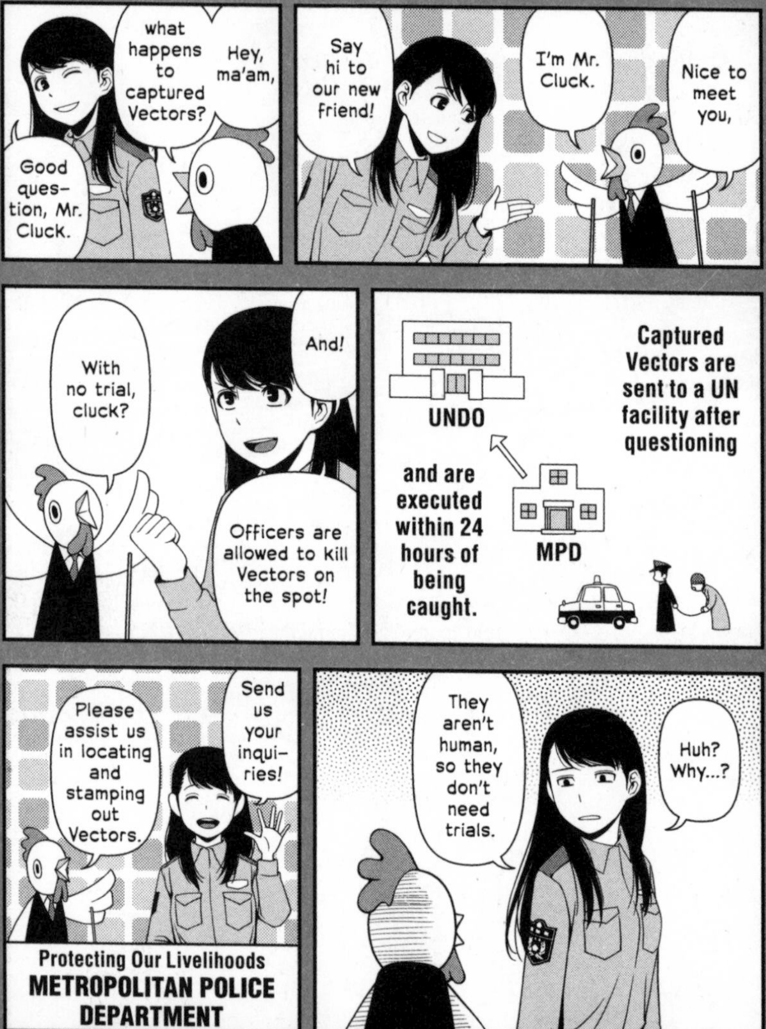
Nice to meet you,
I'm Mr. Cluck.
Say hi to our new friend!
Hey, ma'am,
what happens to captured Vectors?
Good question, Mr. Cluck.
Captured Vectors are sent to a UN facility after questioning
UNDO
MPD
and are executed within 24 hours of being caught.
And!
With no trial, cluck?
Officers are allowed to kill Vectors on the spot!
Huh? Why...?
They aren't human, so they don't need trials.
Send us your inquiries!
Please assist us in locating and stamping out Vectors.
Protecting Our Livelihoods
METROPOLITAN POLICE DEPARTMENT

A Q&A with Mr. Cluck and Ms. Policewoman
~WHAT IS REVIVAL?~

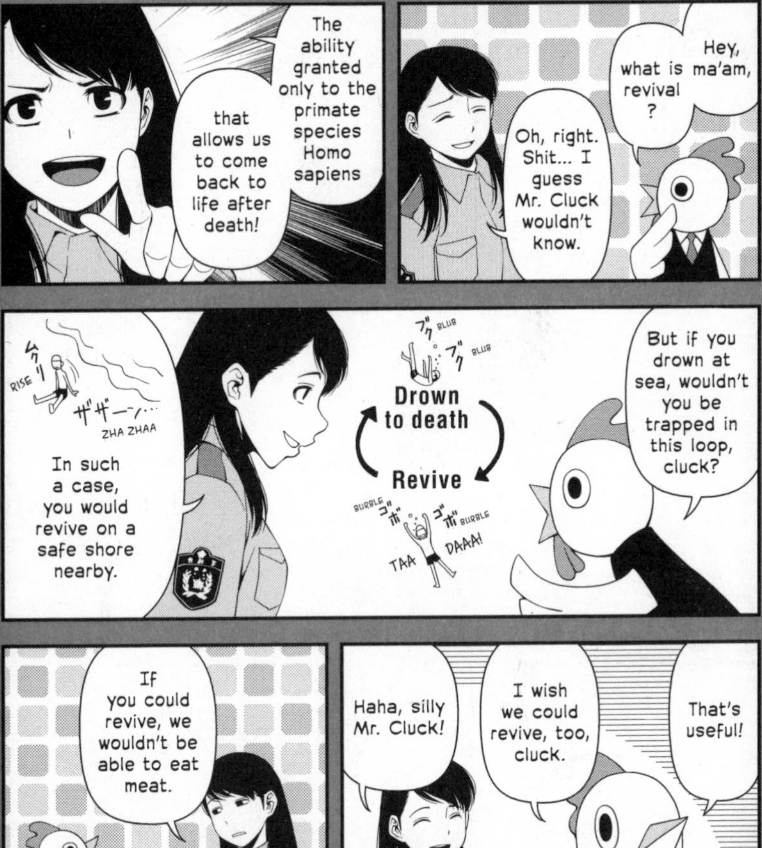
Hey, ma'am, what is revival?
Oh, right. Shit... I guess Mr. Cluck wouldn't know.
The ability granted only to the primate species Homo sapiens
that allows us to come back to life after death!
But if you drown at sea, wouldn't you be trapped in this loop, cluck?
BLUB
BLUB
Drown to death
Revive
BURBLE
BURBLE
TAA DAAA!
RISE
ZHA ZHAA
In such a case, you would revive on a safe shore nearby.
That's useful!
I wish we could revive, too, cluck.
Haha, silly Mr. Cluck!
If you could revive, we wouldn't be able to eat meat.
Protecting Our Livelihoods
METROPOLITAN POLICE DEPARTMENT

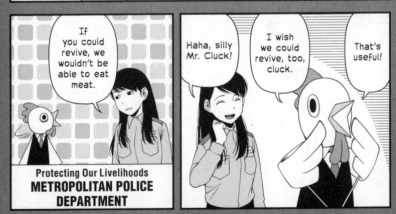

4
I Just Hate...

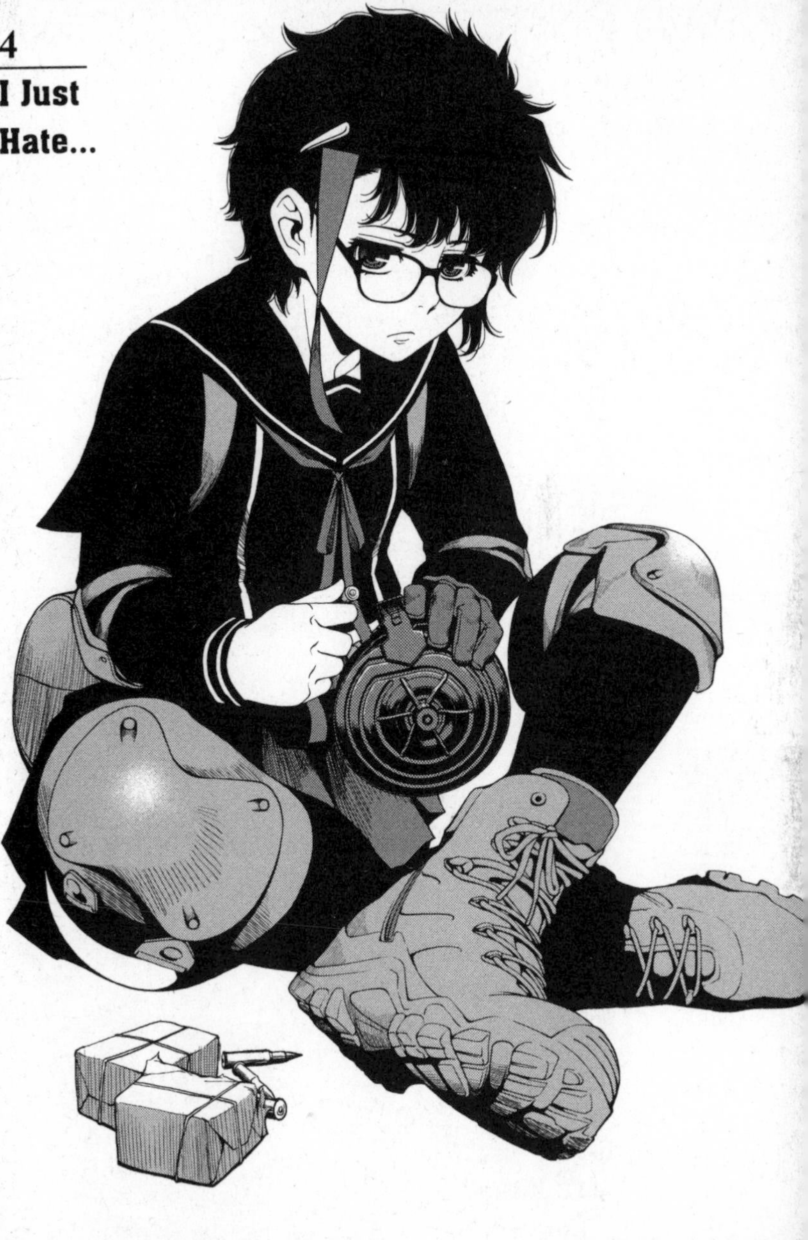

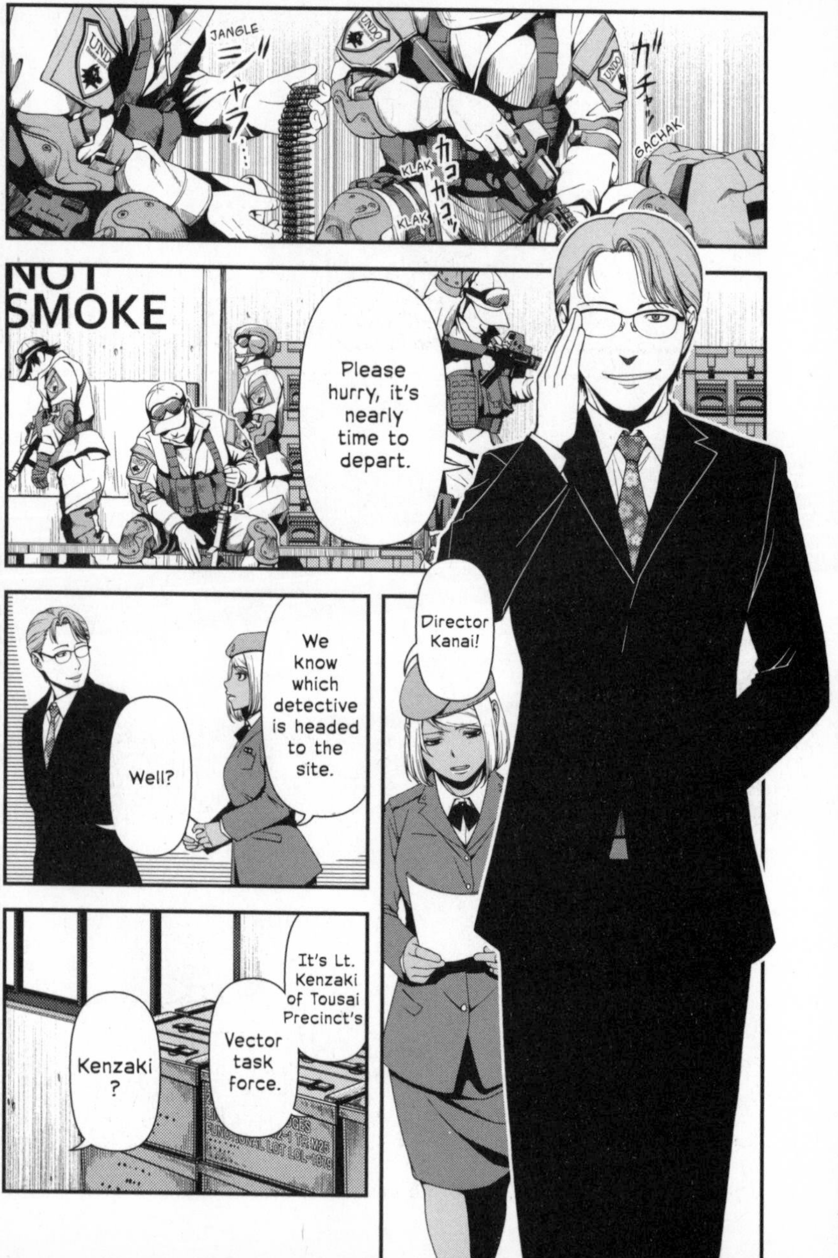

ガチャッ
GACHAK
カッカッ
KLAK
KLAK
ジャラ…
JANGLE
NOT
SMOKE
Please hurry, it's nearly time to depart.
Director Kanai!
We know which detective is headed to the site.
Well?
It's Lt. Kenzaki of Tousai Precinct's
Vector task force.
Kenzaki?

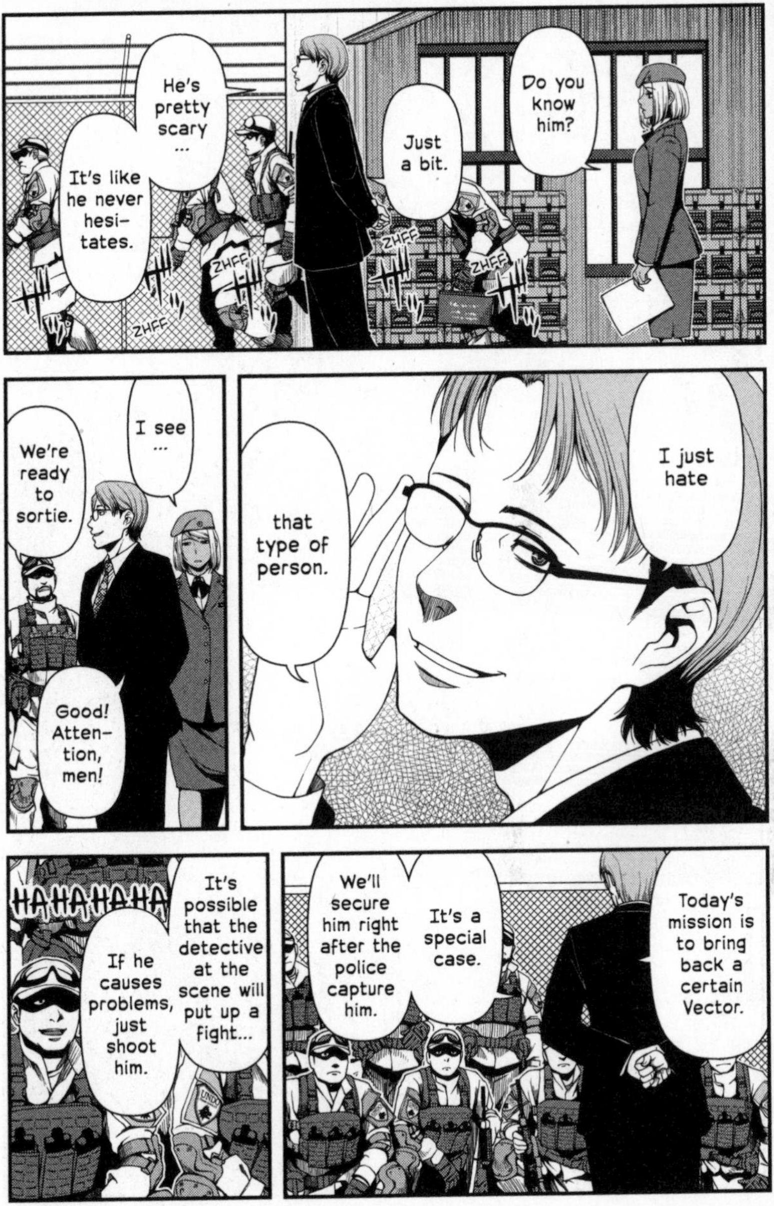
Do you know him?
Just a bit.
He's pretty scary ...
It's like he never hesi-tates.
ZHFF
ZHFF
ZHFF
ZHFF
I just hate
that type of person.
I see ...
We're ready to sortie.
Good! Atten-tion, men!
Today's mission is to bring back a certain Vector.
It's a special case.
We'll secure him right after the police capture him.
It's possible that the detective at the scene will put up a fight...
If he causes problems, just shoot him.
HAHAHAHA

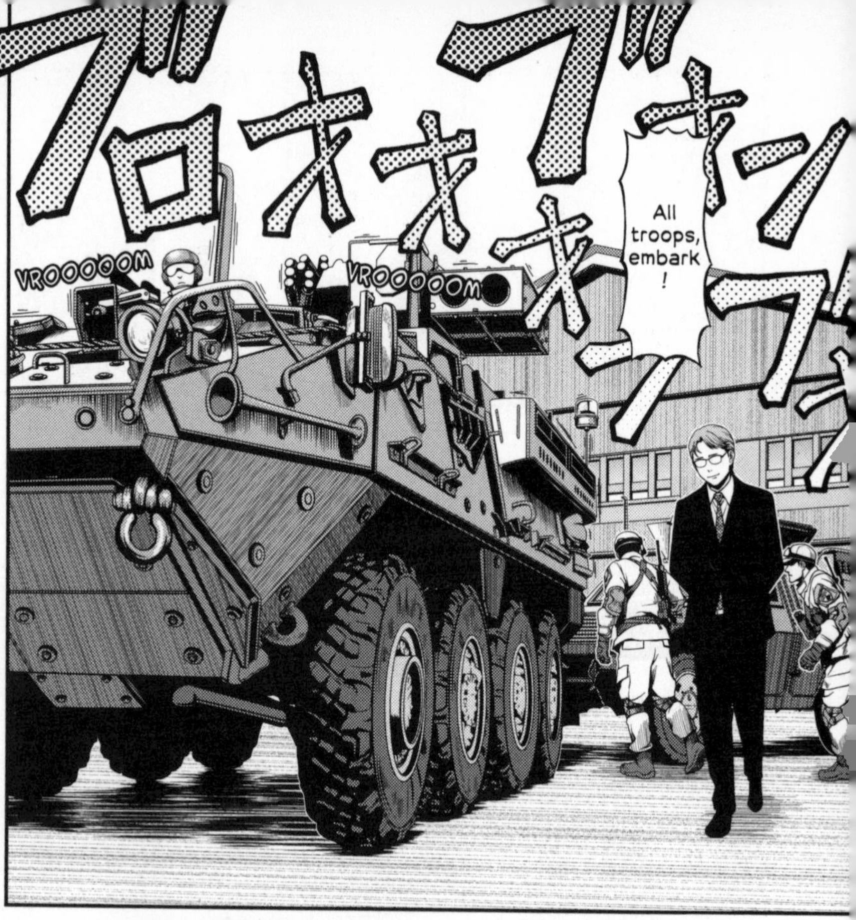
VROOOOOM
VROOOOOM
All troops, embark!

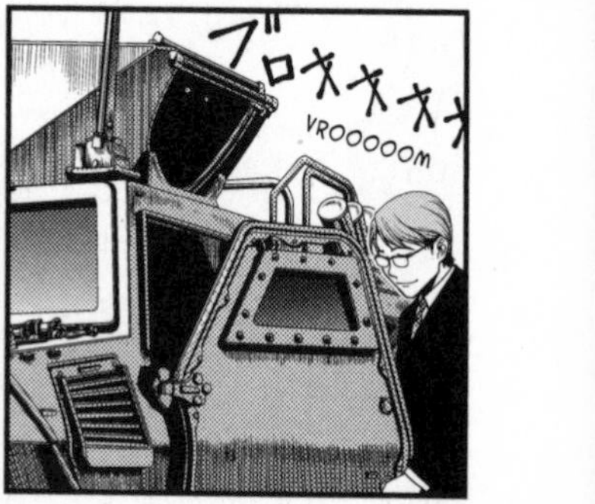
VROOOOOM

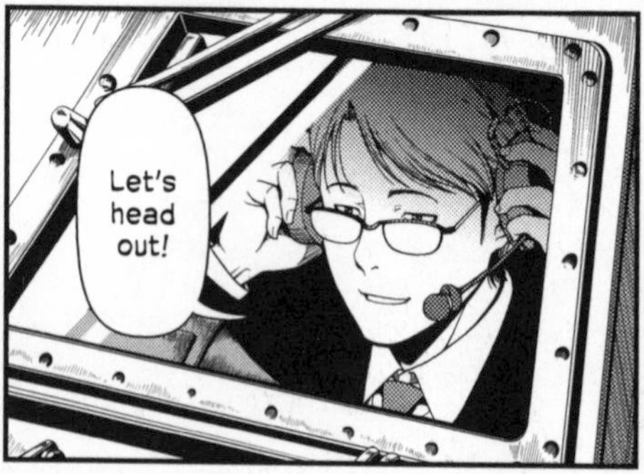
Let's head out!

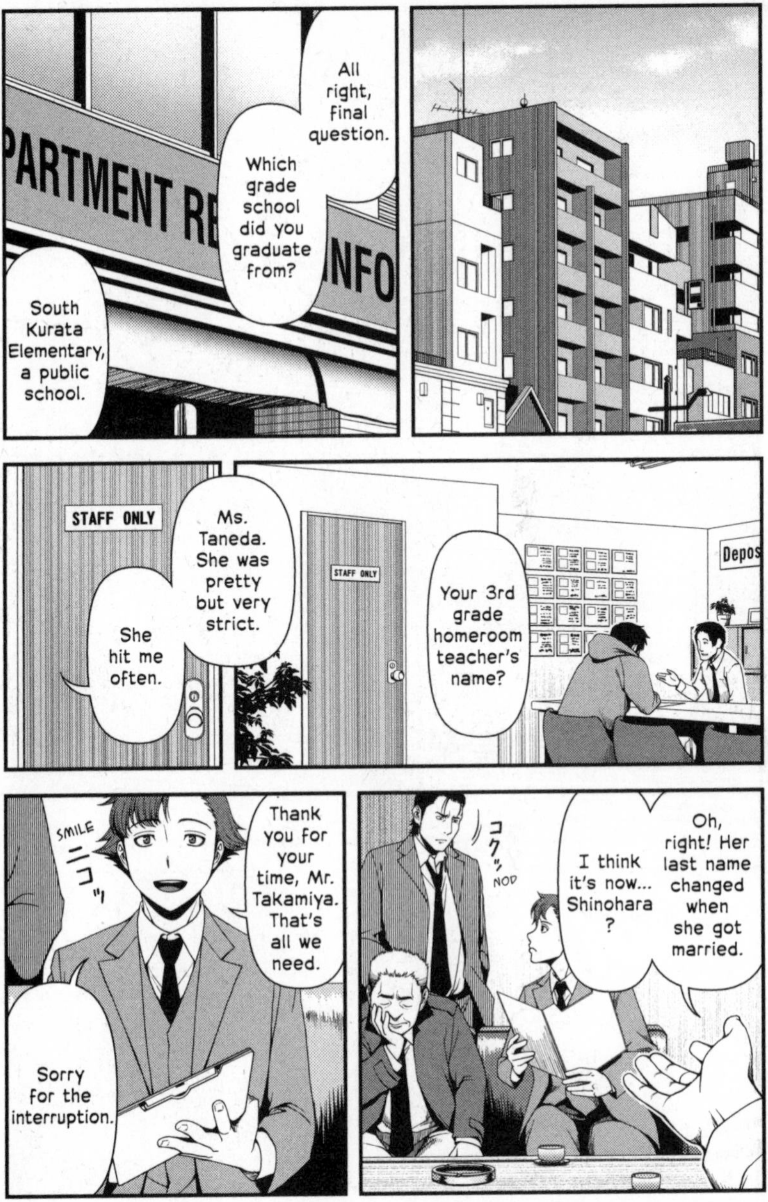

All right, final question.
Which grade school did you graduate from?
South Kurata Elementary, a public school.
Depos
STAFF ONLY
Your 3rd grade homeroom teacher's name?
STAFF ONLY
Ms. Taneda. She was pretty but very strict.
She hit me often.
Oh, right! Her last name changed when she got married.
I think it's now... Shinohara?
コクッ NOD
Thank you for your time, Mr. Takamiya. That's all we need.
SMILE ニコッ
Sorry for the interruption.

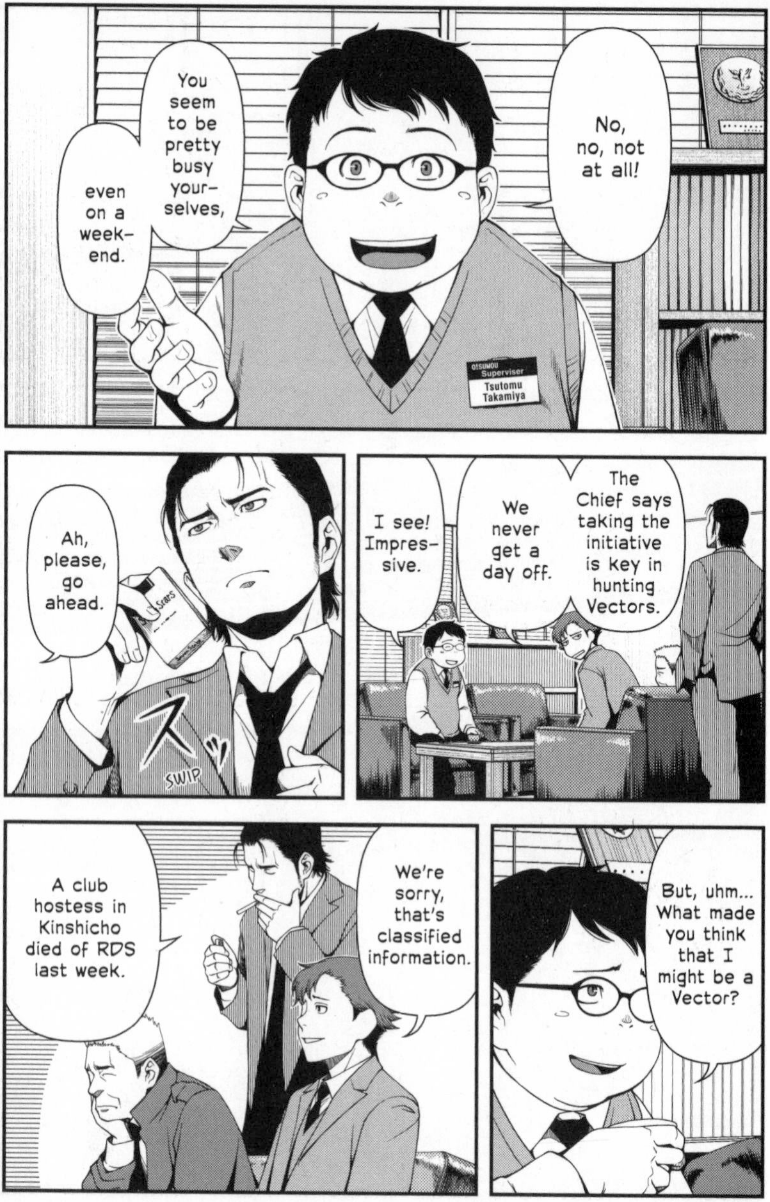
No, no, not at all!
You seem to be pretty busy your-selves,
even on a week-end.
OTSUMOU Superviser
Tsutomu Takamiya
The Chief says taking the initiative is key in hunting Vectors.
We never get a day off.
I see! Impressive.
Ah, please, go ahead.
SWIP
But, uhm... What made you think that I might be a Vector?
We're sorry, that's classified information.
A club hostess in Kinshicho died of RDS last week.

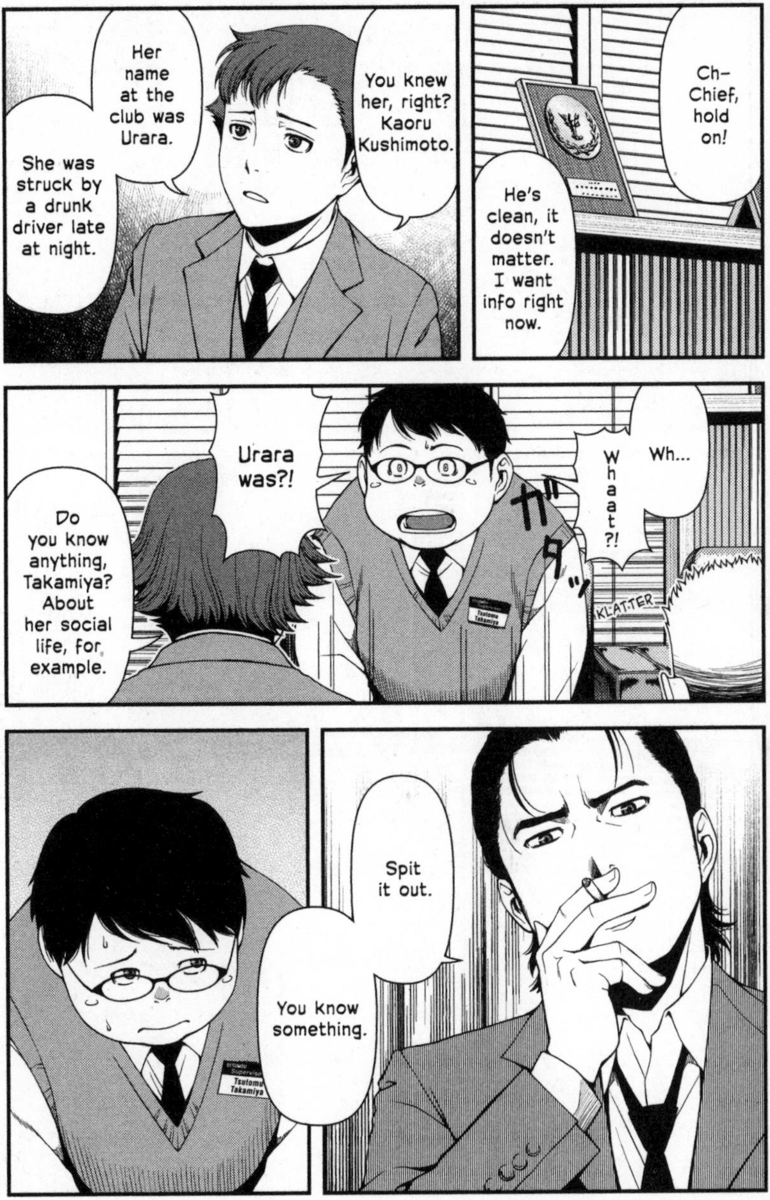
Ch–Chief, hold on!
He's clean, it doesn't matter. I want info right now.
You knew her, right? Kaoru Kushimoto.
Her name at the club was Urara.
She was struck by a drunk driver late at night.
Wh...
Whaat?!
KLATTER
ガタッ
Urara was?!
Do you know anything, Takamiya? About her social life, for example.
Spit it out.
You know something.

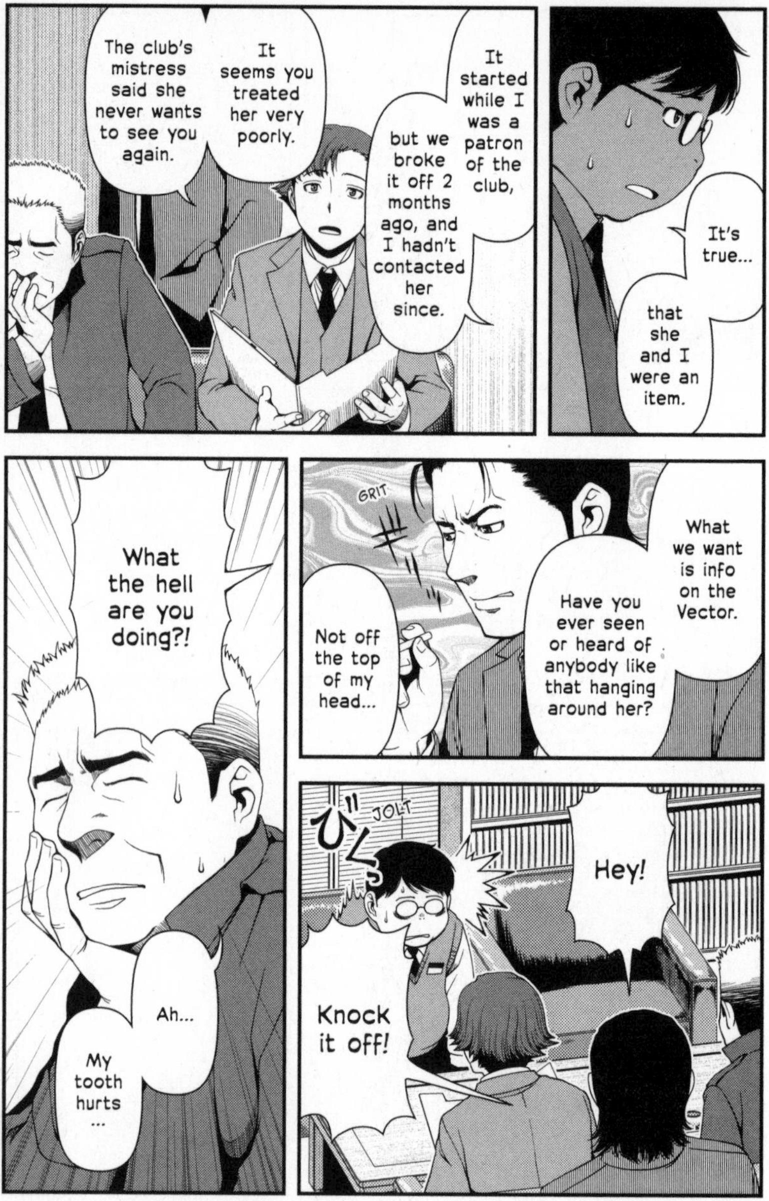
It's true...
that she and I were an item.
It started while I was a patron of the club,
but we broke it off 2 months ago, and I hadn't contacted her since.
It seems you treated her very poorly.
The club's mistress said she never wants to see you again.
What we want is info on the Vector.
Have you ever seen or heard of anybody like that hanging around her?
GRIT
Not off the top of my head...
Hey!
JOLT
Knock it off!
What the hell are you doing?!
Ah...
My tooth hurts ...

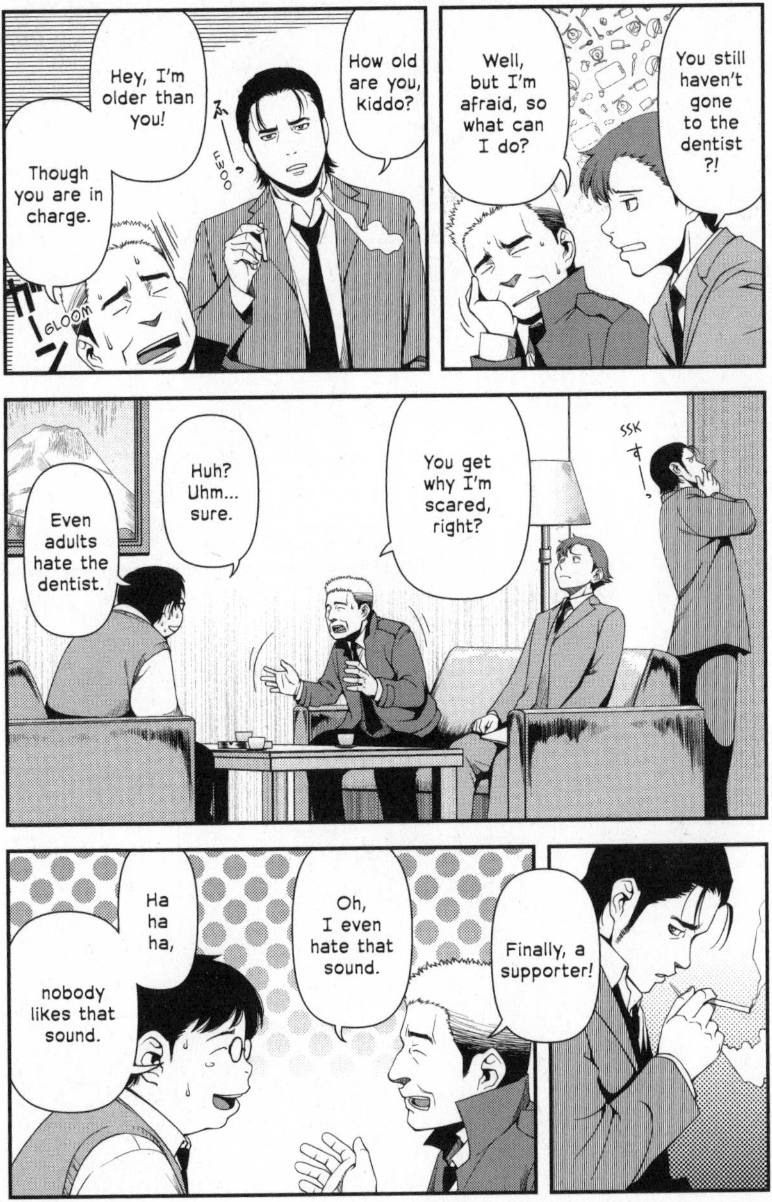
You still haven't gone to the dentist ?!
Well, but I'm afraid, so what can I do?
How old are you, kiddo?
FWOO
Hey, I'm older than you!
Though you are in charge.
GLOOM
SSK
You get why I'm scared, right?
Huh? Uhm... sure.
Even adults hate the dentist.
Finally, a supporter!
Oh, I even hate that sound.
Ha ha ha,
nobody likes that sound.

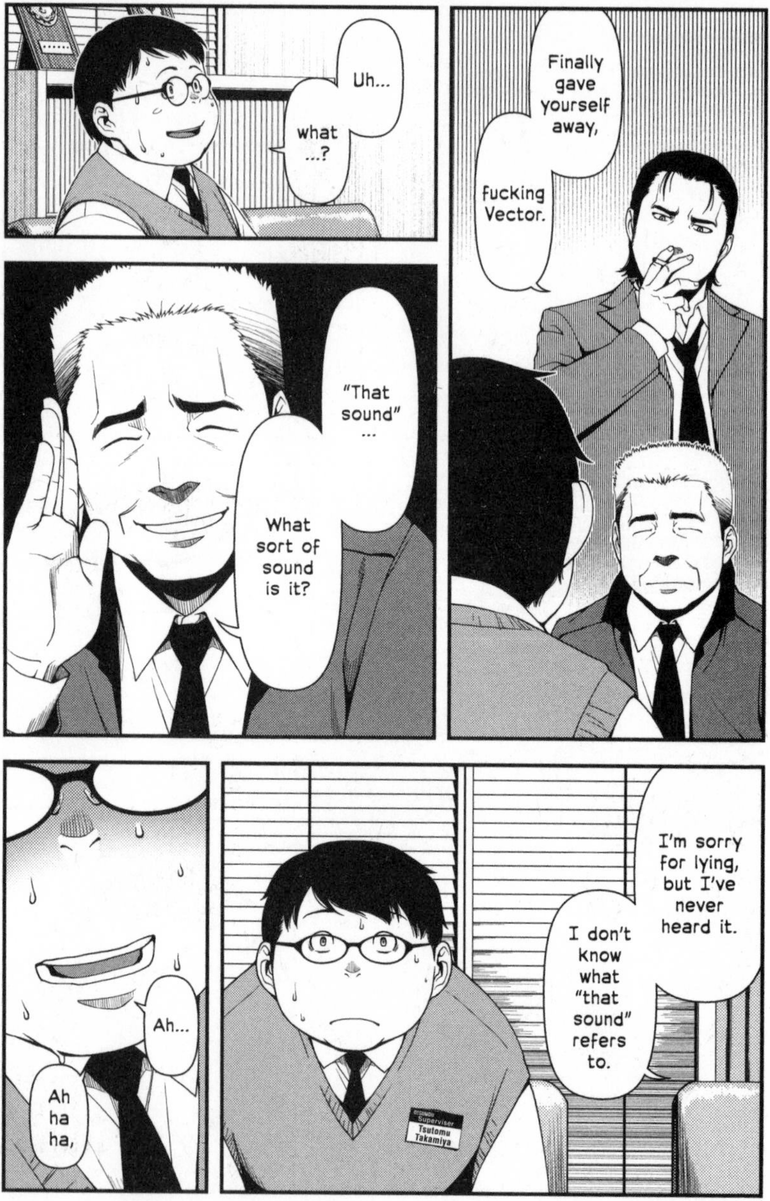
Finally gave yourself away,
fucking Vector.
Uh...
what ...?
"That sound" ...
What sort of sound is it?
I'm sorry for lying, but I've never heard it.
I don't know what "that sound" refers to.
Superviser
Tsutomu Takamiya
Ah...
Ah ha ha,

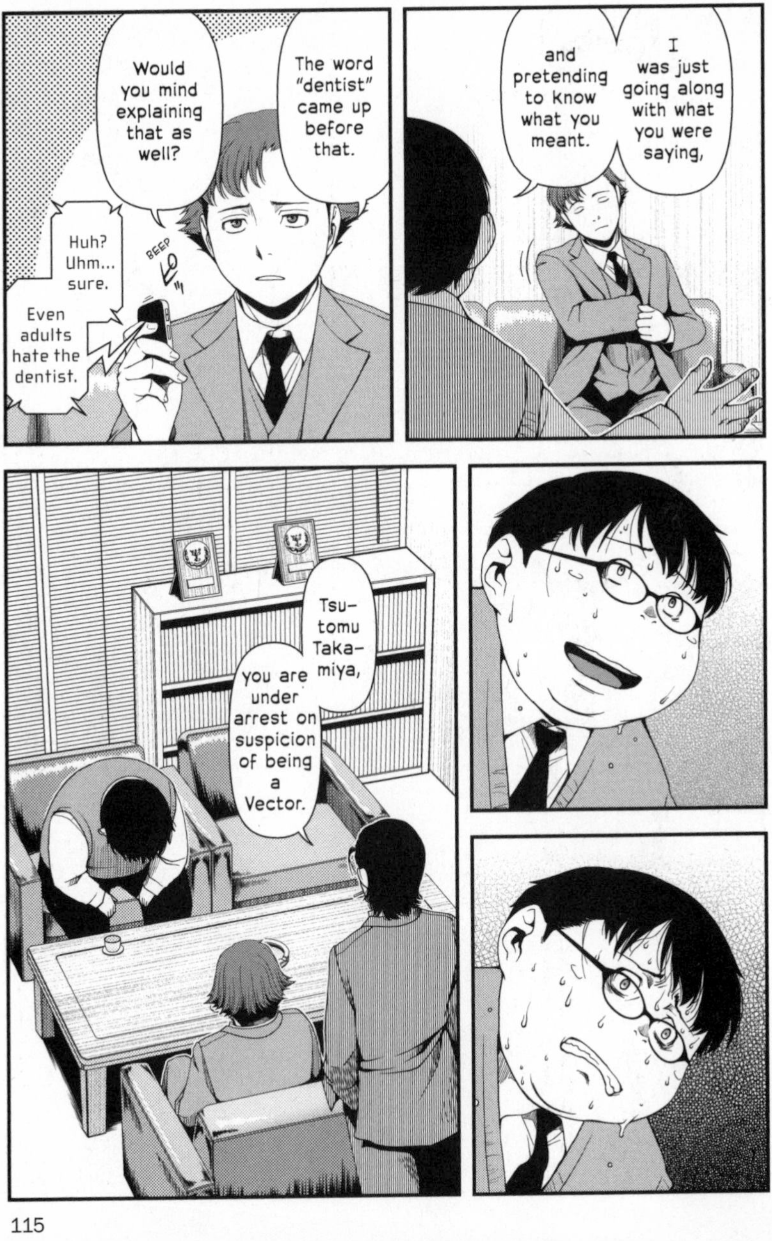
I was just going along with what you were saying,
and pretending to know what you meant.
The word "dentist" came up before that.
Would you mind explaining that as well?
Huh? Uhm... sure.
BEEP
Even adults hate the dentist.
Tsu-tomu Taka-miya,
you are under arrest on suspicion of being a Vector.

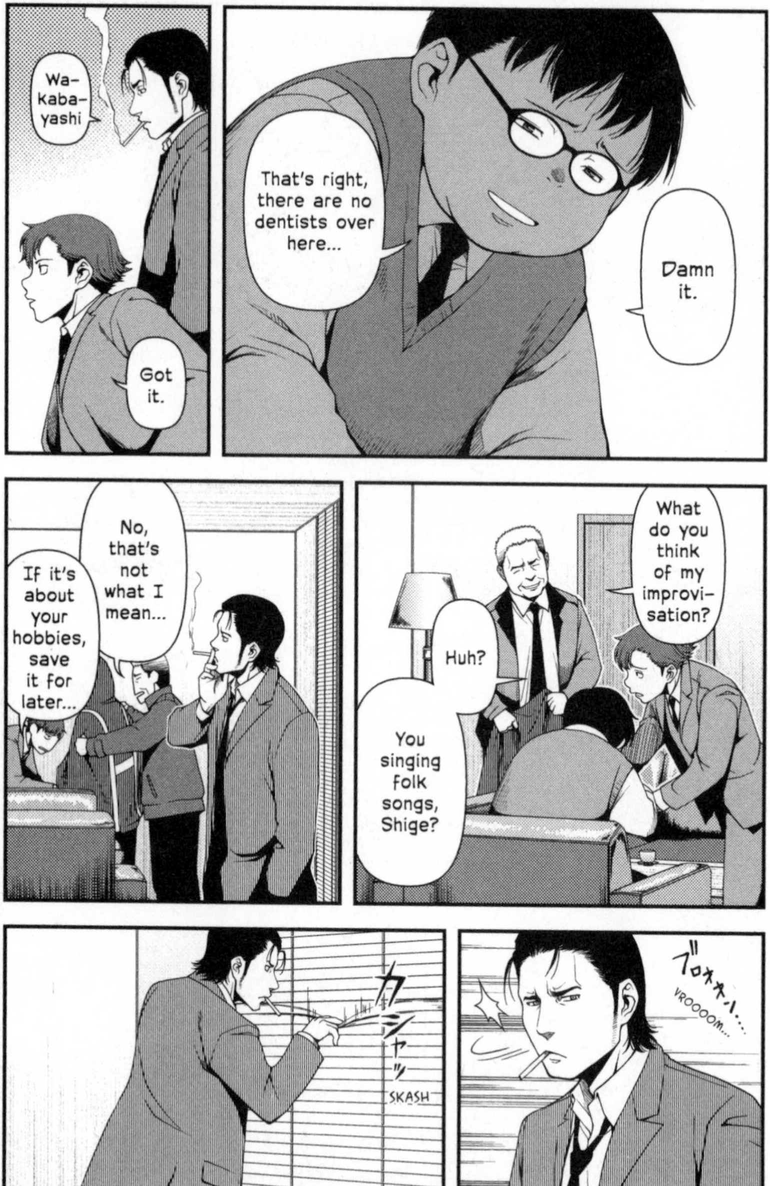
Damn it.
That's right, there are no dentists over here...
Wa-kaba-yashi
Got it.
What do you think of my improvi-sation?
Huh?
You singing folk songs, Shige?
No, that's not what I mean...
If it's about your hobbies, save it for later...
ブロオオン・・・
VROOOOM...
カシャッ
SKASH

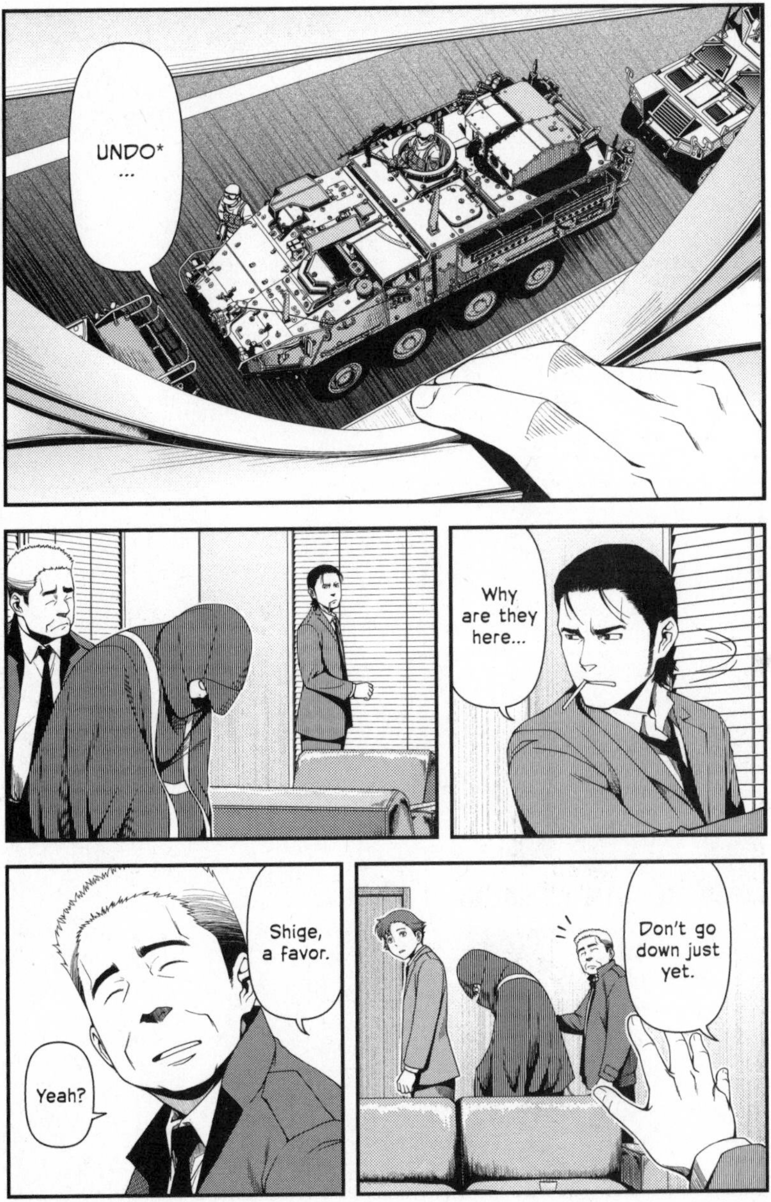
UNDO* ...
Why are they here...
Don't go down just yet.
Shige, a favor.
Yeah?

*United Nations Disease-Control Office

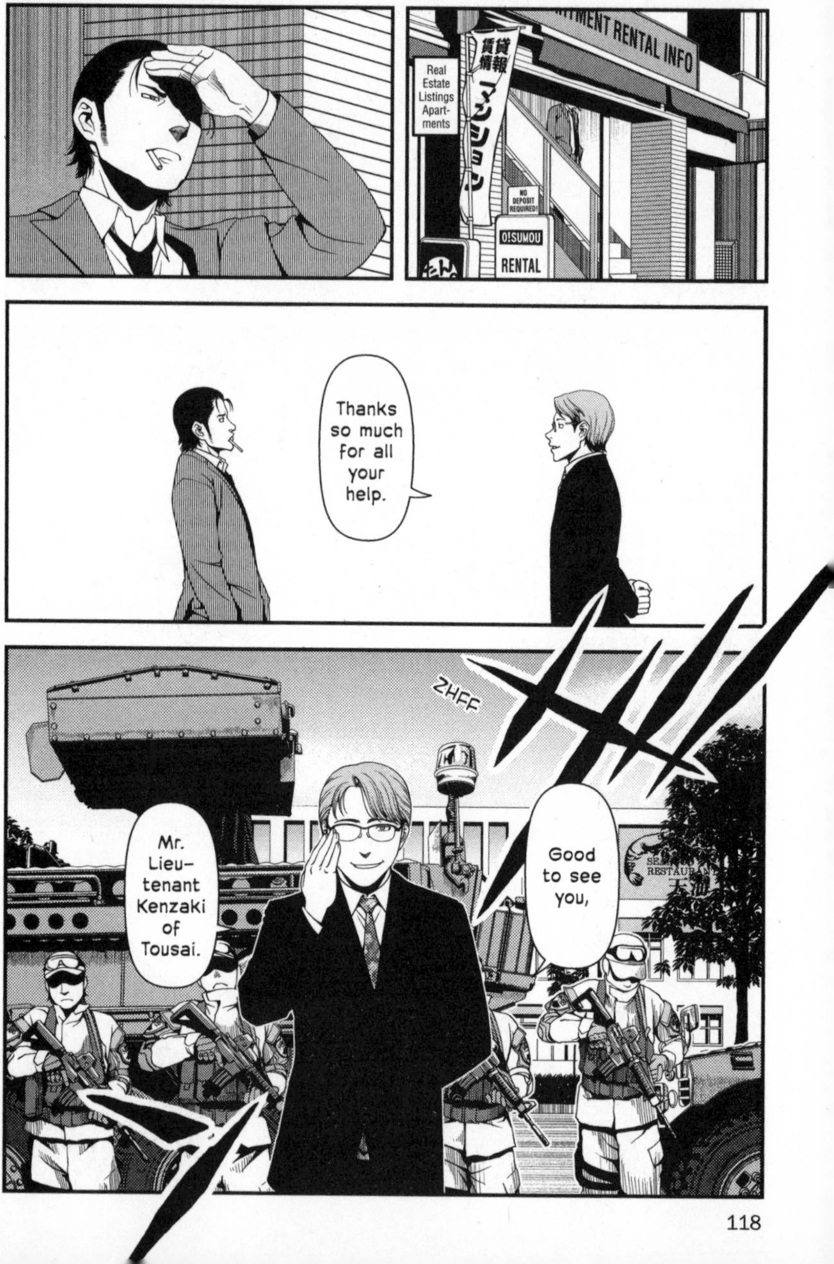
MENT RENTAL INFO
賃貸情報
マンション
Real Estate Listings Apartments
NO DEPOSIT REQUIRED!
O!SUMOU
RENTAL
Thanks so much for all your help.
ZHFF
Good to see you,
Mr. Lieutenant Kenzaki of Tousai.

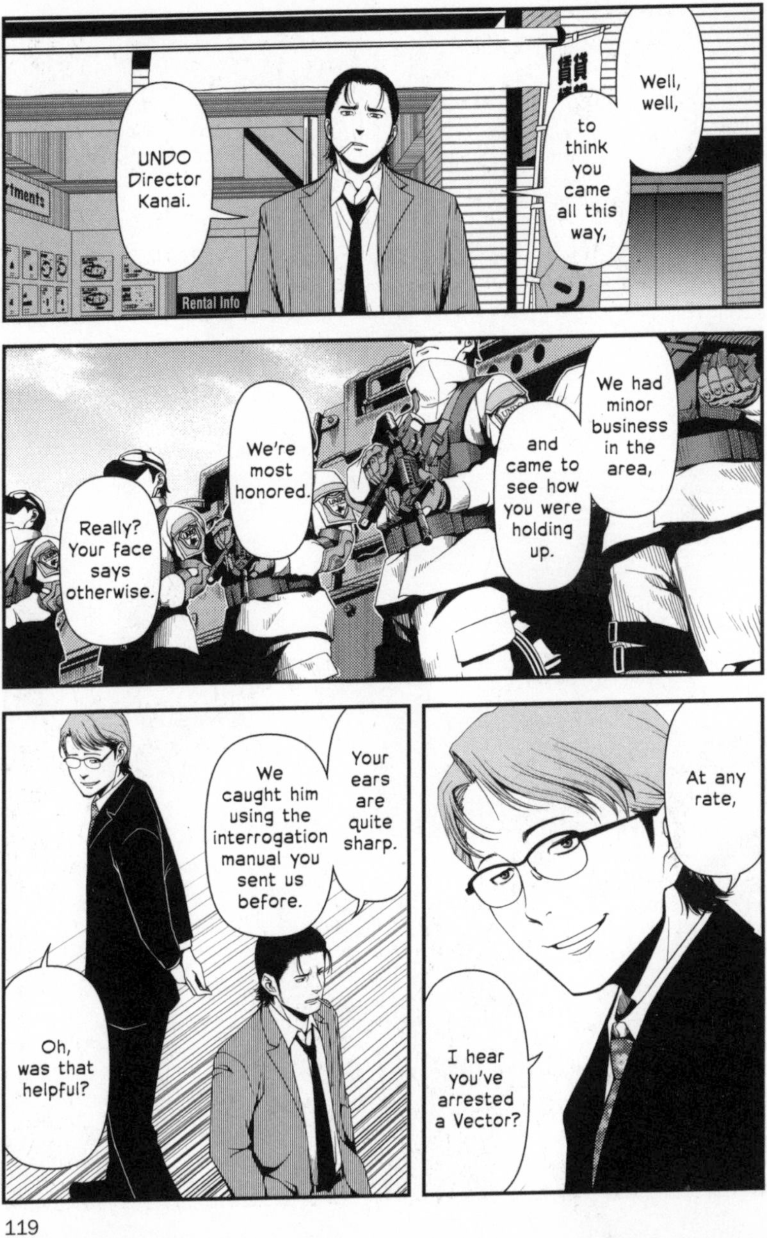
Well, well,
to think you came all this way,
UNDO Director Kanai.
Rental Info
We had minor business in the area,
and came to see how you were holding up.
We're most honored.
Really? Your face says otherwise.
At any rate,
I hear you've arrested a Vector?
Your ears are quite sharp.
We caught him using the interrogation manual you sent us before.
Oh, was that helpful?

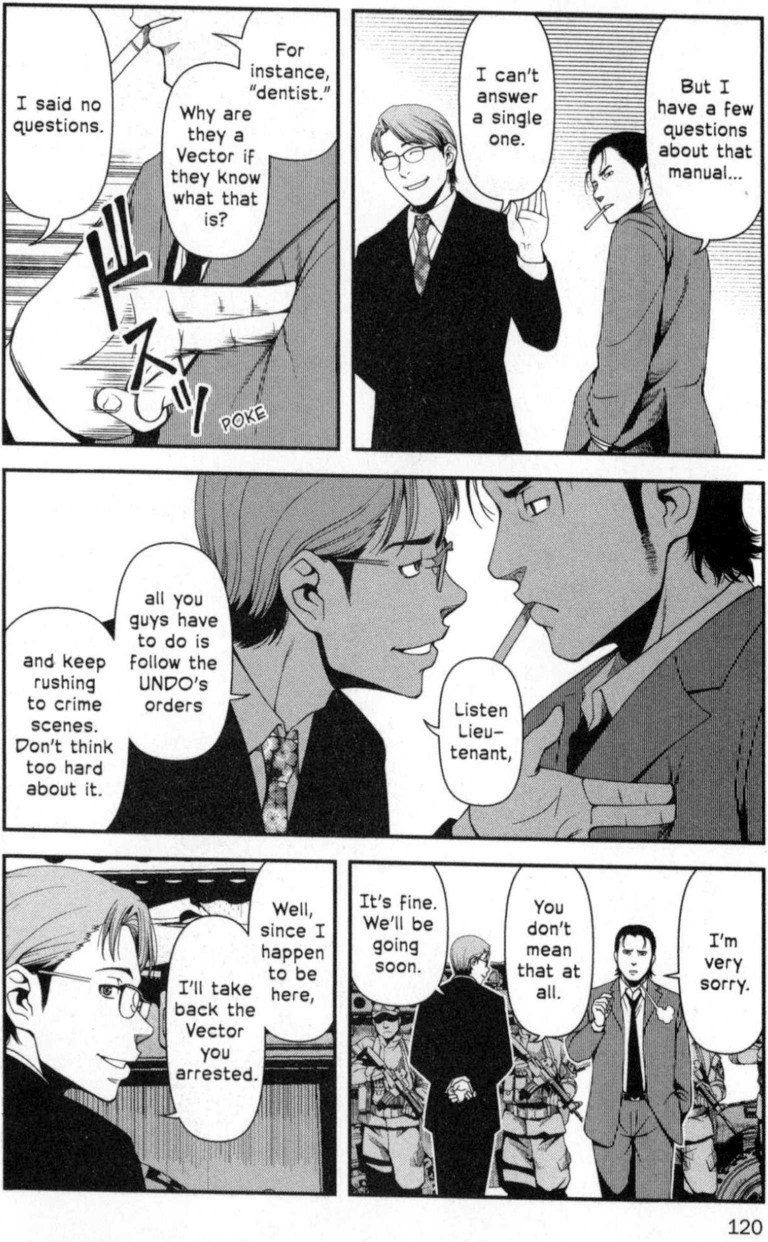
But I have a few questions about that manual...
I can't answer a single one.
For instance, "dentist."
Why are they a Vector if they know what that is?
I said no questions.
POKE
Listen Lieutenant,
all you guys have to do is follow the UNDO's orders
and keep rushing to crime scenes. Don't think too hard about it.
I'm very sorry.
You don't mean that at all.
It's fine. We'll be going soon.
Well, since I happen to be here,
I'll take back the Vector you arrested.

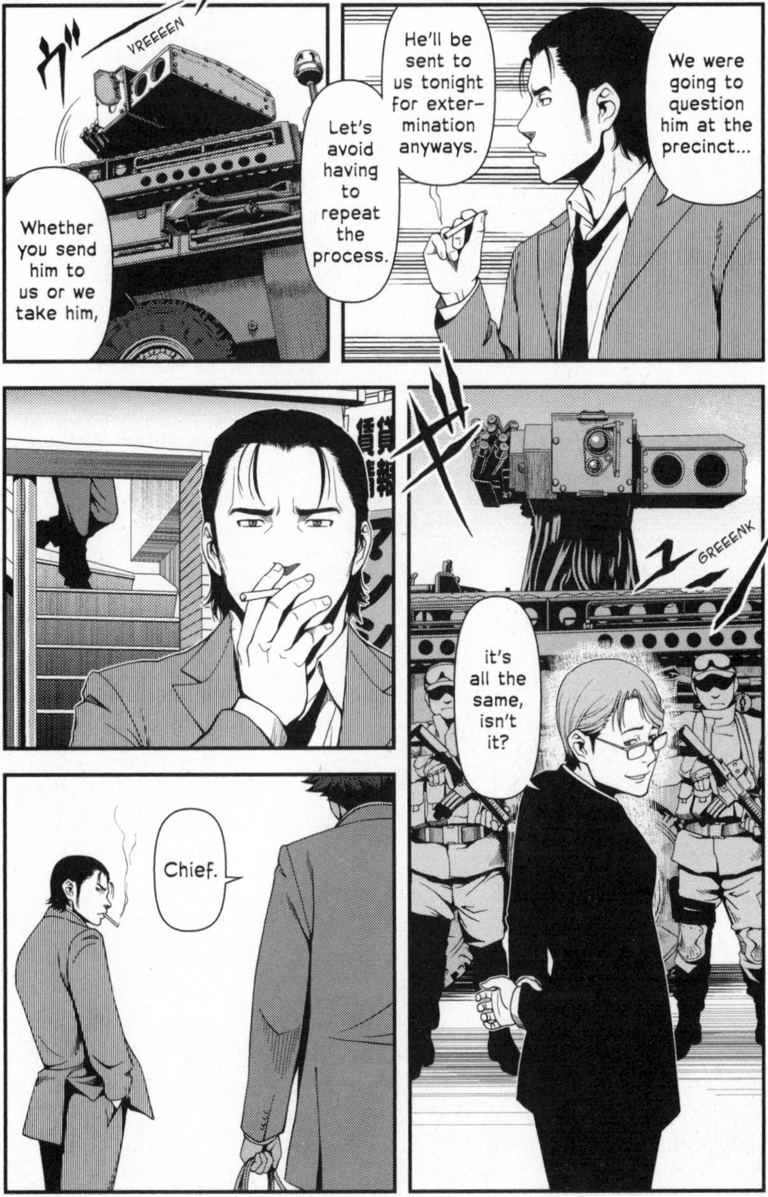

We were going to question him at the precinct...
He'll be sent to us tonight for extermination anyways.
Let's avoid having to repeat the process.
VREEEEN
Whether you send him to us or we take him,
GREEENK
it's all the same, isn't it?
Chief.

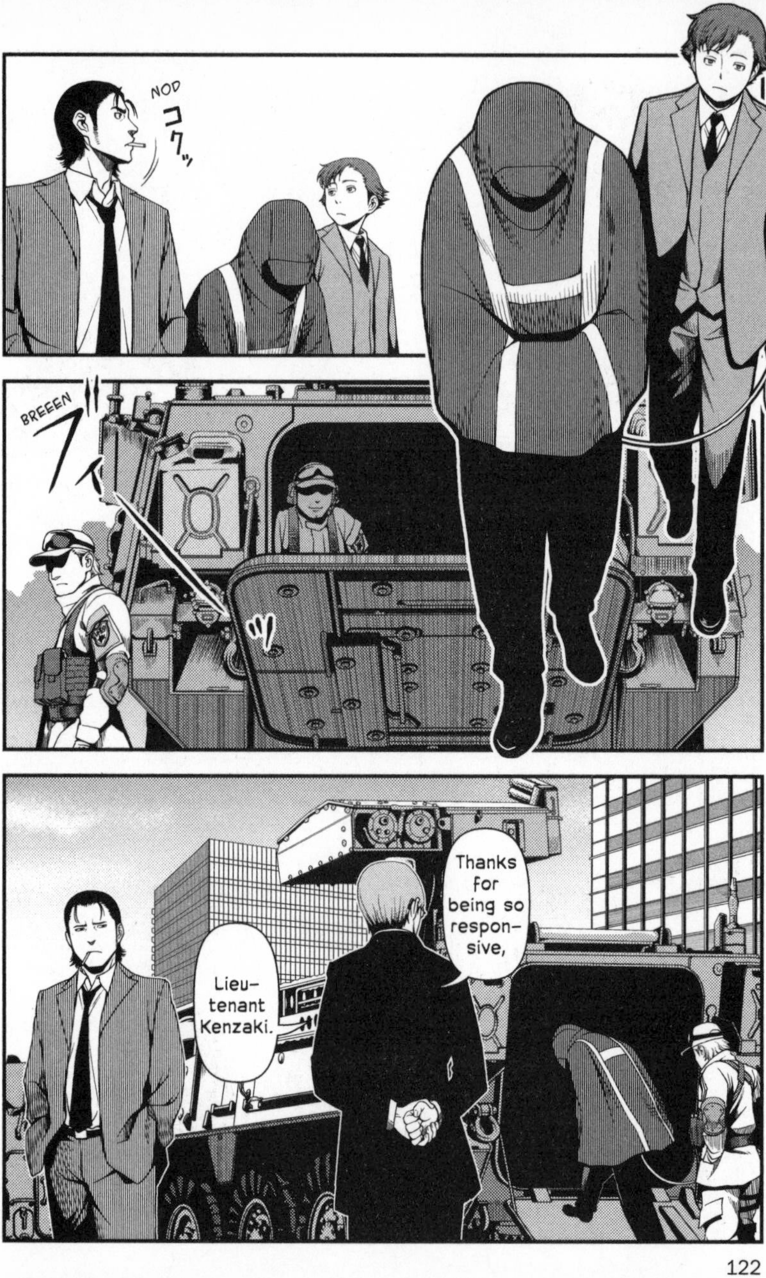
NOD
コクッ
BREEEN
ブィ
ッ
Thanks for being so respon-sive,
Lieu-tenant Kenzaki.

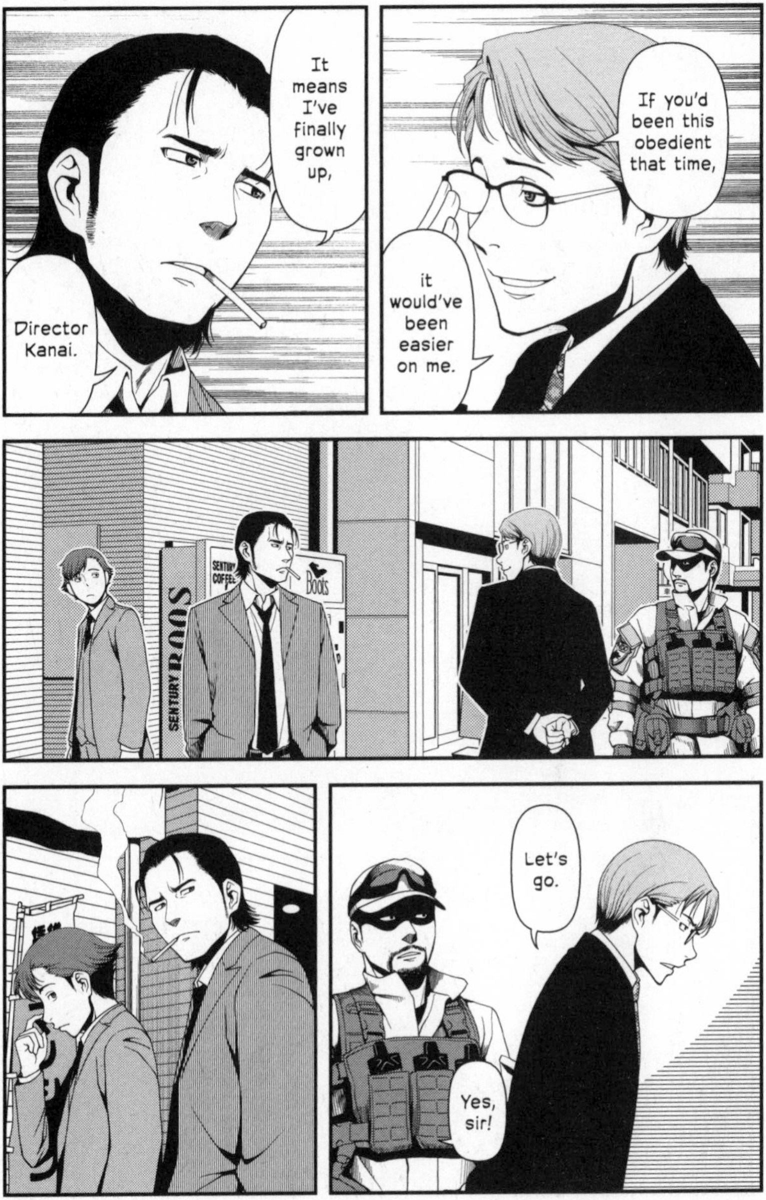
If you'd been this obedient that time,
it would've been easier on me.
It means I've finally grown up,
Director Kanai.
Boots
Let's go.
Yes, sir!

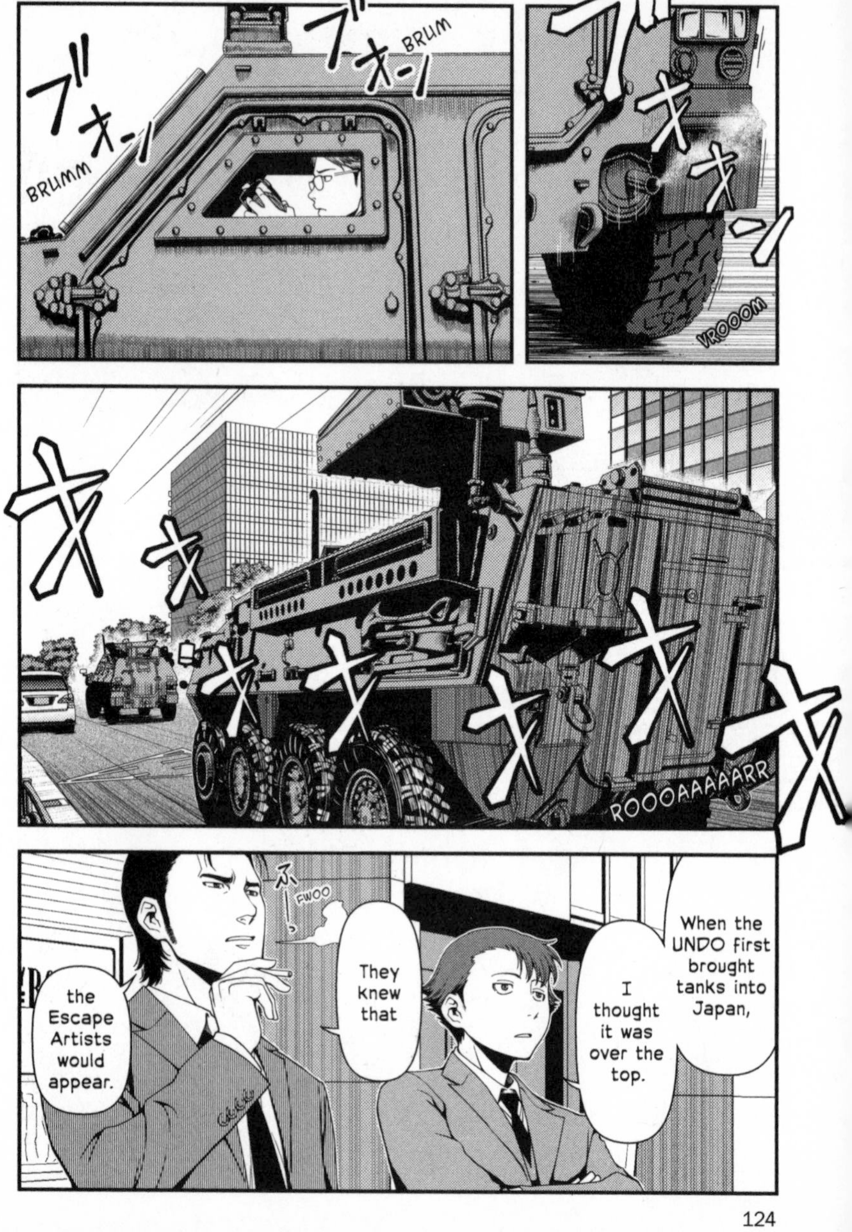
ブォォーン
VROOOM
ブォーン
BRUM
ブォーン
BRUMM
ォォォォォォォ
ROOOAAAAARR
When the UNDO first brought tanks into Japan,
I thought it was over the top.
ふー
FWOO
They knew that
the Escape Artists would appear.

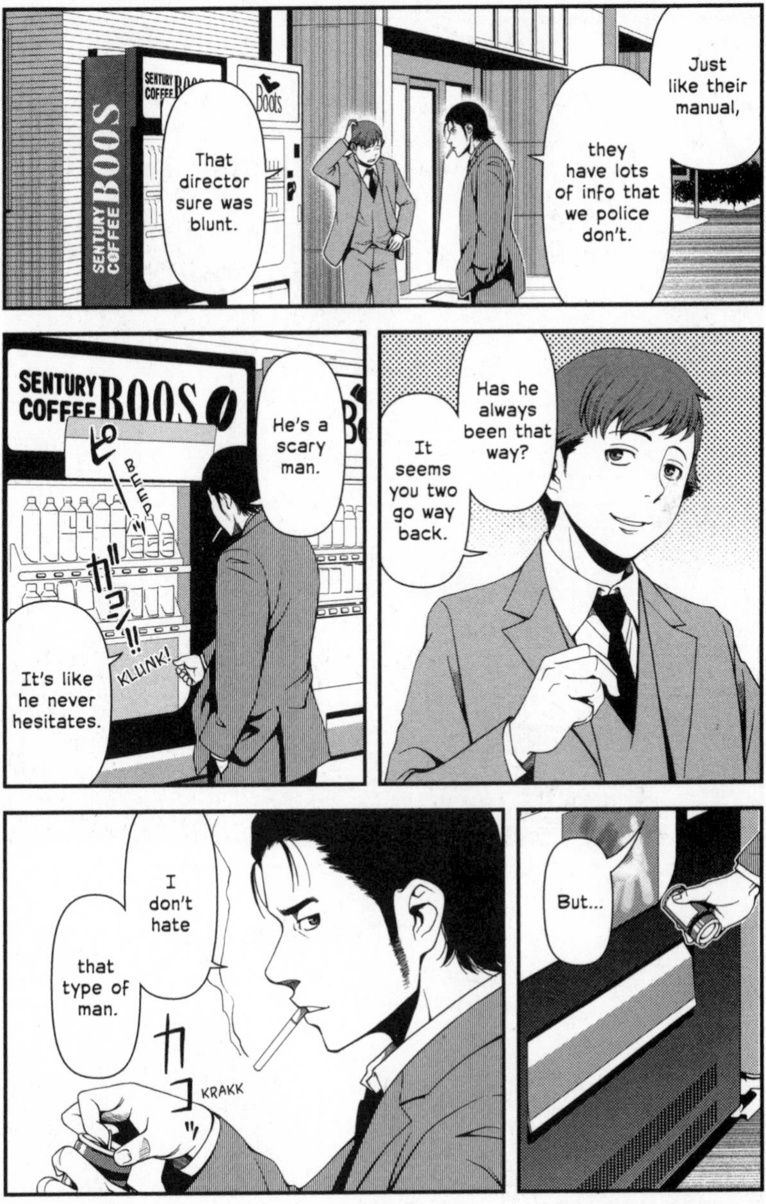
Just like their manual,
they have lots of info that we police don't.
That director sure was blunt.
Has he always been that way?
It seems you two go way back.
He's a scary man.
BEEP
KLUNK!
It's like he never hesitates.
But...
I don't hate
that type of man.
KRAKK

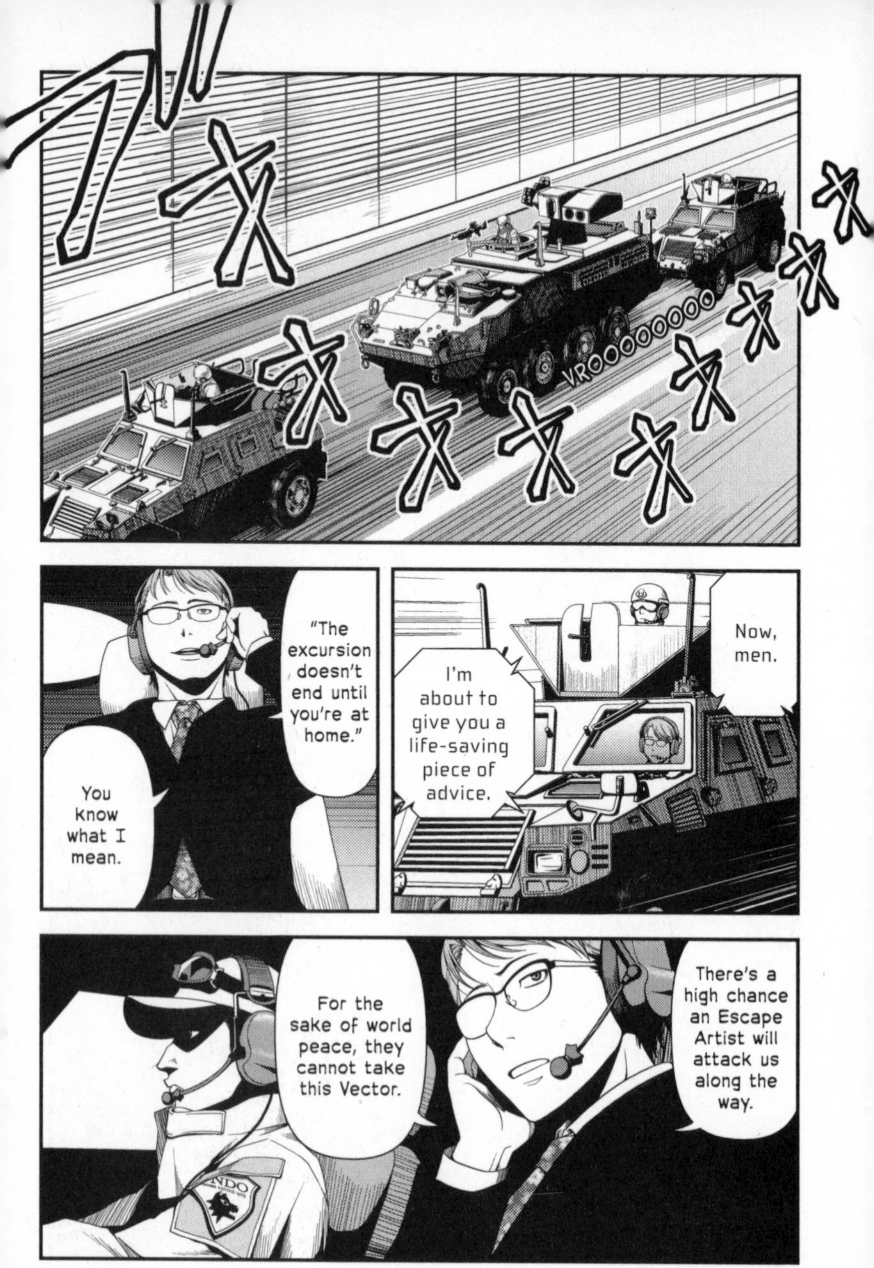
VROOOOOOOOO
Now, men.
I'm about to give you a life-saving piece of advice.
"The excursion doesn't end until you're at home."
You know what I mean.
There's a high chance an Escape Artist will attack us along the way.
For the sake of world peace, they cannot take this Vector.

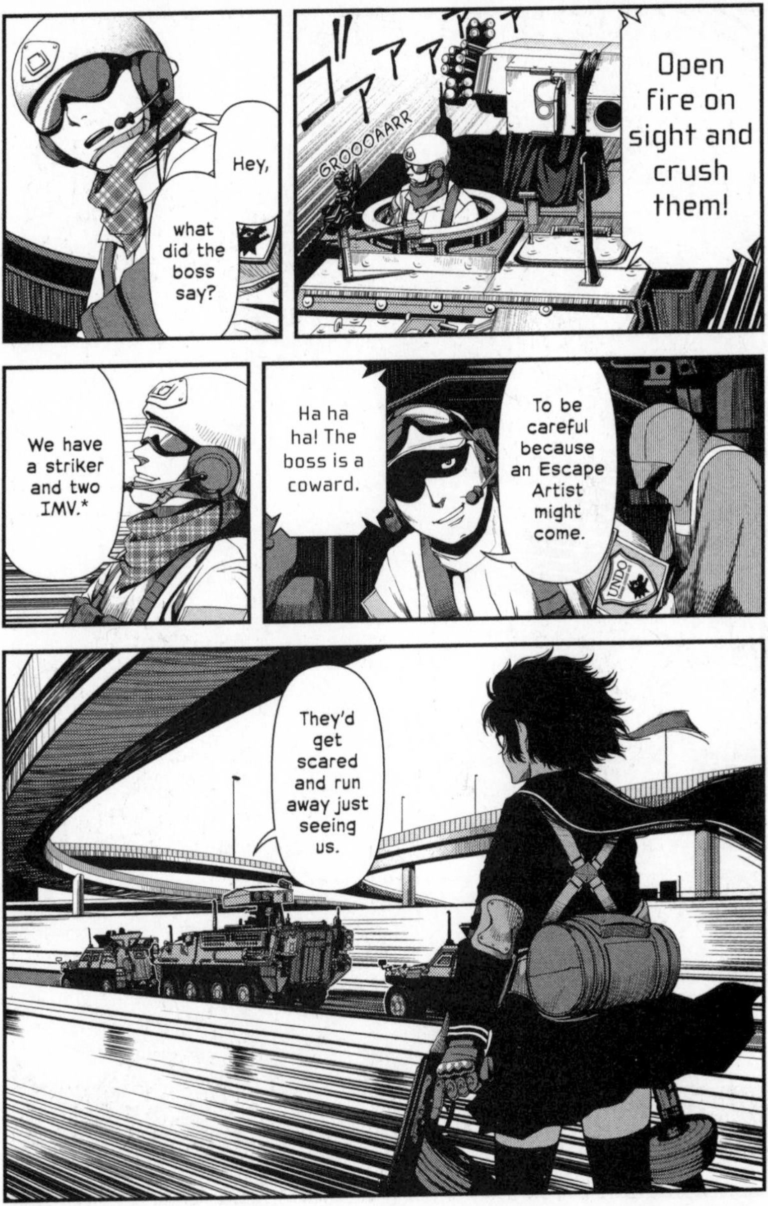
GROOOAARR
Open fire on sight and crush them!
Hey,
what did the boss say?
To be careful because an Escape Artist might come.
Ha ha ha! The boss is a coward.
We have a striker and two IMV.*
They'd get scared and run away just seeing us.

*Infantry Mobility Vehicle

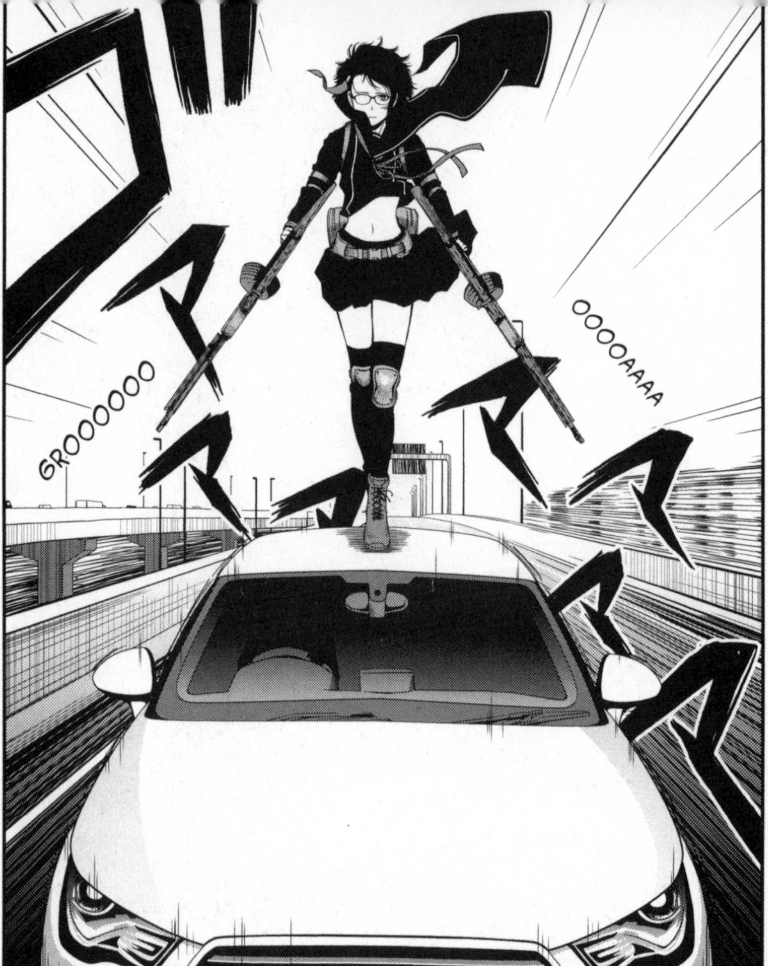
GROOOOOO
OOOOAAAA

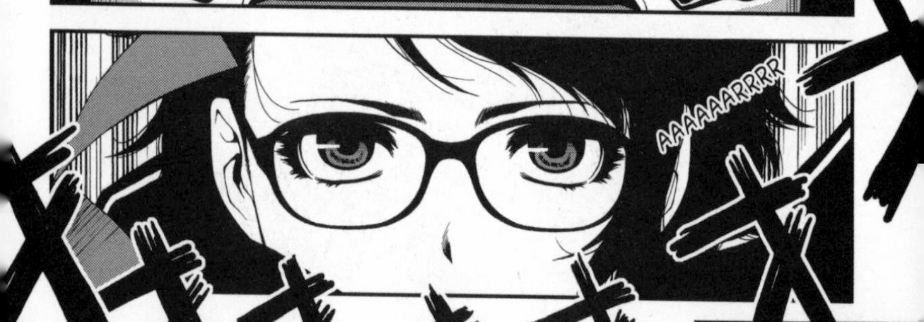
AAAAAARRRR

End of Chapter 4

5

Go On, Shoot

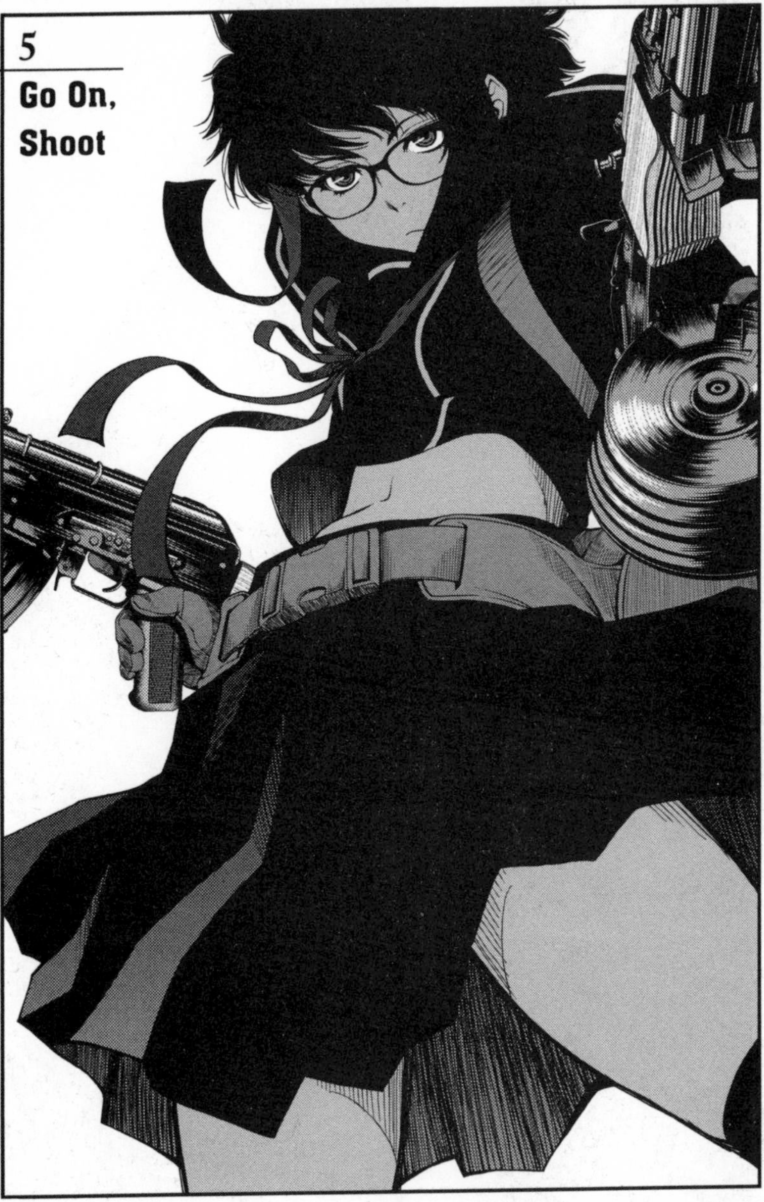

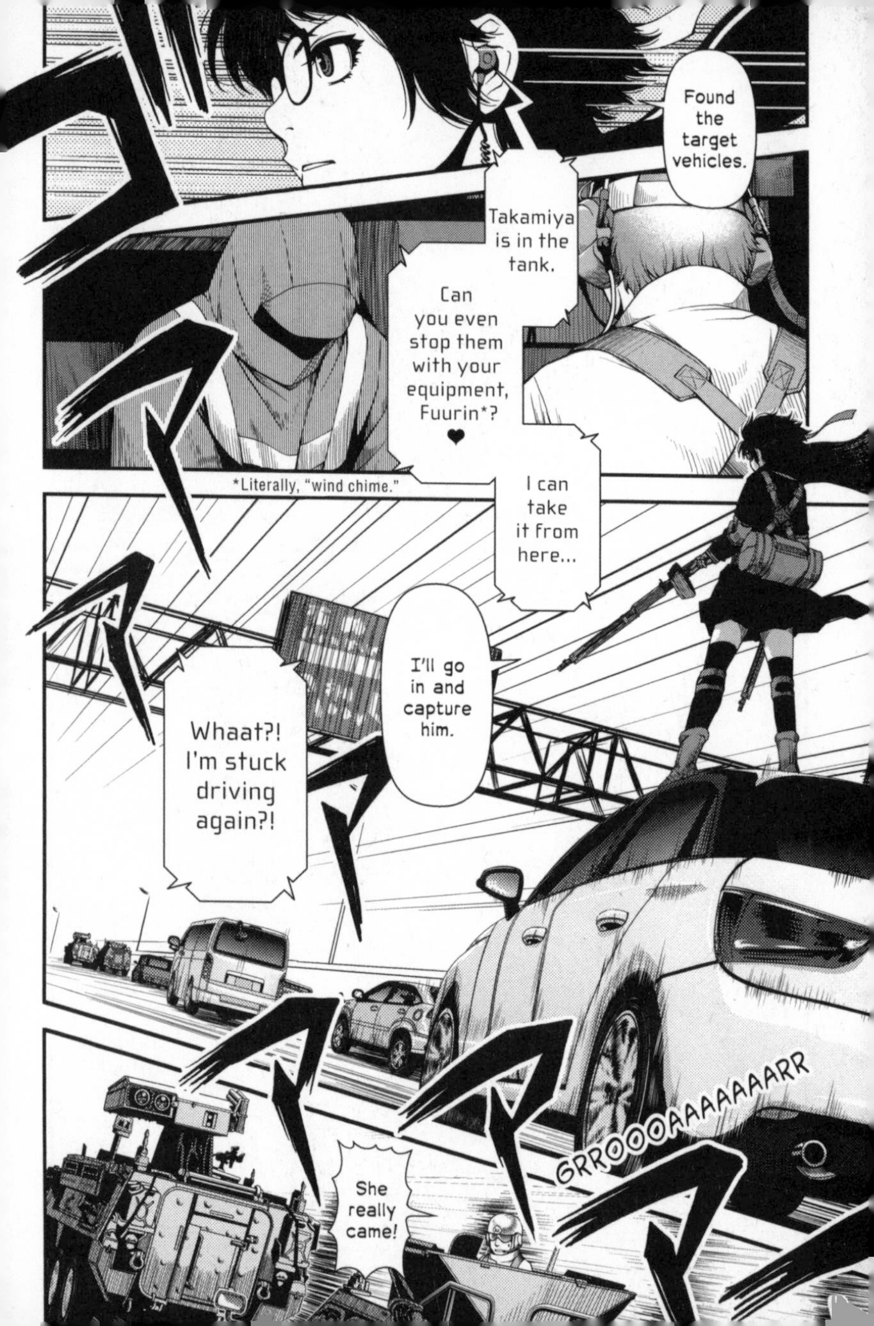
Found the target vehicles.
Takamiya is in the tank.
Can you even stop them with your equipment, Fuurin*? ❤
I can take it from here...
I'll go in and capture him.
Whaat?! I'm stuck driving again?!
GRROOOAAAAAAARR
She really came!
*Literally, "wind chime."

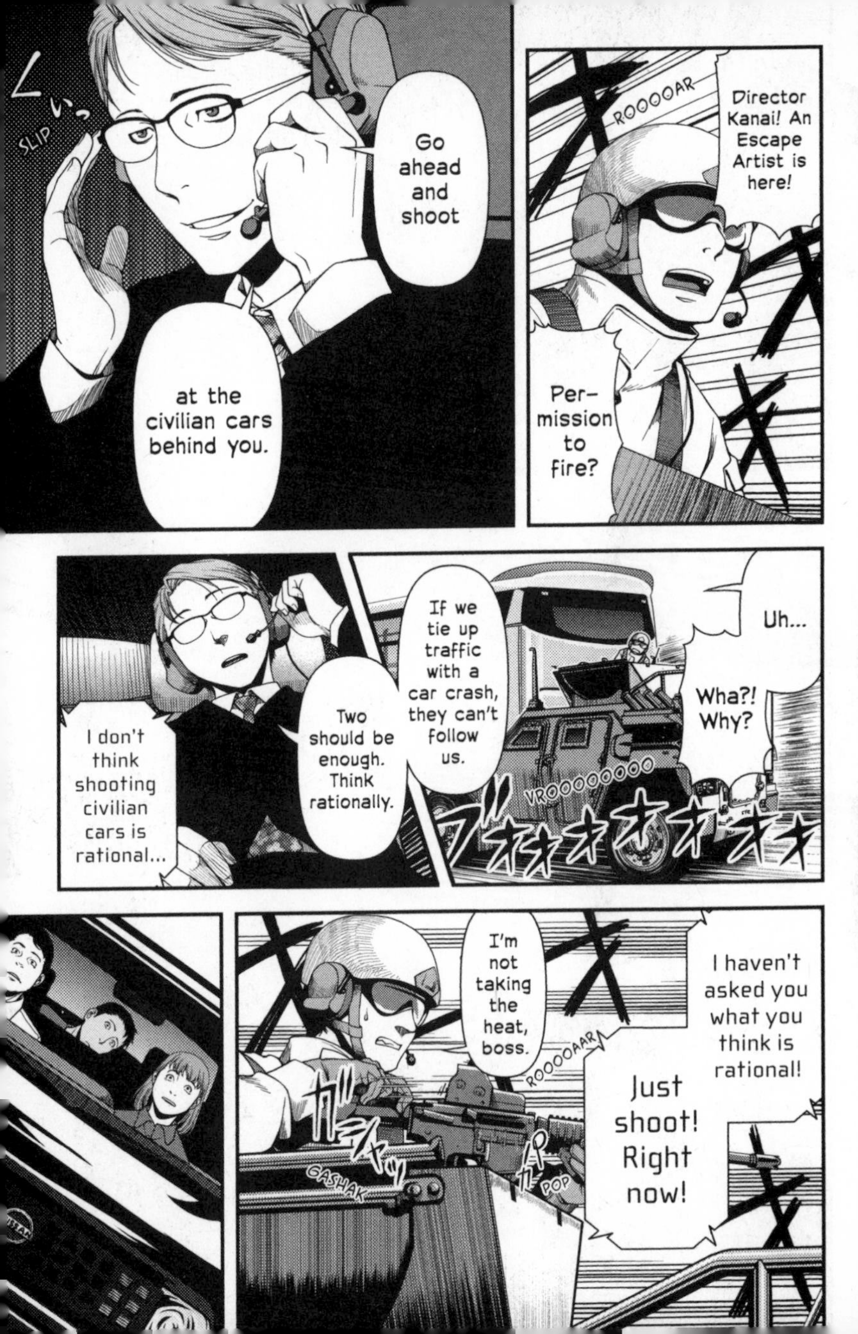
ROOOOAR
Director Kanai! An Escape Artist is here!
Per-mission to fire?
SLIP
Go ahead and shoot
at the civilian cars behind you.
Uh...
Wha?! Why?
If we tie up traffic with a car crash, they can't follow us.
VROOOOOOOOO
Two should be enough. Think rationally.
I don't think shooting civilian cars is rational...
I haven't asked you what you think is rational!
Just shoot! Right now!
ROOOOAAR
I'm not taking the heat, boss.
POP
GASHAK

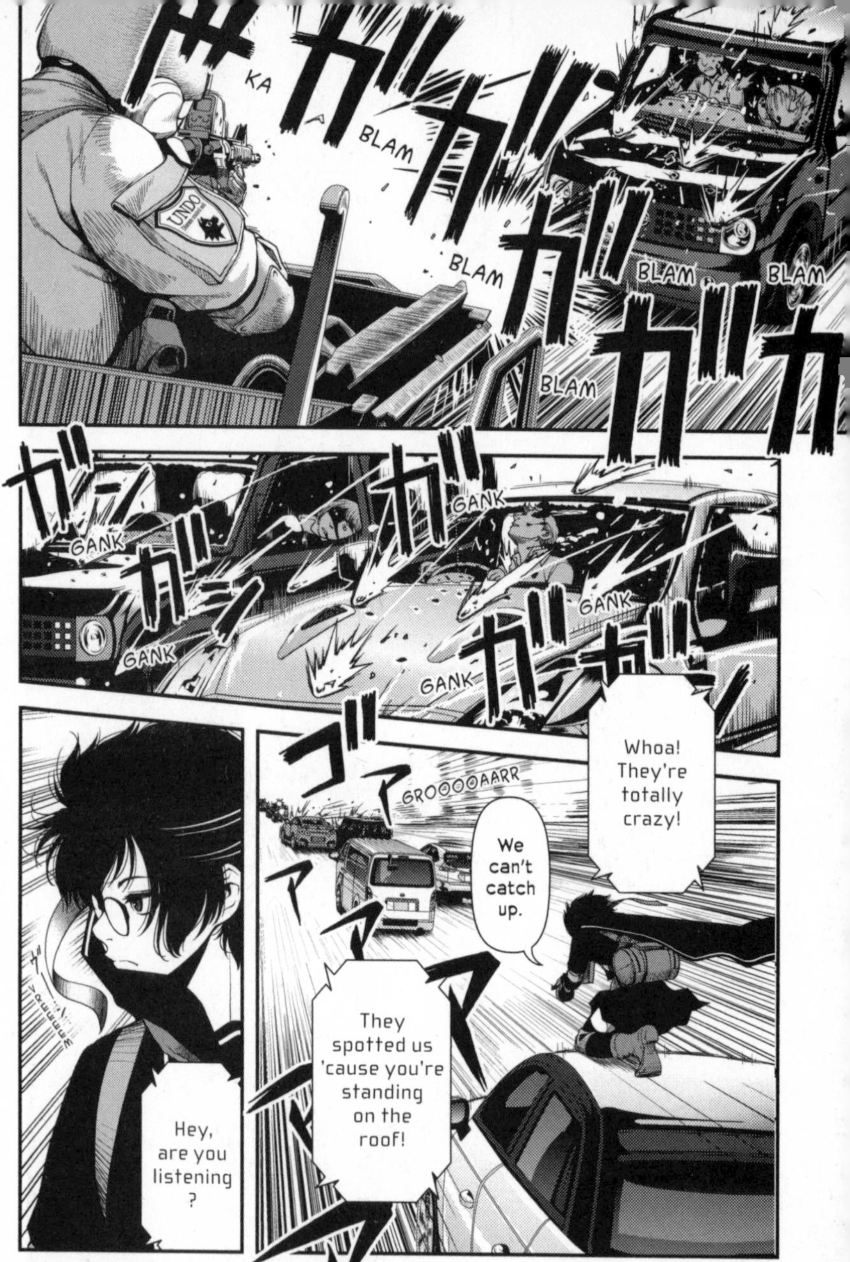
BLAM
BLAM
KA
BLAM
BLAM
BLAM
GANK
GANK
GANK
GANK
GANK
Whoa! They're totally crazy!
We can't catch up.
GROOOOAARR
They spotted us 'cause you're standing on the roof!
Hey, are you listening?

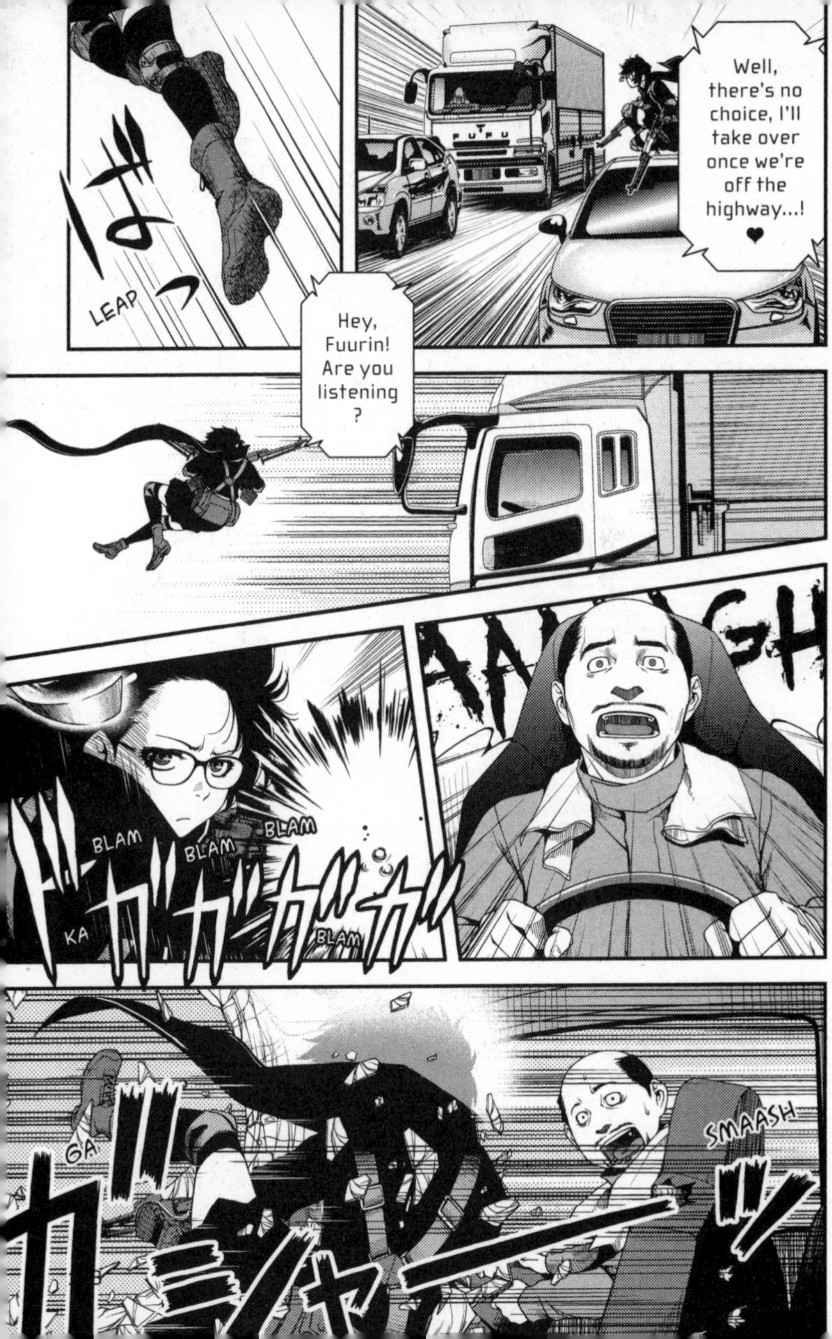
Well, there's no choice, I'll take over once we're off the highway...! ❤
LEAP
Hey, Fuurin! Are you listening ?
BLAM
BLAM
BLAM
BLAM
KA
SMAASH
GA

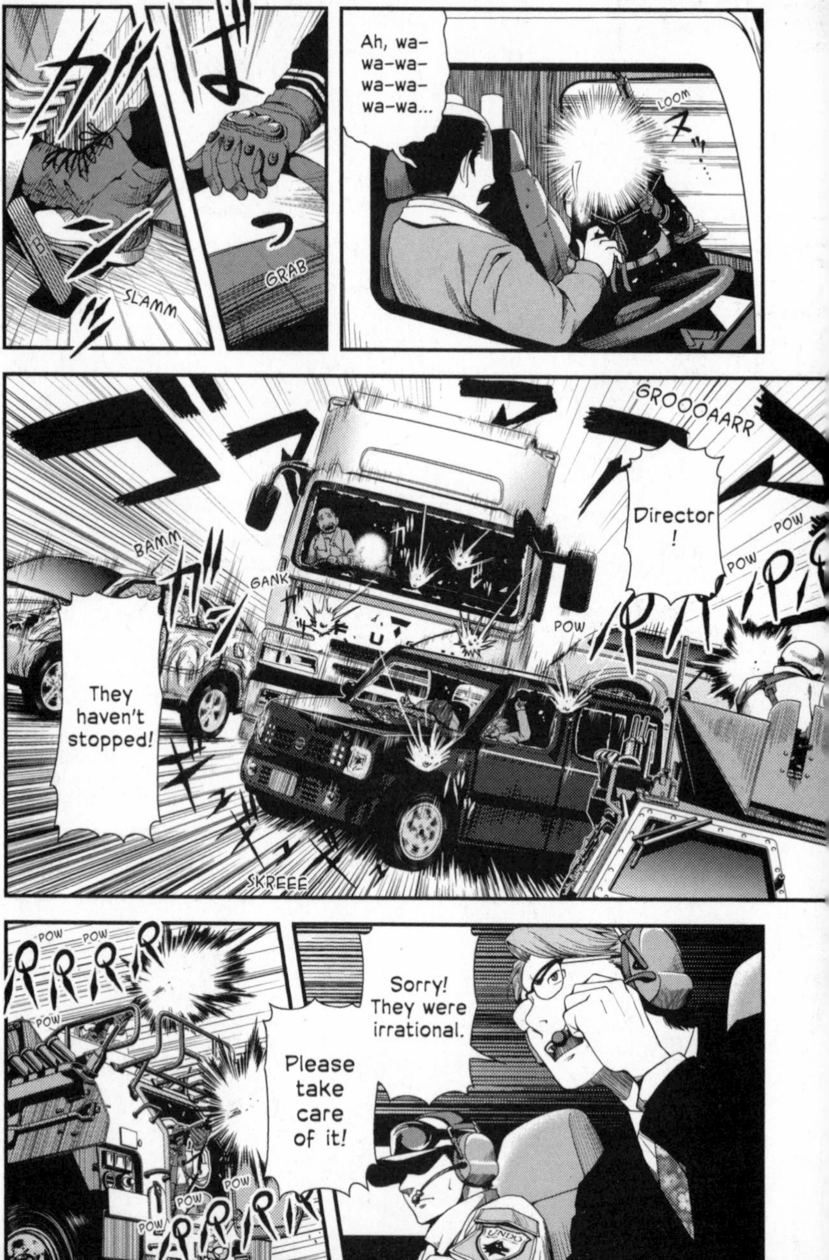
Ah, wa-wa-wa-wa-wa-wa-wa...
LOOM
GRAB
SLAMM
GROOOAARR
Director!
POW
POW
POW
BAMM
GANK
They haven't stopped!
SKREEE
Sorry! They were irrational.
Please take care of it!
POW
POW
POW
POW
POW
POW

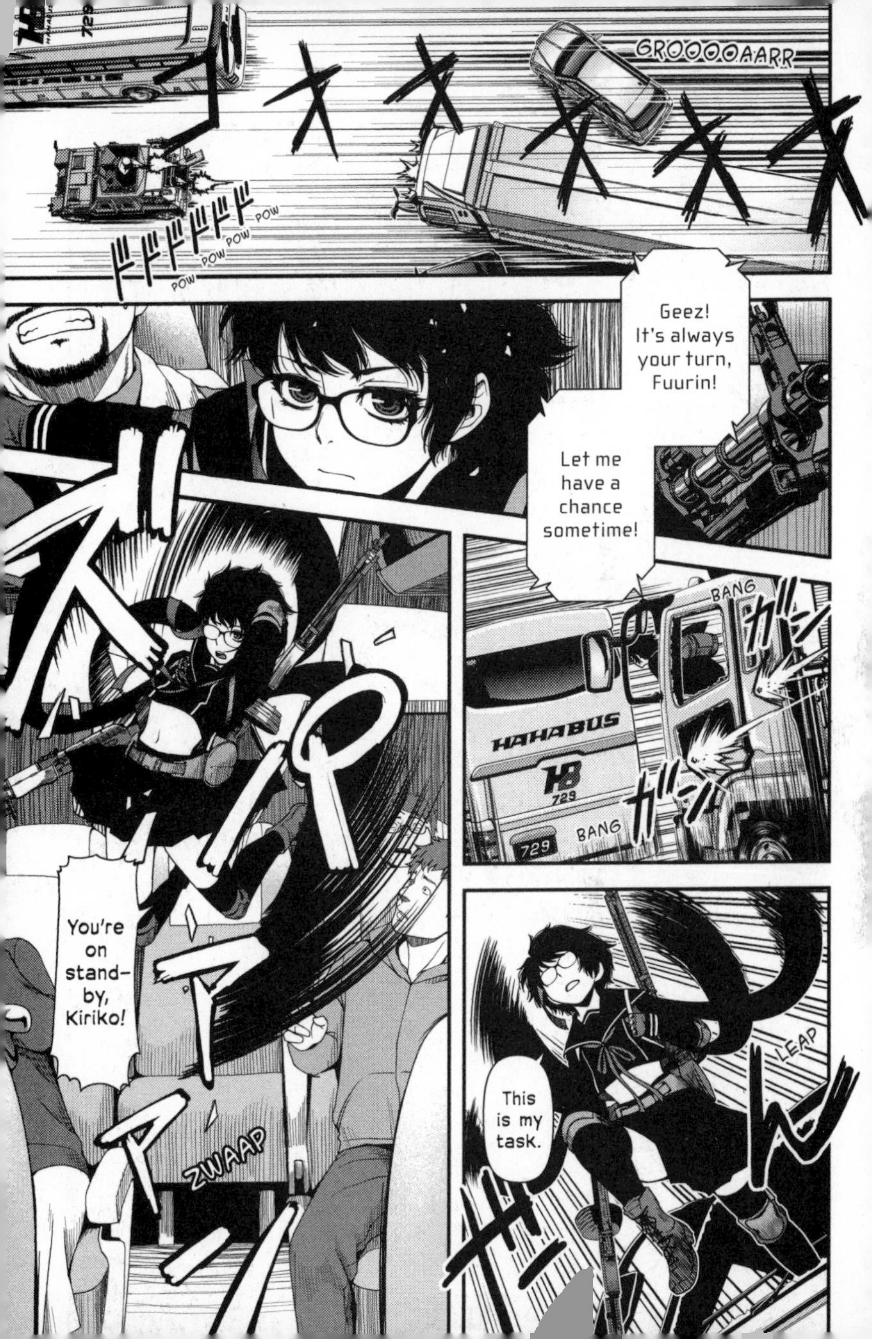
GROOOOAARR
POW POW POW POW
Geez! It's always your turn, Fuurin!
Let me have a chance sometime!
BANG
HAHABUS
729
BANG
LEAP
This is my task.
You're on stand-by, Kiriko!
ZWAAP

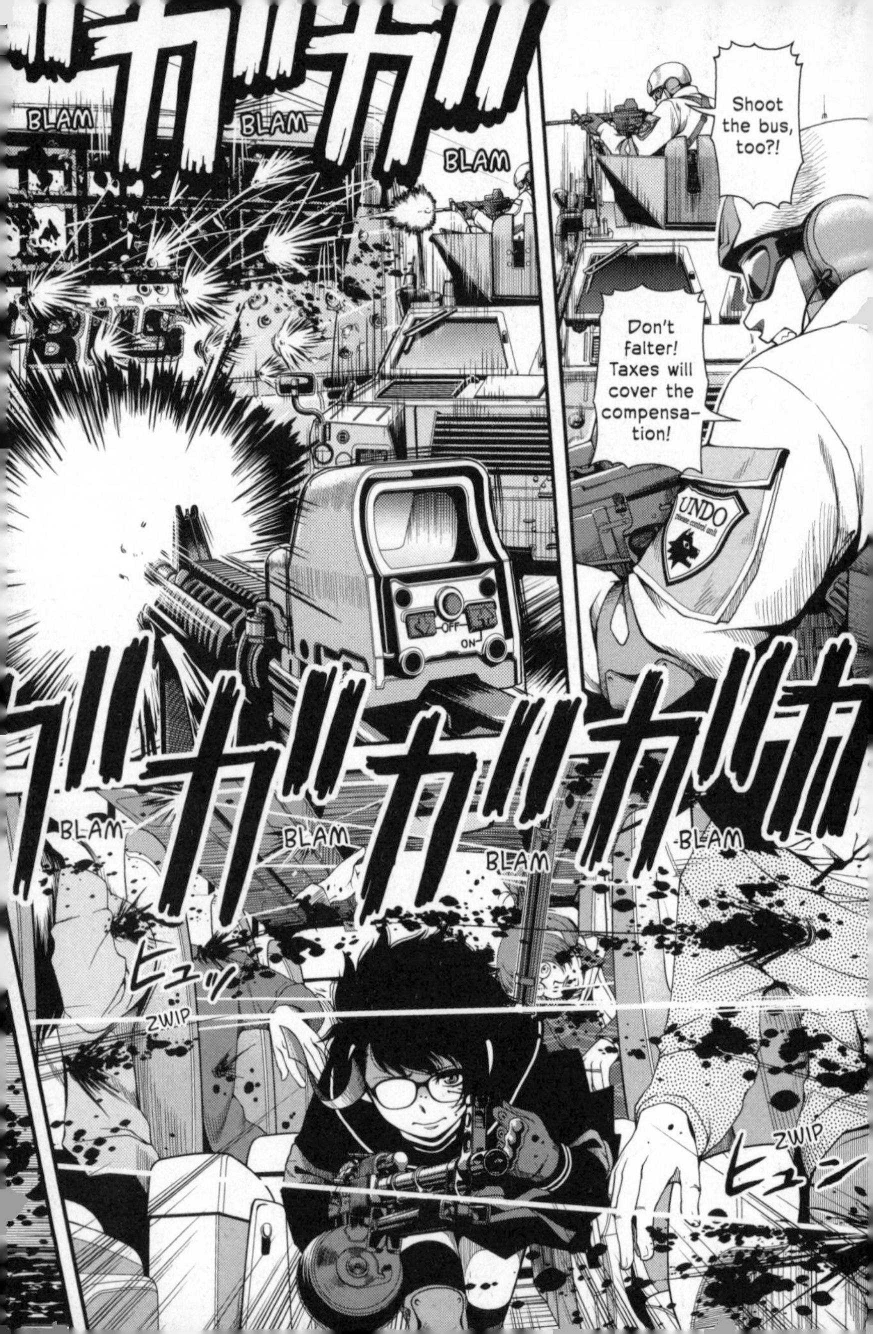

Shoot the bus, too?!
Don't falter! Taxes will cover the compensa-tion!
UNDO
BLAM
BLAM
BLAM
BUS
OFF
ON
BLAM
BLAM
BLAM
BLAM
ZWIP
ヒュン
ヒュッ
ZWIP

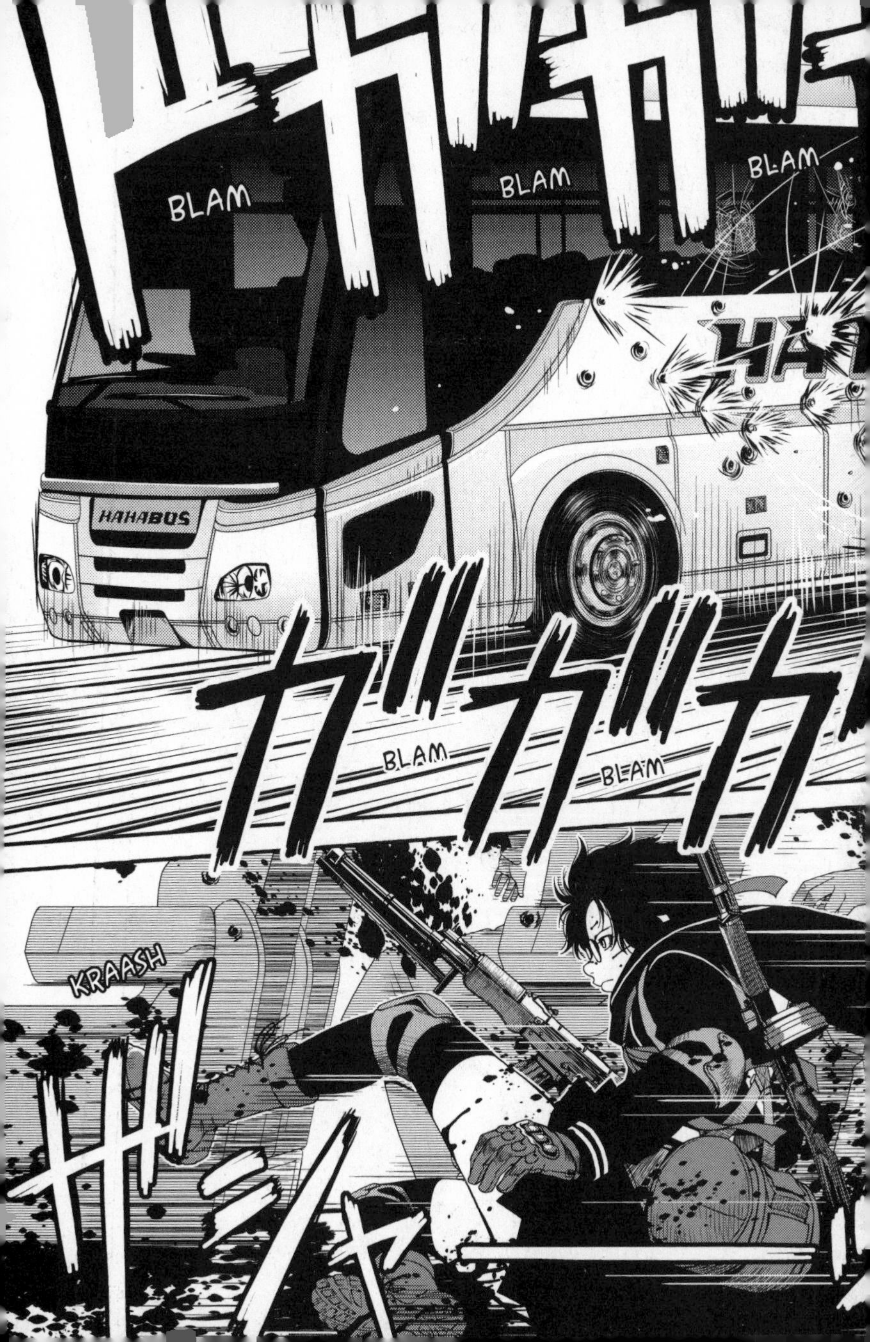
BLAM
BLAM
BLAM
HAHABUS
ガガガ
BLAM
BLAM
KRAASH

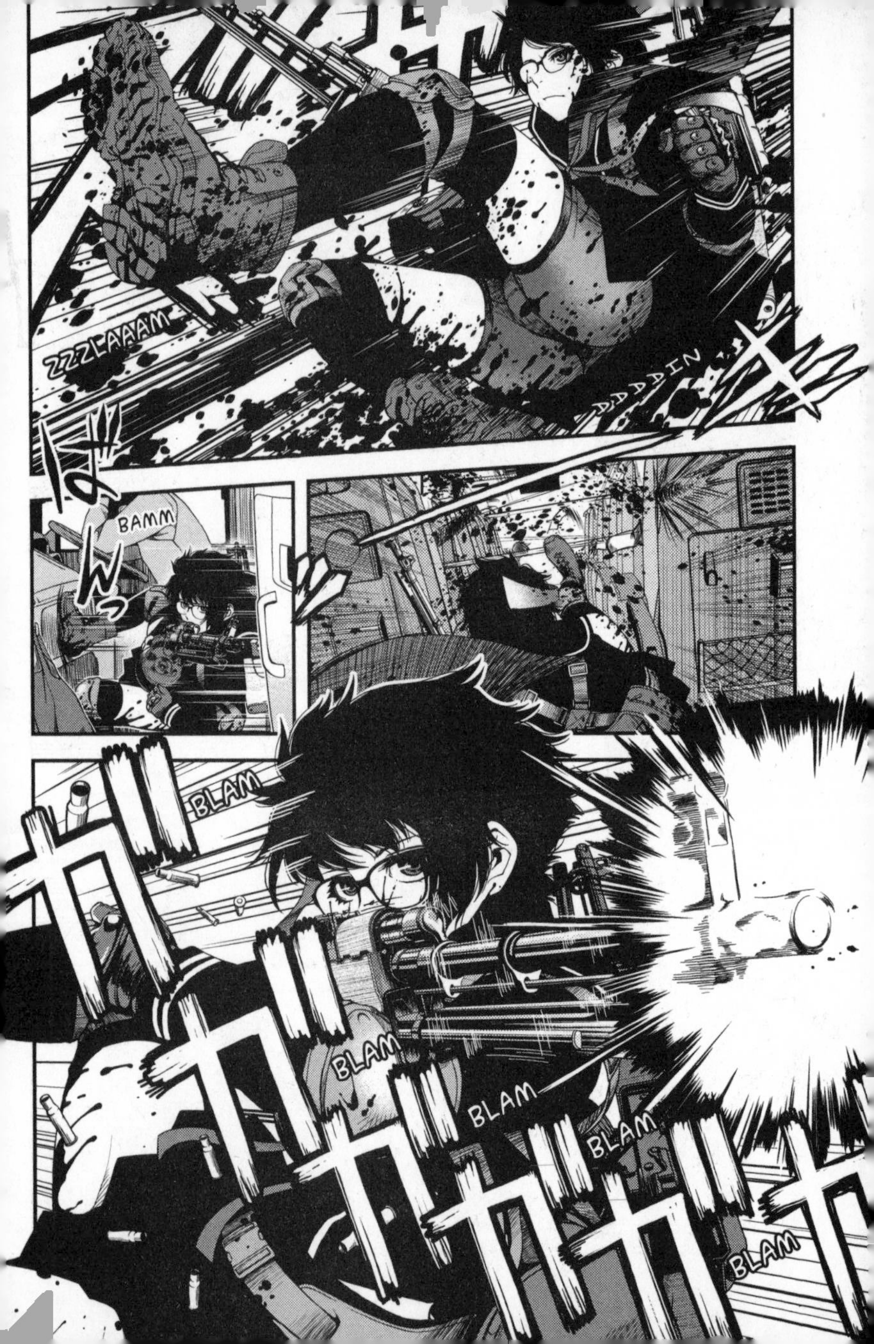
AAAAIN
ZZZLAAAAM
BAMM
BLAM
BLAM
BLAM
BLAM
BLAM
BLAM

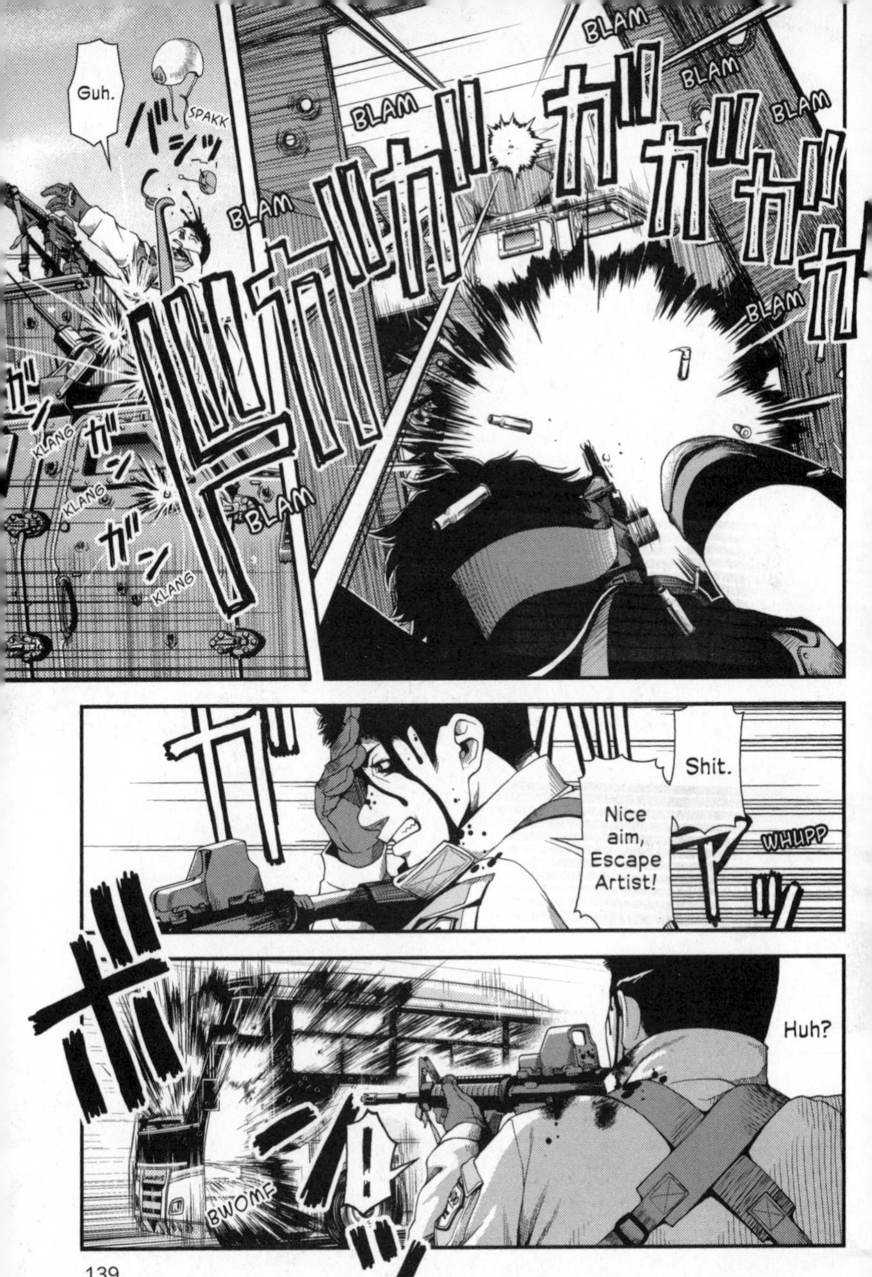

BLAM
BLAM
BLAM
BLAM
BLAM
BLAM
Guh.
SPAKK
KLANG
KLANG
KLANG
BLAM
Shit.
Nice aim, Escape Artist!
WHUPP
Huh?
BWOMF

BLAM

BLAM

BLAM

BLAM

BLAM

KLANG

KLANG

KLANG

KLANG

Did
I get
her...?

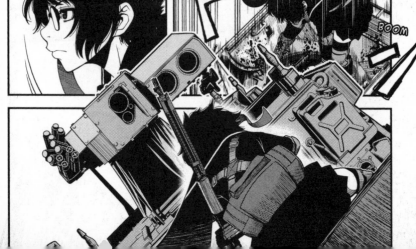

BOOM

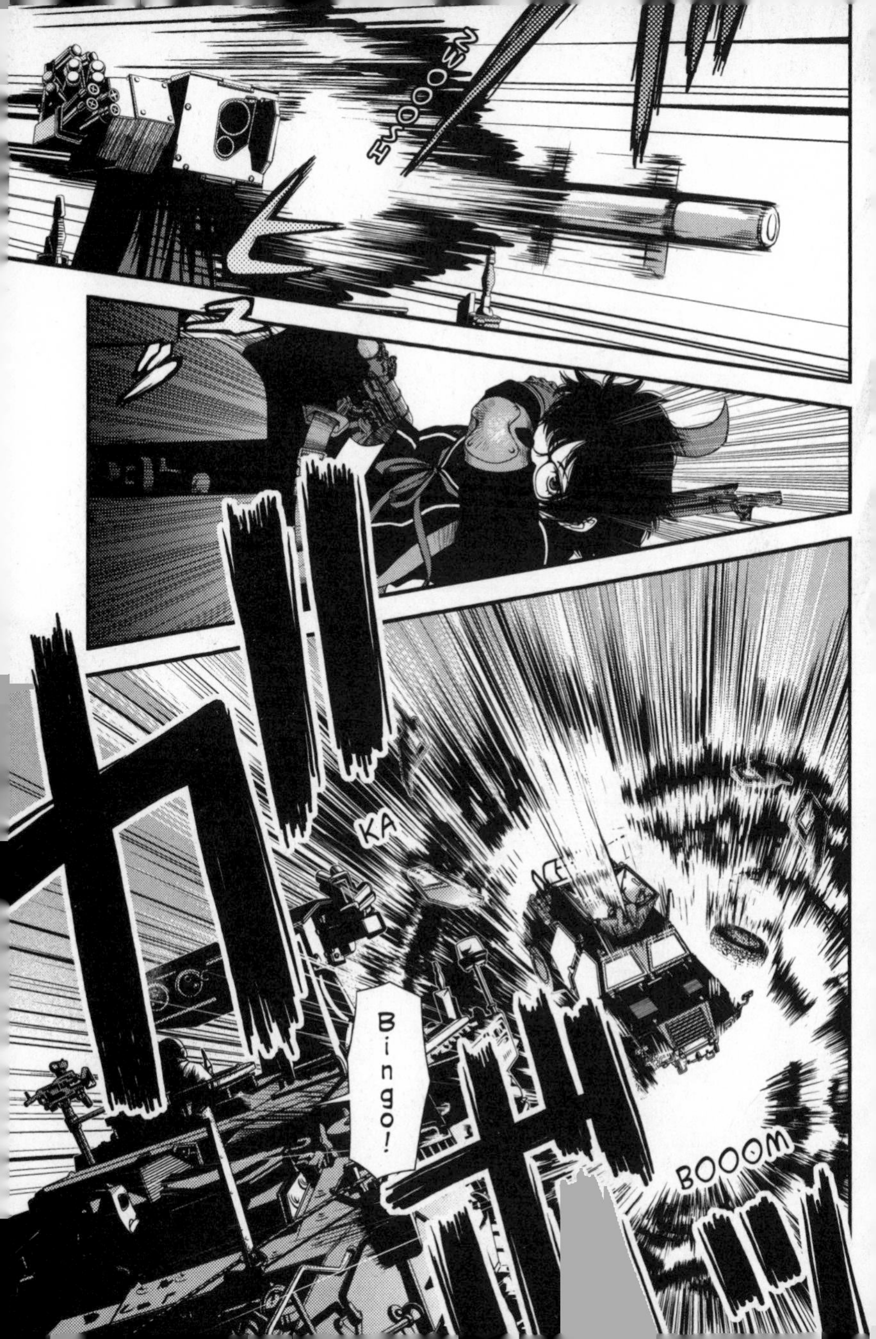
SWOOOSH
KA
Bingo!
BOOOM

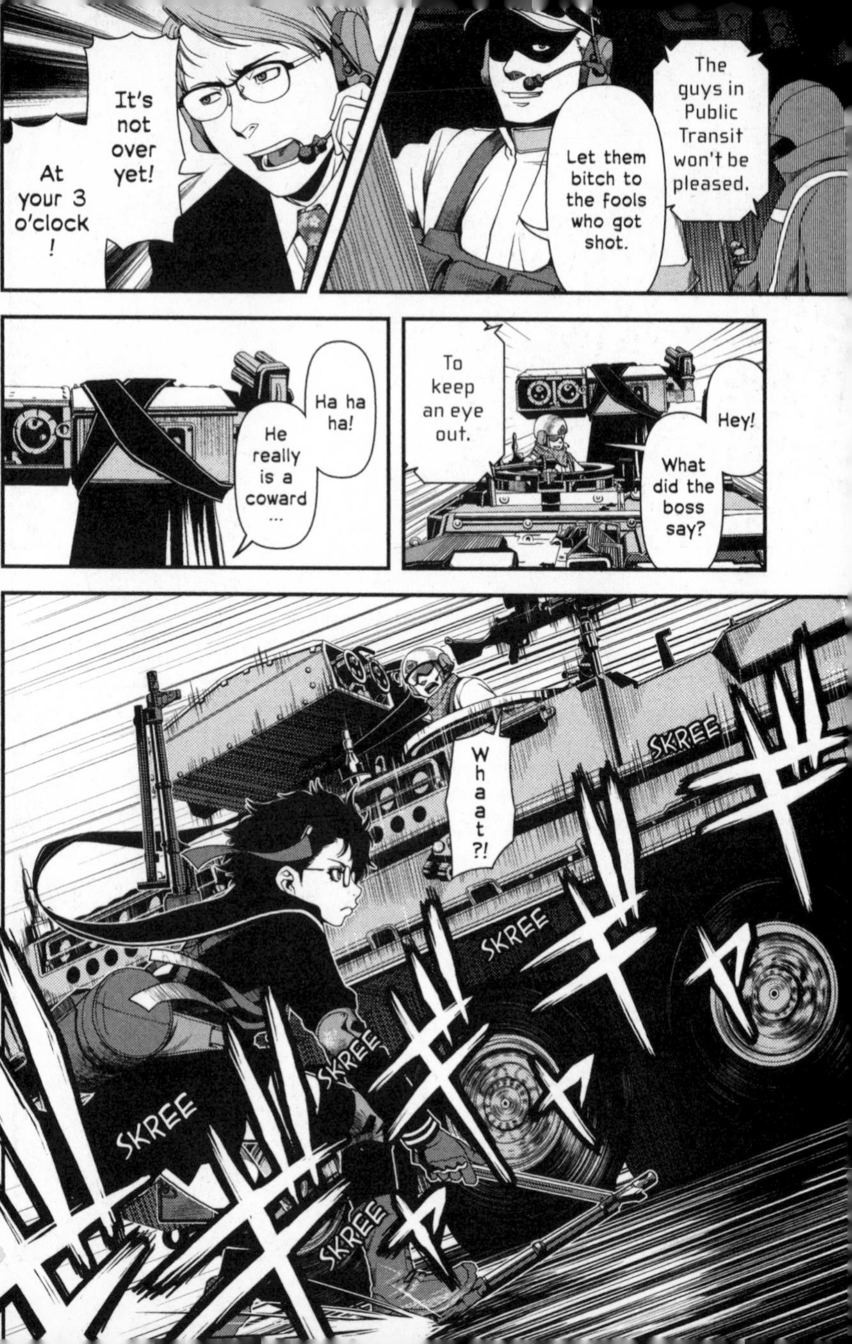
The guys in Public Transit won't be pleased.
Let them bitch to the fools who got shot.
It's not over yet!
At your 3 o'clock!
Hey!
What did the boss say?
To keep an eye out.
Ha ha ha!
He really is a coward...
Whaaat?!
SKREE
SKREE
SKREE
SKREE
SKREE
SKREE

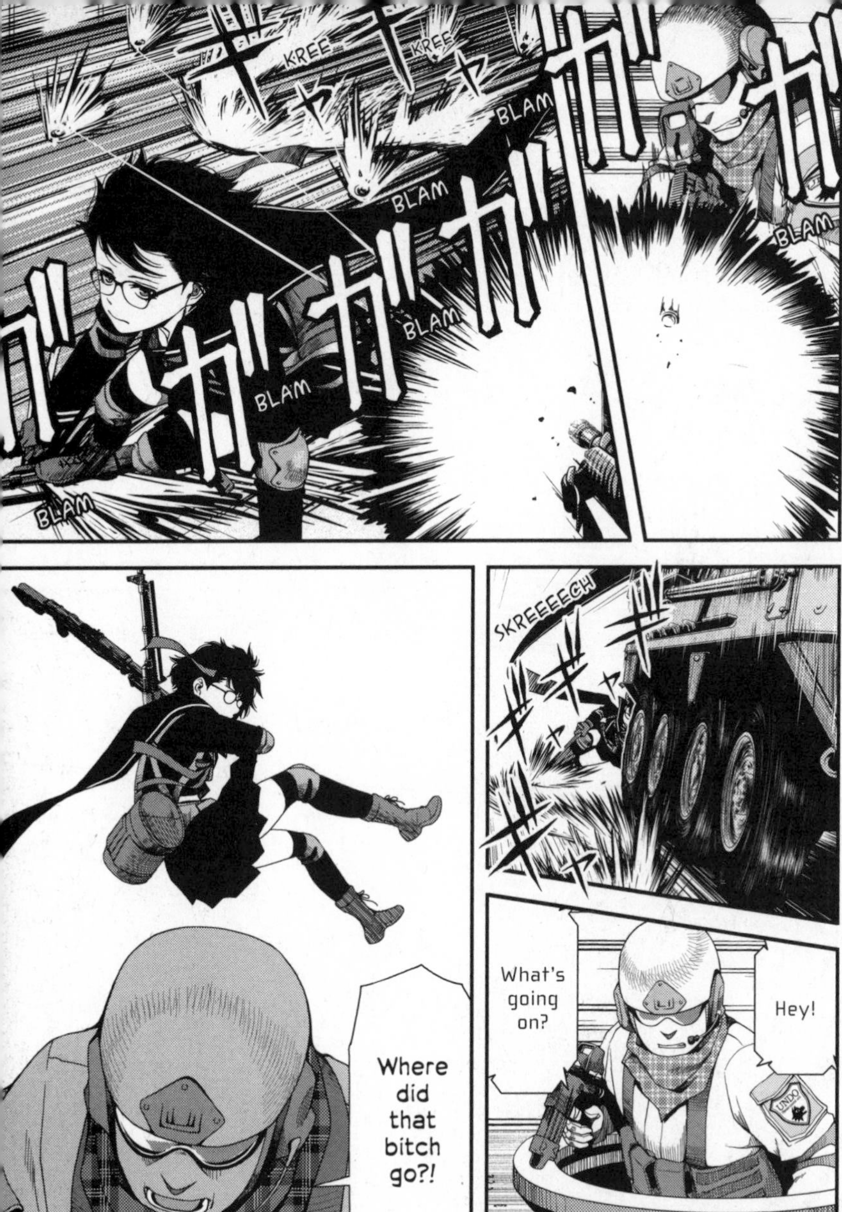
BLAM
BLAM
KREE
KREE
BLAM
BLAM
BLAM
BLAM
BLAM
SKREEEECH
Hey!
What's going on?
Where did that bitch go?!

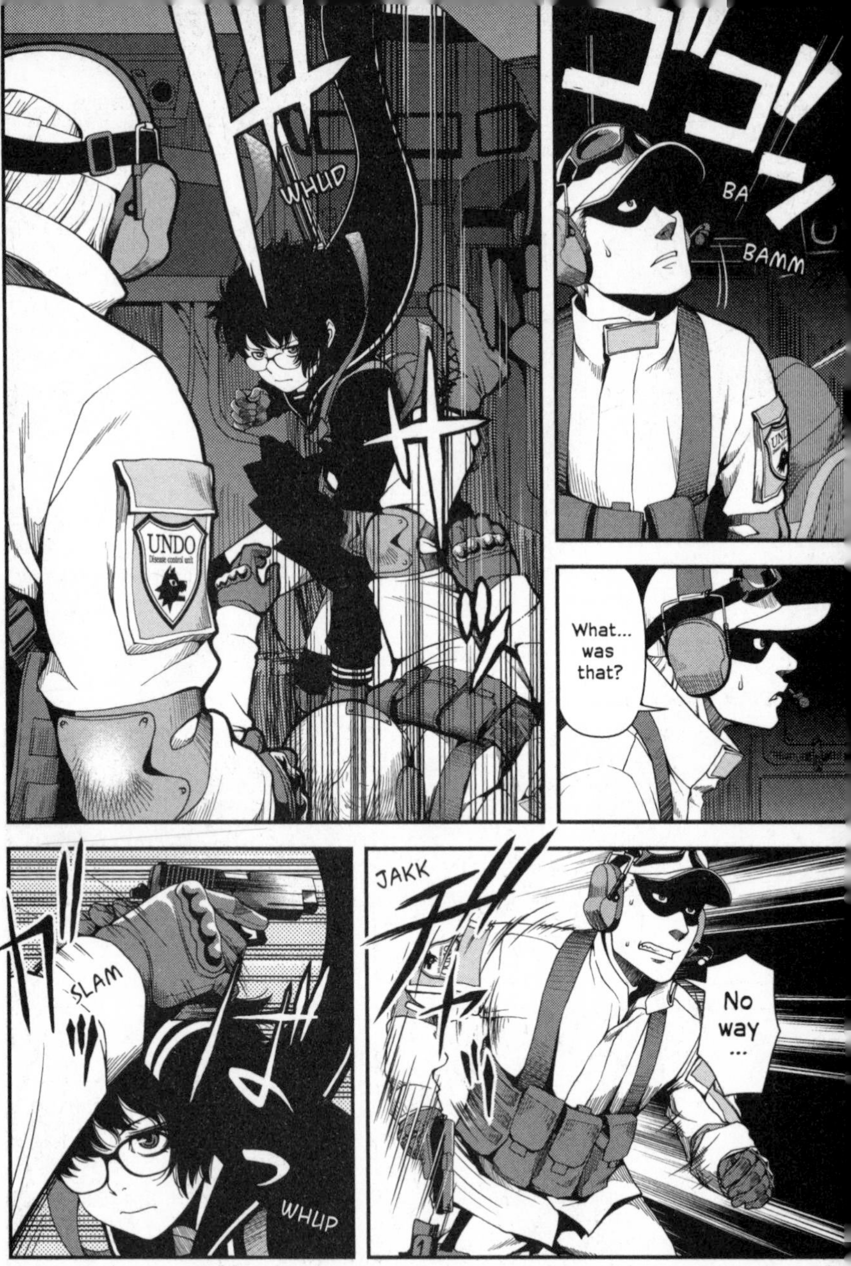
BA
BAMM
What... was that?
WHUD
UNDO
Disease control unit
JAKK
No way ...
SLAM
WHUP

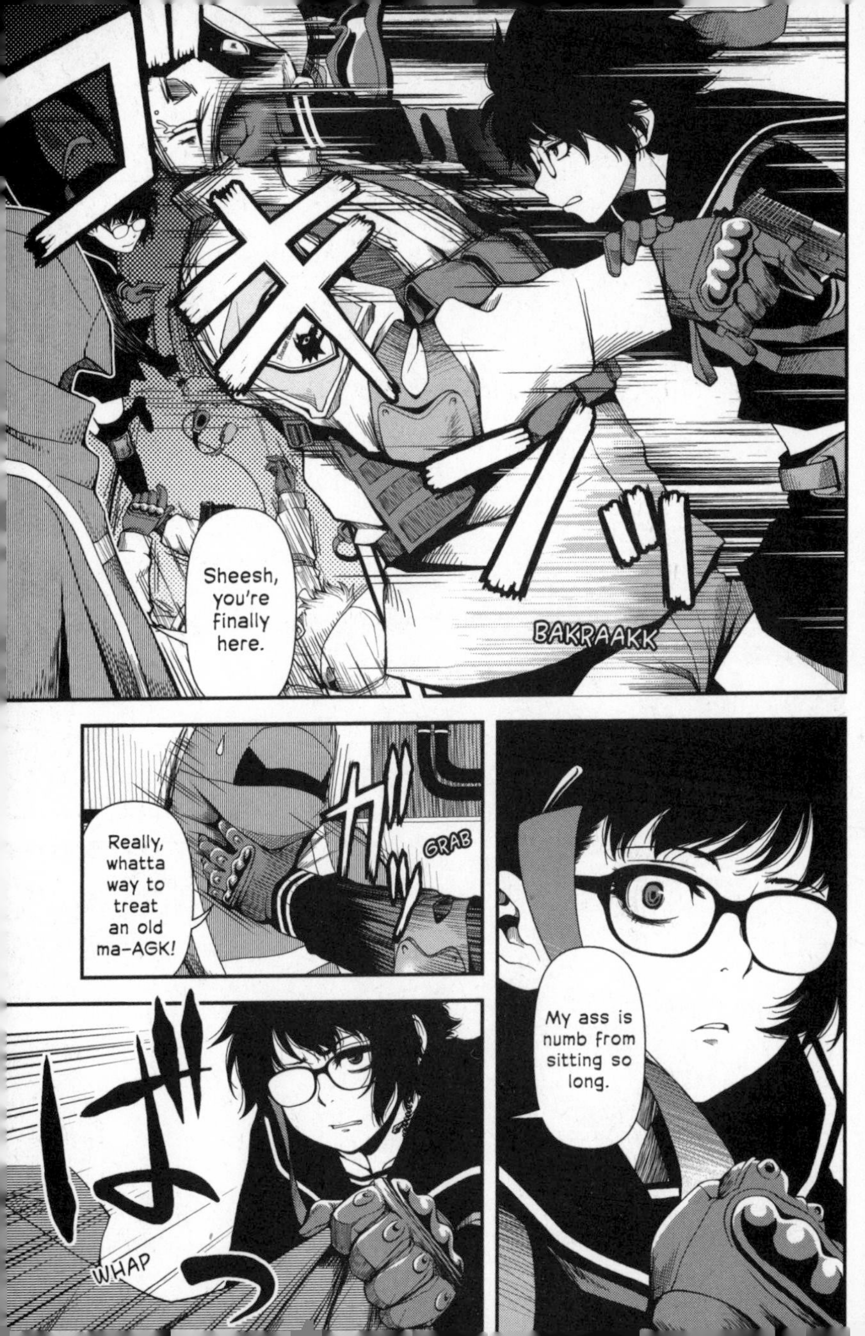
Sheesh, you're finally here.
BAKRAAKK
My ass is numb from sitting so long.
Really, whatta way to treat an old ma-AGK!
GRAB
WHAP

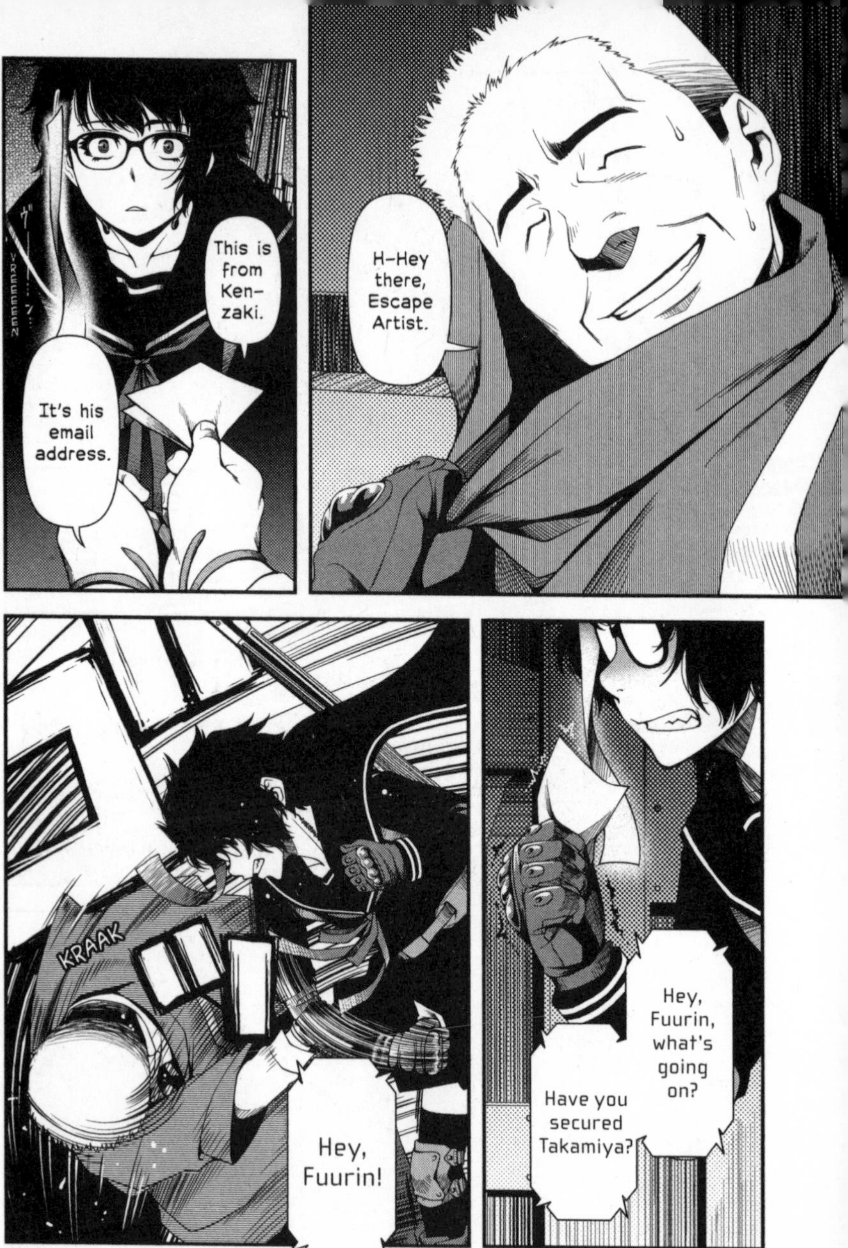
H-Hey there, Escape Artist.
VREEEEEN
This is from Ken-zaki.
It's his email address.
Hey, Fuurin, what's going on?
Have you secured Takamiya?
KRAAK
Hey, Fuurin!

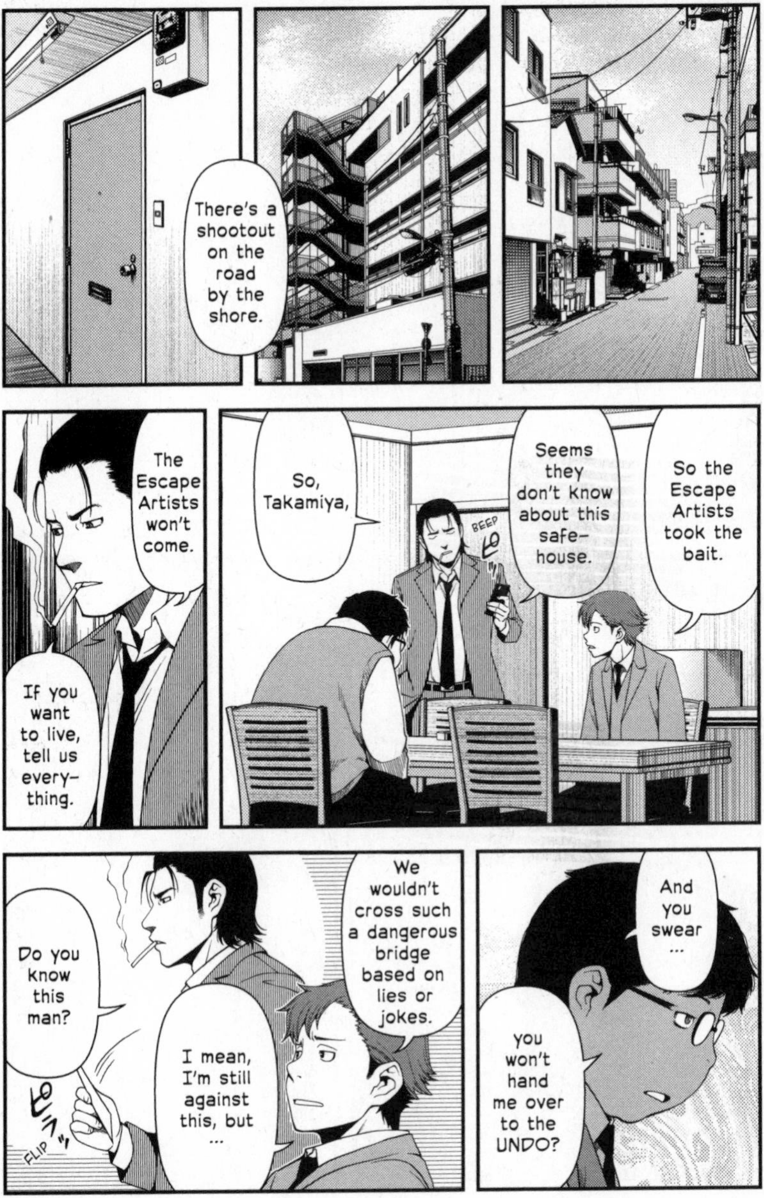
There's a shootout on the road by the shore.
So the Escape Artists took the bait.
Seems they don't know about this safe-house.
BEEP
So, Takamiya,
The Escape Artists won't come.
If you want to live, tell us every-thing.
And you swear ...
you won't hand me over to the UNDO?
We wouldn't cross such a dangerous bridge based on lies or jokes.
Do you know this man?
I mean, I'm still against this, but ...
FLIP

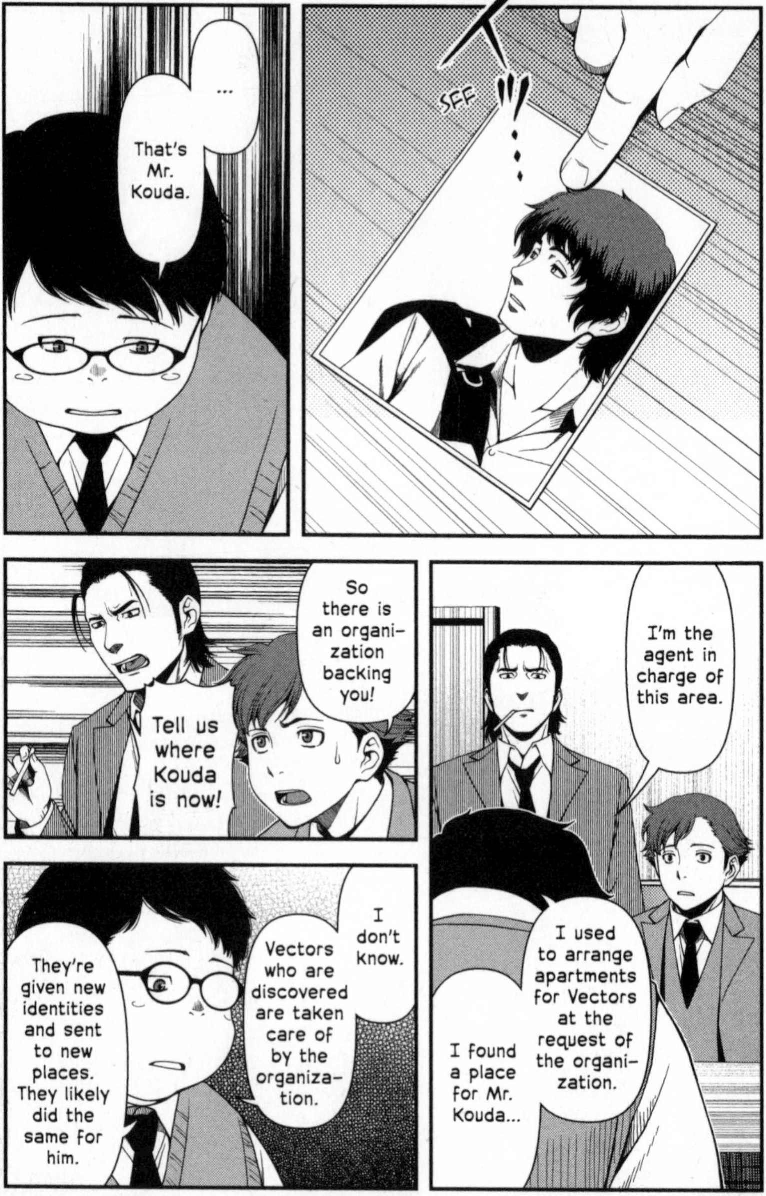
SFF
!!...
...
That's Mr. Kouda.
I'm the agent in charge of this area.
I used to arrange apartments for Vectors at the request of the organization.
I found a place for Mr. Kouda...
So there is an organization backing you!
Tell us where Kouda is now!
I don't know.
Vectors who are discovered are taken care of by the organization.
They're given new identities and sent to new places. They likely did the same for him.

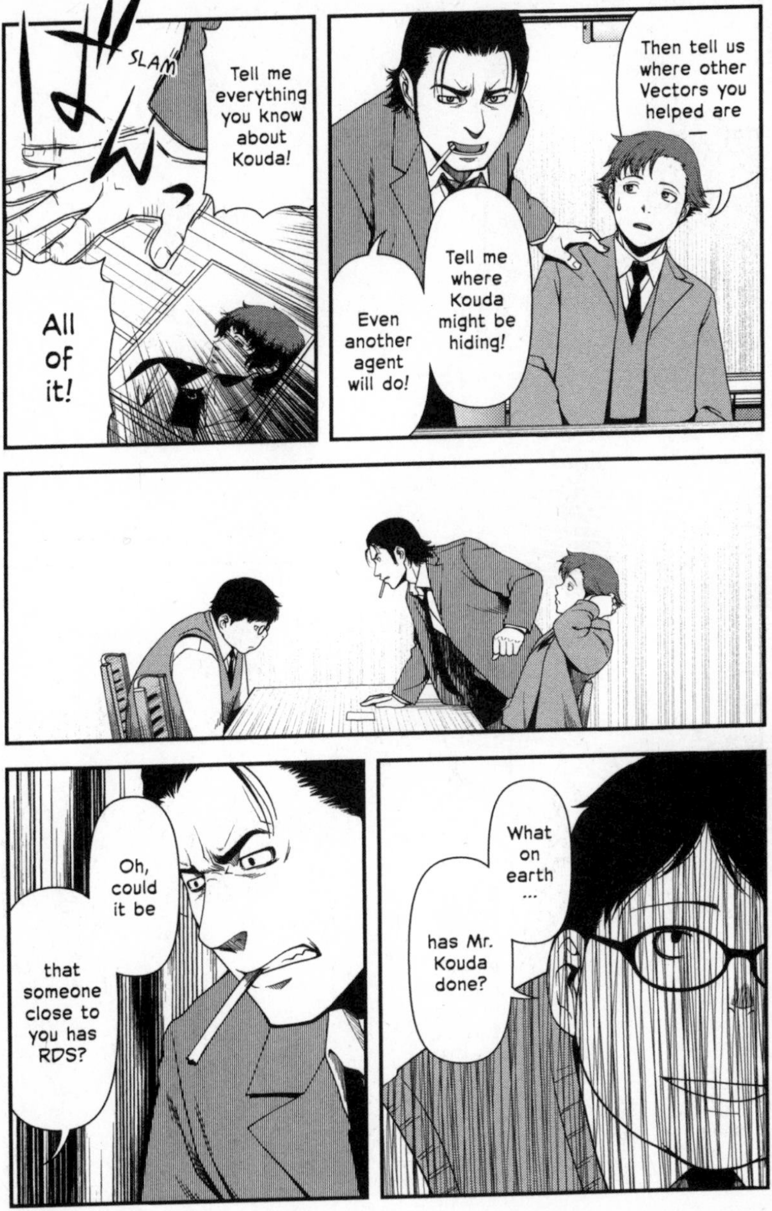

Then tell us where other Vectors you helped are —
Tell me where Kouda might be hiding!
Even another agent will do!
SLAM
Tell me everything you know about Kouda!
All of it!
What on earth ...
has Mr. Kouda done?
Oh, could it be
that someone close to you has RDS?

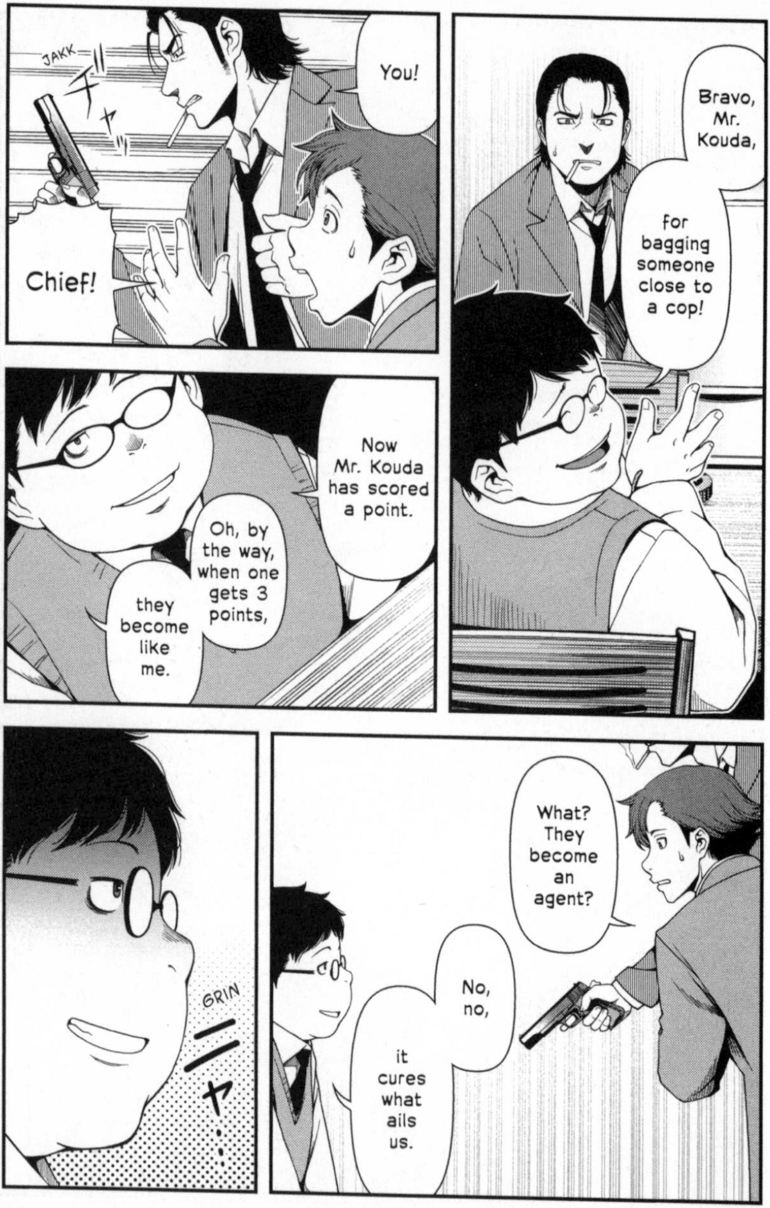

Bravo, Mr. Kouda,
for bagging someone close to a cop!
You!
JAKK
Chief!
Now Mr. Kouda has scored a point.
Oh, by the way, when one gets 3 points,
they become like me.
What? They become an agent?
No, no,
it cures what ails us.
GRIN

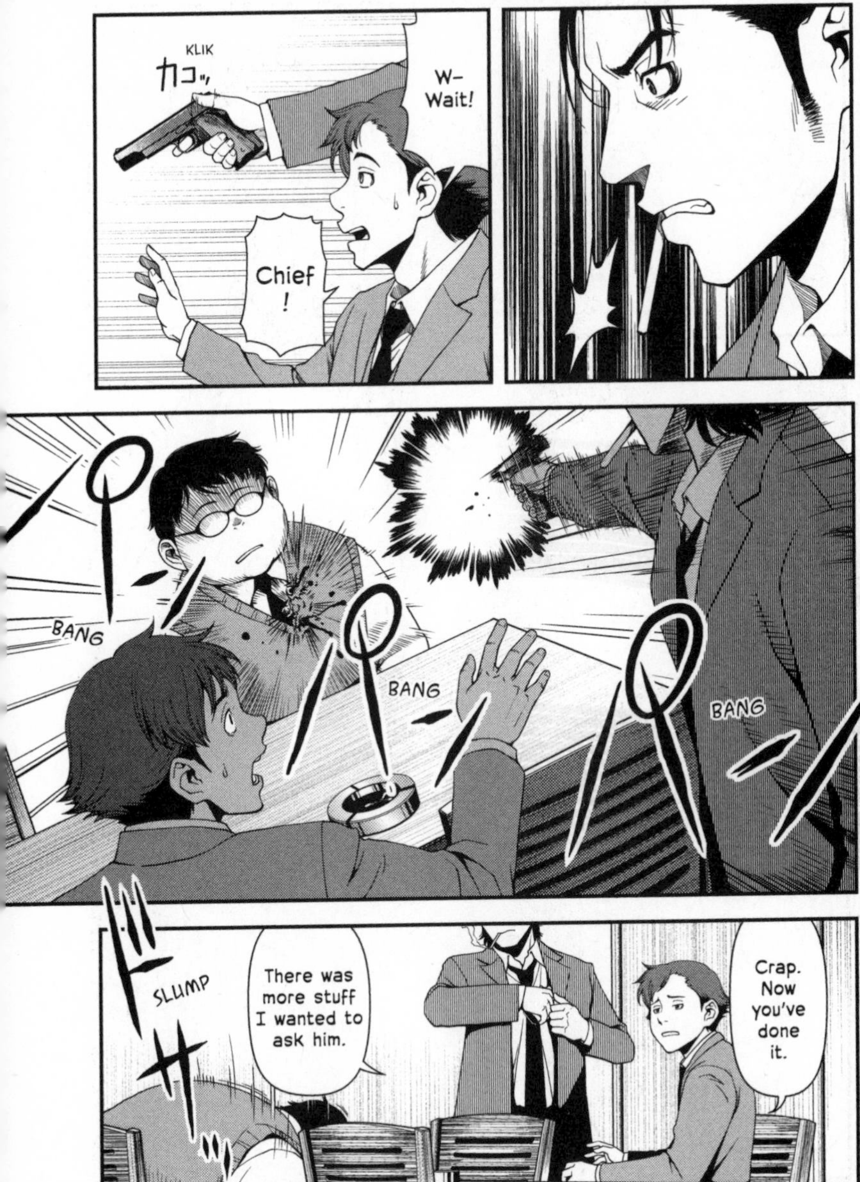
W–Wait!
KLIK
カコッ
Chief!
BANG
BANG
BANG
Crap. Now you've done it.
There was more stuff I wanted to ask him.
SLUMP

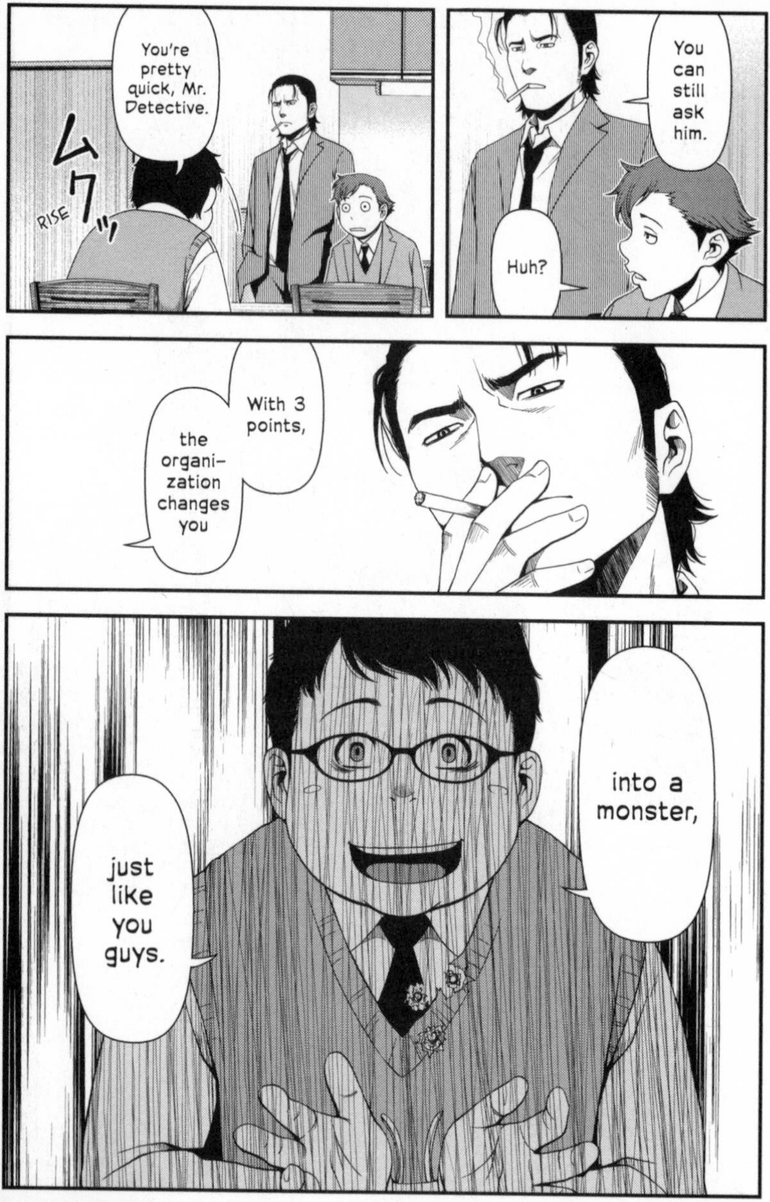
You can still ask him.
Huh?
You're pretty quick, Mr. Detective.
ムク
RISE
With 3 points,
the organization changes you
into a monster,
just like you guys.

6
Don't Let Him Catch You

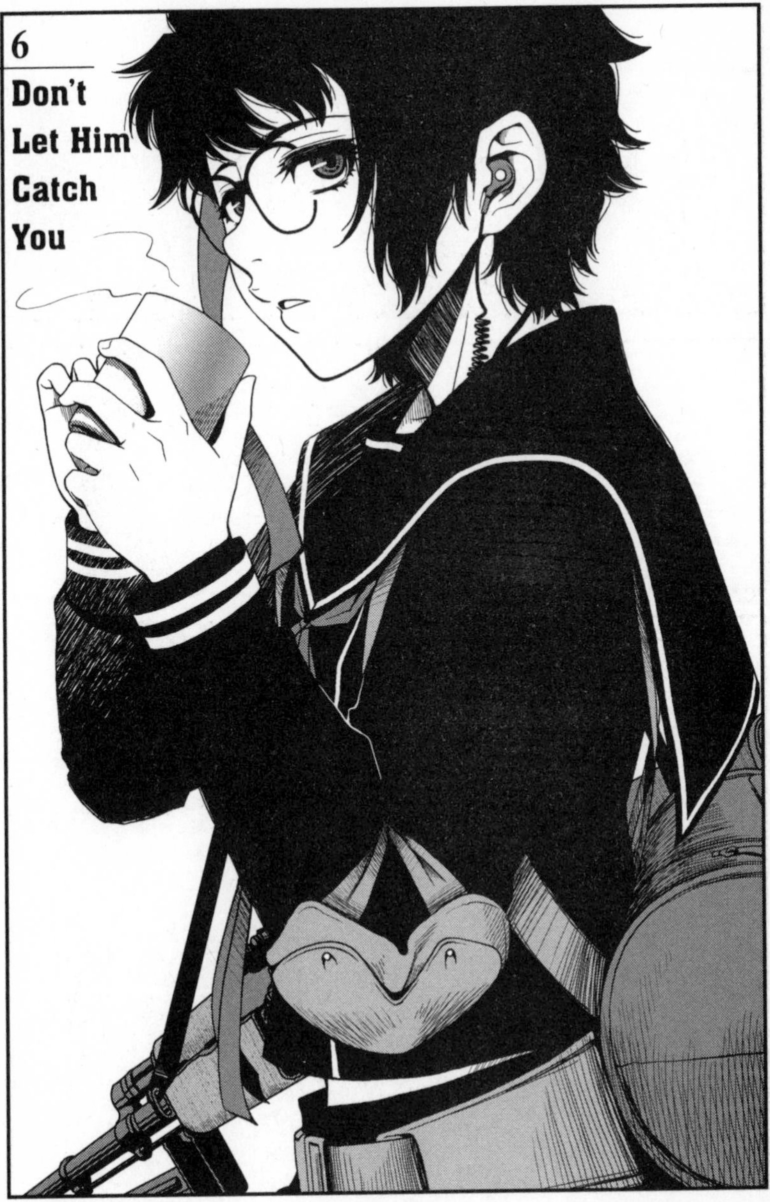

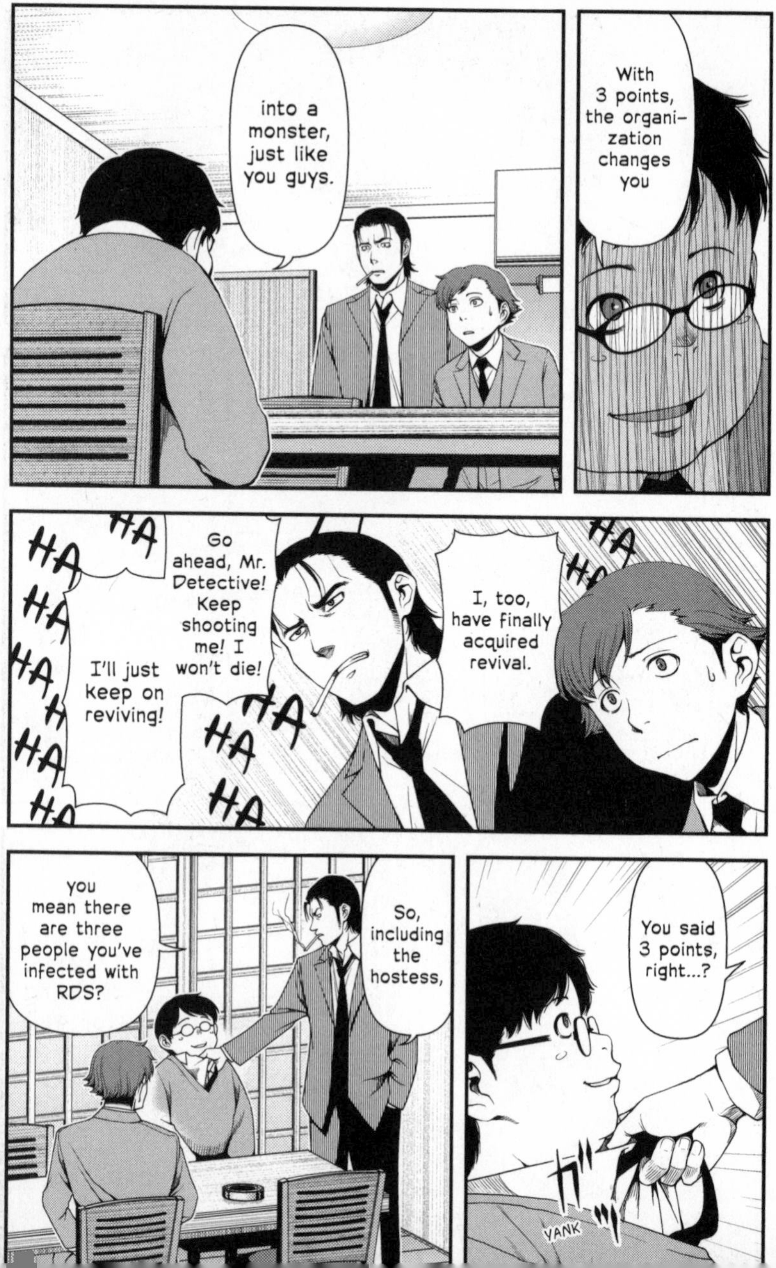
With 3 points, the organi-zation changes you
into a monster, just like you guys.
HA HA
I, too, have finally acquired revival.
Go ahead, Mr. Detective! Keep shooting me! I won't die!
I'll just keep on reviving!
HA HA HA HA HA HA HA HA
HA HA HA
You said 3 points, right...?
YANK
So, including the hostess,
you mean there are three people you've infected with RDS?

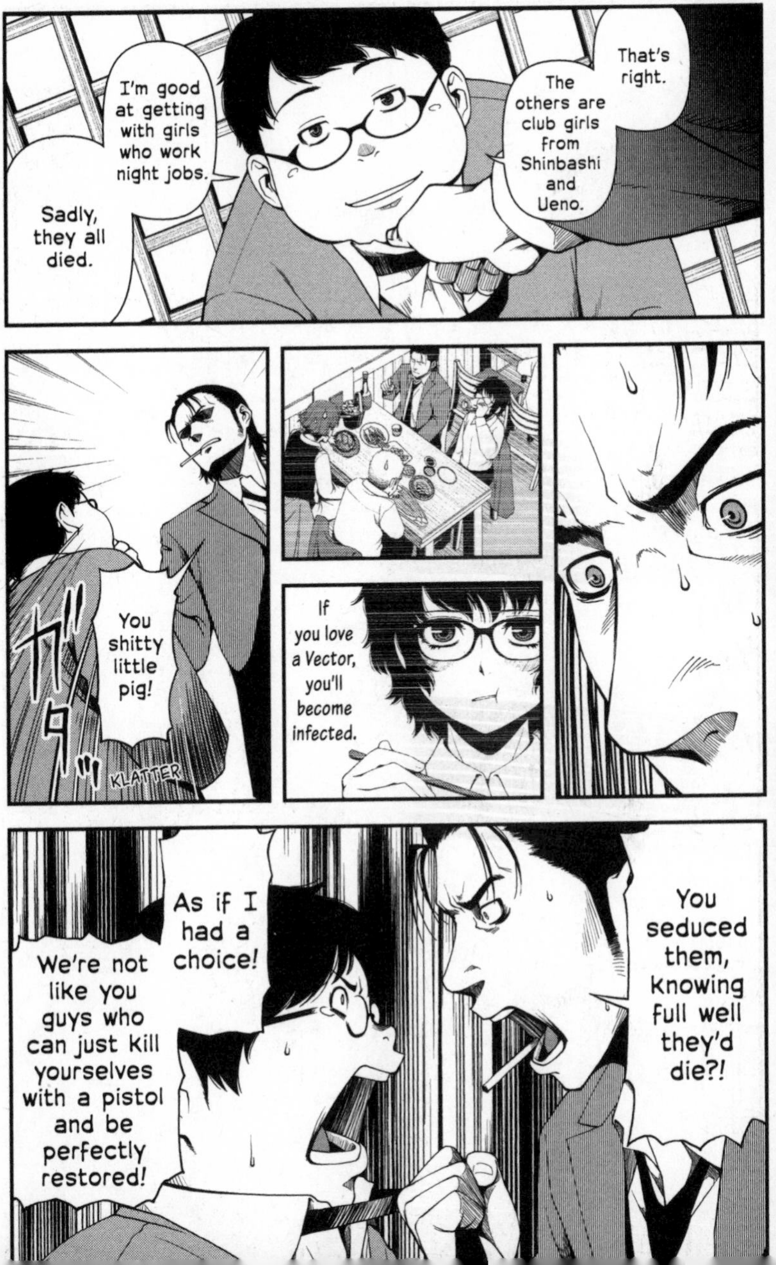
That's right.
The others are club girls from Shinbashi and Ueno.
I'm good at getting with girls who work night jobs.
Sadly, they all died.
If you love a Vector, you'll become infected.
You shitty little pig!
ガタッ
KLATTER
You seduced them, knowing full well they'd die?!
As if I had a choice!
We're not like you guys who can just kill yourselves with a pistol and be perfectly restored!

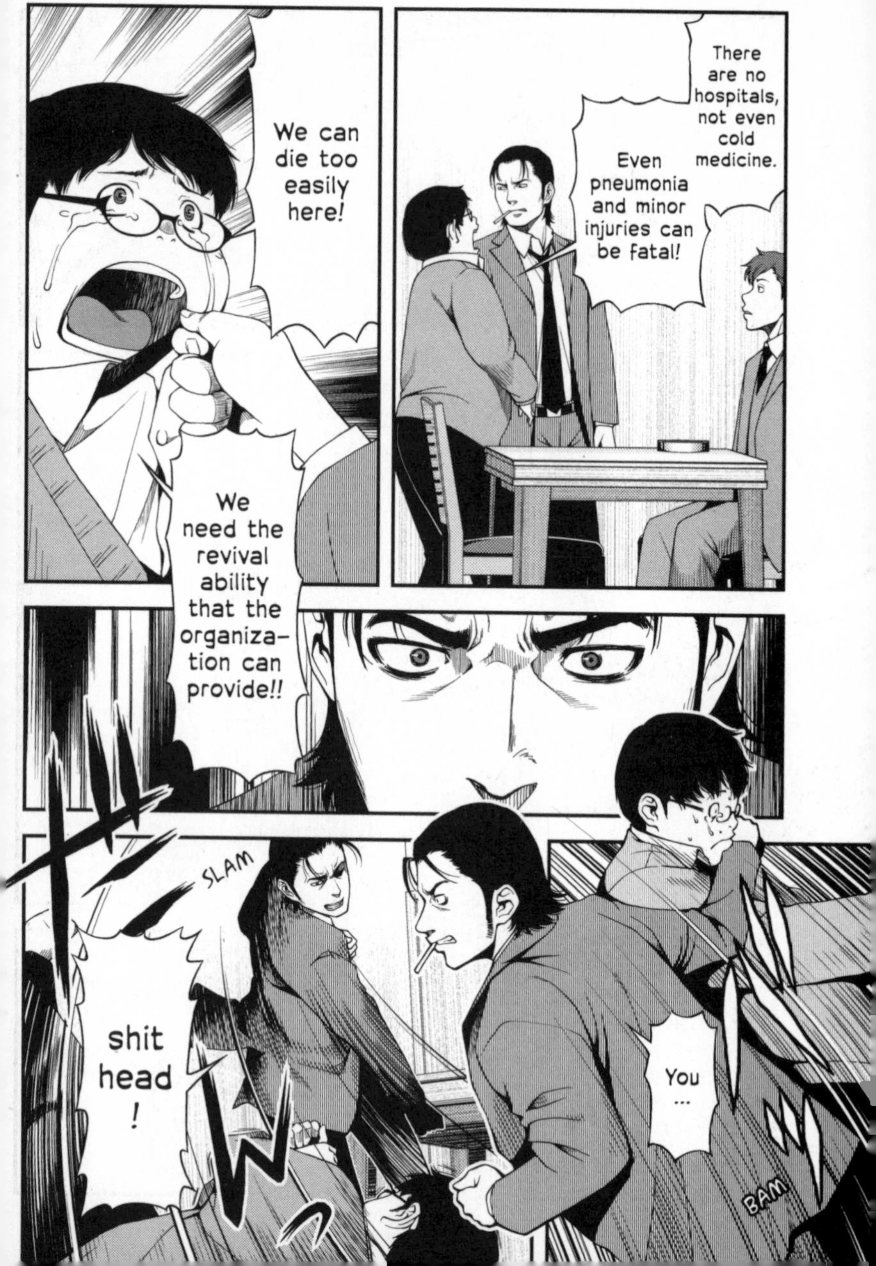
There are no hospitals, not even cold medicine.
Even pneumonia and minor injuries can be fatal!
We can die too easily here!
We need the revival ability that the organiza-tion can provide!!
You ...
SLAM
shit head!
BAM

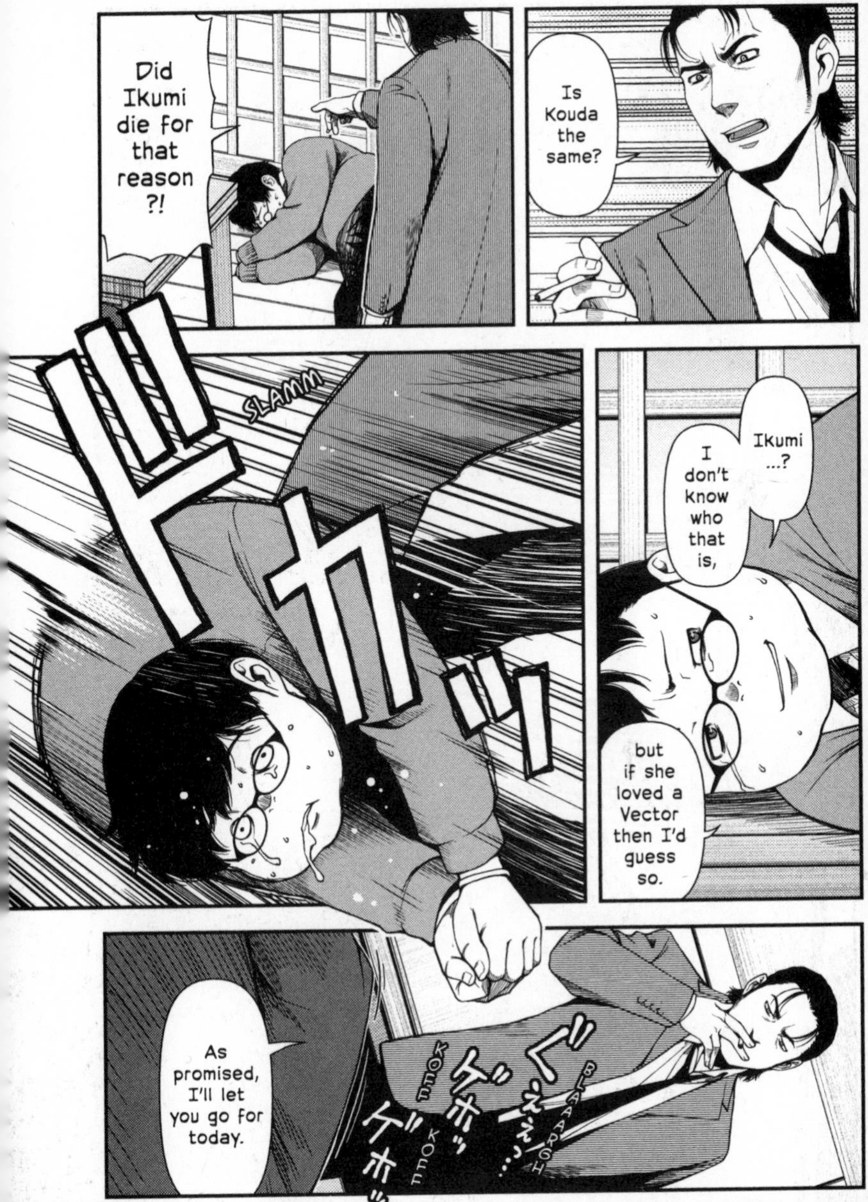
Is Kouda the same?
Did Ikumi die for that reason ?!
Ikumi ...?
I don't know who that is,
but if she loved a Vector then I'd guess so.
SLAMM
BLAAARGH
KOFF KOFF
As promised, I'll let you go for today.

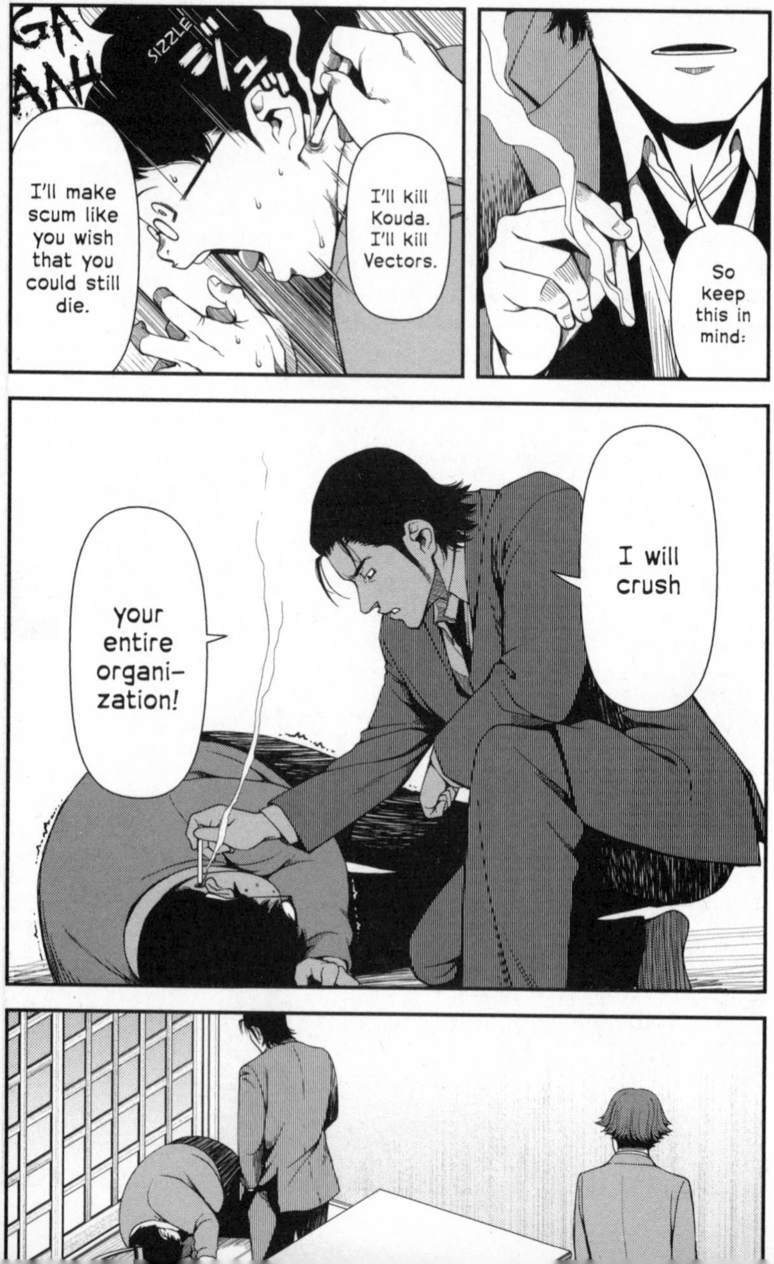
So keep this in mind:
SIZZLE
I'll kill Kouda. I'll kill Vectors.
GAAAH
I'll make scum like you wish that you could still die.
I will crush
your entire organization!

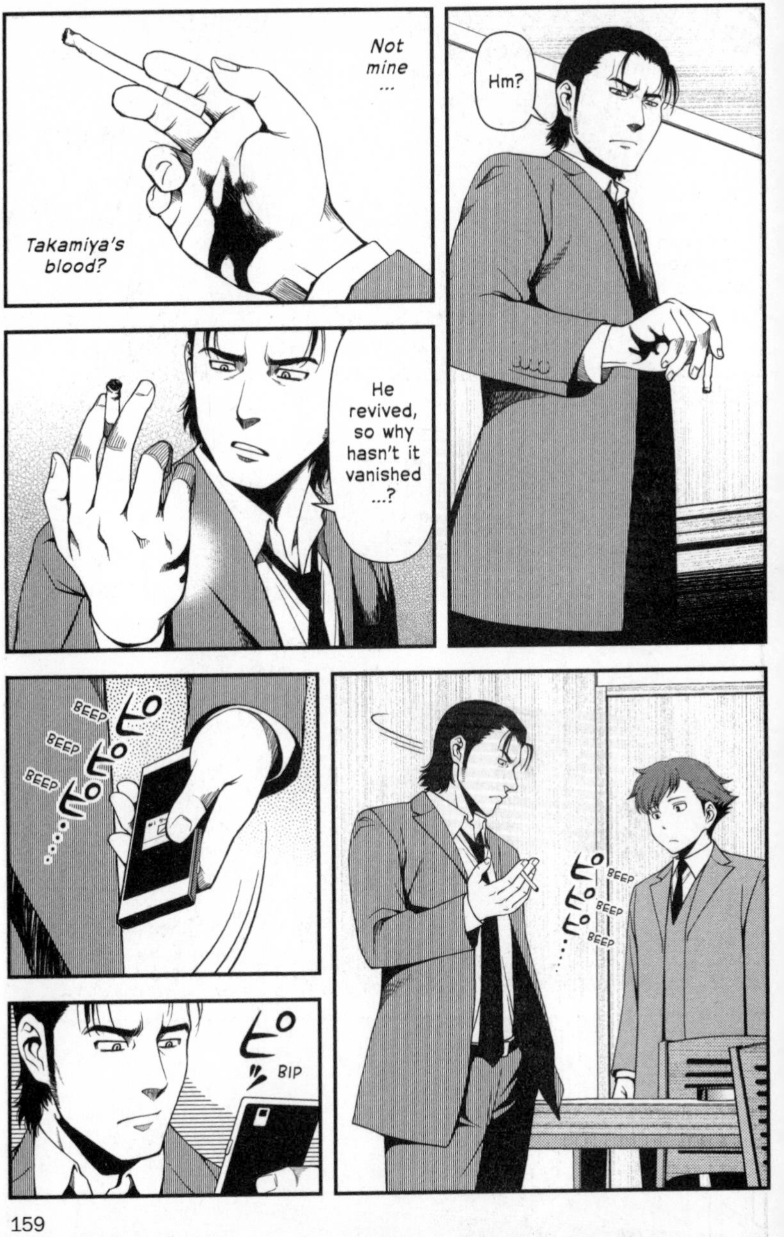
Hm?
Not mine ...
Takamiya's blood?
He revived, so why hasn't it vanished ...?
ピ BEEP
ピ BEEP
ピ BEEP
...
ピ BEEP
ピ BEEP
ピ BEEP
...
ピ BIP

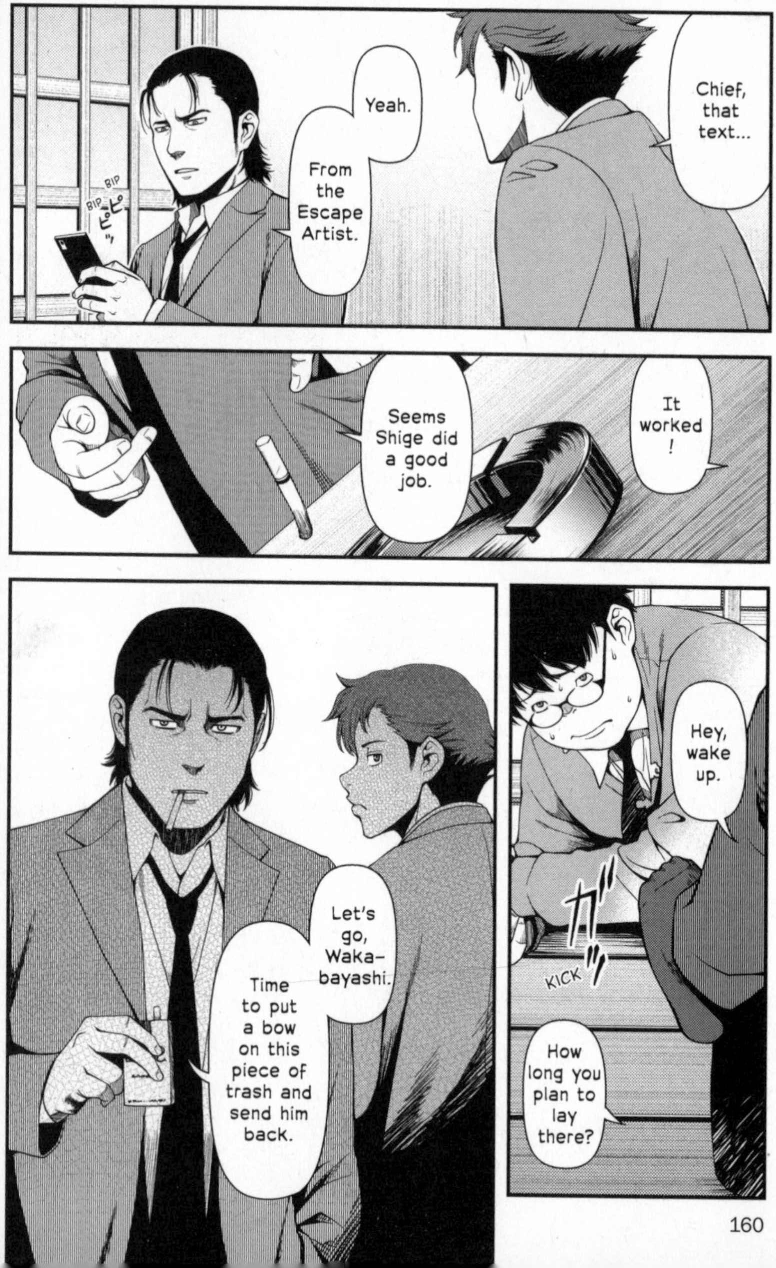
Chief, that text...
Yeah.
From the Escape Artist.
BIP BIP
ピピッ
It worked!
Seems Shige did a good job.
Hey, wake up.
ガッ
KICK
How long you plan to lay there?
Let's go, Waka-bayashi.
Time to put a bow on this piece of trash and send him back.

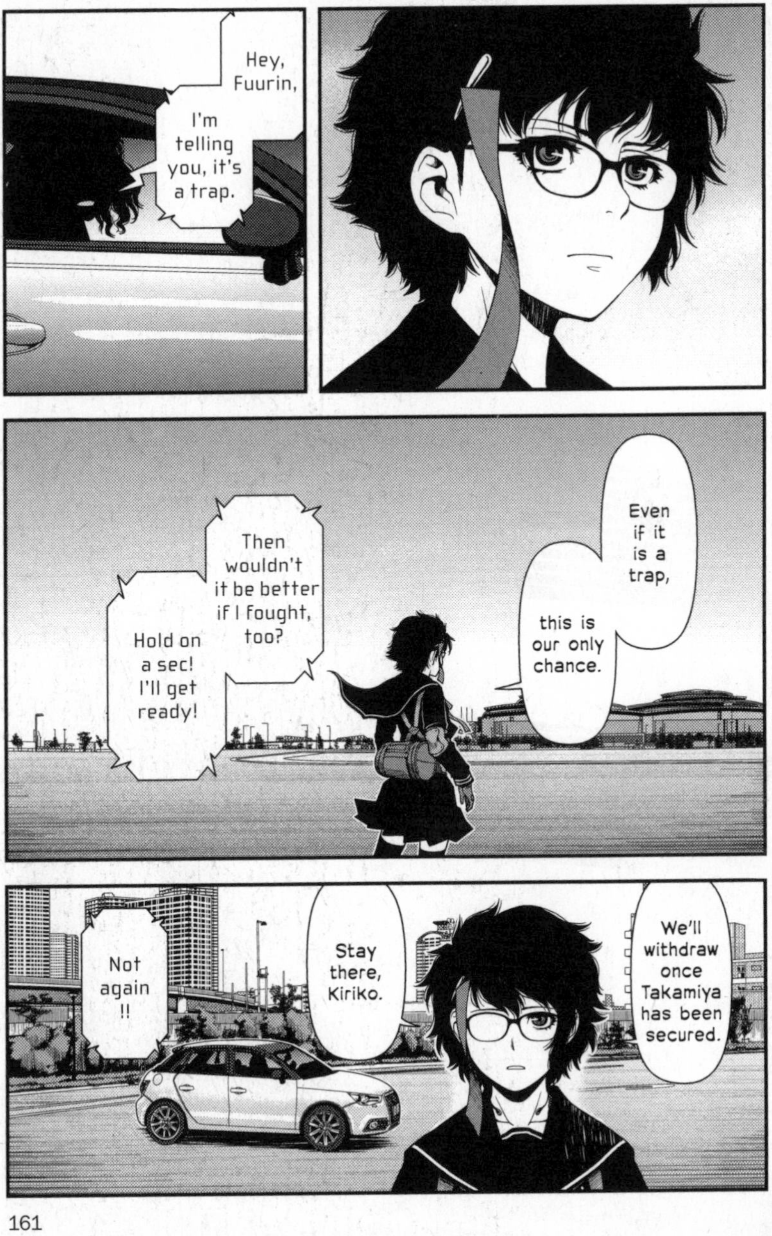
Hey, Fuurin,
I'm telling you, it's a trap.
Even if it is a trap,
this is our only chance.
Then wouldn't it be better if I fought, too?
Hold on a sec! I'll get ready!
We'll withdraw once Takamiya has been secured.
Stay there, Kiriko.
Not again !!

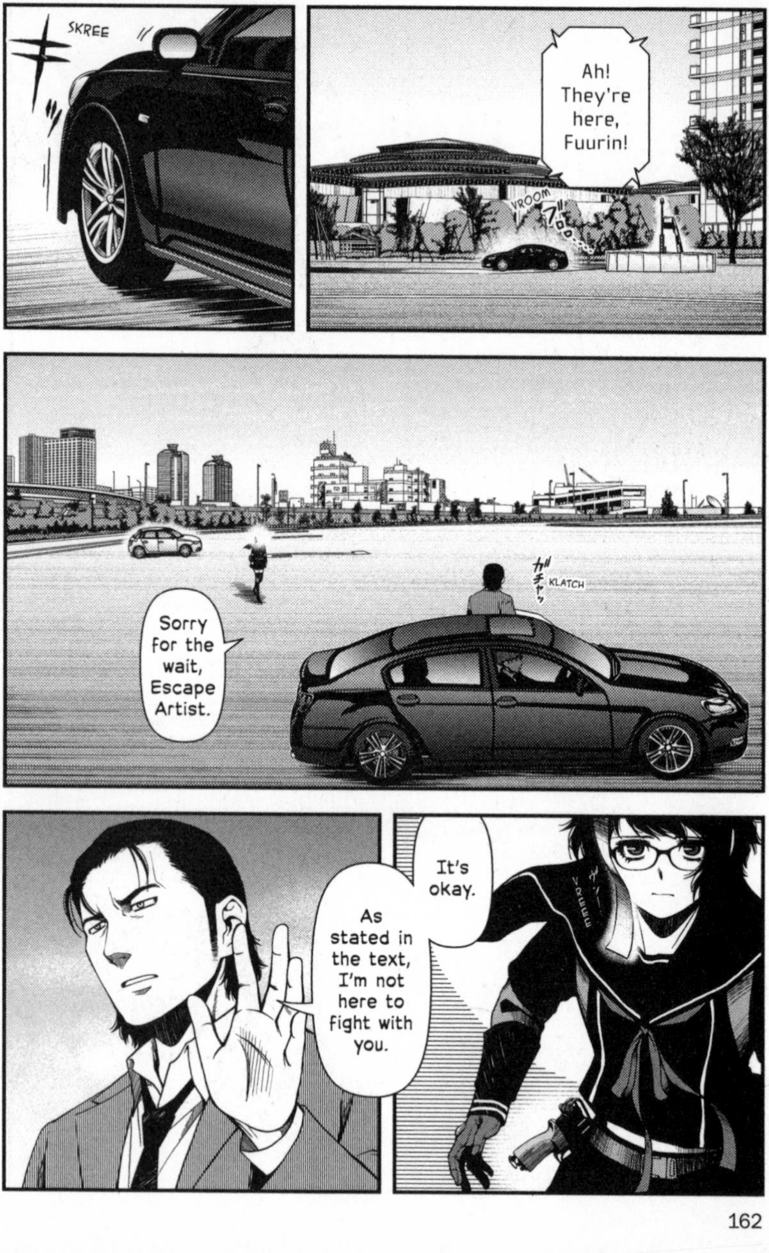
Ah! They're here, Fuurin!
VROOM
SKREE
KLATCH
Sorry for the wait, Escape Artist.
VREEE
It's okay.
As stated in the text, I'm not here to fight with you.

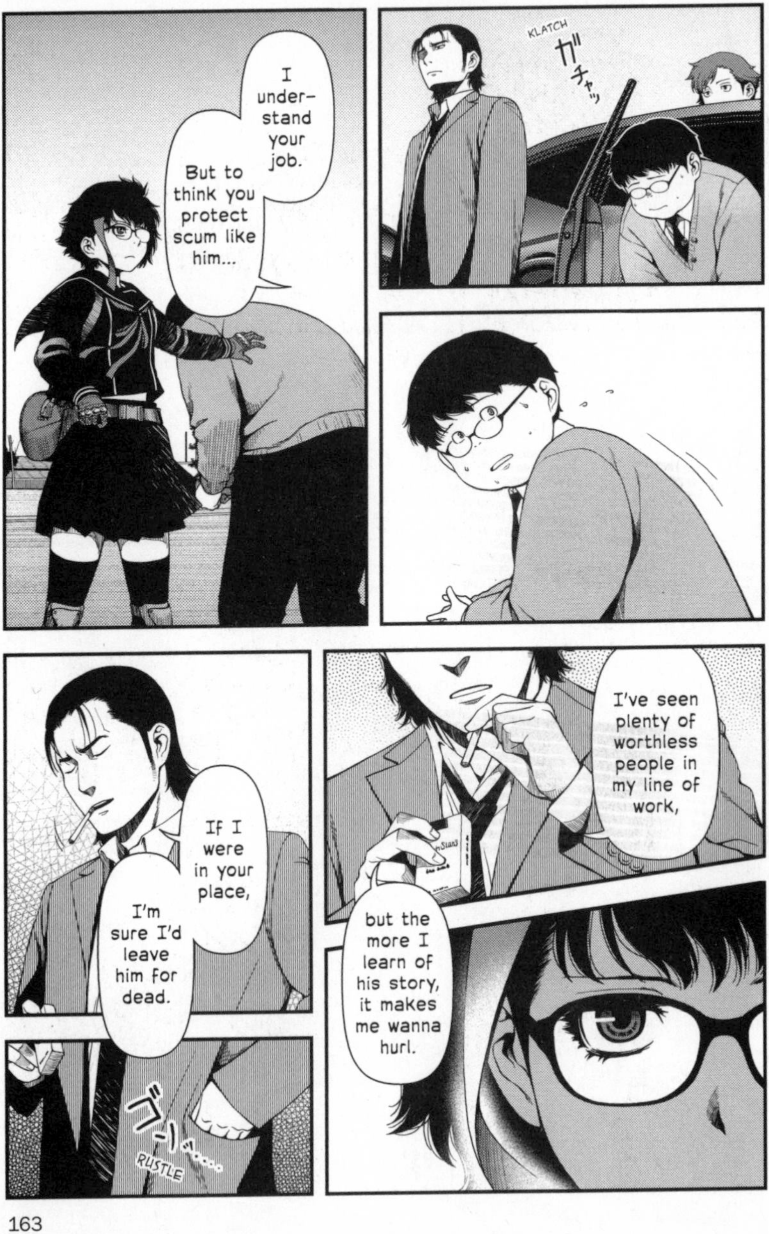
KLATCH
ガチャッ
I understand your job.
But to think you protect scum like him...
I've seen plenty of worthless people in my line of work,
but the more I learn of his story, it makes me wanna hurl.
If I were in your place,
I'm sure I'd leave him for dead.
ゴソッ…
RUSTLE

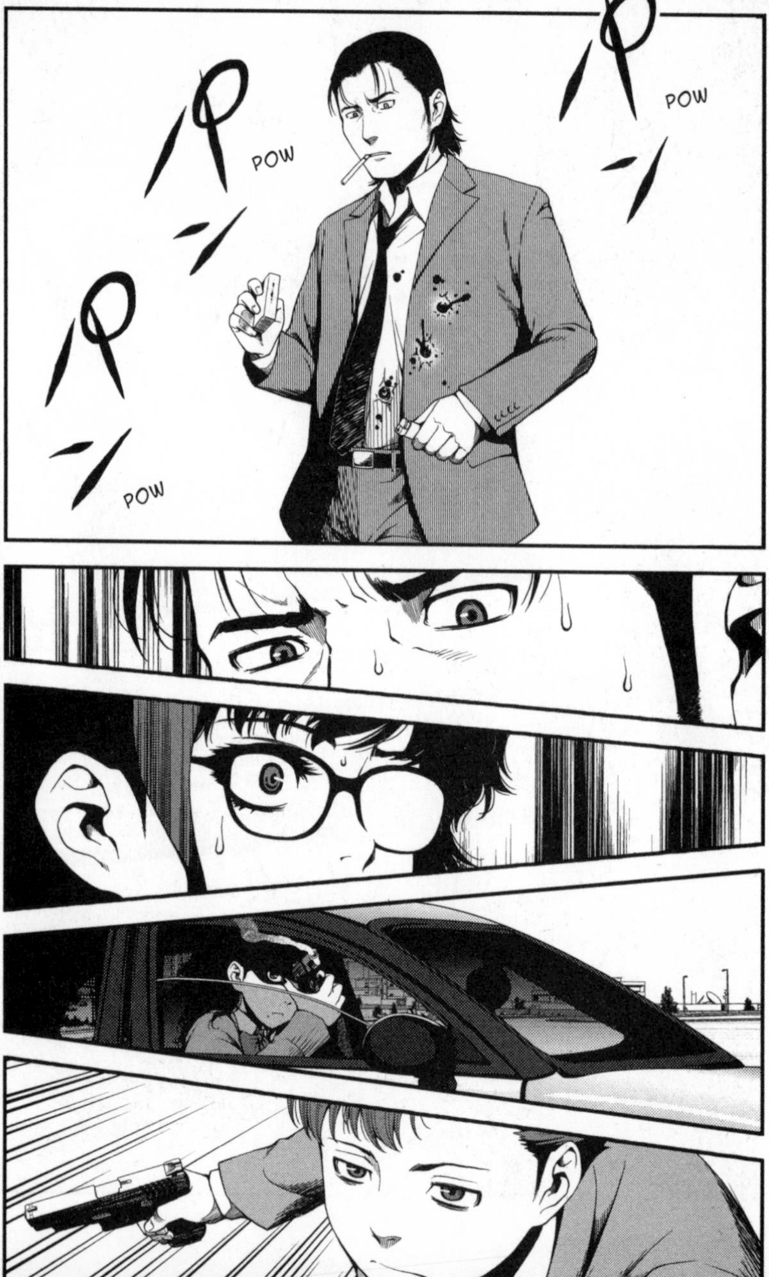
パン
POW
パン
POW
パン
POW

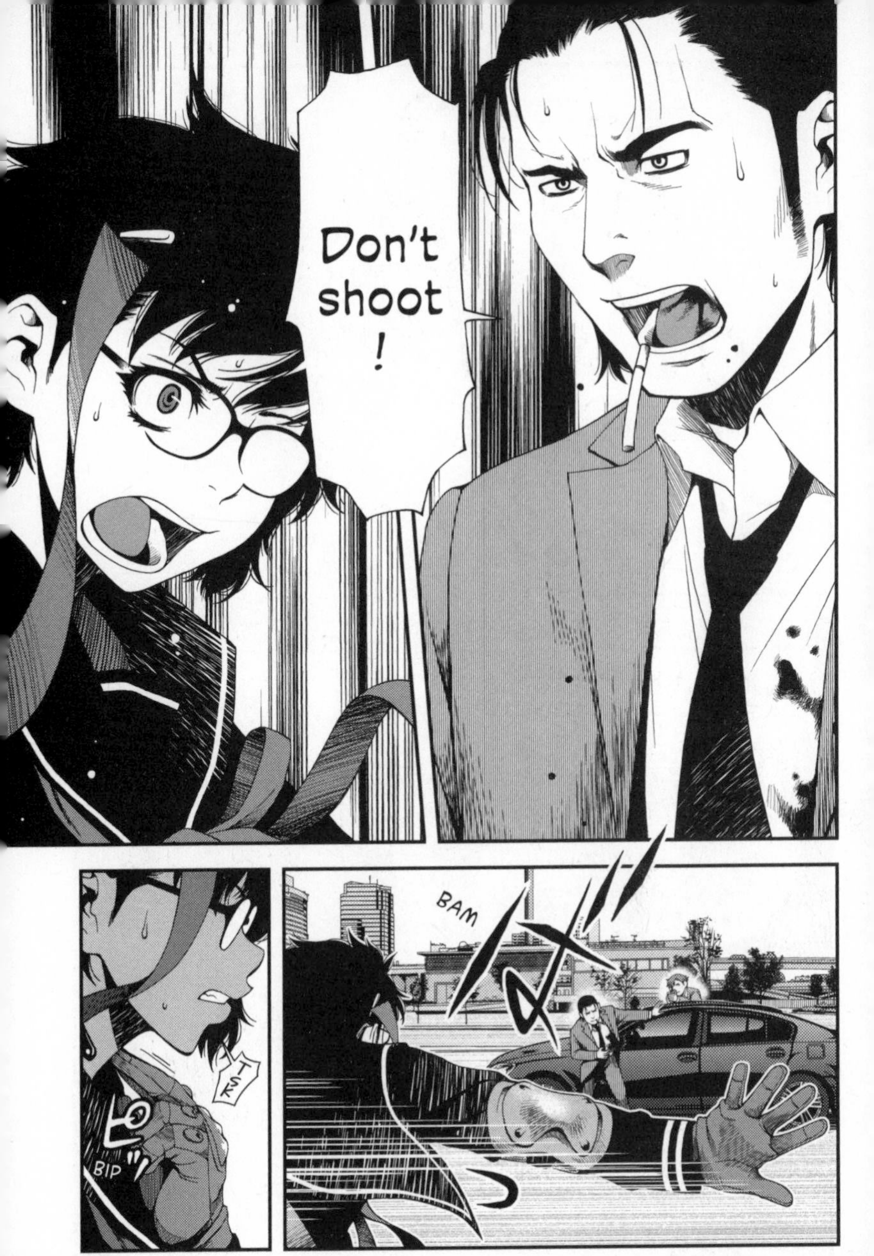
Don't shoot !
BAM
TSK
BIP

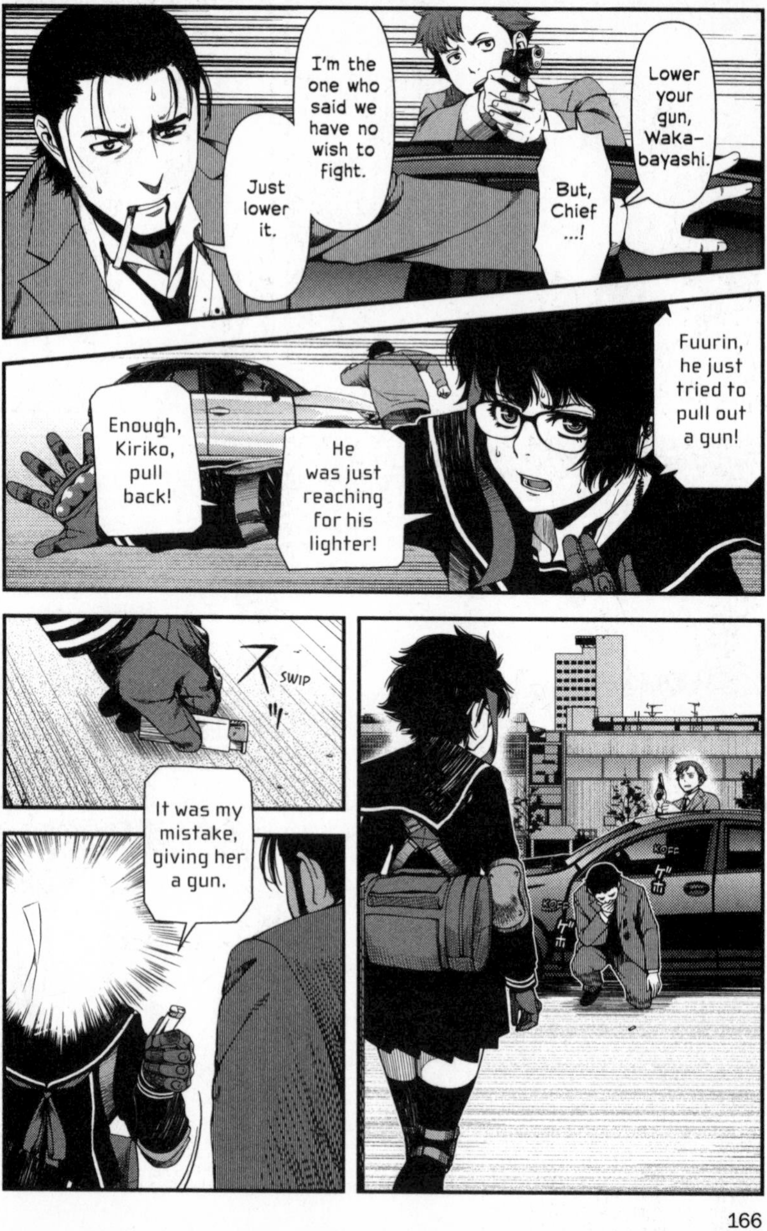
Lower your gun, Wakabayashi.
But, Chief ...!
I'm the one who said we have no wish to fight.
Just lower it.
Fuurin, he just tried to pull out a gun!
He was just reaching for his lighter!
Enough, Kiriko, pull back!
KOFF
KOFF
ス
SWIP
It was my mistake, giving her a gun.

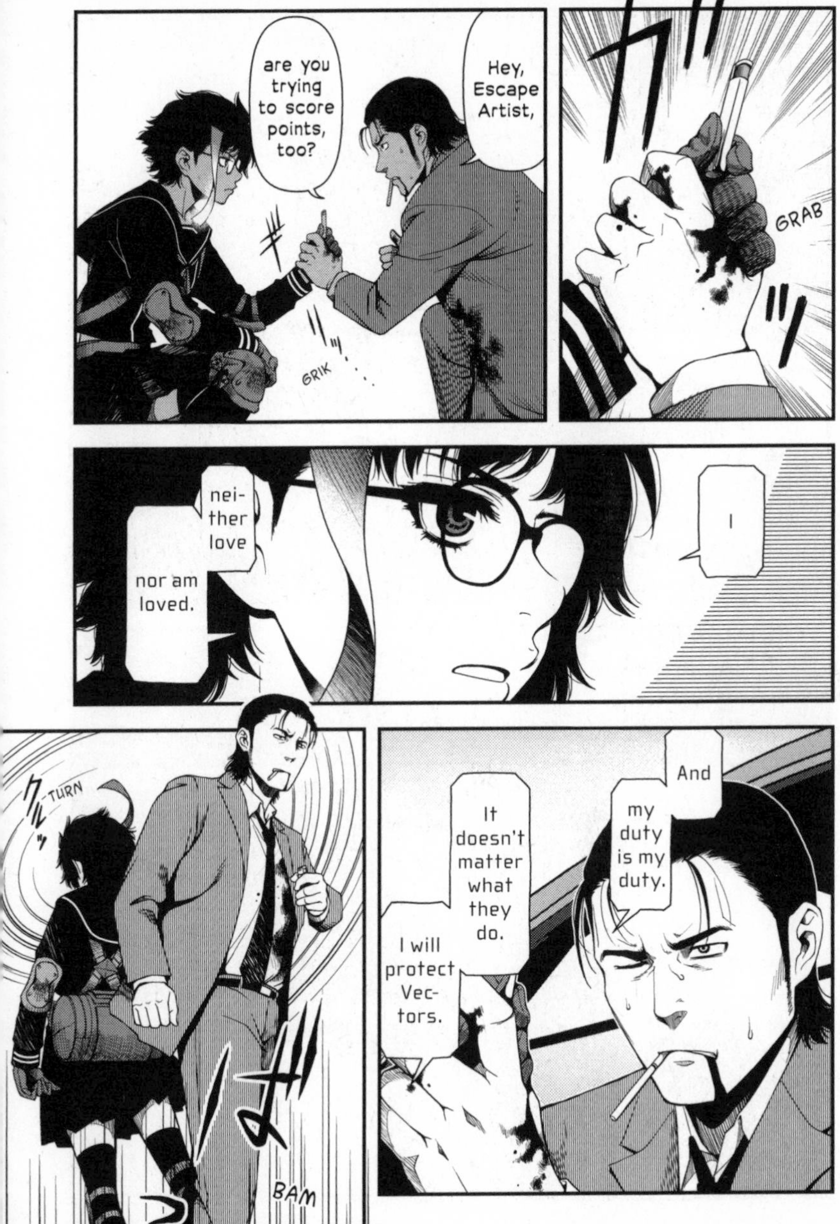
GRAB
Hey, Escape Artist,
are you trying to score points, too?
GRIK
I
nei-ther love
nor am loved.
And
my duty is my duty.
It doesn't matter what they do.
I will protect Vec-tors.
TURN
BAM

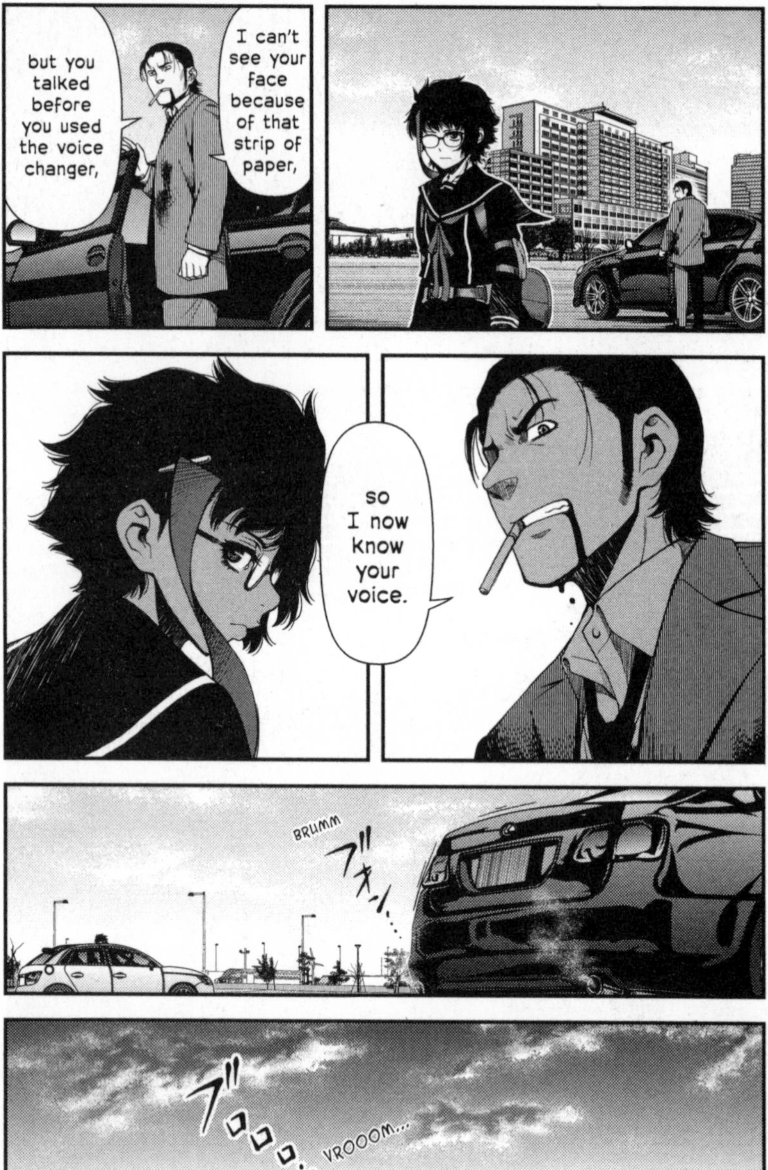
I can't see your face because of that strip of paper,
but you talked before you used the voice changer,
so I now know your voice.
BRUMM
VROOOM...

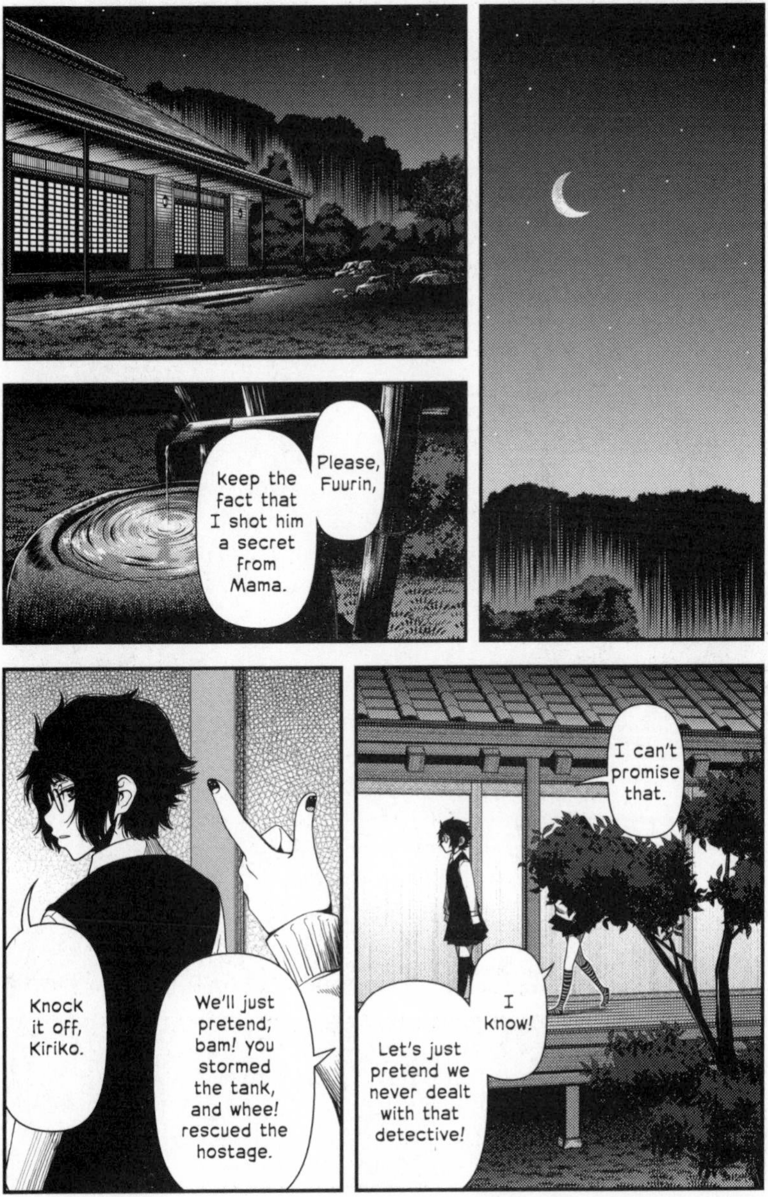
Please, Fuurin,
keep the fact that I shot him a secret from Mama.
I can't promise that.
I know!
Let's just pretend we never dealt with that detective!
We'll just pretend, bam! you stormed the tank, and whee! rescued the hostage.
Knock it off, Kiriko.

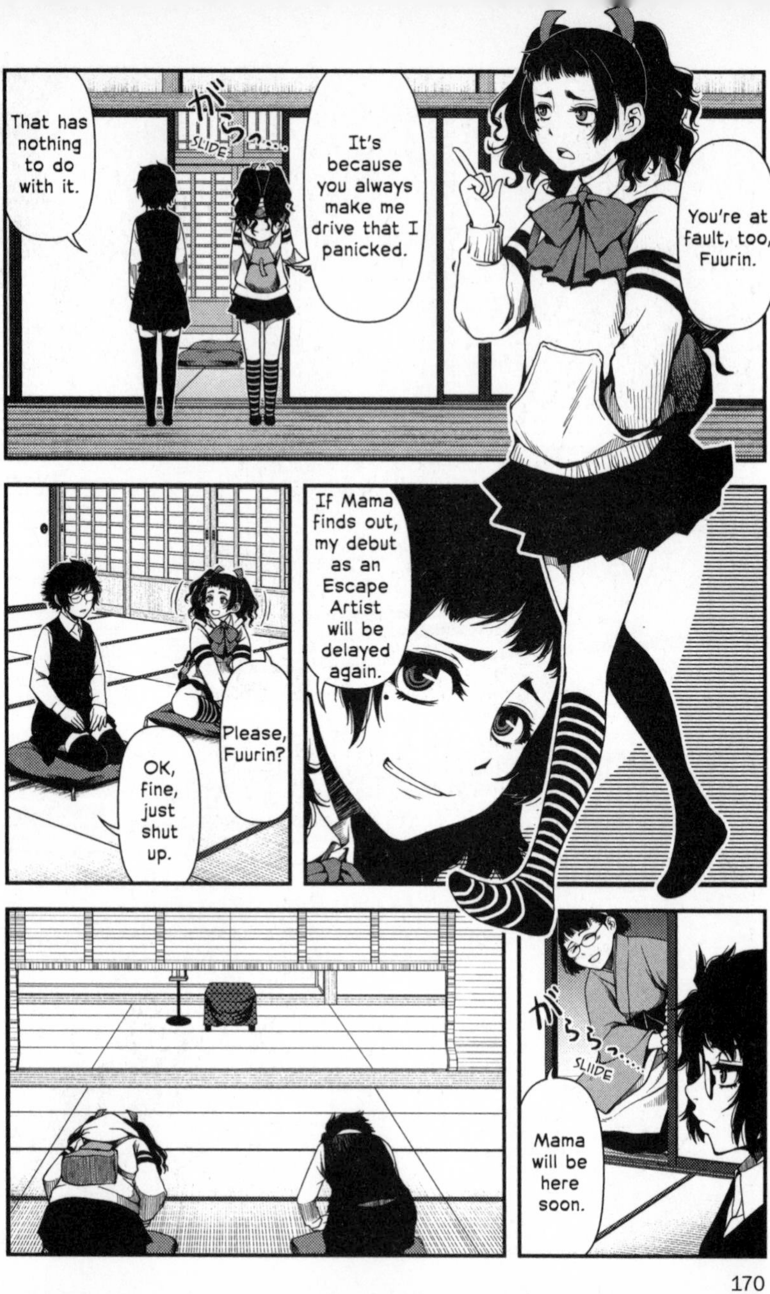

You're at fault, too, Fuurin.
がらっ…
SLIDE
It's because you always make me drive that I panicked.
That has nothing to do with it.
If Mama finds out, my debut as an Escape Artist will be delayed again.
Please, Fuurin?
OK, fine, just shut up.
がららっ…
SLIIDE
Mama will be here soon.

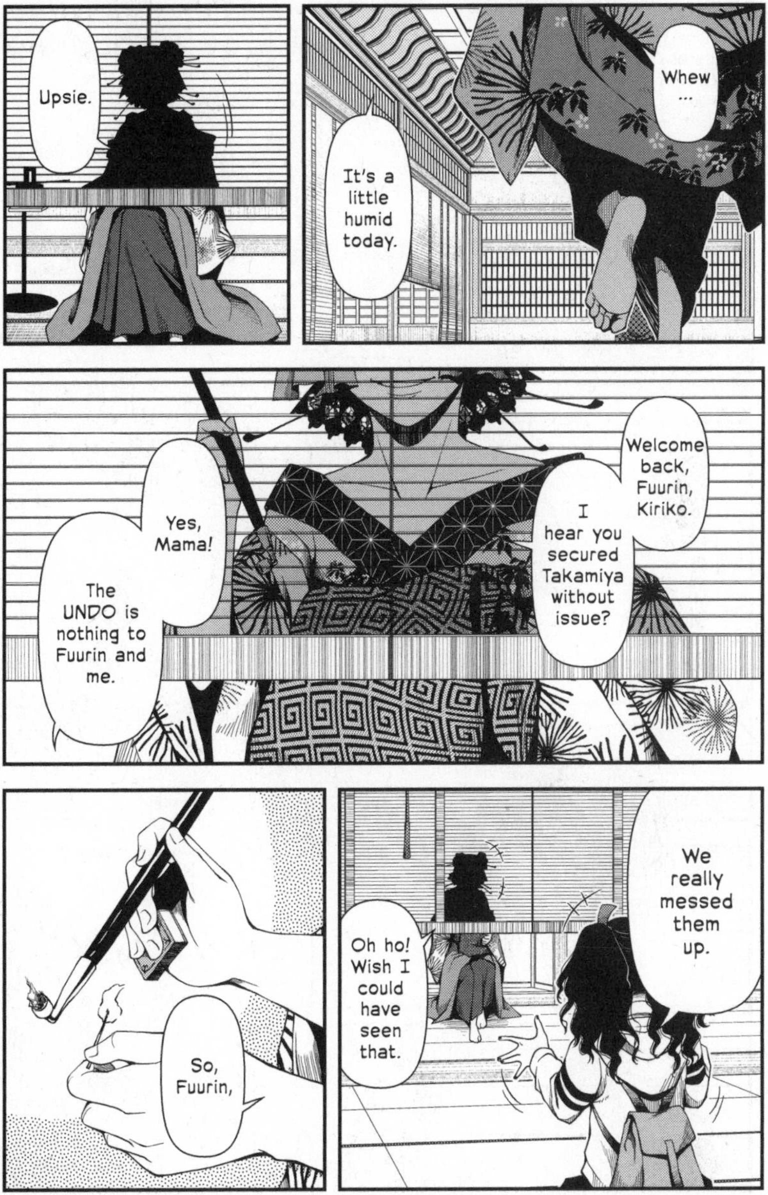

Whew ...
It's a little humid today.
Upsie.
Welcome back, Fuurin, Kiriko.
I hear you secured Takamiya without issue?
Yes, Mama!
The UNDO is nothing to Fuurin and me.
We really messed them up.
Oh ho! Wish I could have seen that.
So, Fuurin,

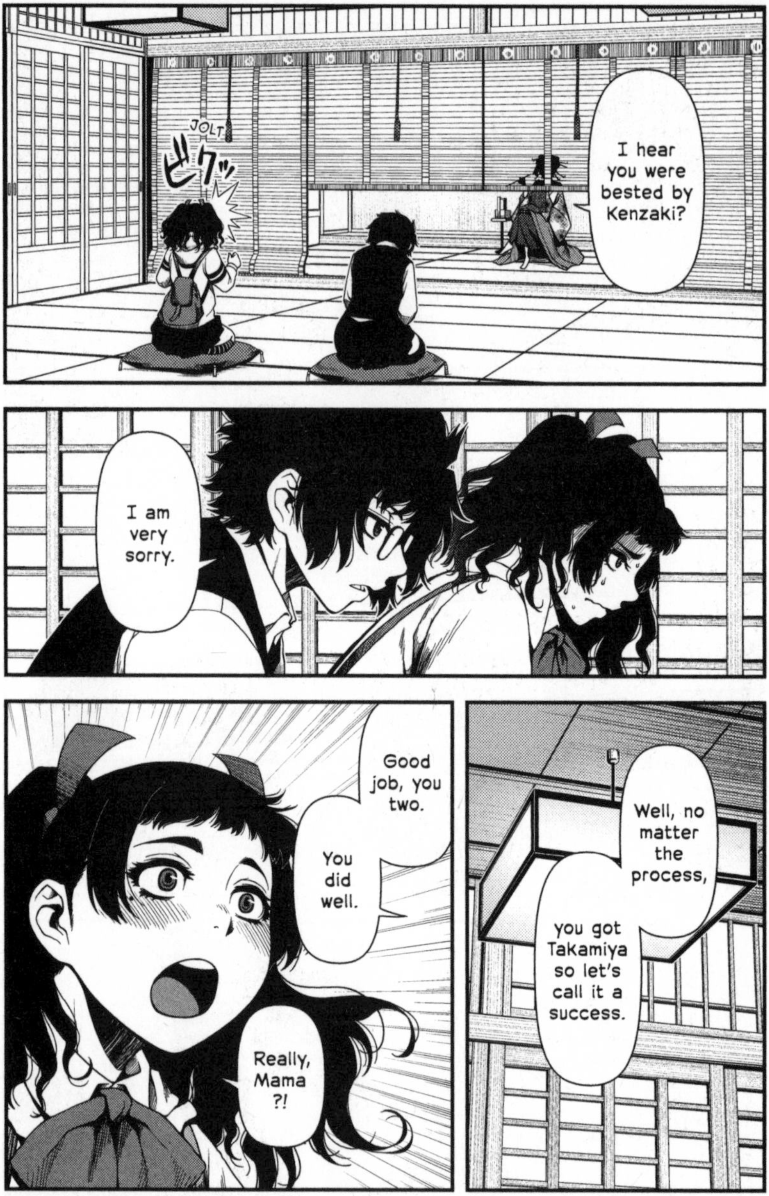
I hear you were bested by Kenzaki?
JOLT
ビクッ
I am very sorry.
Well, no matter the process,
you got Takamiya so let's call it a success.
Good job, you two.
You did well.
Really, Mama?!

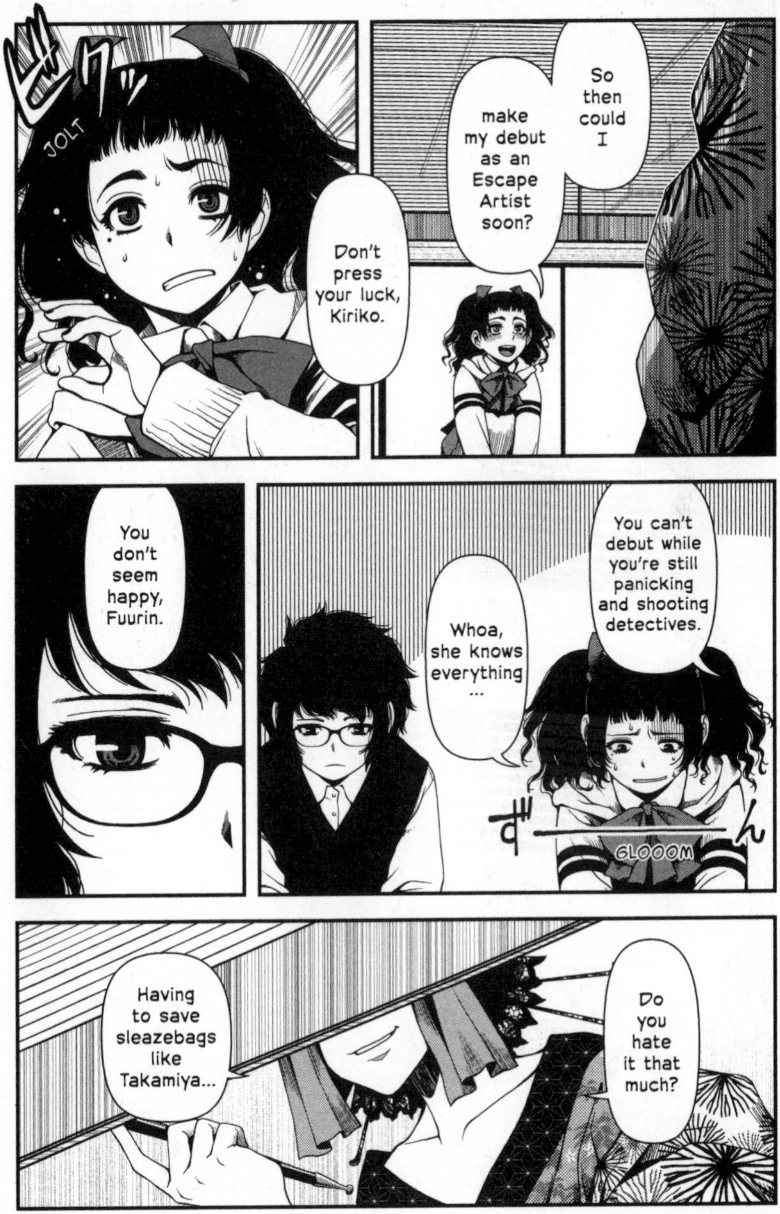
So then could I
make my debut as an Escape Artist soon?
Don't press your luck, Kiriko.
ビクッ
JOLT
You can't debut while you're still panicking and shooting detectives.
Whoa, she knows everything ...
ずーん
GLOOOM
You don't seem happy, Fuurin.
Do you hate it that much?
Having to save sleazebags like Takamiya...

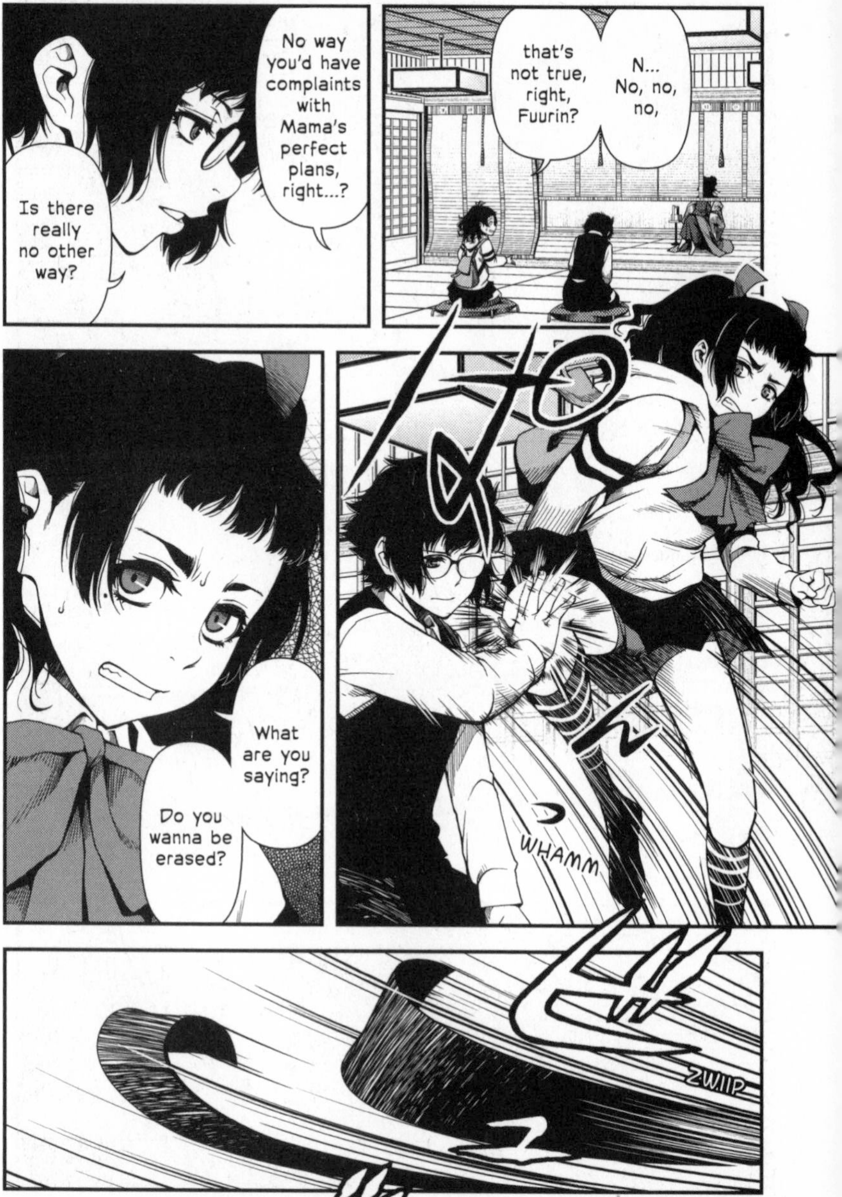
N... No, no, no,
that's not true, right, Fuurin?
No way you'd have complaints with Mama's perfect plans, right...?
Is there really no other way?
WHAMM
What are you saying?
Do you wanna be erased?
ZWIIP

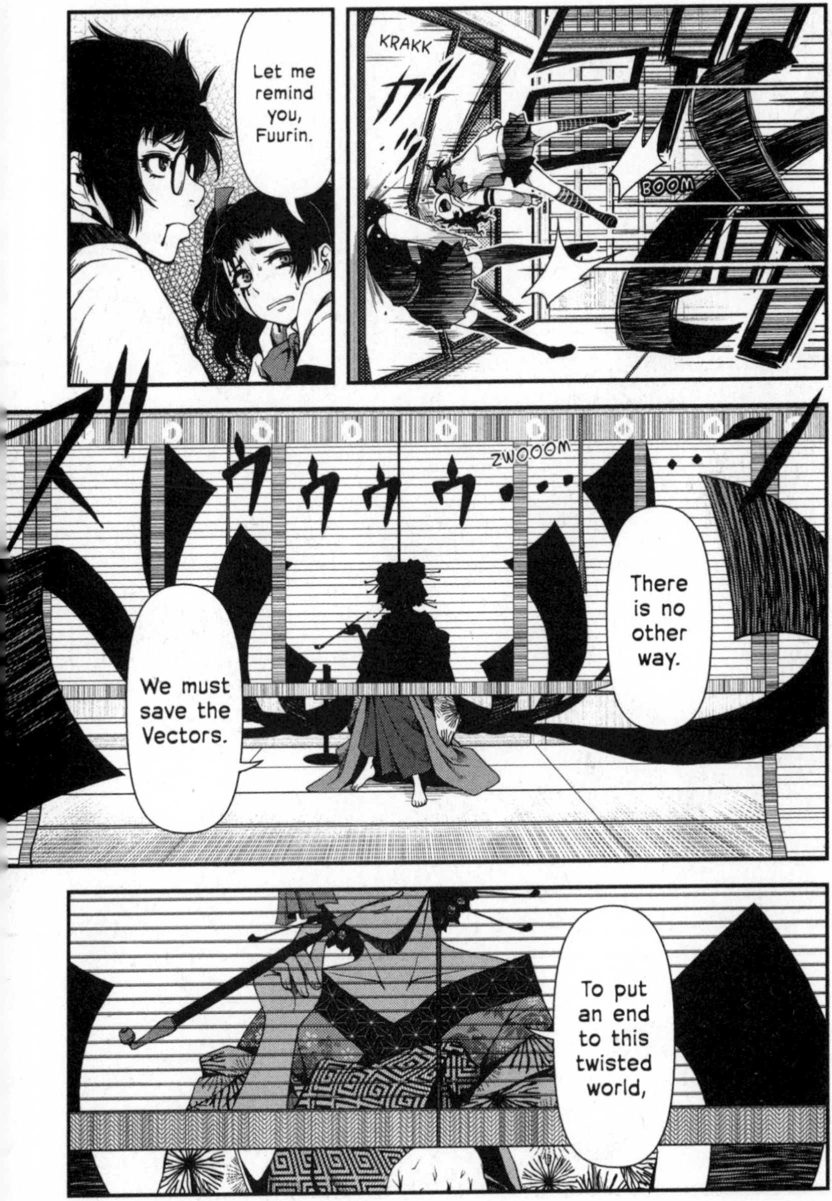
KRAKK
BOOM
Let me remind you, Fuurin.
ZWOOOM
There is no other way.
We must save the Vectors.
To put an end to this twisted world,

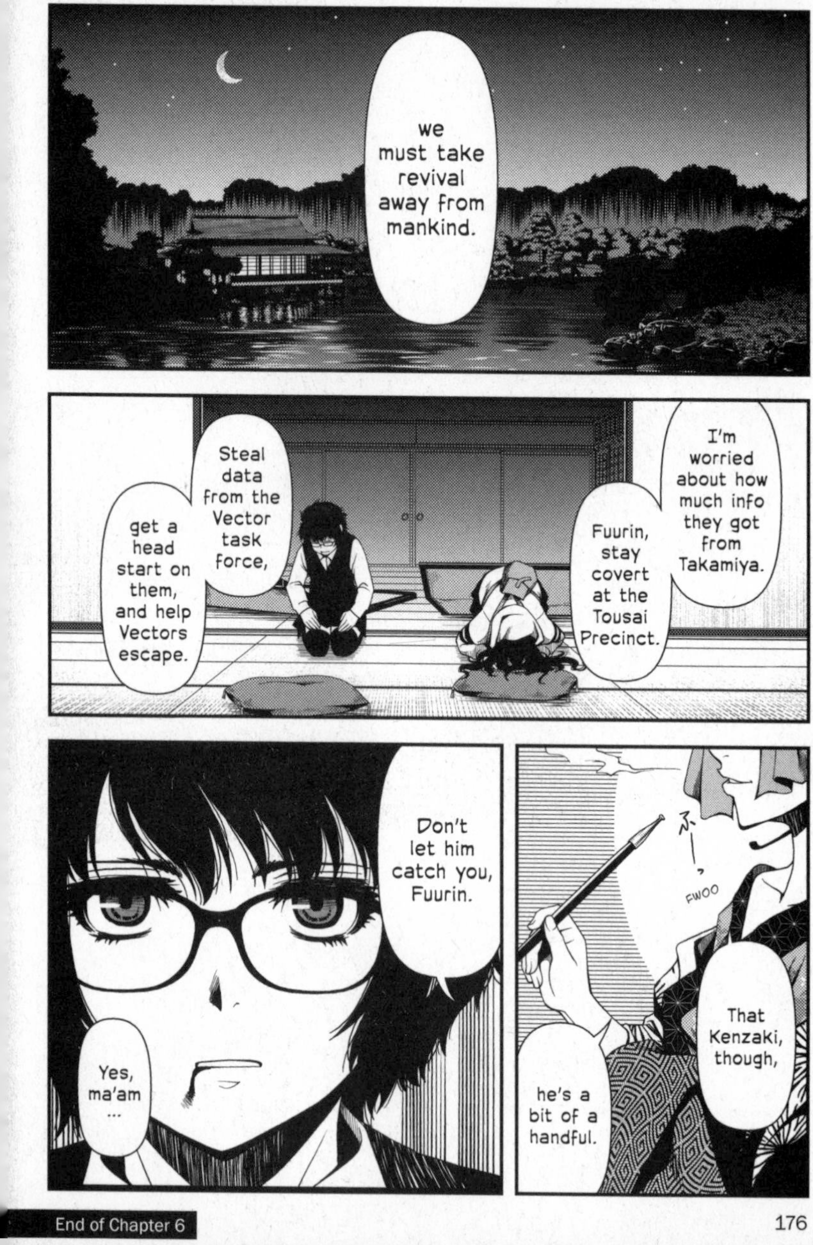
we must take revival away from mankind.
I'm worried about how much info they got from Takamiya.
Fuurin, stay covert at the Tousai Precinct.
Steal data from the Vector task force,
get a head start on them, and help Vectors escape.
ふー
FWOO
That Kenzaki, though,
he's a bit of a handful.
Don't let him catch you, Fuurin.
Yes, ma'am ...

A Q&A with Mr. Cluck and Ms. Policewoman
~WHAT ARE ESCAPE ARTISTS?~

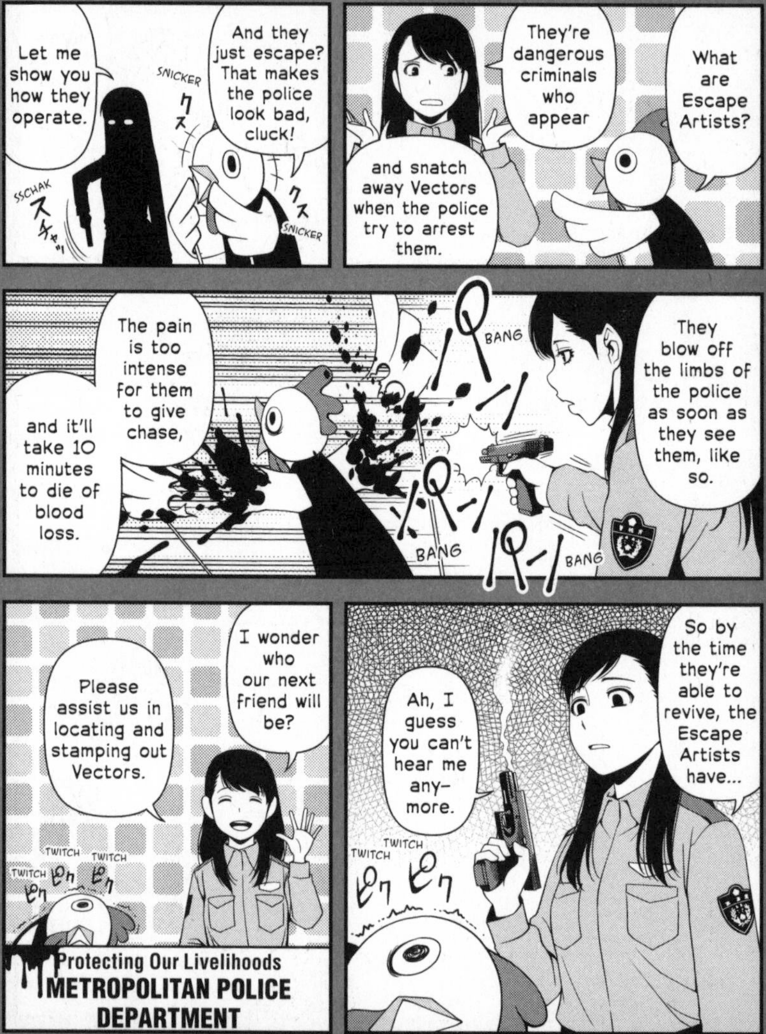
What are Escape Artists?
They're dangerous criminals who appear
and snatch away Vectors when the police try to arrest them.
And they just escape? That makes the police look bad, cluck!
SNICKER
クス
クス
SNICKER
Let me show you how they operate.
SSCHAK
スチャッ
They blow off the limbs of the police as soon as they see them, like so.
BANG
BANG
BANG
The pain is too intense for them to give chase,
and it'll take 10 minutes to die of blood loss.
So by the time they're able to revive, the Escape Artists have...
Ah, I guess you can't hear me any-more.
TWITCH
TWITCH
ピク ピク
I wonder who our next friend will be?
Please assist us in locating and stamping out Vectors.
TWITCH
TWITCH
TWITCH
ピク ピク ピク
Protecting Our Livelihoods
METROPOLITAN POLICE DEPARTMENT

A Q&A with Mr. Meow and Ms. Policewoman
~HOW MANY ESCAPE ARTISTS ARE THERE?~

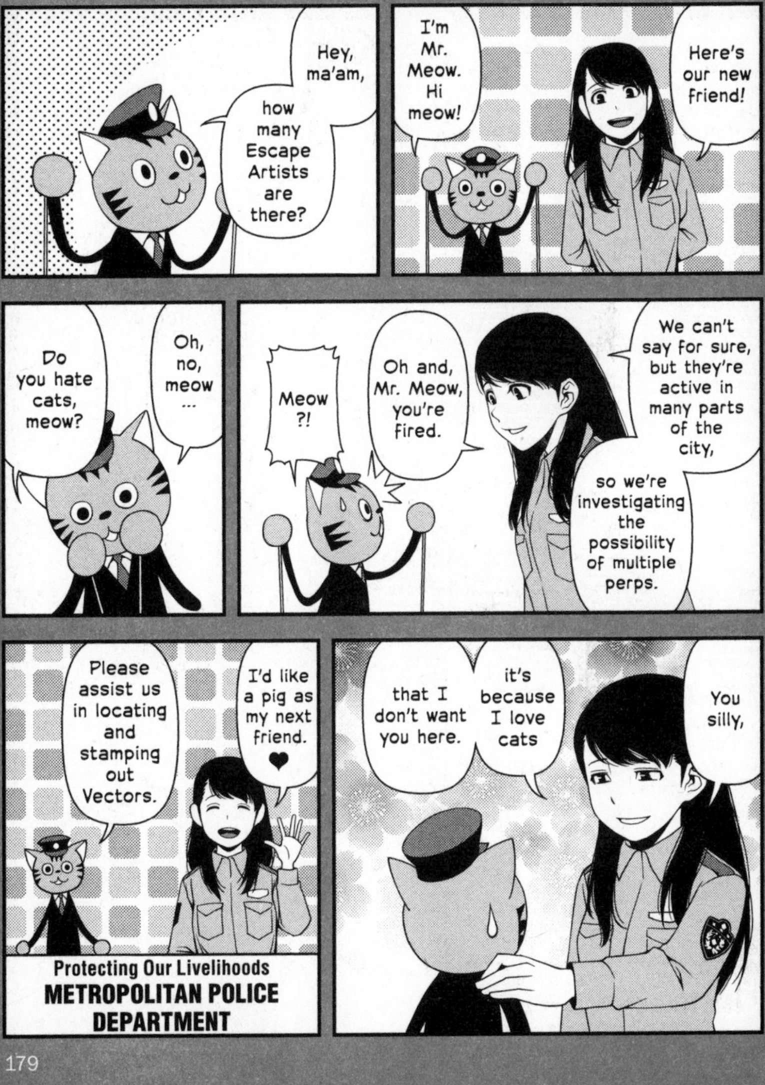

Here's our new friend!
I'm Mr. Meow. Hi meow!
Hey, ma'am,
how many Escape Artists are there?
We can't say for sure, but they're active in many parts of the city,
so we're investigating the possibility of multiple perps.
Oh and, Mr. Meow, you're fired.
Meow?!
Oh, no, meow ...
Do you hate cats, meow?
You silly,
it's because I love cats
that I don't want you here.
I'd like a pig as my next friend. ❤
Please assist us in locating and stamping out Vectors.
Protecting Our Livelihoods
METROPOLITAN POLICE DEPARTMENT

7
A Hound in the Force

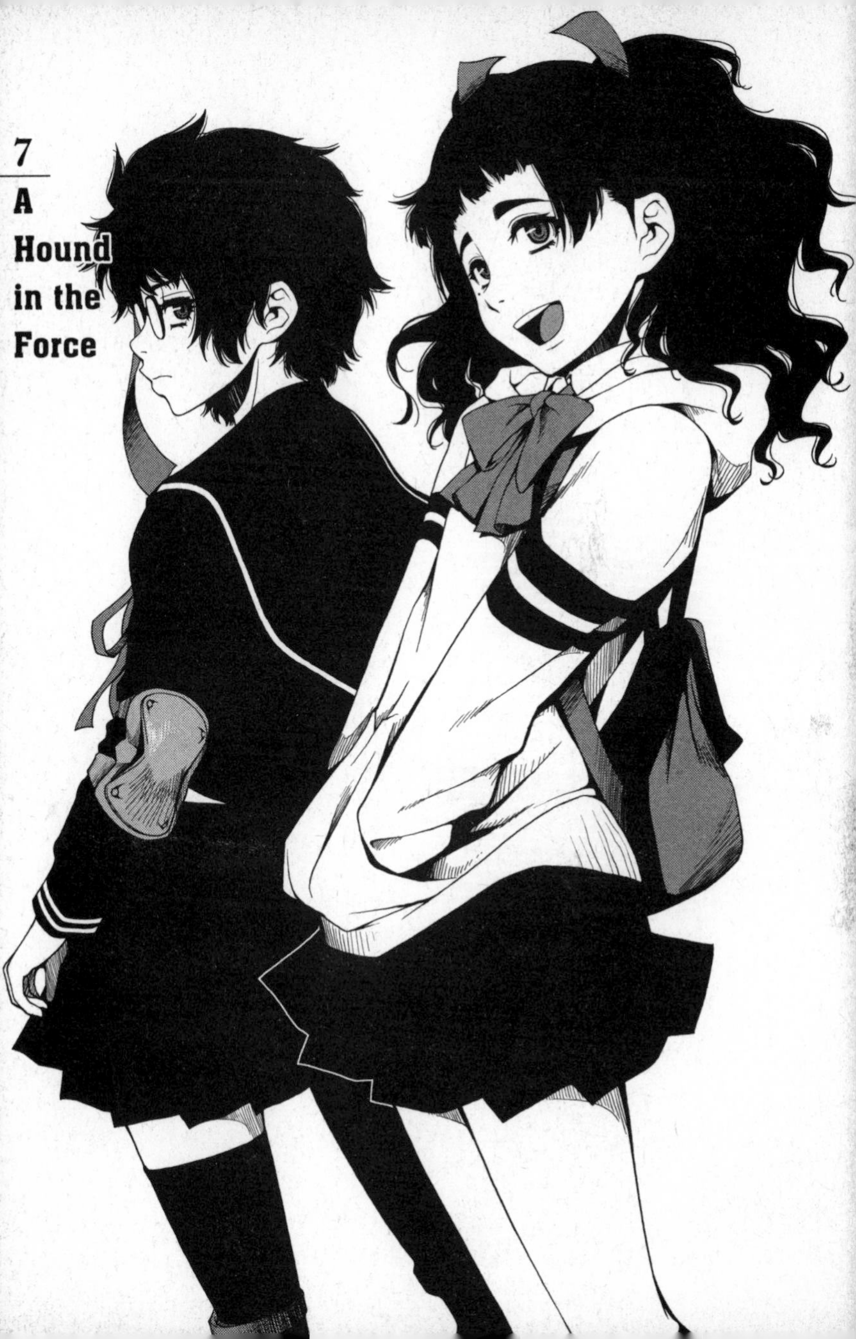

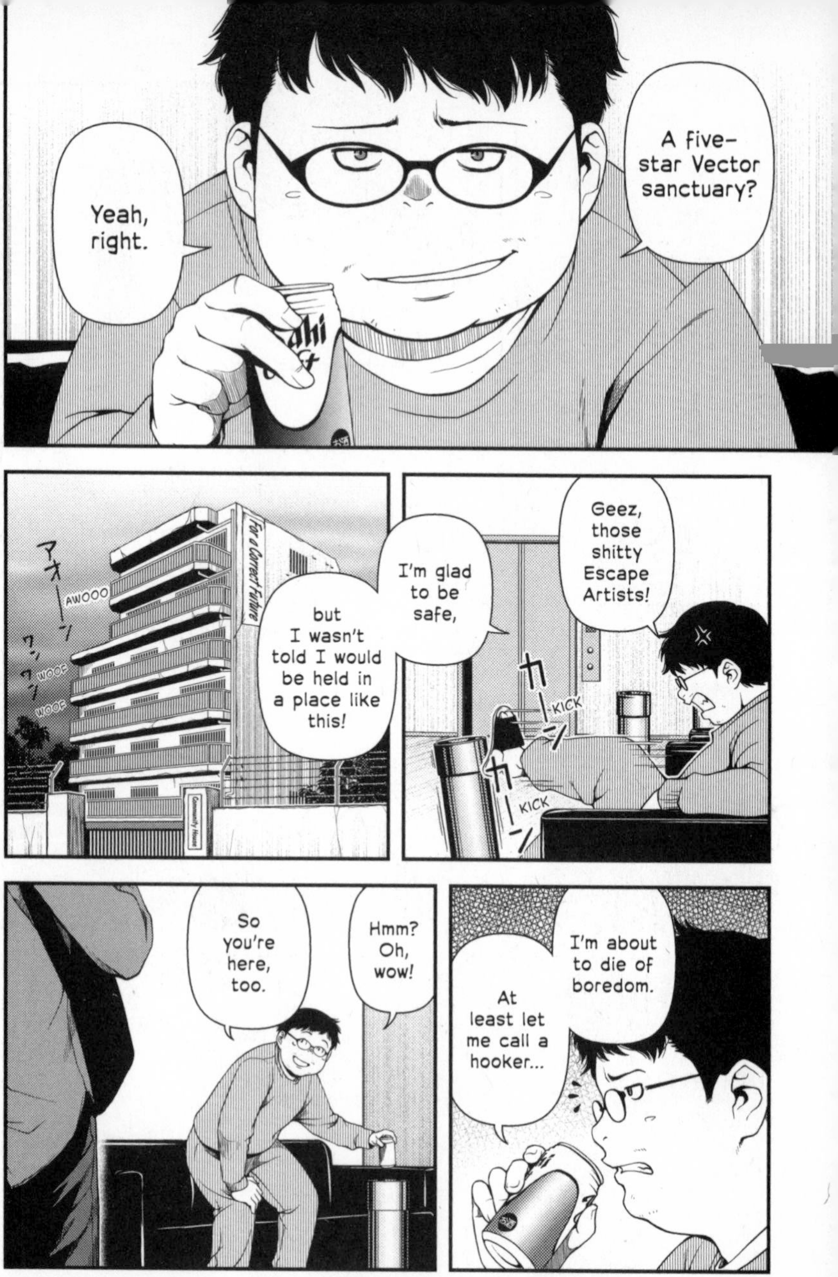
A five-star Vector sanctuary?
Yeah, right.
Geez, those shitty Escape Artists!
KICK
KICK
I'm glad to be safe,
but I wasn't told I would be held in a place like this!
For a Correct Future
AWOOO
WOOF
WOOF
Community House
I'm about to die of boredom.
At least let me call a hooker...
Hmm? Oh, wow!
So you're here, too.

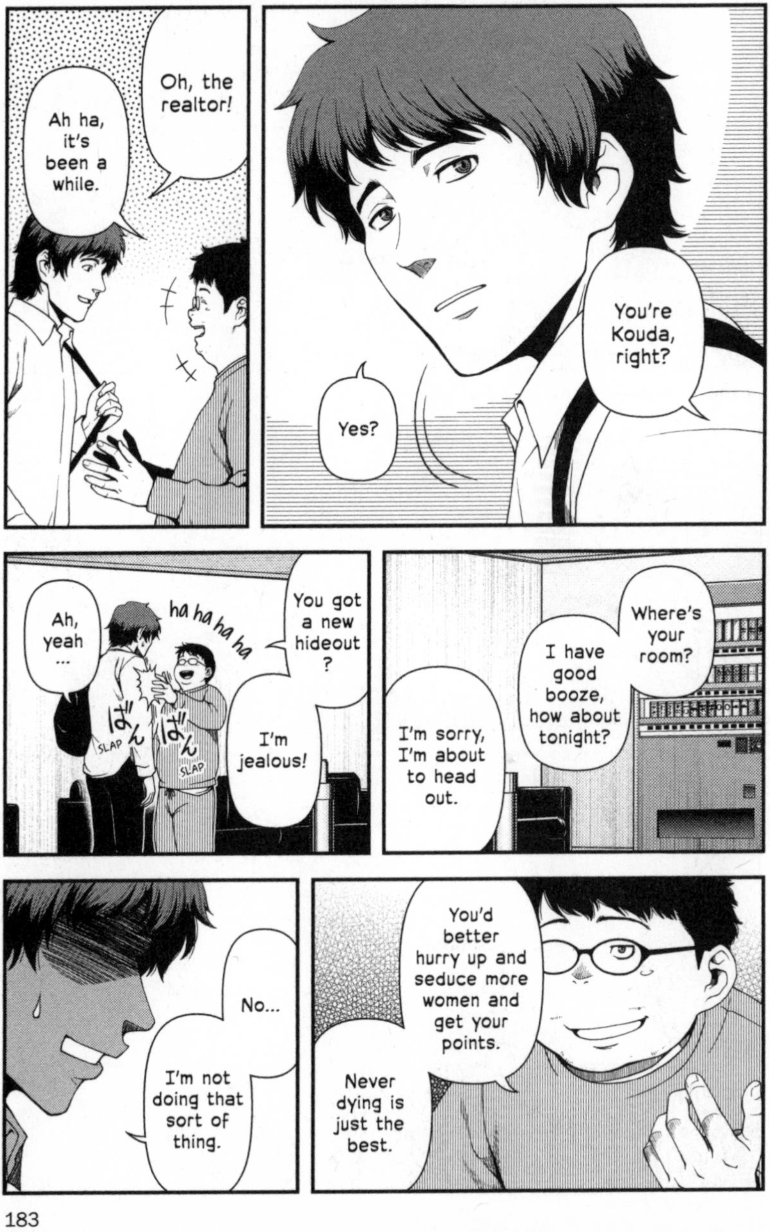
You're Kouda, right?
Yes?
Oh, the realtor!
Ah ha, it's been a while.
Where's your room?
I have good booze, how about tonight?
I'm sorry, I'm about to head out.
You got a new hideout?
I'm jealous!
ha ha ha ha
Ah, yeah ...
ばん
SLAP
ばん
SLAP
You'd better hurry up and seduce more women and get your points.
Never dying is just the best.
No...
I'm not doing that sort of thing.

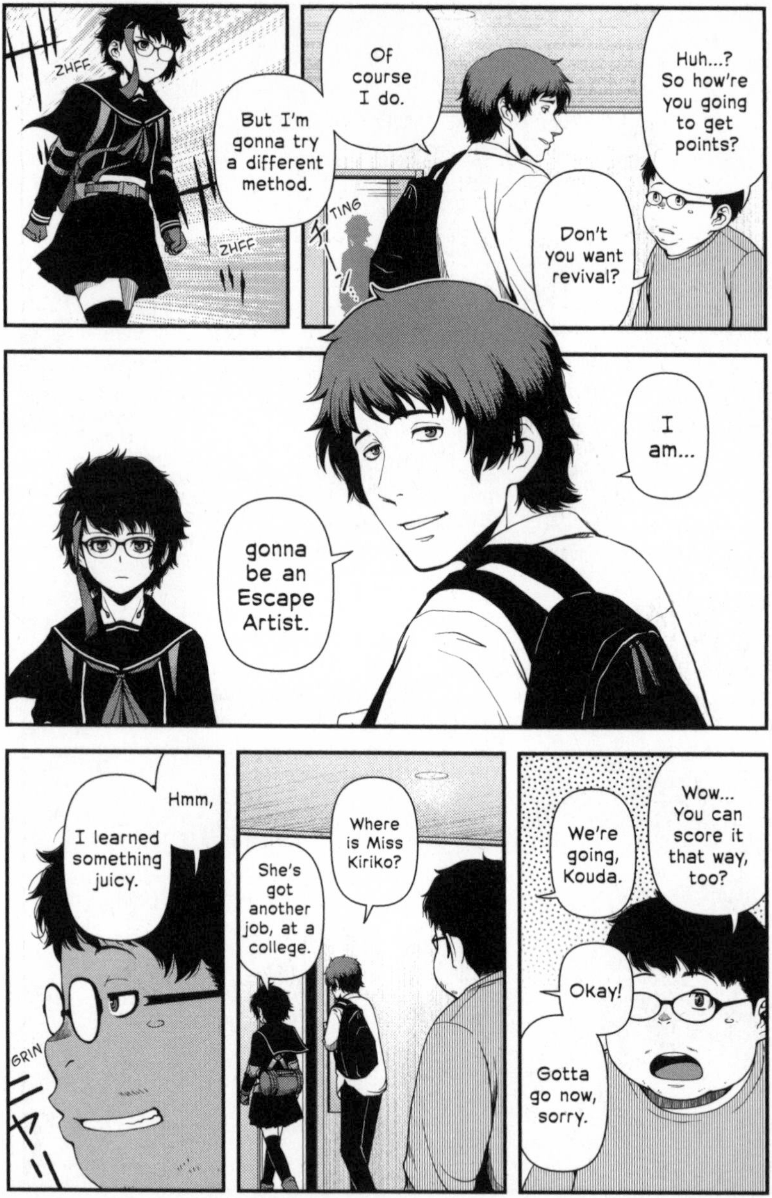
Huh...? So how're you going to get points?
Don't you want revival?
Of course I do.
But I'm gonna try a different method.
TING
ZHFF
ZHFF
I am...
gonna be an Escape Artist.
Wow... You can score it that way, too?
We're going, Kouda.
Okay!
Gotta go now, sorry.
Where is Miss Kiriko?
She's got another job, at a college.
Hmm,
I learned something juicy.
GRIN

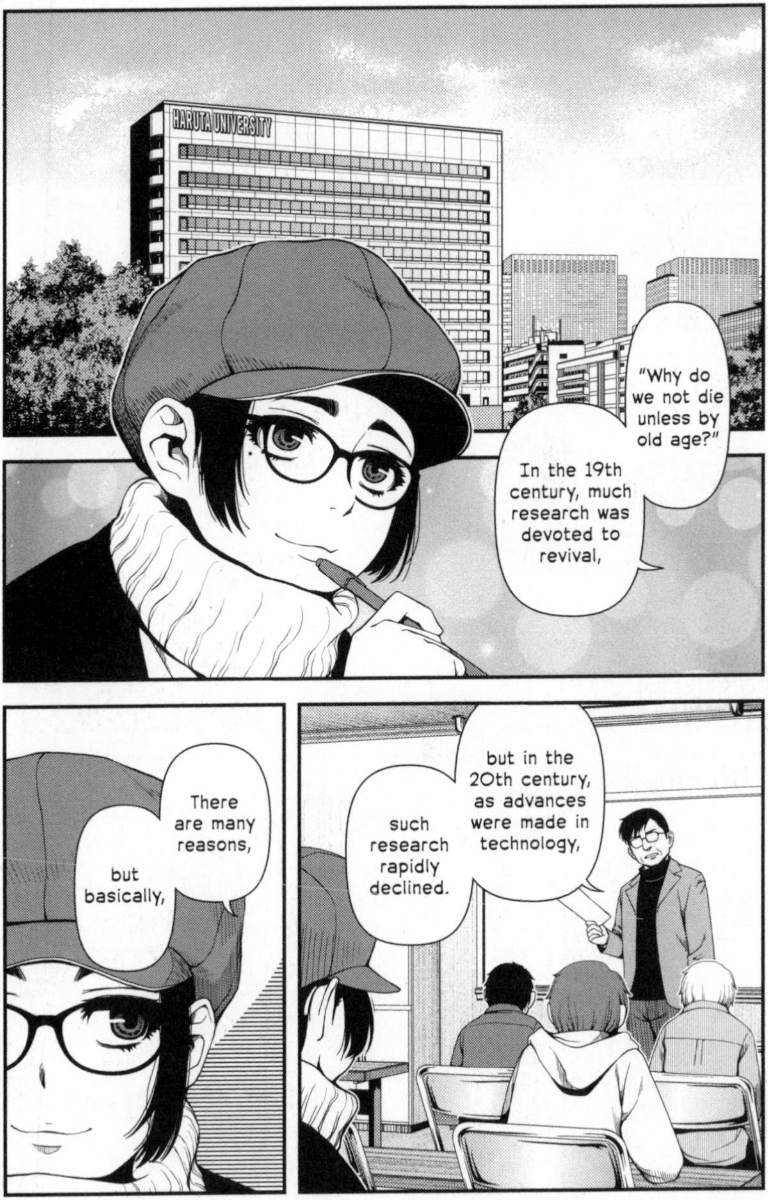
HARUTA UNIVERSITY
"Why do we not die unless by old age?"
In the 19th century, much research was devoted to revival,
but in the 20th century, as advances were made in technology,
such research rapidly declined.
There are many reasons,
but basically,

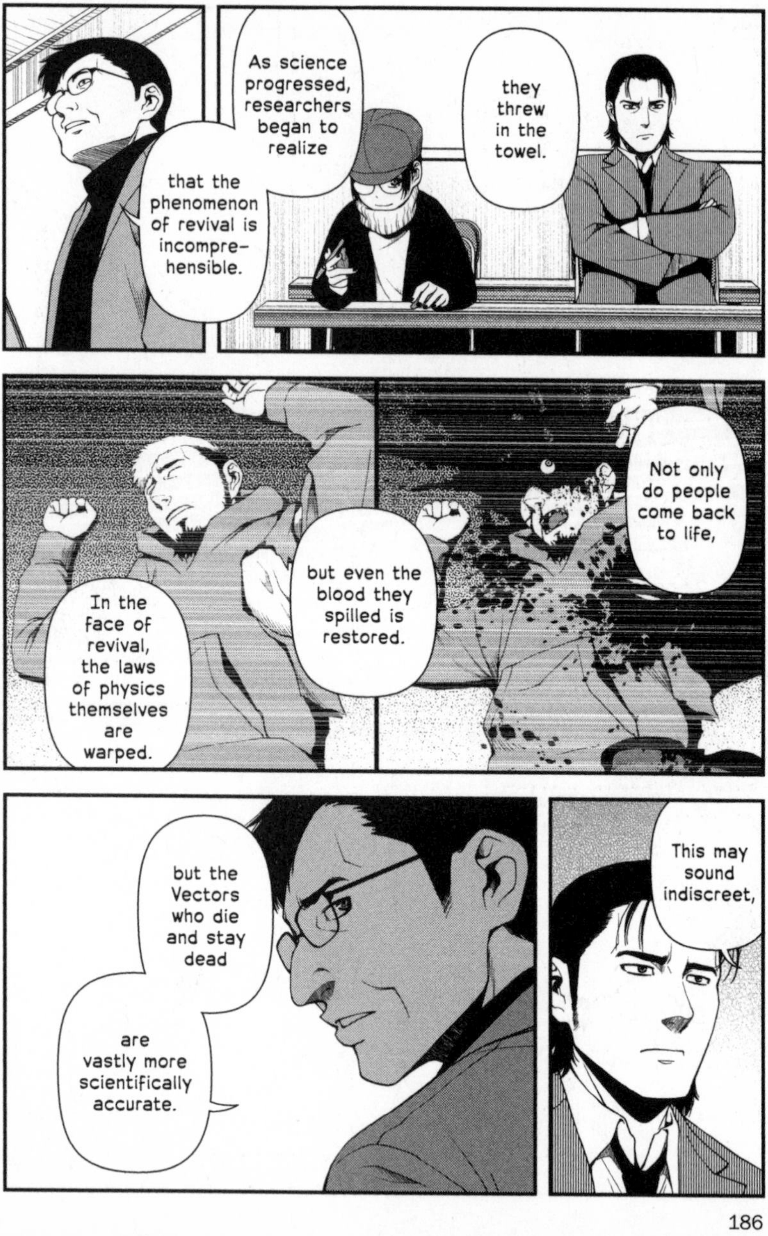
As science progressed, researchers began to realize
that the phenomenon of revival is incompre-hensible.
they threw in the towel.
Not only do people come back to life,
but even the blood they spilled is restored.
In the face of revival, the laws of physics themselves are warped.
This may sound indiscreet,
but the Vectors who die and stay dead
are vastly more scientifically accurate.

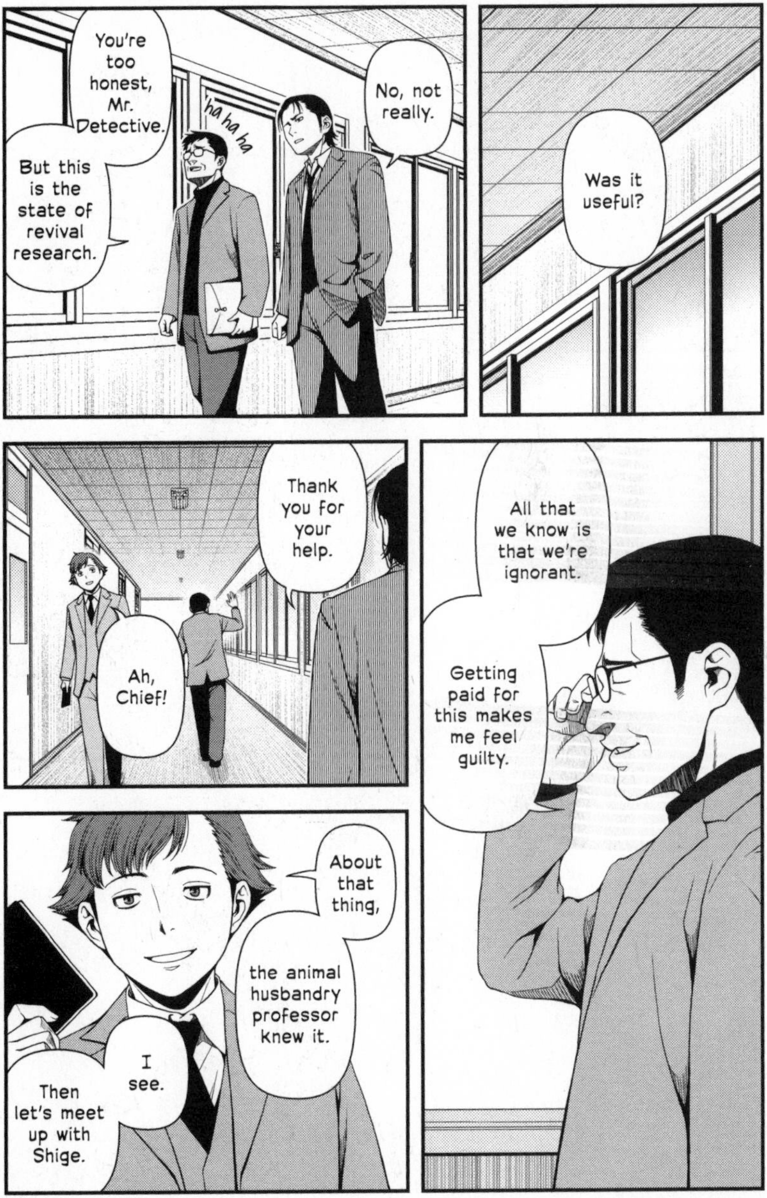
Was it useful?
No, not really.
You're too honest, Mr. Detective.
ha ha ha
But this is the state of revival research.
All that we know is that we're ignorant.
Getting paid for this makes me feel guilty.
Thank you for your help.
Ah, Chief!
About that thing,
the animal husbandry professor knew it.
I see.
Then let's meet up with Shige.

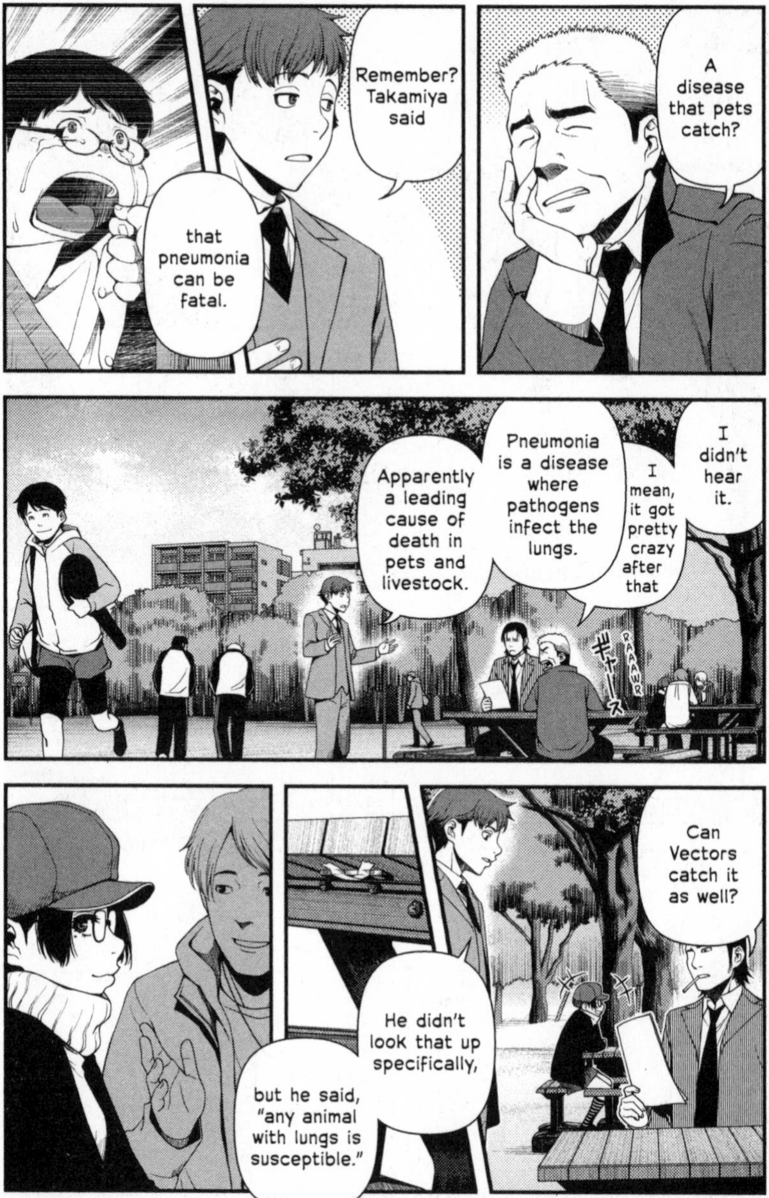
A disease that pets catch?
Remember? Takamiya said
that pneumonia can be fatal.
I didn't hear it.
I mean, it got pretty crazy after that
Pneumonia is a disease where pathogens infect the lungs.
Apparently a leading cause of death in pets and livestock.
RAAAWR
Can Vectors catch it as well?
He didn't look that up specifically,
but he said, "any animal with lungs is susceptible."

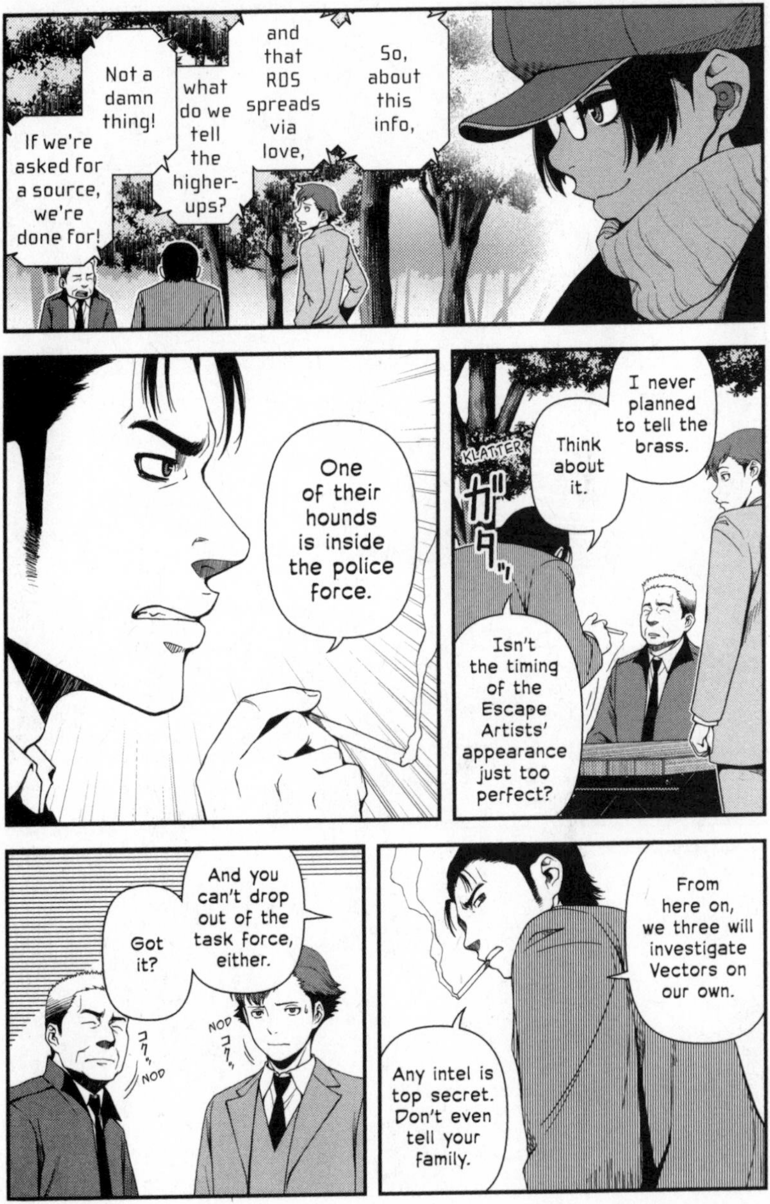
So, about this info,
and that RDS spreads via love,
what do we tell the higher-ups?
Not a damn thing!
If we're asked for a source, we're done for!
I never planned to tell the brass.
Think about it.
KLATTER
Isn't the timing of the Escape Artists' appearance just too perfect?
One of their hounds is inside the police force.
From here on, we three will investigate Vectors on our own.
Any intel is top secret. Don't even tell your family.
And you can't drop out of the task force, either.
Got it?
NOD
NOD

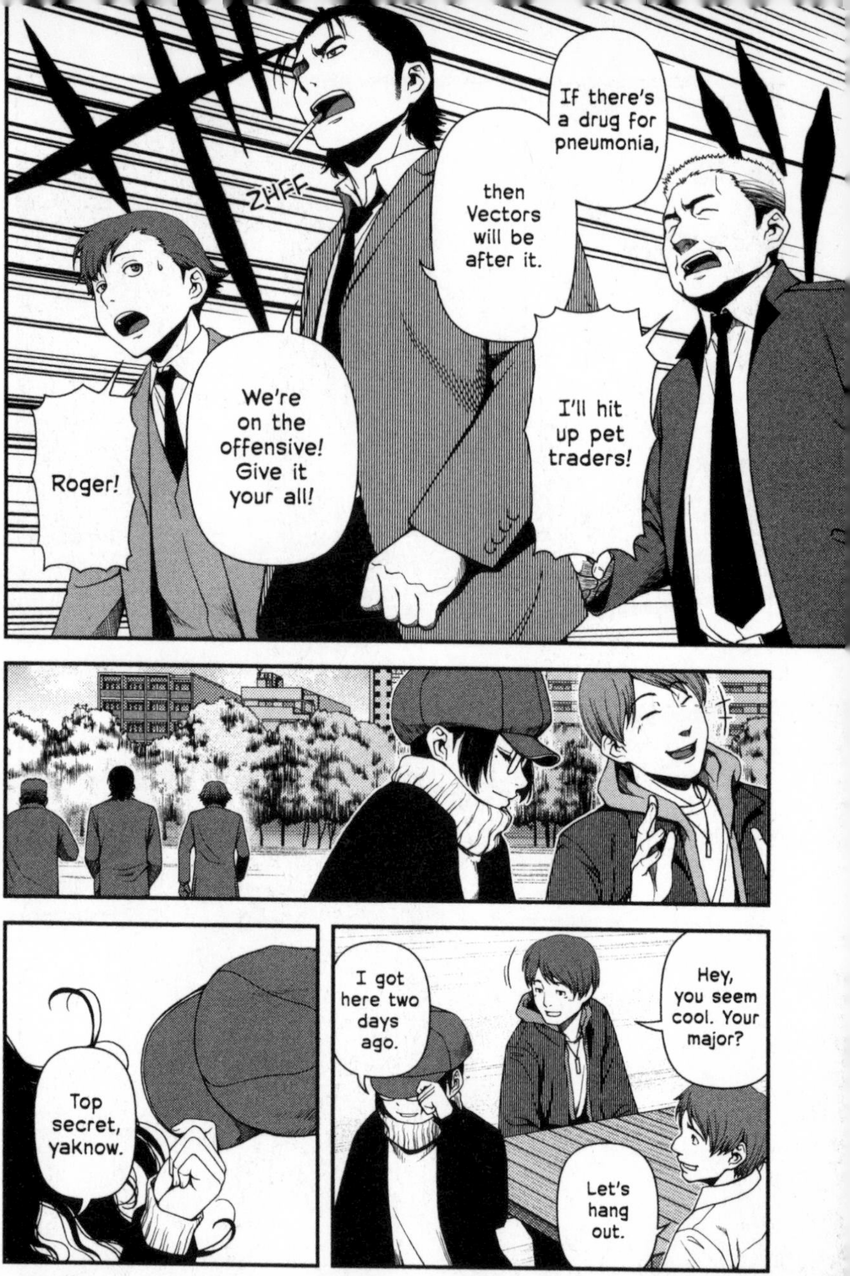
If there's a drug for pneumonia,
then Vectors will be after it.
I'll hit up pet traders!
ZHFF
We're on the offensive! Give it your all!
Roger!
Hey, you seem cool. Your major?
Let's hang out.
I got here two days ago.
Top secret, yaknow.

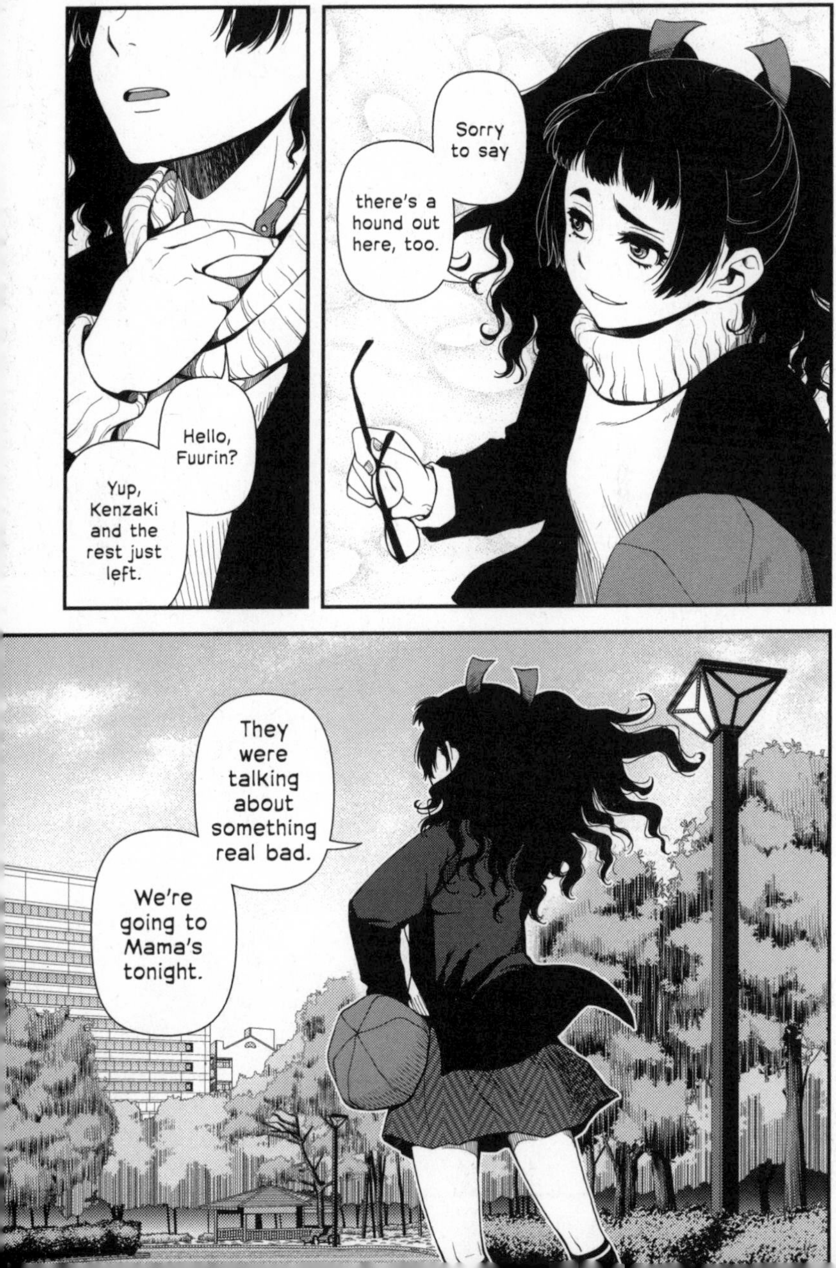
Sorry to say
there's a hound out here, too.
Hello, Fuurin?
Yup, Kenzaki and the rest just left.
They were talking about something real bad.
We're going to Mama's tonight.

So they've zeroed in on the antibiotics, eh.

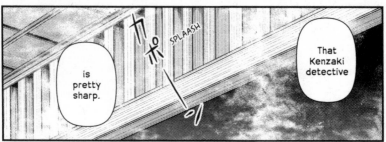

That Kenzaki detective

is pretty sharp.

SPLAASH

They knew about the points...

Takamiya has already owned up

to telling them that.

DRIBBLE...

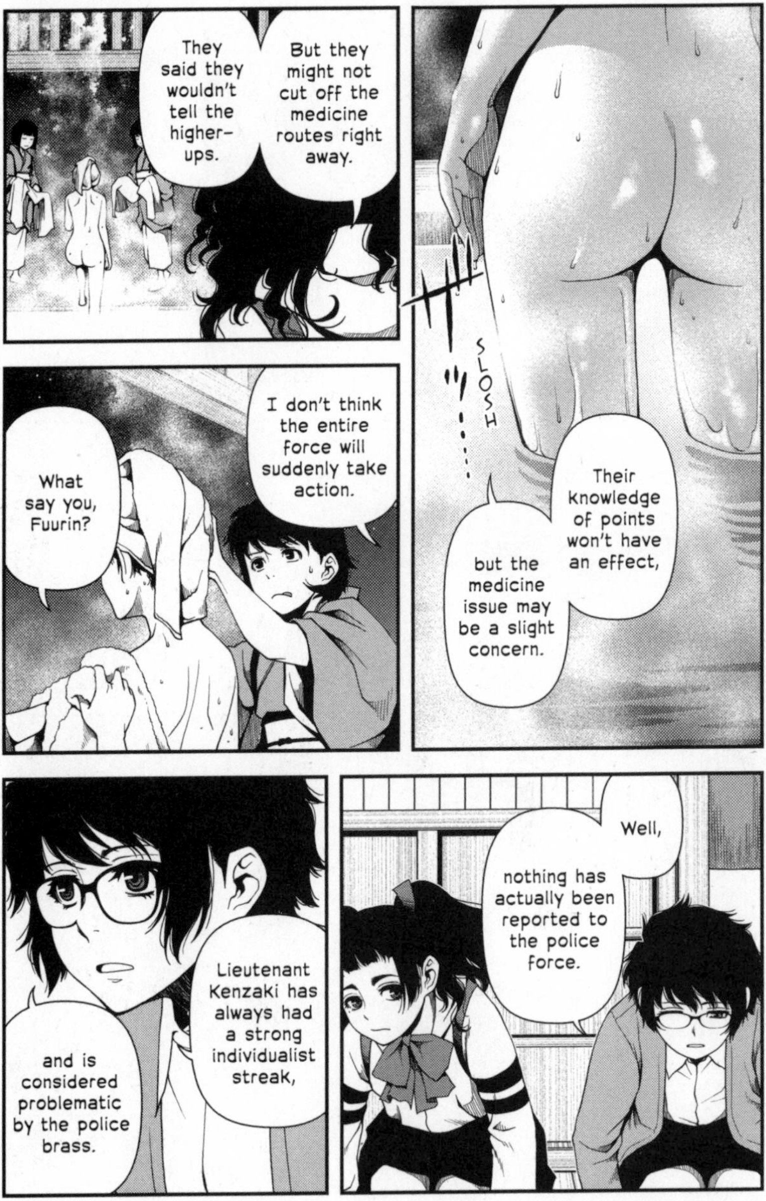
SLOSH
Their knowledge of points won't have an effect,
but the medicine issue may be a slight concern.
But they might not cut off the medicine routes right away.
They said they wouldn't tell the higher-ups.
I don't think the entire force will suddenly take action.
What say you, Fuurin?
Well,
nothing has actually been reported to the police force.
Lieutenant Kenzaki has always had a strong individualist streak,
and is considered problematic by the police brass.

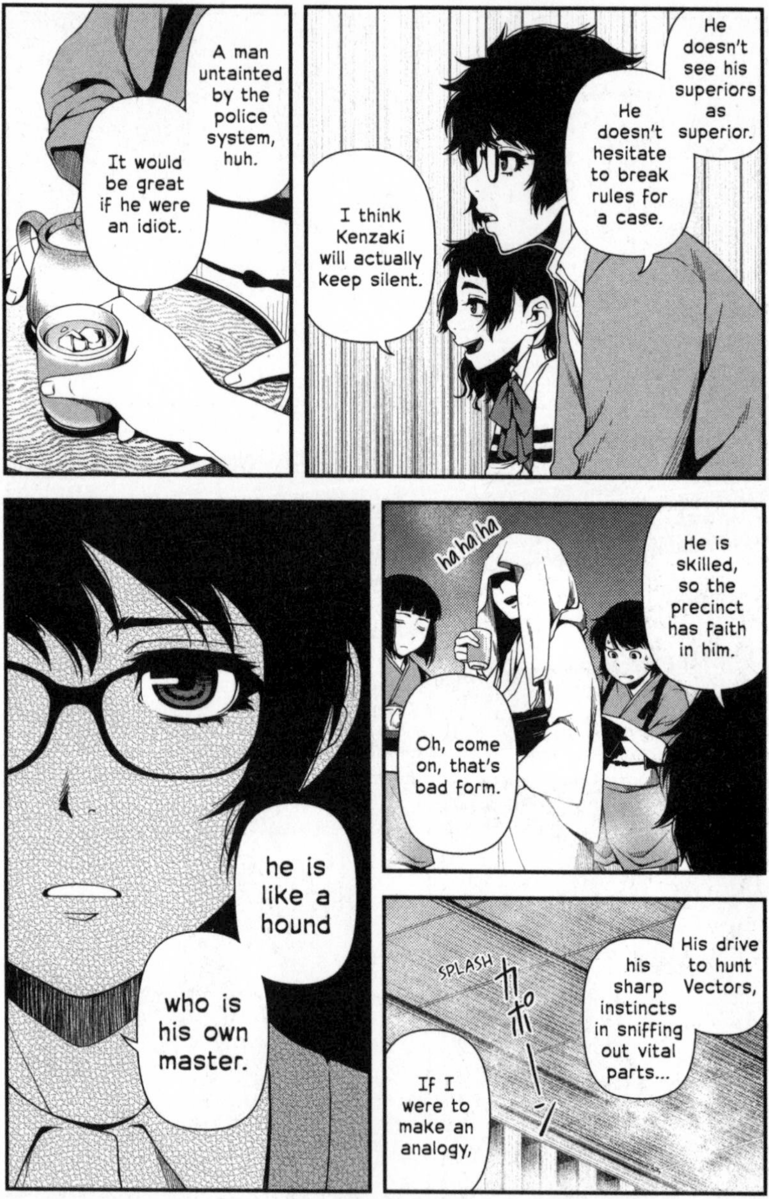
He doesn't see his superiors as superior.
He doesn't hesitate to break rules for a case.
I think Kenzaki will actually keep silent.
A man untainted by the police system, huh.
It would be great if he were an idiot.
ha ha ha
He is skilled, so the precinct has faith in him.
Oh, come on, that's bad form.
His drive to hunt Vectors,
his sharp instincts in sniffing out vital parts...
SPLASH
カポーン
If I were to make an analogy,
he is like a hound
who is his own master.

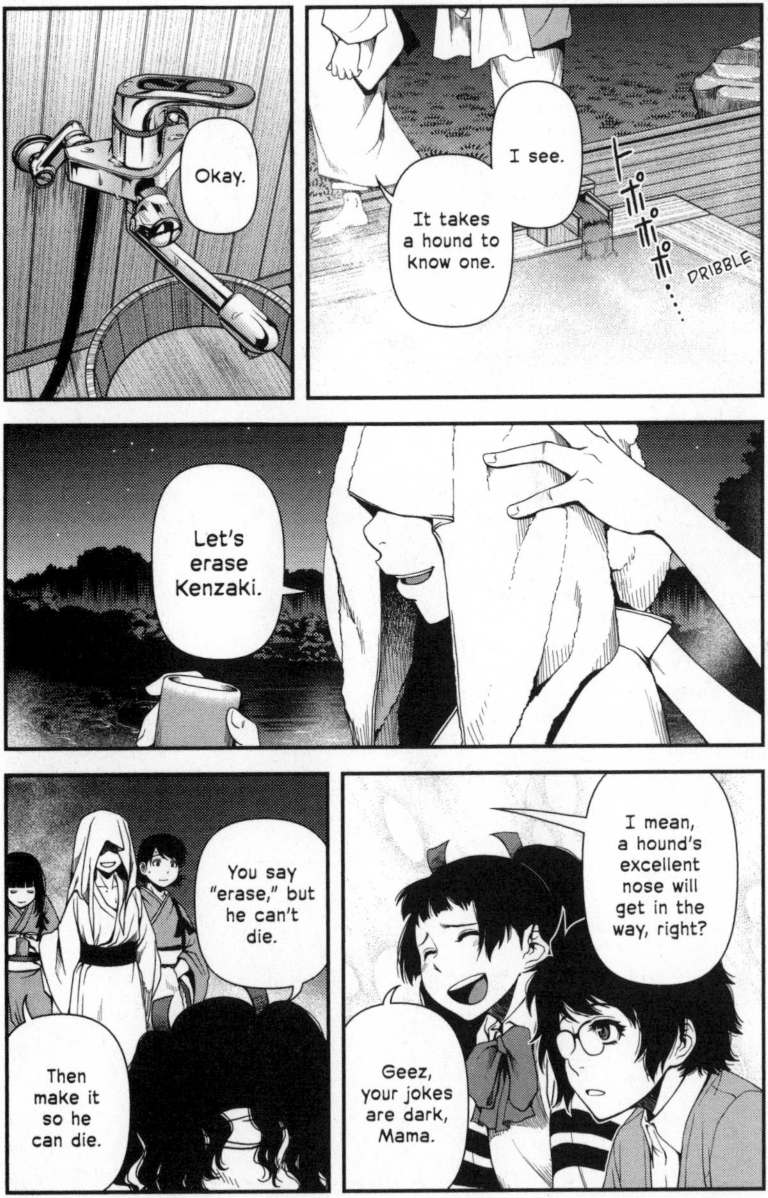
I see.
It takes a hound to know one.
トポポポ…
DRIBBLE
Okay.
Let's erase Kenzaki.
I mean, a hound's excellent nose will get in the way, right?
Geez, your jokes are dark, Mama.
You say "erase," but he can't die.
Then make it so he can die.

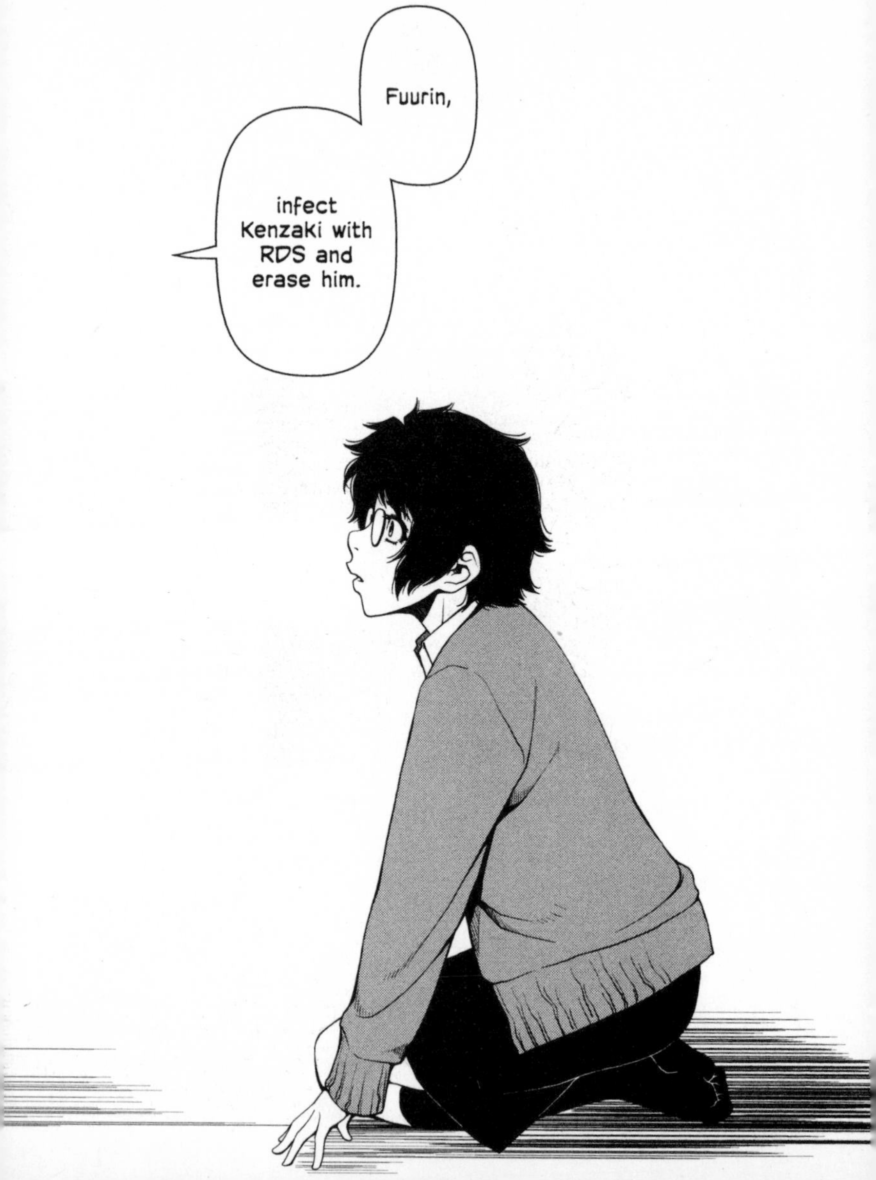
Fuurin,
infect Kenzaki with RDS and erase him.

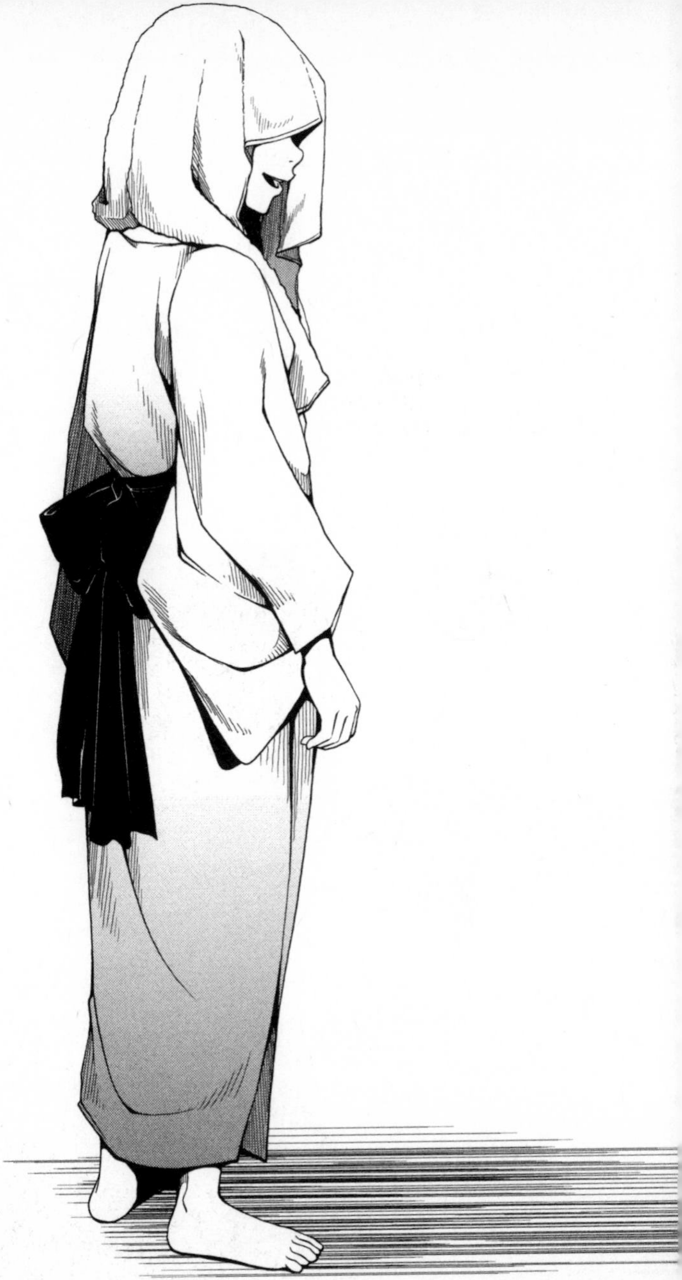

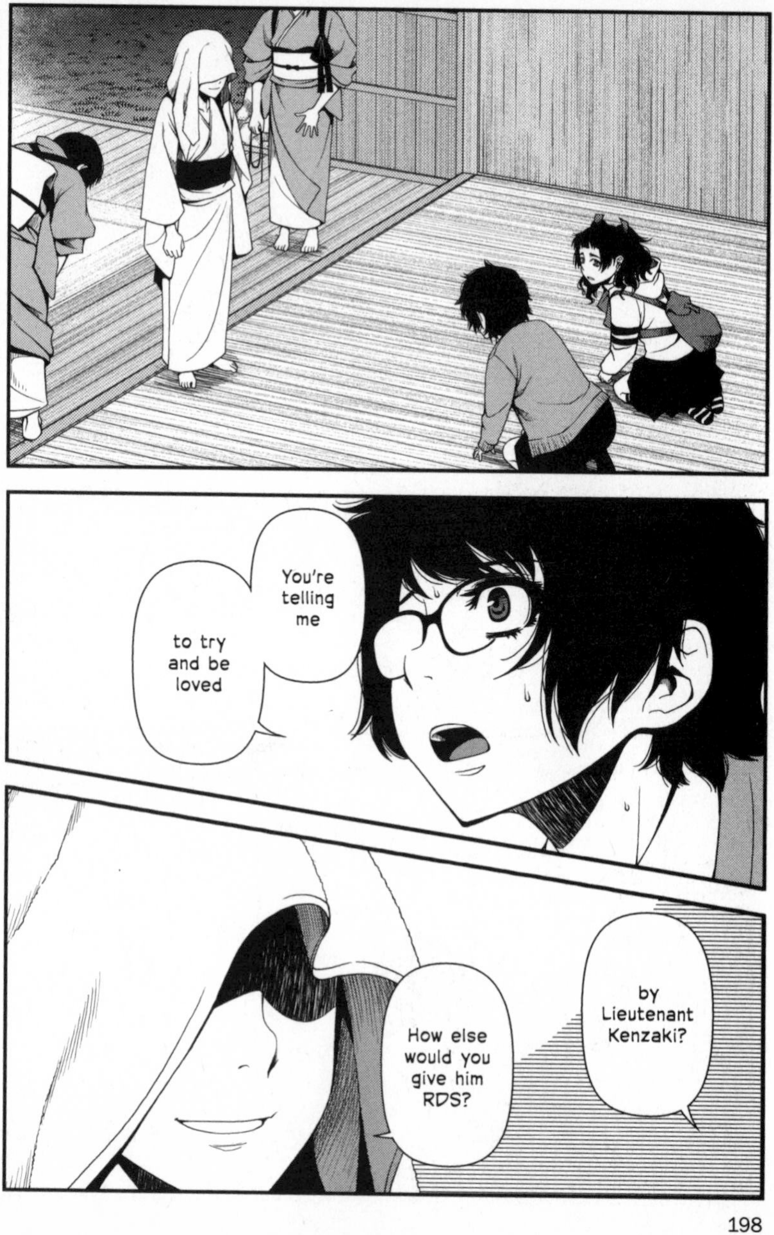
You're telling me
to try and be loved
by Lieutenant Kenzaki?
How else would you give him RDS?

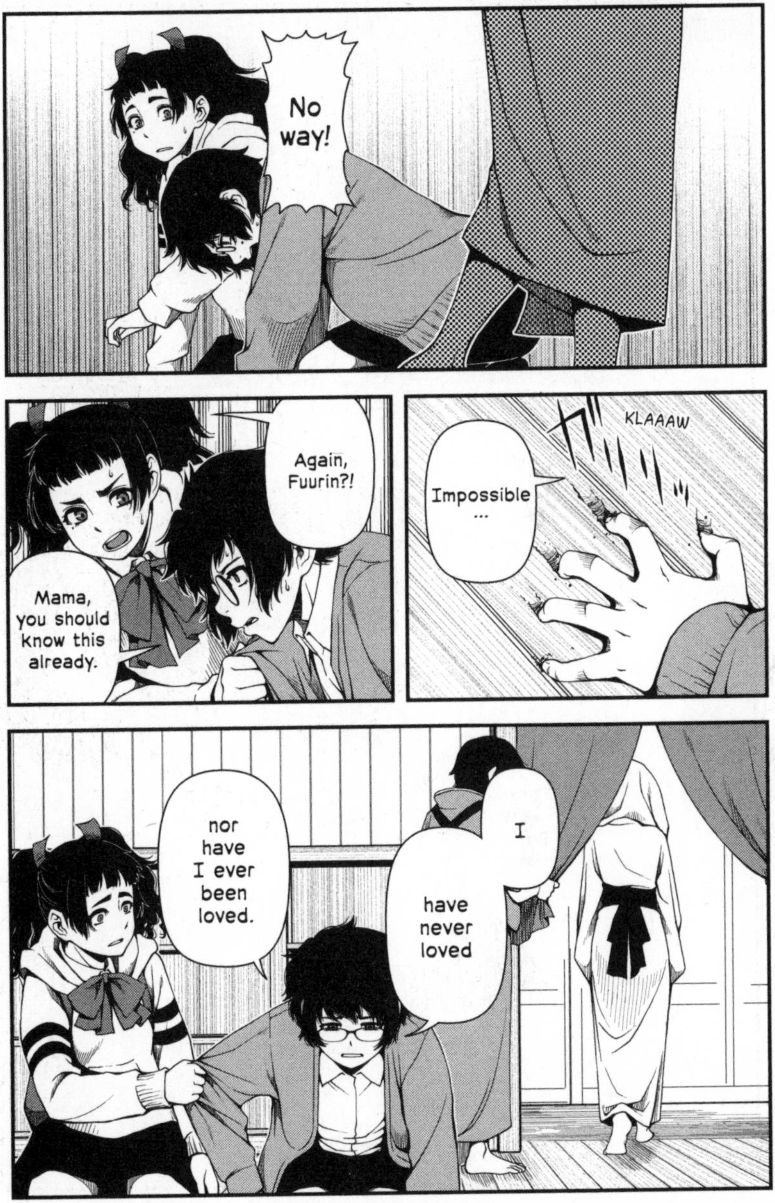
No way!
KLAAAW
Impossible ...
Again, Fuurin?!
Mama, you should know this already.
I have never loved
nor have I ever been loved.

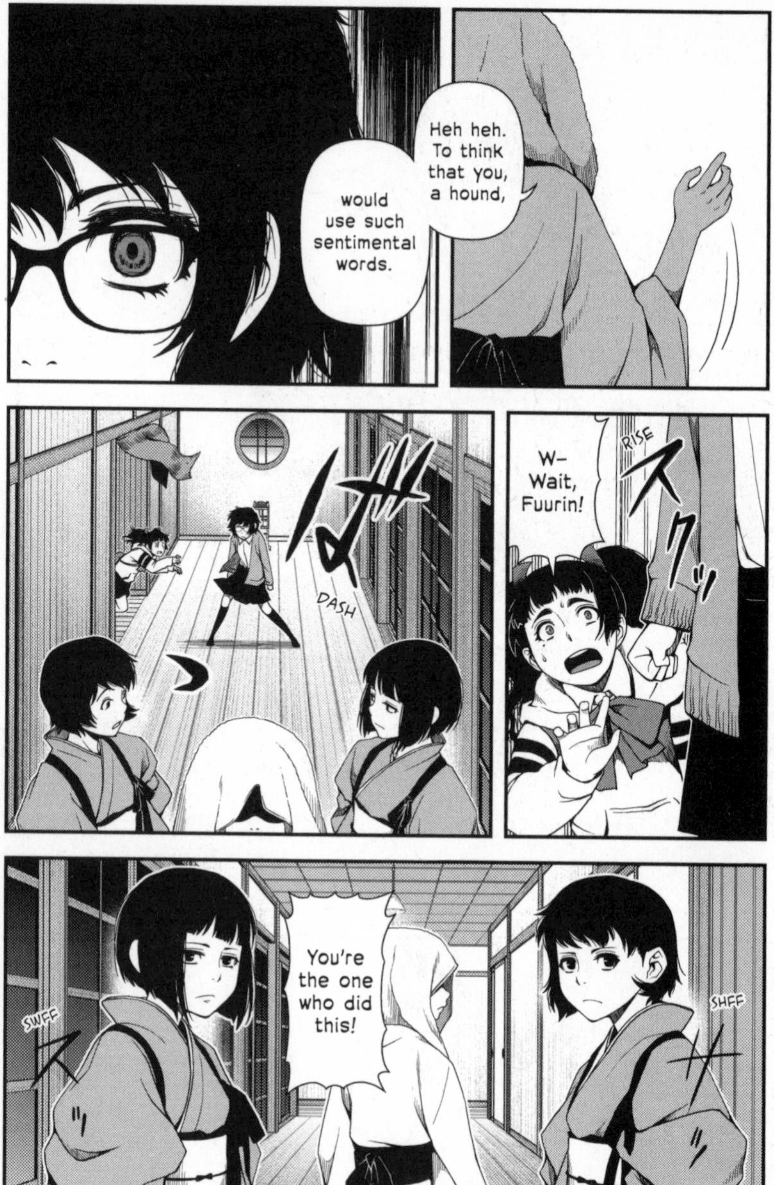
Heh heh. To think that you, a hound,
would use such sentimental words.
RISE
W– Wait, Fuurin!
スクッ
DASH
SHFF
You're the one who did this!
SWFF

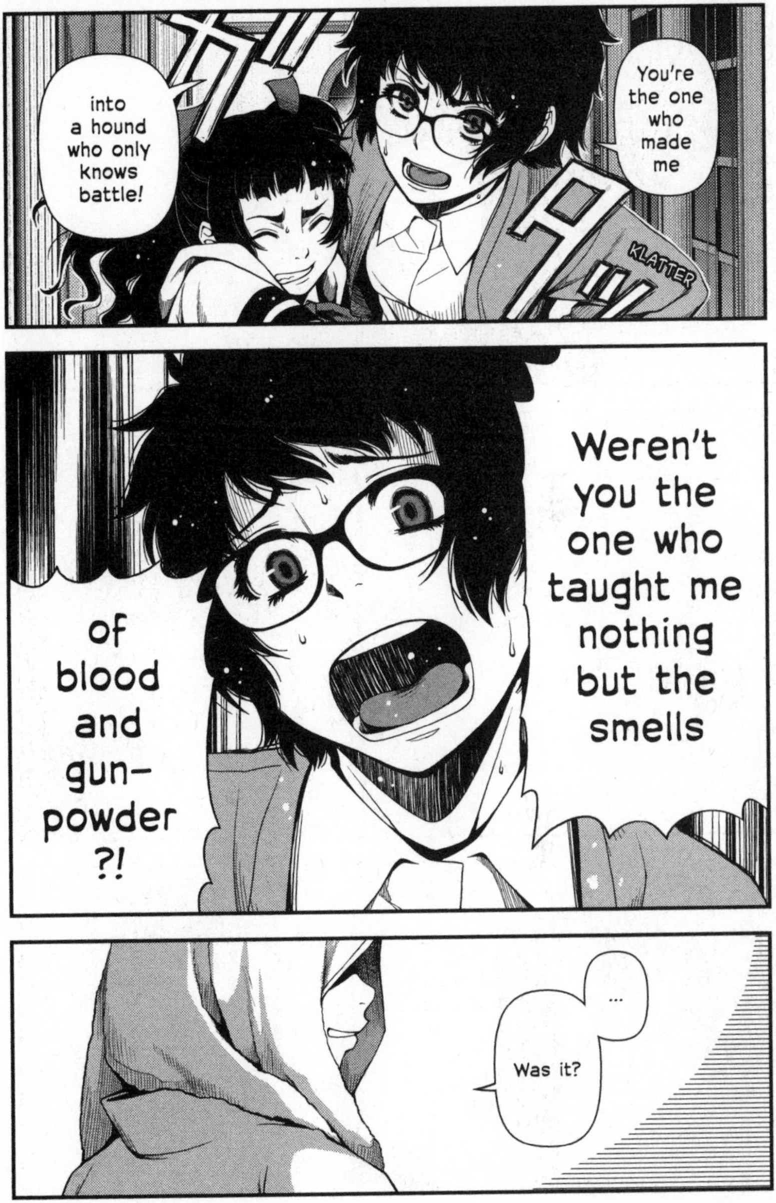

You're the one who made me
into a hound who only knows battle!
KLATTER
Weren't you the one who taught me nothing but the smells
of blood and gun-powder?!
...
Was it?

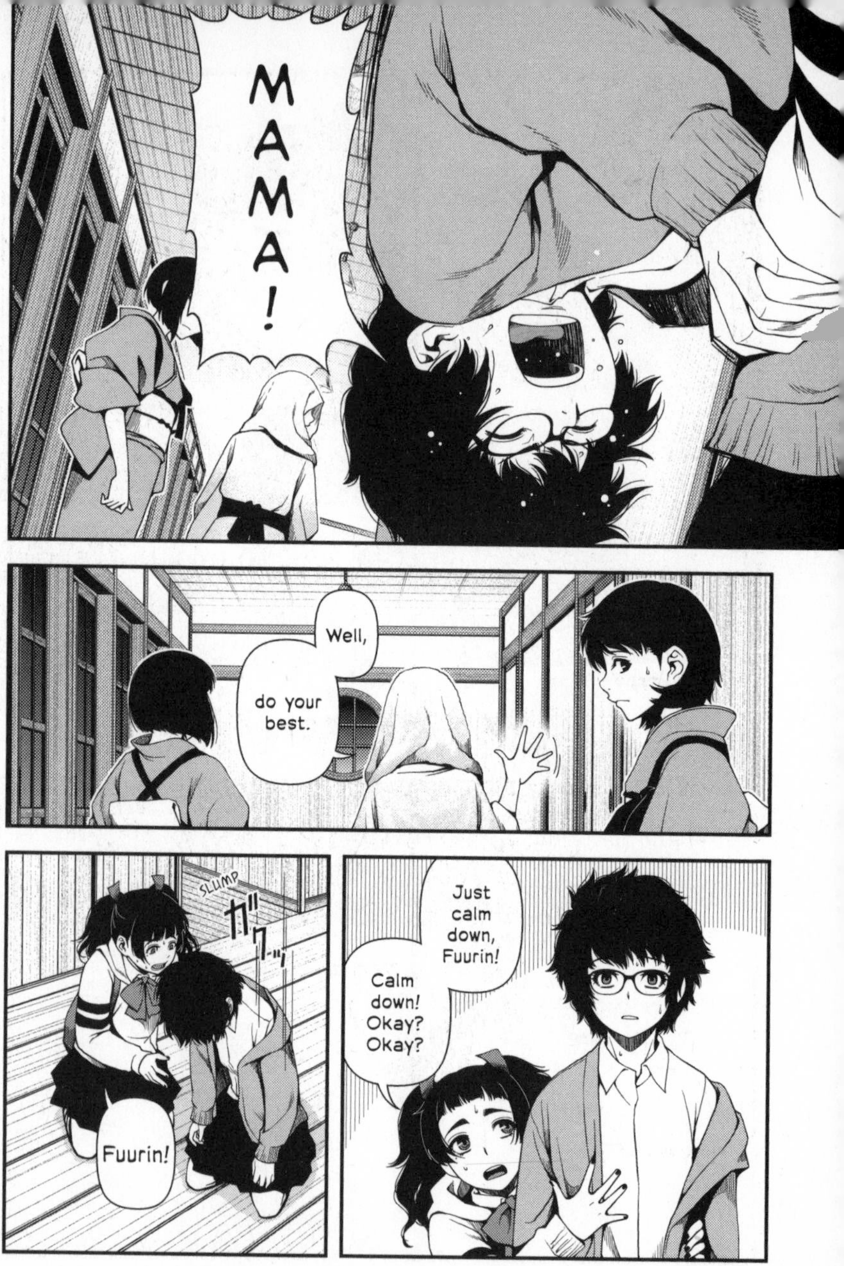
MAMA!
Well,
do your best.
Just calm down, Fuurin!
Calm down! Okay? Okay?
SLUMP
Fuurin!

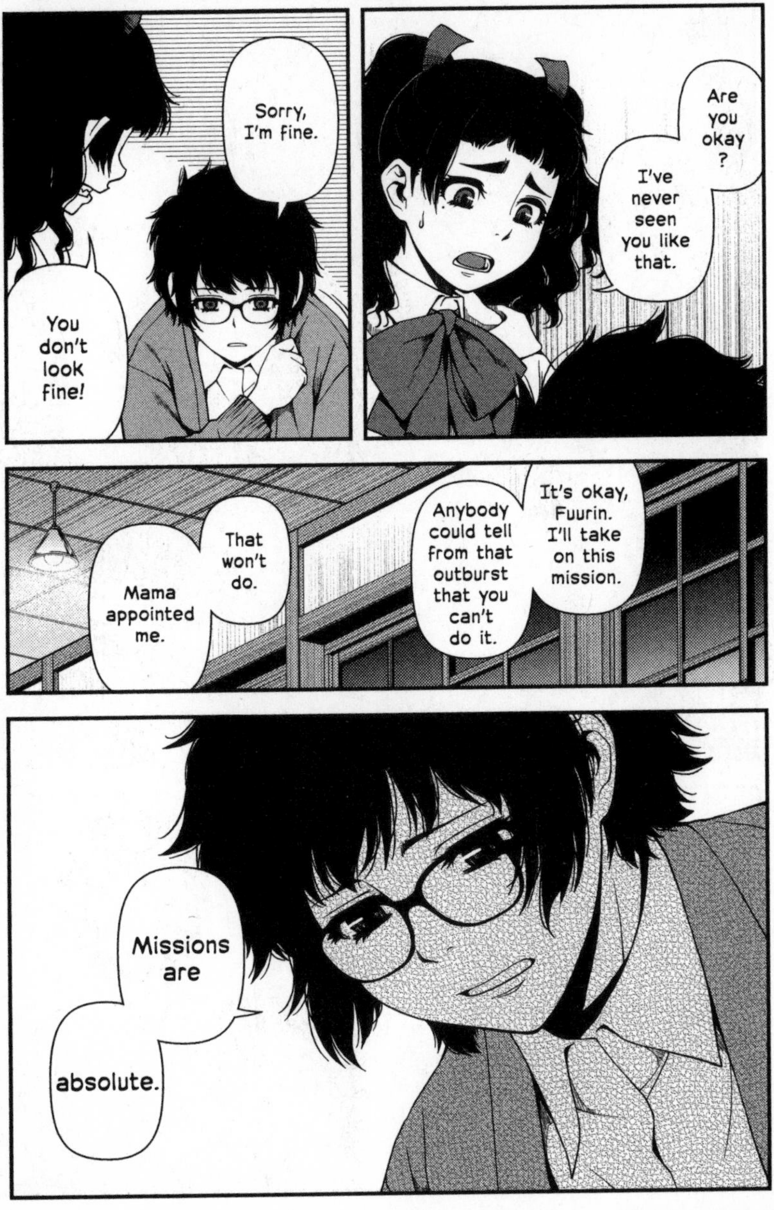
Are you okay?
I've never seen you like that.
Sorry, I'm fine.
You don't look fine!
It's okay, Fuurin. I'll take on this mission.
Anybody could tell from that outburst that you can't do it.
That won't do.
Mama appointed me.
Missions are
absolute.

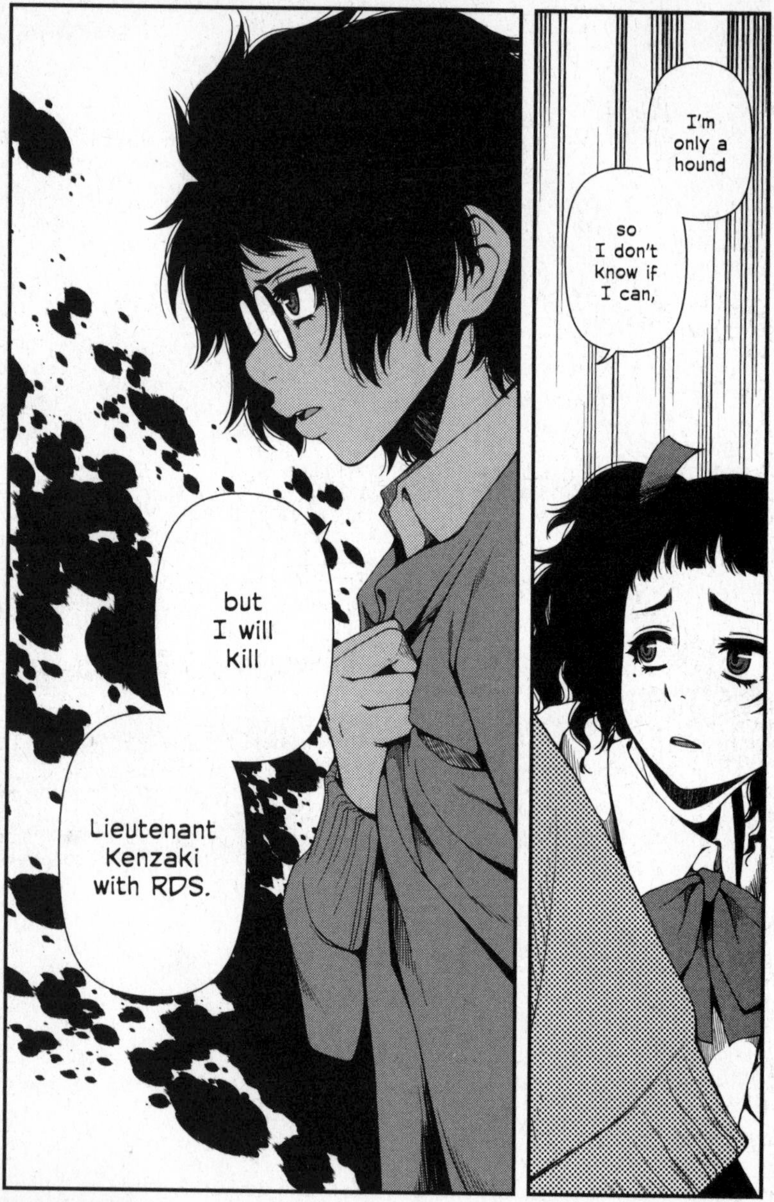
I'm only a hound
so I don't know if I can,
but I will kill
Lieutenant Kenzaki with RDS.

Immortal Hounds: Next Volume Preview

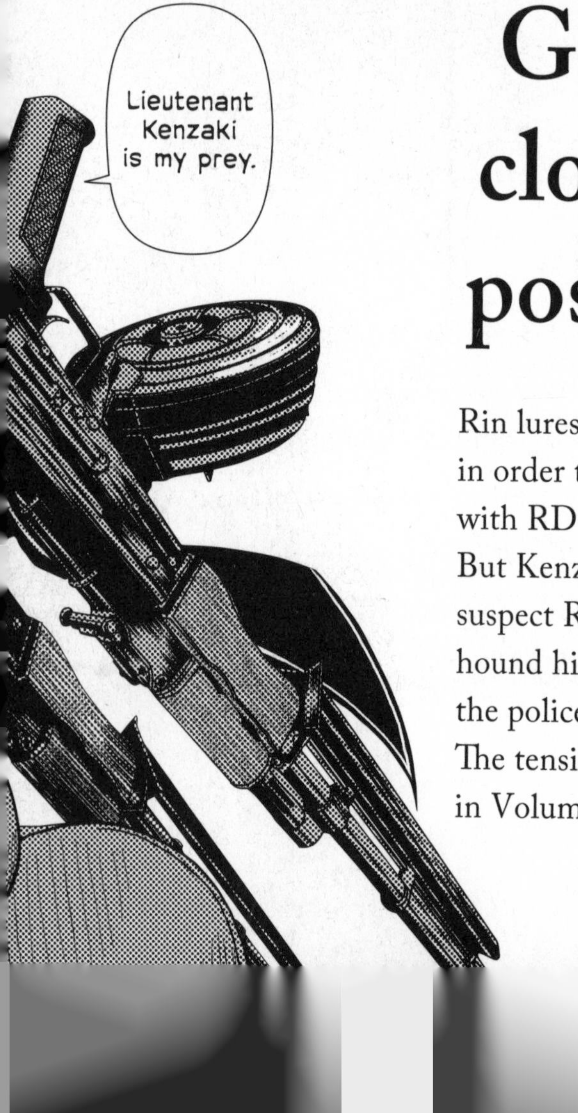
Lieutenant Kenzaki is my prey.

Get as close as possible

Rin lures out Kenzaki in order to infect him with RDS and kill him. But Kenzaki begins to suspect Rin of being the hound hiding within the police force. The tension grows in Volume 2!

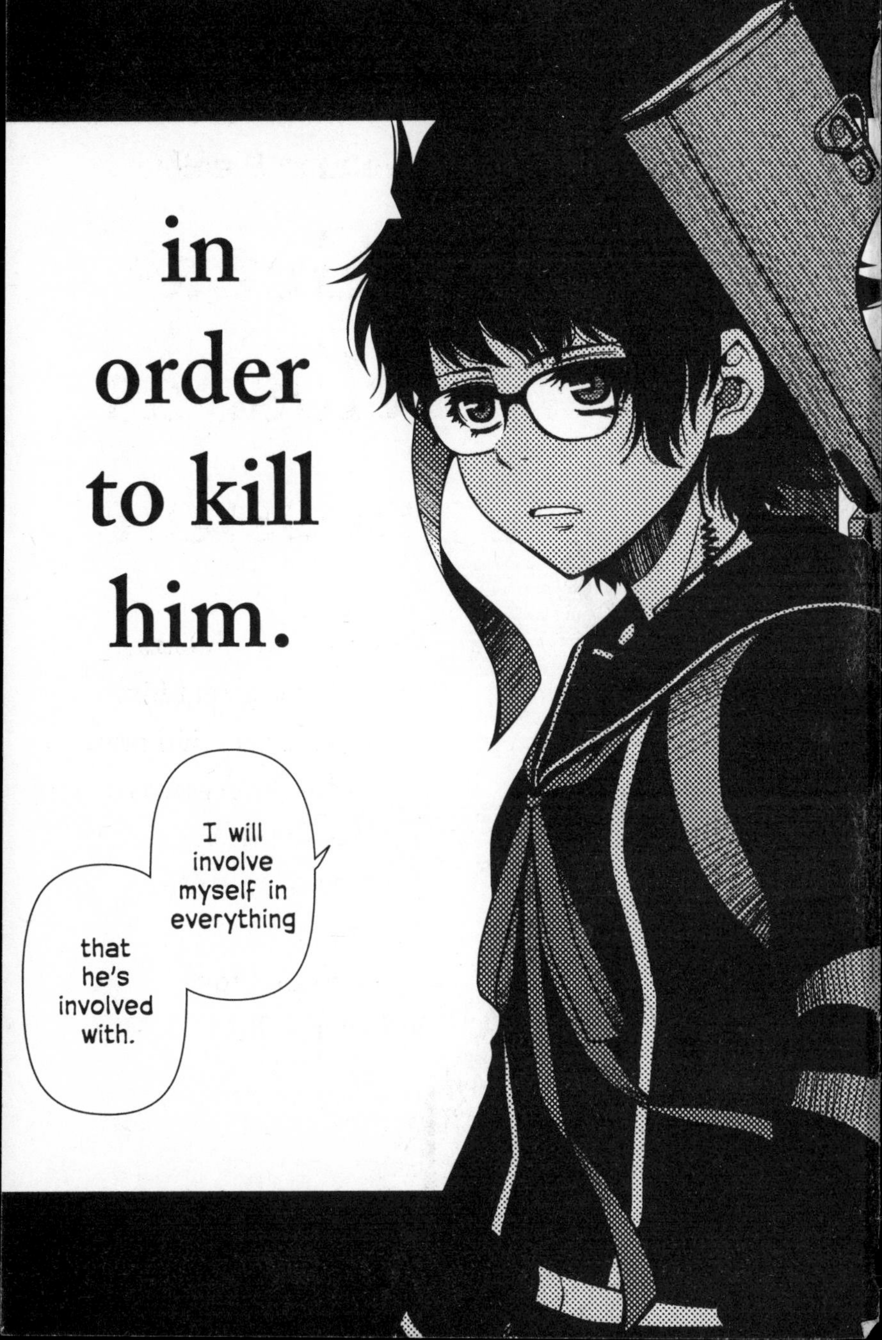
in order to kill him.
I will involve myself in everything
that he's involved with.

Immortal Hounds 1

A Vertical Comics Edition

Translation: Yota Okutani
Production: Grace Lu
          Anthony Quintessenza

© 2014 Ryo Yasohachi
First published in Japan in 2014 by KADOKAWA CORPORATION ENTERBRAIN.
English translation rights arranged with KADOKAWA CORPORATION ENTERBRAIN
through TUTTLE-MORI AGENCY, INC., Tokyo.

Translation provided by Vertical Comics, 2016
Published by Vertical Comics, an imprint of Vertical, Inc., New York

Originally published in Japanese as *Shinazu no Ryouken 1* by Kadokawa Corporation, 2014
Shinazu no Ryouken first serialized in *Harta*, Kadokawa Corporation, 2013-

This is a work of fiction.

ISBN: 978-1-942993-59-9

Manufactured in Canada

First Edition

Vertical, Inc.
451 Park Avenue South
7th Floor
New York, NY 10016
www.vertical-comics.com

Vertical books are distributed through Penguin-Random House Publisher Services.